Sir Robert Peel

SIR ROBERT PEEL
by Henry William Pickersgill
(National Portrait Gallery)

A. A. W. RAMSAY

Sir Robert Peel

A daring pilot in extremity
Pleased with the danger when the waves ran high
DRYDEN

CONSTABLE
LONDON

Published by Constable and Company Ltd
10 Orange Street, London WC2
First published 1928
Reissued 1971
Copyright © 1971 by the Estate of A.A.W. Ramsay

ISBN 0 09 458290 4

Reproduced and Printed in Great Britain by
Redwood Press Limited, Trowbridge & London

IN MEMORY OF
CAROLINA JEAN PENTLAND

GENERAL EDITOR'S PREFACE

ἐκεῖνος δυνατὸς ὢν τῷ τε ἀξιώματι καὶ τῇ γνώμῃ, χρημάτων
τε διαφανῶς ἀδωρότατος γενόμενος, κατεῖχε τὸ πλῆθος ἐλευθέρως,
καὶ οὐκ ἤγετο μᾶλλον ὑπ' αὐτοῦ ἢ αὐτὸς ἦγε, διὰ τὸ μὴ κτώμενος
ἐξ οὗ προσηκόντων τὴν δύναμιν πρὸς ἡδονήν τι λέγειν, ἀλλ'
ἔχων ἐπ' ἀξιώσει καὶ πρὸς ὀργήν τι ἀντειπεῖν.

*To character, judgment and crystal-clear integrity he
owed his unfettered power over the people ; ever a leader,
not a follower, and relying on no dishonest arts, he did
not seek to speak them pleasant things ; but, such was the
esteem in which they held him, he dared, if need be, to oppose
them and incur their anger.*

THIS judgment of Thucydides on the great Athenian statesman
is no less true of Peel, one of our greatest statesmen of the nineteenth century. Peel's reputation suffered in his lifetime, and has
since suffered to some extent by the responsibility he took for two
acts of policy, Catholic Emancipation and the Repeal of the Corn
Laws, both of them contrary to his own previously expressed
opinions, and both of them devastating to the unity of the great
party he led. But, in fact, as Miss Ramsay makes clear in this
volume, both acts are illustrations of the highest form of statesmanship, if by statesmanship we mean the capacity to guide a
country through imminent dangers to stability and security without too meticulous consideration of the statesman's verbal consistency. We naturally demand a reasonable consistency in the
expressed opinions of our statesmen, but emergencies sometimes
arise in which a policy honestly pursued in the past for its value
to the strength of the country may prove fatal to its existing peace.
Such were the emergencies in 1827 and 1846 ; and fortunate is the
country which at such a time has a statesman wise and unselfish
enough, as Peel proved to be, to neglect his own past and follow
what he believes to be the only safe course, however revolutionary.

Peel may have proved to be a lost leader ; it was assuredly not for a handful of silver he left those who had followed him, honoured him ; but because he saw more clearly than they that the old road led to destruction, and had the courage to alter the direction before they came on the precipice.

Peel has also suffered somewhat in reputation for his cold and undemonstrative manner. He had none of the engaging characteristics of some great leaders of men, a winning way with his immediate helpers, or an electric power over the masses. But here again Miss Ramsay well brings out how the absence of these not negligible gifts was well atoned for by the transparent honesty and the strength and nobility of character of the man who in all his changes of policy never lost the respect of the nation or even of the party who felt themselves left in the lurch. The greatest tribute to this character of Peel's is that no other statesman of his time, few at any other time, could have carried through so easily and successfully two such changes, almost revolutionary, in the policy of the party and the country.

We have been fortunate in having several statesmen who have kept high the standard of public life more even by what they are and are felt to be than by what they do. Peel was not the least of these. His achievements in statesmanship were great, but greater far are the high ideals set before the country by the man he was.

BASIL WILLIAMS.

Edinburgh, *Sept.* 1927.

FOREWORD

I MUST thank for invaluable advice and assistance my editor, Professor Basil Williams; and thank also, for information and help of various kinds, Mr. and Mrs. Hammond; Mr. George Peel; the Deputy-Keeper of Manuscripts in the British Museum; Mr. William Mitchell, K.C.; Mr. A. E. Pairman of the Commercial Bank of Scotland; Mrs. M. Whitaker, and my mother and father. Mr. G. Kitson Clarke kindly informed me of the title and scope of his forthcoming book on Peel. I feel also that this book owes an incalculable amount to the lectures of Professor J. F. Rees, and of the late Professor J. Shield Nicholson, which first introduced me to the study of economics when I was a student at Edinburgh University.

A. A. W. RAMSAY.

CONTENTS

CHAPTER I

SPINNING JENNY

DURING the long reign of George the Third a great revolution took place in Britain : a revolution so far-reaching in its effects that there was no part of the national life—social, industrial, political, religious, aesthetic—that it did not touch and alter, for better or worse. It changed the face of the country and the minds of the people. The material effects of the revolution were complicated and in part altered—its intellectual effects were greatly intensified —by the revolution, equally great but different in its nature, which during the same period took place in France.

In Britain the revolution was first of all the transformation of an agricultural country into an industrial country. A new system of social organisation replaced the old one. The town became the dominant factor in the national life, instead of the village. The agricultural interest lost its commanding position : the factory hand instead of the cotter or farm labourer, the tradesman instead of the farmer, the cottonmaster and the banker instead of the landlord, became the typical units of the national organisation. Political change necessarily accompanied these economic changes. The new forces claimed their share of influence in political life ; but it was long before they could enforce their claim, and the struggle confused and embittered the economic disorders.

The effects of such a revolution must have been in any case profound and disquieting. New powers, hitherto unknown in the world's history, were let loose, and no one was wise enough to understand, or strong enough to control them. Much suffering must inevitably have followed ; but unfortunately the situation was complicated by political events in reality unconnected with it. The energies of the country were absorbed in the greatest international struggle it had yet experienced, and the minds of the ruling classes preoccupied with ideas ill understood. The great revolution was allowed to work itself out without let or guidance ; and many evils that might have been checked in the

A

beginning were able to grow to such proportions that it seemed centuries of reform could not eradicate them.

This change pressed most hardly on the country labourer. For him agricultural improvements often meant the loss of his common rights and little plot, and the alternative before him might be to cling to the land, struggling on a starvation wage, or to leave home and seek his fortune in the towns, where he became the pawn of an unorganised and chaotic industry, living from hand to mouth, and dependent on the fluctuations of trade. But there was another class that suffered almost as much. The small freeholders —the yeomanry, long belauded as the source of England's strength and the mainstay of English freedom—were often put to it to live. There was no place for the small farmer, without knowledge or capital, in scientific agriculture and large-scale production, and the yeomanry began to decline.

At worst, the small freeholder might sink to the level of the labourers around him, or even be driven from the land to the town. Some sold their land and turned tenant farmer. A few who were luckier, or wealthier, or more intelligent might prosper under the new system. Others took advantage of the very forces that threatened their existence; and their industry and shrewdness found new channels. They transferred their energies from agriculture to trade; and the old agricultural middle class became an important element in the formation of the new commercial and industrial middle class, which was to become, for a time, the dominant power in the country.

Such a yeoman family, of the name of Peele, had settled near Blackburn in Lancashire in the seventeenth century, and William Peele bought the little estate called Peelfold in 1731, and bequeathed it and not much else to his eldest son, Robert. This William is said to have been spendthrift and improvident, but his son was a man of different metal. It was he who dropped the final 'e' out of the family name, remarking that 'it was of no use as it did not add to the sound,'[1] and this strong sense of utility he displayed in all his affairs.

Like many others of their class, the Peels seem to have engaged in handloom weaving on a small scale in their own home; and when in 1744 a relaxation of the law allowed printed cottons to be manufactured in England, Robert Peel was one of the first to see

---

[1] *Lawrence Peel*, p. 13.

the possibilities of the new industry. Even by mortgaging Peel-fold, however, he could not raise the capital he needed, and he and his brother-in-law, Haworth, therefore approached one Yates, landlord of the *Black Bull* at Blackburn, and entered into partner-ship with him. In the new firm, Yates supplied the capital, Haworth the technical skill, and Peel, one may guess, the organis-ing power and business ability.

Haworth went up to London to learn the newest processes of the manufacture, and, about the year 1764, a little factory for cotton printing was set up at Blackburn, and weaving and spinning mills were added. There was considerable prejudice to contend against. A family tradition relates that a skilled mechanic, brought from outside, had to be concealed in Haworth's house while he plied his mysteries. Later, the handloom weavers and hand-spinners rose and wrecked the machines ; but the firm was now too solidly established to be injured permanently. Peel removed to Burton-upon-Trent, built three new mills and a canal, and prospered more than ever. For reasons of convenience, the original partnership was dissolved. Peel set up an independent business, and Yates and Haworth took into their concern, as a junior partner, their old friend's third son, another Robert. Robert II was as energetic and capable as his father : he was one of a large family, and at eighteen years old he had remarked that ' they were too thick on the ground,' and suggested that he should be given £500 and sent out into the world to seek his fortune. He did not get it ; but this independent spirit may account for the fact that he chose to enter the firm of Haworth and Yates rather than that of his father. They set up their factories at Bury, and young Peel married Yates' daughter Ellen, a girl nearly twenty years younger than himself, whom he selected as his future bride while she was still almost in the nursery.

In the factory at Bury many innovations were made, of great importance in the history of the cotton trade. It was one of the first mills to employ the spinning jenny, and some mechanical improvements were made there in the machinery. James Har-greaves, inventor of the jenny, is said to have worked for the firm. Peel took a leading part in the successful attempt of the cotton masters to oppose Arkwright's attempt to enforce the patents of his machinery.[1] It was Peel, too, who hit on the novel scheme of

[1] Wheeler, *History of Manchester*, p. 521.

importing paupers wholesale from London poorhouses, and, in particular, of employing pauper children to tend the machines. The senior partners died or retired : Peel & Co., as the firm now was, began to extend its operations on all sides. New factories sprang up in various districts, and the direct personal connection of the proprietor with all of these could not be maintained. His remained the guiding brain, but the practical management of the mills was delegated to others, while Peel himself soared into higher spheres. He had built up, by thrift, industry, and intelligence, a fortune at that time almost unequalled in England, and he now determined to enter politics. For this the possession of land was necessary, and Peel acquired a pocket borough, Tamworth, and bought the manor of Drayton, near by. In 1790 he entered Parliament as member for Tamworth, and became a loyal adherent of the younger Pitt, then at the zenith of his power.

His parliamentary career was not undistinguished. Pitt respected his knowledge, and is said to have consulted him upon financial questions. When the European War broke out, he contributed £10,000 and raised a corps of volunteers at his own expense, and in recognition of his generosity Pitt gave him a baronetcy in 1800. In economic theory Peel was not generally in advance of his fellows, but his practical good sense was great. He wrote a pamphlet entitled *The National Debt productive of National Prosperity*, and strongly disapproved of the resumption of cash payments ; but, on the other hand, he prevented, for the time being, the imposition of a tax on raw cotton, and strenuously opposed the Corn Laws of 1815. He also took the lead in urging the Government to give a monetary reward to Samuel Crompton, the inventor of ' the mule.' [1]

His abilities were, in fact, those of a practical man of business, not of a statesman or great financier ; and his tastes and disposition continued to be those of the class from which he had sprung. He was keen, sober, and conscientious in a narrow way ; ambitious, but no snob ; sometimes pompous and affected, but in private relapsing into the more genial and homely ways of his youth. His letters to his eldest son read like extracts from *The Fairchild Family ;* but when he read in the newspapers of that son's political career, he would slap his knee and cry joyfully, ' Robin's the lad ! '

[1] See French, *Life of Crompton.* Crompton was awarded £2000 by Parliament.

It is in relation to the employment of children that Sir Robert
Peel, first baronet, made his most important contribution to the
cotton trade—or, indeed, to industry in general. Not only was he
the first to introduce infant labour into the factories,[1] but he was
also the first to give to the child labourer the protection of the law.

Peel & Co., in their early days, had certainly an evil reputation.
It seems probable that, while Peel himself was still acting manager,
conditions were not so bad. He was friendly to those of his em-
ployees who showed industry and ambition : he encouraged them
to set up for themselves, and always took an interest in their subsequent careers. Long afterwards it was found that his old workmen ' spoke of him with respect, and some with affection.' [2] When,
however, his personal connection with the business was less
close, Peel's mills became as bad as any in the trade. They were
built on the model of Arkwright's original factory,[3] which was
planned solely for the purpose of accommodating the machinery,
and therefore the ventilation was insufficient. Cleanliness was
also neglected. The children were at times worked fourteen or
fifteen hours a day. Peel's orders that they should have proper
medical attendance in all cases of sickness were apparently disobeyed. The mill at Radcliff Bridge, near Manchester, was in a
particularly disgraceful state. Here the children were kept for
almost a year at a time on night work. Under this system they
actually worked shorter hours (10-$10\frac{1}{2}$ working hours), but the
injury to their health was great, partly because the same beds were
used for the two shifts,—the ' night children ' entering the beds
just left by the ' day children '—and partly because the misguided
little ' night children ' *would* go out to play in the sunlight instead
of sensibly going to sleep, and so did not get sufficient rest. Peel
himself admitted that conditions at Radcliff Bridge were ' very
bad.' [4] This was one of the factories where the epidemic fever
started, which in 1796 roused the indignation of Dr. Percival, and
so drew the attention of the public for the first time to the condition of the factory children.

[1] Of course children were employed in the spinning industry under the
domestic system long before this.

[2] W. Cooke Taylor, *Tour in the Manufacturing Districts of Lancashire*, p. 102.

[3] ' We all looked up to him (Arkwright) and imitated his mode of building.'
—Evidence of Sir R. Peel, *Report of the Commission on the employment of Children
in Manufacture*, 1816, p. 134.

[4] *Report of the Committee of* 1816, p. 138.

The pauper children were entirely dependent on their masters for support, and it is probable that Peel's ' little hands ' were better fed and better clothed than in some smaller and less prosperous concerns, where it was the direct interest of the master to save money on their keep.[1]   Sir Robert contended that the dress of his children was always ' pretty good,' and that ' he had not a doubt that they were well fed,' [2] but it is clear that if asked point blank whether they subsisted on roast beef and plum duff or on water gruel, he would have been put to it to give a definite answer.

For these conditions Sir Robert Peel cannot be held entirely responsible. ' I could not be in two places at once,' he said later. ' It was not often in my power to visit the factories, but whenever such visits were made, I was struck with the uniform appearance of bad health, and in many cases stinted (*sic*) growth of the children.' [3]   He repeatedly ordered his overseers not to work the ' little hands,' under any circumstances, more than twelve hours a day ; but he found it impossible to get his orders obeyed. The old practices went on when his back was turned ; and this was not surprising, because the overseers were paid according to the output. It does not seem to have occurred to Peel to alter the mode of payment ; and when one of the Factory Commissioners of 1816 asked him why he did not dismiss the disobedient overseers, the honourable baronet seems to have lost his temper. ' If my business had been in hands equally competent with those of the honourable member,' he replied, ' perhaps that practice might have been resorted to ; but with the best knowledge I had I conducted my business, and I think, with as much humanity, in general, as other gentlemen.' [4]

It took several years to rouse Peel to do more than ' gently ask and demand ' that his overseers should reform ; but he did finally see that more active intervention was necessary, and he succeeded in carrying through Parliament the Health and Morals of Apprentices Act, 1802. By this Act the hours of apprentices in the cotton trade were limited to twelve, and special provisions were made for their being properly clothed and educated, and for the mills being cleaned and ventilated. A cynic might point out that by intro-

---

[1] The feeding and clothing of Peel's ' little hands ' was under a separate authority, not under the control of the overseer of the works.

[2] *Report of the Committee of* 1816, p. 135.

[3] *Ib.* p. 132.   [4] *Ib.* p. 142.

ducing an Act of Parliament, instead of reforming his own mills, Peel protected himself against trade losses by ensuring that rival manufacturers should be equally subjected to limitation of hours and increased expenses ; but the cynic would be wrong. Peel's position was now too securely established to be threatened by competition, and he was beyond doubt actuated by a sincere desire to improve the state of the factory children. He was a slow and unsympathetic man, and entirely lacking in imagination, but his feelings had at last been roused, and he came to take a great pride in his honourable position as the children's protector.

The Act of 1802 was a very ineffective piece of legislation. The penalties for violating it were ridiculously small, and in some districts no attempt whatever was made to enforce it. The better class of cotton master, however, did make some attempt to follow its provisions, partly out of respect for the law, but more because the passing of the Act had, however slightly, roused public opinion in favour of the children. In Peel's own mills it was certainly observed very fairly. From this time he himself received a regular weekly report of the health of the children, and ' Magistrates who were the inspectors,' he proudly boasted, ' declared it was of no use to visit factories in which I had a concern, because the children were more healthy than any other children of poor people.' [1]

The Act of 1802 applied only to apprentices, and with the advent of steam power, pauper apprentice labour and the country mill gave place to free labour and the town factory. The ' free ' child labourer was exploited just as unscrupulously as the apprentice had been, and Robert Owen and his friends desired to supplement the old Act with one regulating free labour. They approached Sir Robert Peel, who readily promised to introduce a Bill, and who secured the appointment of the first Factory Commission, that of 1816, usually called ' Peel's Committee.' The original provisions of the Bill were an advance on 1802. No child under ten years old was to be employed in the textile trades, and no child under sixteen years for more than eleven hours a day. The Bill, however, was circulated during the recess of Parliament, Peel was unwise enough to favour an attempt to obtain limitation of hours for adults also, and so strong an opposition grew up that he was obliged to make large concessions. The age of employment was

[1] *Report of the Committee of* 1816, p. 137.

lowered to nine, and the time limit raised to twelve hours. Peel's own evidence, given before the Committee, is of great interest. It shows him an honest man, but with no clear grasp of the economic principles which either his friends or his opponents had brought to bear upon the question.[1] The Bill was long delayed, partly owing to opposition, partly to Peel's ill-health, but it was at length passed, in its mutilated form, in 1819—the first of that long succession of Factory Acts that form one of the greatest achievements of the nineteenth century.

The Act of 1819, like the Act of 1802, remained to a great extent a dead letter; but it was of inestimable value, for it asserted clearly and for the first time the great principles, that it is the duty of the State to protect from industrial exploitation those who cannot protect themselves, and that the theory of freedom of contract cannot apply to a child. The assertion of these principles was far more impressive, because the man who was responsible for the passing of the Act was no mere scholar or visionary, but was himself a master manufacturer and one of the pioneers of the cotton trade.

Peel himself was hardly conscious of the significance of his action. He was the true child of the Industrial Revolution: representing in himself the energy, the enterprise, the hard practical sense, the keen but narrow ambition, and the strong individualism that the revolution had set free. Where he rose above his fellows was in his capacity, however limited, of detaching himself from the conditions of his life, and perceiving their defects. He had no general conception of the problems raised by the industrial revolution: he simply tried to remedy an individual instance of suffering that came under his own eye.

One of the Peels, when asked why it was that the new firm under Sir Robert had so far outstripped the old one managed by his father, replied, after a little thought, ' I think it was because they had more brains.' [2] Sir Robert Peel united to his father's shrewdness and industry a new originality and enterprise. By the undiscoverable processes of nature, the next generation saw the hard common sense and practical ability of the Peels transmuted, by some touch of divine fire, into political genius.

---

[1] See, for example, the extraordinarily confused and meaningless speech on the subject of foreign competition.—*Report*, p. 141.

[2] *Lawrence Peel*, p. 37.

Mr. Pitt, leaving the House of Commons one day, encountered his friend Peel in the doorway, accompanied by a little Harrow boy. ' Is this your son, Mr. Peel ? ' said the Primè Minister, whose fondness for boys is well known. ' It is,' was the answer ; and Pitt took the little fellow's hand and led him into the House. So the eighteenth century and the nineteenth touched hands.[1]

[1] See a letter from Samuel Oldknow, who witnessed the incident, 22nd July, 1826. H.O. 44, 16.

CHAPTER II

THE EDUCATION OF A TORY

WHILE the factory children were spending twelve hours a day at the wheels (and half an hour a day in religious exercises) in Sir Robert Peel's mills, a blooming flock of little ones was growing up in his house at Drayton. The Peels went in for large families, but in this generation there was no need for them to feel themselves 'too thick upon the ground;' there was ample provision for all. The girls were heiresses. The boys went to Harrow and Oxford, and were destined for politics, the army, or the Church—not to follow their father in business. But the characteristics acquired in generations of trade clung to them. Received now as equals in the houses of the Tory aristocracy, the Peels remained, in their whole moral and intellectual outlook, essentially practical men, essentially middle class.

The household at Drayton was still very different from the great and splendid houses in the English counties, where the statesmen of the next generation were now growing up, and the childhood of the young Peels was very unlike that of the little Lord Ashley, a lonely, neglected boy, starved by servants and terrified by his parents; or of young 'Jack Spencer, Viscount Althorp,' growing up the close companion of footmen and stable-boys; or of little Lord John Russell, learning from his tutor to bet and gamble, and spending every night of his holidays at the theatre. Life at Drayton was strict, simple and orderly, and, for the times, pious. The association of parents and children, though formal, was close and affectionate. It suggests one of those domestic interiors so skilfully portrayed by Charlotte Mary Yonge; and the eldest son of the house might well have been the original of one of Miss Yonge's prim and conscientious young heroes.

The time was drawing near when a struggle must inevitably arise between the new commercial middle class, growing daily more powerful, wealthier, more self-conscious, and the old landed aristocracy, who still held the monopoly of political influence in

the country. Who could be a fitter guide or mediator in such a
struggle than the son of such a house as this—sharing in the life of
the old aristocracy, yet representing the traditions and the characteristics of the new ?

Possibly with some unconscious premonition of this—but more
likely owing to a more commonplace ambition—old Sir Robert
Peel had set his heart upon having his eldest son a statesman.
The child's career was decided while he was still in the cradle and
his education directed for this sole purpose. He was a pretty little
fair boy, with a round, smiling face, very docile and sedate, and not
much liked by other children because he was always held up to
them as an example by the elders. No doubt this rather injudicious treatment helped to heighten and develop an innate
priggishness. He was shy, over-sensitive, and terrified of being
laughed at. He was born in 1788, before the migration to Drayton ; and the rough country boys at Bury, who shouted at him as
he went home from his tutor's, had been a source of real unhappi-
ness to him. With all this, however, he had at the same time
plenty of self-confidence and pluck. It was noticed that in games
with other children he always managed to impose his own will
upon theirs. At thirteen he was sent to Harrow, where he at once
showed his independence. Thinking himself within his lawful
rights, he refused to fag, and was brutally thrashed by a bigger
boy. A romantic tale, which relates that little Byron rushed
forward in tears and begged to take half the punishment, seems to
be entirely mythical.

After this inauspicious opening, he seems to have been happy at
school. His industrious habits, his popularity with his masters,
and his shirking of games, which might have made him disliked,
seem to have been counterbalanced by his imperturbable good-
nature and his readiness to do other people's exercises for them.
He was a reserved, solitary boy, with a habit of taking long walks
alone, ' communing with nature,' as a schoolfellow describes it,
and shooting any birds he encountered with a gun he had concealed at a cottage. This method of ' communing with nature '
may be considered rather one-sided, but it was uncommonly useful
to young Peel in after life. He was a first-rate shot, and a keen
shot, and this talent served to recommend him to the Tory
aristocracy who were to be his associates.[1]

[1] See Parker, *Peel*, vol. i. chap. i. ; *Lawrence Peel*, p. 48 ff.

In the meantime his education went on at home also.   Since his
earliest years, Sir Robert had trained his son in public speaking.
Every Sunday little Robert was called upon to repeat the sermon
he had heard at church that morning, and this exercise proved an
excellent training.   It developed in the boy extraordinary powers
of accuracy, and taught him early to listen to and memorise long,
formal, and uninteresting orations.   ' His memory is so tenacious
and correct,' was said of him long after, ' that they (*i.e.* his political
opponents) never can make any mistakes without his detecting
them ; and he is inconceivably ready in all references to former
debates and their incidents, and the votes and speeches of individual members.' [1]   More than this, the training helped to overcome his natural diffidence and self-consciousness, which might
otherwise have been a serious obstacle to a political career, so
that he was never so much at ease, never so little awkward, as
when speaking in public.

In 1805 he went up to Oxford.   True to his plans, old Sir
Robert had selected for him the aristocratic college of Christ
Church, where the boy became a gentleman commoner.   He was
by no means a mere student : he shot, rode (very badly), went into
society, and took a great deal of interest in his clothes.   Nevertheless he worked himself into a fever before his examination, lost
his nerve, and wrote home to say he could not go up, as he was sure
he should fail.   His father answered him with sensible encouragement, advising more amusement and less application.   Peel took
his advice, and passed brilliantly, being the first man to obtain a
double first, in mathematics and classics, under the new regulations.   He was now almost twenty-one, and his father bought him,
as a nice coming-of-age present, the Irish borough of Cashel, and
he was free to begin his political career.

He had now grown up into a personable young man, tall and
well-built, with blue eyes, bright yellow hair, and a fair complexion
that blushed and paled very readily.   The sly expression of the
eyes, which his enemies declared meant cunning, is, as Lord Rosebery pointed out, really the indication of a sense of humour.   He
had never outgrown his shyness, and was handicapped by a very
awkward manner, disagreeably stiff and cold, and sometimes even
more disagreeably suave.   He was reserved and exceedingly
sensitive, and part of this awkwardness was due to an attempt to

----

[1] *Greville*, iii. p. 239.

guard his own feelings. In spite of all his shyness, however, he was very confident in his own powers, very ambitious, and very proud. He had a violent temper, which he commonly managed to control, but which sometimes broke loose, with disastrous effects. His moral character was irreproachable, and had never given his parents the slightest anxiety. His amusement was shooting, his interests were literary and artistic, his chief pleasure was hard work.

He entered Parliament, of course, as a Tory. All his short, contented life he had been surrounded by an atmosphere of Toryism.

He was brought up by his father in the traditions of the 'nineties to think that the French Revolution was the greatest disaster in history ; to think that revolution and reform were indissolubly connected ; that concession meant disaster ; that to give the lower classes in the State a hand in the government was to court destruction ; that to keep down the forces of anarchy with the strong hand was the first duty of government and the first condition of national prosperity. Nothing in his education had counteracted this teaching. He had never associated with members of the other political party. The Whigs were still so much discredited that he had but little opportunity of seeing their case fairly stated in the public press. The Radicals were as yet almost non-existent. ' Democracy ' meant for him the mob that had sacked Birmingham ; ' Reform ' was the catchword of the Jacobin clubs.

Always docile and receptive, he had accepted the ideas presented to him without criticism or consideration. In any case, he had not had time at his age to form an independent judgment ; but he was not naturally critical, and he had never been taught to think for himself, to search for truth, to weigh a question on its merits, or to analyse his own mental attitudes. The great virtue of any educational system is that it should teach the child to think ; but it is scarcely an exaggeration to say that this was the last thing considered by the system under which Peel had been educated. At school, of course, he had learnt nothing but Latin and Greek grammar : even mathematics he had only taken up of his own accord upon leaving school. As an example of the educational theories of the day, an extract may be given from a letter of congratulation sent to Peel by his old headmaster :

' Now remember what I say. Give the last high finish to all that you now possess by the continual reading of Homer. Let no day pass without your having him in your hands. Elevate your own mind by the continual meditation of the vastness of his comprehension and the unerring accuracy of all his conceptions. If you will but read him four or five times every year, in half a dozen years you will know him by heart. . . . He alone possesses the great secret of knowing how far ornament should be carried, what degree of it gives strength to a sentiment, and what overwhelms and oppresses it.' [1]

Obviously to Dr. Jackson the requisite qualifications for a young man entering political life were a mind steeped in classical literature, a habit of hard work, and the careful study of oratory ; and the way in which he thought these might be attained was by reading, five times in the year, a romantic epic written in a foreign language three thousand years before.[2]

Such, then, was the young man who entered political life in 1809. A gift for oratory had been perhaps over-cultivated, producing a tendency towards the pompous and artificial style. He had a natural, inherited power of application, a remarkable memory, and a good knowledge of mathematics and of classical literature. He was entirely ignorant of economic theory, and he knew very little of the actual conditions of life around him— even those of his father's business. He had acquired to admiration the mechanism of an educated mind, without the inquiring spirit which gives it its real value.

The natural result was that his outlook was narrow, prejudiced, and self-satisfied. Flung while still almost a boy into political life, and immersed in the cares and routine of office, it did not seem likely that experience would correct this. Against the danger young Peel had only one safeguard—his own fundamental honesty. Ignorant he might be, but he would never wilfully deceive himself. This intellectual honesty might in time pierce through conventions and traditions and reach the truth ; but the atmosphere of parliamentary life, with its admired pretences and reverend shams, was not favourable to its preservation.

A baseless tradition of later days relates that Sir Robert Peel warned his official friends that it would be well to get young Robert into harness speedily, as, if he were not given some office, he might drift into a junction with the Whigs. The story is

[1] Parker, *Peel*, i. p. 28.

[2] In justice to Peel I must state that I have never found any indication that he followed his master's advice.

absurd on the face of it, for what did the Prime Minister care for
the politics of a young fellow of one-and-twenty without aristocratic connections ?   Nor is there any indication that young Peel
displayed any liberal tendencies at this time.   Visiting his relations in London, he on one occasion surprised them by delivering
a flaming panegyric on Napoleon, so that on his departure his uncle
remarked with a sigh that he wished Robert were half as liberal
in home as in foreign politics.   But this seems to have been merely
a piece of boyish hero-worship.   The Whigs, moreover, at this
time displayed certain tendencies which were singularly unsympathetic to Peel, not only then, but at every period of his life.

The outbreak of the French Revolution had thrown the whole
party system in Britain into confusion : it had placed both Whigs
and Tories in an equally false position, and as a result of this, Peel,
being obliged to join one party or other, found himself in a false
position also.

By the declaration of war on France in 1793, Britain, the free
self-governing State, was plunged into a struggle *à outrance* with
a Power which represented all that was best, most liberal, most
hopeful in Europe, just as surely as afterwards it came to represent
a dangerous and aggressive tyranny that must, for Europe's safety,
be destroyed.   This confusion of ideals abroad was reflected in the
confusion of British politics at home.   Pitt, who had seemed born
to reorganise the domestic life of the nation, who seemed of all
men the most capable of steering the country through the
dangerous waters of economic change on which she was now
launched—Pitt was pledged to an external struggle that absorbed
all his energies.   His half-hesitating touch, in '93, had let loose a
strong current of national feeling that swept him away upon its
crest, a patriotic fervour that never failed until the power of
France was broken and the threat of Napoleonic Empire ended.
He was the national hero—' The pilot that weathered the storm '—
and his death, worn-out and broken-hearted, in the midst of the
disasters of 1805, was the signal for a nation's mourning.   Nevertheless his later career had been the falsification of all his early
promise.   All his powers absorbed in the great struggle, his eye
blinded by long years in office, and his perceptions deadened by his
habit of subsisting chiefly on port, he had lost touch with the spirit
of progress and reform.   Indiscriminate coercion was all that he
could offer for the solution of internal problems ; and at the same

time as he gathered round him all that was best of the patriotic devotion of the nation, he gathered also all that was worst of bigotry, corruption, and greed.

Upon the Whig party the effects of the war were equally disastrous. It led at once to the break-up of the party and its destruction, for the time being, as an effective political force. Burke and Grenville seceded and supported the Tory Government. Fox and his friends were stanch to the principles of the Revolution, and thereby lost their hold on the people, who regarded them as traitors, or at best lukewarm friends to their country. Some of them at least justified this opinion by sneers at patriots, and by an opposition spiteful and factious. So completely discredited did they become that the great chiefs withdrew from parliamentary life, leaving Tiernay to head what remained of their party.

With the opening of the nineteenth century the position of the Whigs improved. After the rupture of the Peace of Amiens, the war became so clearly a war for national existence that they could conscientiously support it, and they were able to form an administration after the death of Pitt. Unfortunately, they gained but little credit from their short tenure of power. They did not prosecute the war with energy, and dallied with unfounded hopes of peace. The army and the navy were allowed to deteriorate. In 1807 an intrigue on the subject of Catholic Emancipation destroyed the Government, and they once more yielded to the temptation of factious and malicious opposition, which revived all the popular distrust of their motives.

To young Peel, brought up in a house where Pitt was the hero, and endowed with a strong sense of public duty, all this was very unpleasing, and alone would have prevented his leaning towards the Whigs. Thus the best as well as the worst tendencies of his nature led him to join the Tories, the party so strangely compounded of ignorant reaction and lofty public spirit.

It was in April, 1809, that Peel came up to London—a little London, where green fields lay where now are streets of brick, and a vast ash-heap occupied the site of the present London University ; where Regent Street was not built, nor Regent's Park laid out ; where gentlemen walking at night went armed, and the Bow Street runners, in red waistcoats, haunted thieves' kitchens in search of prey ; and where the old Houses of Parliament still stood, a huddle of low, mean-looking roofs, filling the space between the Abbey and the water, and Westminster Hall rose high above them, peerless then as now. When the new member took his seat there, it was in the midst of a Cabinet crisis of a very disagreeable nature.

There had been divisions in the Tory party ever since Pitt resigned over Catholic Emancipation in 1802. Mr. Canning and Lord Castlereagh, the pupils of Pitt, both favoured the removal of the Catholic disabilities; but the Chancellor, Eldon, the Home Secretary, Spencer Perceval, and the great bulk of the party were opposed to it. The Prime Minister, the Duke of Portland, had not the strength or capacity to hold the Government together, and personal rivalries added to his difficulties. Lord Sidmouth had never forgiven Canning for cruel personal attacks in the past, and had refused to sit in the same Cabinet with him. Worse, there was jealousy between Canning and Castlereagh.

One was Foreign Secretary, one Secretary at War, and their duties overlapped in the continental warfare now developing. Canning thought himself inadequately supported, and in March, 1809, he told Portland that he would resign unless Castlereagh were transferred to another office. He wished that the new Secretary at War should be Lord Wellesley, whose character and ante-cedents promised that he would be a very malleable instrument in Canning's hands. Portland agreed, but he was dying and was in no condition to undertake the unpleasant job of tackling Castlereagh. After three months Canning discovered that nothing had been done, and protested. The other members of the Cabinet were now informed, and Perceval thought Castlereagh was not being fairly treated. It was suggested that Portland, who was failing rapidly, should resign at once, and, amid a general reorganisation of the Cabinet, Castlereagh's change of office would pass un-noticed. But who was to succeed Portland? Canning at once declared that he would serve under no one in the Commons; that Perceval could not serve under him, and that the latter should retire to the House of Lords. Perceval, who had no mind to be shelved, suggested that he and Canning should keep their present positions, under a Prime Minister in the Upper House. Meantime the Walcheren Expedition, which had been Castlereagh's chosen scheme and conducted entirely by him, was ending in disaster, and Perceval urged the impropriety of insisting on the fulfilment of Portland's promise now. Canning resigned.

At this moment Castlereagh became aware, for the first time, that Canning had continued to act with him as colleague and maintain the most intimate relations with him, while all the time urging his removal. He instantly sent a challenge, and Canning, instead of offering an explanation,[1] accepted it. A duel was fought, in which Canning was slightly wounded. Castlereagh and Portland had both resigned, and a new Ministry was formed under Perceval, from which both Canning and Castlereagh, the two ablest of the Tory leaders, were necessarily excluded. The whole story was made public, and Canning was left with a reputation for intrigue which, however unjustly, clung to him for the remainder of his life.

Peel had sat for two months under the Portland Government without speaking; but when the new session opened, in January, 1810, he at once attracted attention. It was then, as now, the custom to choose some promising young man to make his maiden speech in seconding the Address to the Throne, and Perceval invited Peel to do so. It was an occasion of some importance, for the Government were anxiously awaiting an attack upon the Walcheren Expedition, and Peel's speech consisted chiefly of a defence of the Government's policy. The House is always kind on such an occasion, but Peel's speech was a triumph. His father, with his younger son, William, stood listening in the gallery opposite, and when loud applause broke out, tears of joy and pride rolled down Sir Robert's face.

In March the young member spoke again, this time in defence of the Walcheren Expedition, and in April Perceval offered him an Under-Secretaryship at the Colonial Office. A friend, meeting him, congratulated him on his promotion, and he replied that 'he thought it no subject for congratulation, that he only accepted it in deference to his father, and wished to have been free to form his own opinion independently upon it.'[2] This may have been the affectation of a diffident and self-conscious young man; but it may also hint at a real reluctance, a real dread of being committed to a definite course before he had found his footing, an instinctive clutch at his intellectual integrity and independence.

---

[1] Canning declared that he thought all along that Castlereagh had been informed. It is just possible that he may have thought so up till June, but after that time he knew it was not so.

[2] Parker, *Peel*, i. p. 30.

But he had always been more or less passive under his father's guidance, and he did not rebel now. He was launched on an official career, and for eight years, the critical years from twenty-two to thirty, he was to be immersed in the daily routine of administration and the feverish excitement of party warfare in the House of Commons. Had he joined the Opposition, necessity might have fostered a more critical turn of mind ; but as a member of the Tory Government, which stood for the established order of things, he was called upon to defend, not to criticise, to preserve, not to attack, and the natural bent of his mind was intensified.

He remained at the Colonial Office for two years, and thus became well acquainted with his future chief, Lord Liverpool, then Secretary of State for War and Colonies. He was too unimportant a person to play any part, save by casting his vote, in the great struggle over the Regency Bill, though he seems to have shared in the general enthusiasm for Perceval roused in the Tory party by the Prime Minister's unexpected display of courage, vigour and straightforwardness.[1] He entertained at dinner parties, where ' the conversation was almost exclusively political,' [2] his parliamentary contemporaries—Palmerston, two years his elder, who had already been two years in office as Secretary at War ; Manners Sutton, afterwards for many years Speaker ; Robinson, a future Prime Minister ; Goulburn, for long Peel's loyal colleague ; and John Wilson Croker, who became his close friend. Croker, then Secretary to the Admiralty, was a man of some ability and of sterling honesty and courage ; but there was an ugly element in his character, a strain of cruelty and malice that showed itself chiefly in his literary work, and Peel was one day to discover it.

In 1812 his position was suddenly changed. As the Prime Minister was entering the House of Commons one day, a stranger met him on the steps, said in a loud voice, ' I am John James Bellingham, a merchant of Liverpool,' and, drawing a pistol, shot him through the heart. Perceval dropped with a cry of ' Murder ! ' He was lifted into the Vote Office, but died in a few moments. The assassin was proved to be insane, but, in an age less tender of lunatics than ours, was speedily sentenced and hanged.

[1] Plumer Ward, *Memoirs*, i. pp. 340-1.
[2] Parker, *Peel*, i. p. 31.

Perceval had made himself very popular by his courage, honesty, and unassuming simplicity, and it was believed that only this had held together the Tory ministry during two stormy years, and that a Whig Government must be the inevitable sequel to his death. The first attempt of the Regent was to commission Wellesley and Canning, who approached the Whigs. Grenville and Grey, however, received the advances with haughty coldness, and made demands so intolerable to the Prince that the affair fell through. Liverpool was then sent for, and his first effort was to secure Canning. Castlereagh, who had entered the Perceval Cabinet some months before, offered to resign to Canning the Foreign Secretaryship, but he would not give up the lead in the House of Commons also, and Canning demanded both. He believed he was indispensable, and that he could soon make what terms he pleased. So he threw away his chance, as the Whigs had thrown away theirs : the Liverpool Government, apparently so weak, was to last for fourteen years.

The new Cabinet was exclusively Tory in character. Castlereagh was Foreign Secretary, Eldon Chancellor, Sidmouth went to the Home Office, and Palmerston was still ' at War,' where he remained for sixteen years, the most stable element in a shifting political system. ' Ultra ' peers for the most part made up the rest of the Cabinet. Liverpool was but little pleased with the quality of his administration. ' I have no resource but to bring forward the most promising of the young men,' he wrote.[1] He selected his late subordinate, Robert Peel, as Secretary for Ireland.

---

[1] Parker, *Peel,* i. p. 32.

CHAPTER III

ORANGE PEEL, 1812-1818.

THERE was at this period a complete Irish Administration : an Irish Chancellor of the Exchequer, Solicitor-General, and Attorney-General managed financial and legal business ; two Under-Secretaries in Dublin undertook civil and military affairs, and there was a third Under-Secretary in London. At the head of all was the Lord Lieutenant ; but he was chiefly the King's representative, he was always a peer, and resided in Dublin. It was the Chief Secretary who was the working head of the Administration, and who was responsible to Parliament for the doings of all the rest. Neither the Viceroy nor, with rare exceptions, the Secretary had a seat in the Cabinet. The exact division of authority between these two varied according to the character of the individuals who held the posts ; but the position of Chief Secretary was one of little glory and much peril, for, whatever Government might be in power, the state of Ireland was likely to be the weakest point in its administration, and thither the attacks of the Opposition would most frequently be directed.

Parliamentary government was in reality out of place in Ireland. The English in Ireland were alien conquerors ruling a hostile population which was in chronic disorder and periodic revolt. There was no scope for democratic institutions here, for a real representative assembly would at once have voted Ireland out of the Union. But there it was, and they had to make the best of it. The Irish Parliament had been merged in that of the United Kingdom in 1801 : a hundred Irish members sat at Westminster, and twenty peers. A franchise, nominally the same as that of England, but in reality much more democratic, gave almost every peasant a vote. This representative government was, however, a fiction. At bottom, the power of England in Ireland rested, as the power of an alien conqueror must always rest, on force ; but an outward respect for parliamentary institutions must be preserved, and the Irish administration worked through an elaborate system of corruption and pretence.

The threat of force, of course, hung always in the background : both parties remembered '98. A large army of occupation was maintained and, in the absence of any efficient police, was necessary to keep any semblance of order. But the Government were sincerely reluctant to use this means more than was necessary. They relied on other safeguards.

Ireland was a Catholic country ; but the Catholics had been, in the past century, disfranchised and oppressed. The old penal laws had been repealed by Grattan's Parliament, and when the Union with Britain took place in 1801 the complete emancipation of the Catholics had been promised. The promise, however, was not kept : the opposition of the King and the strong feeling of a large part of the British people had made its fulfilment impossible. The Irish Catholic could vote, but not sit in Parliament ; enter the army or navy or the professions, but not rise to the higher ranks. The Universities and all the important posts of the Civil Service were closed to him.

Roughly, about one-sixth of the population of Ireland was Protestant, and on this the Government relied to maintain their hold over the Catholic majority. The Protestant Dissenters of Northern Ireland were a privileged people. They occupied the only province that could by any stretch of language be called wealthy and prosperous. They had long been used to a monopoly of Government's favour, and they feared any increase of Catholic influence, lest it should bring revenge and confiscation. They had not yet forgotten ' The Troubles ' of Stafford's day. They called themselves Irish now, but they were not sufficiently Irish to trust their fellow-countrymen. The Government could rely upon their loyalty ; but the loyalty which would have been so desirable if more widely spread was sometimes embarrassing when so highly concentrated. The Protestants formed themselves into Orange Clubs, and provoked disorder by insulting demonstrations against the Catholics, and occasionally even by armed attacks.

The Government relied also upon the support of the landlords, who were almost all Protestant. The influence of the landlords made the democratic franchise a fiction. Numbers of ' 40s. freeholders ' were artificially created, who must vote as their landlords dictated, or be turned out; and through these parliamentary elections were controlled.[1]

More important even than this, it was believed, was the influence of the Established Church of Ireland, a branch of the Anglican Church. It is difficult to understand why this institution should have been considered of such priceless value. It was an abuse so flagrant that it might have been thought the most reckless tyrant would have hesitated to insult a conquered people by its presence, much less a Government which was anxious to act with justice and moderation. It was a State Church which represented the religion of a small minority of the people. It was one of the wealthiest of churches, supported by one of the most poverty-stricken countries in Europe. The Catholic peasant was taxed to support the Protestant Church, and the whole authority of the State was called in to support the demand; while the Catholic Church, the religion of the great majority of the people, was not merely unrecognised, but penalised, by the State. In as many as a hundred and forty parishes there existed a Protestant church without a single Protestant parishioner to attend it, and the Protestant clergyman recited (or did not recite) the service to empty benches. It might seem impossible that any respectable man— much less a minister of the Christian Church—would willingly place himself in a situation so degrading; yet there was never any lack of Anglican clergymen to fill Irish benefices—indeed, there was red-hot competition for them. How this institution could do anything to uphold the Government—how it could do anything but embitter Irish feeling against the Government—it is difficult at the present day to perceive.

The last, and perhaps the chief, means by which the Government maintained their position in Ireland was corruption. A vast patronage was in their gift, both civil and ecclesiastical, and by this the upper classes were retained in the official interest. Land-owners sold their pocket boroughs for peerages, and all classes their services for places in the Revenue, the Law, and the Church.

---

[1] ' Could you tell me . . . whether you think there is any probability of a contest for the county of Sligo at the next election ? I could at the present moment make from 280 to 290 voters by giving leases to tenants who are now holding at will. If there is any chance of their being of use next year, I will do so forthwith and register them in time. If not, I should perhaps postpone giving 21 years leases till matters look a little more propitious to the payment of rents.'—Lord Palmerston to Mr. Peel, 19th August, 1817. (Parker, *Peel*, i. p. 256.)

Newspapers were retained in the Government interest by payments and patronage from Dublin Castle. The Government of the United Kingdom was at this time corrupt ; but it was a model of purity compared with the Irish system. Naturally, where political corruption existed private corruption was rife. Every official, from the Chief Secretary downwards, used whatever influence he had to grab whatever he could for his friends and relatives. Bribes were habitually taken. Public funds were wasted and misused. The Irish Administration was the Tom Tiddler's Ground where the great aristocratic houses, and all their hangers-on, expected to pick up gold and silver.

Upon this unpleasing scene entered Mr. Peel, twenty-four years old, and with such knowledge of the world as three years in Parliament and two in a subordinate office might give him. He was surrounded by officials of long experience, men far older than himself, to whom this hoary corruption was familiar and natural as the air they breathed. Had he succumbed to the universal influence it would not have been very surprising. Nevertheless, during his six years of office, he contrived to make himself supreme head of the Irish Government ; to introduce a number of reforms ; and, to a considerable extent, to purify the administration.

In this task he started with several advantages. In the first place, the Lord Lieutenant, the Duke of Richmond, resigned only ten months after his arrival, and the permanent chief of the civil department left at the same time. The double change offered an opportunity to the new Secretary to strengthen his position and increase his power, and Peel was not the man to let such a chance slip.

Secondly, he had no connections in Ireland. He sat, indeed, for an Irish borough, but the election had been merely a money transaction, managed by his father, and had not required his presence. He had no friends or relatives in Ireland—no marriage alliance with needy and noble Irish houses. No horde of hangers-on, therefore, beset him, claiming that blood was thicker than water, and resenting his failure to rise to the occasion.

It was, of course, beyond the power even of the best-intentioned to put an end to the system of political corruption as it then existed. Not in Ireland only, but in England, and still more in Scotland, a certain proportion of places and preferments were the undeniable perquisite of the Government's supporters. The first attempt to check political corruption, however, had just been made : Curwen's Act, to prevent the sale of seats in Parliament for money, passed in 1812. It was not an effective measure ; seats continued to be bought and sold. Still, the Act obliged the Government, if no one else, to preserve an outward show of decency in dealing with transactions of this kind, and Peel at once got rid of his own Irish seat, leaving it to his father to procure him another seat in England—by means best not mentioned.

' I am placed in a delicate situation enough here,' he wrote to Croker—' Bound to secure the Government interests . . . but still more bound to faint with horror at the mention of money transactions, to threaten the unfortunate culprits with impeachment if they hint at an impure return, and yet to prevent those strongholds, Cashel, Mallow, and Tralee, from surrendering to the enemies who besiege them.' [1]

Peel's grasp of reality, his bold facing of such facts as came before him, was of service to him here. He entered into no wild crusade against corruption, which would have made him distrusted as visionary and quixotic. He saw that the nature of the Irish Administration was artificial, and regretted it. ' I believe an honest, despotic Government would be by far the fittest for Ireland,' he said straightforwardly. One cannot help feeling that even in England ' an honest, despotic Government ' would have been rather congenial to Mr. Peel ; it would have afforded more scope than parliamentary government for his administrative genius and his imperious temper ; but he could not get this, and he accepted the fact with all its implications.

' I shall be glad,' he wrote to the Prime Minister, ' when the time arrives that the government of this country can be conducted on different principles from what it at present is, when you can look for support (and I do not mean merely parliamentary support, but that effectual support which active and loyal men can afford in this country) to an honest conviction of its necessity and a pure sense of duty. But that time is not yet arrived, and till it does arrive you must either try to carry on the Government without such support, or you must (and I fear there is no misapplication of the term) purchase it.' [2]

Peel began by doing what he could—which was to keep his own hands clean. ' I found in Ireland,' he wrote after, ' that every official man . . . thought he had a right to quarter his family on

<hr/>

[1] Parker, *Peel*, i. p. 47.   [2] *Ib.* i. pp. 112-3.

the patronage of Government. I took the course that you have done, in order to enable me to resist with effect such extravagant pretensions. I determined never to gratify any private wish of my own by the smallest Irish appointment.'[1] As an example of the conduct of the highest officials may be mentioned that of the great Lord Plunket, the Irish patriot. He was appointed Attorney-General in 1822, and immediately made his youngest son, who had just taken orders, Vicar of Bray, and his second son a (paid) Commissioner of Judicial Inquiry. His son's tutor was made an assistant barrister, and his friends ' received almost every valuable office which has been at the disposal of the Crown.'[2] In 1825 he tried to secure for his eldest son the Deanery of Clogher, value £1200 a year, and in 1832 actually appointed his son Dean of Down, though Plunket himself had been, in the previous year, member of a Commission which had recommended the separation of the six benefices which composed the Deanery of Down on the next vacancy. This sort of thing Peel was determined not to tolerate. Political corruption he might be obliged to accept, but private corruption, so far as he could control it, stopped. He put an end to the sale of offices, and also to the practice of dismissing officials who voted against the Government. Cases of malversation or peculation of Government funds he visited with severe punishment, and, however distinguished were the patrons or relatives of the culprits, they implored in vain for mercy.

' Mr. A. gives but a lame justification of himself. Through fear of the Brownes he suffered two unfortunate women to be transported. . . . The Sheriff made no defence, but probably told a falsehood, which I shall detect if it be one. The fact that the nephew, who is, I suppose, a voter, was to get the unfortunate creature's property at her departure, makes the whole case worse than ever. It is quite melancholy to read her letter recommending her child, if she herself does not get her liberty, which she is afraid she will not do, as she has no person to look to for justice. But if it is in my power to get justice for her she shall have it.'

' I am very much obliged to you for your letter respecting the shameful abuses which have been discovered with respect to the

[1] Parker, *Peel* i. p. 60. Peel to Goulburn, 6th January, 1826. Plunket is the person whose name is left blank in this letter.

[2] Goulburn to Peel, 2nd January, 1826. (*Peel Papers*, British Museum, 40,332, p. 3.)

sale of the office of gaoler. I will consider of the application of a remedy without delay.'

' I cannot be responsible for his continuance in office,' he wrote of an official who had misappropriated public funds, and was eagerly defended by the Irish Attorney-General. ' I cannot as an honest man defend him in Parliament. Please let me know whether I am authorised to state that he has been suspended. . . . I am quite tired of and disgusted with the shameful corruption which every Irish inquiry brings to light.' [1]

The Pension Fund,[2] which was more susceptible of reform, he eagerly defended from spoliation. He had only been a year in office before he was at grips with the Lord Lieutenant himself on the subject—and the Lord Lieutenant gave way. In 1816 he wrote with some pride to Lord Whitworth, who had succeeded the Duke of Richmond, and who supported the Secretary's reforms : ' You have made it impossible for anyone to complain of the abuse of the pension list. No member of Parliament has benefited by it, no vote has been influenced by it.'

The political patronage which he was obliged to give, he determined should be given as the reward of services rendered—he at least would make no bargains.

' Sir A. B. hinted Lord D.'s readiness to return a friend of the Government, if a promise were given of the next ribbon to Lord D. and of a baronetage to C. I laughed at such a monstrous proposition, and said he might return whom he pleased.' Any sort of impertinence he instantly checked, and an influential peer, who had demanded a place in hectoring terms, received a cutting rebuke. When, however, the said peer appeared in his office ' nearly crying ' and apologised humbly, Mr. Peel's tender heart relented, and he wrote to Lord Whitworth : ' The truth is Lord D. is a great blockhead, puffed up with his own importance, but meaning no harm. . . . In point of justice, after what has passed, I think you are at liberty to refuse giving him the office ; but in point of policy I would advise you to give it to him. His two members have supported us throughout, have attended constantly, and have got nothing.' [3]

---

[1] Parker, *Peel*, i. pp. 279, 282.

[2] The sum of £80,000 a year was available for pensions in Ireland and £90,000 a year in England.

[3] Parker, *Peel*, i. pp. 273, 275.

As a rule, however, the great majority of such applications were refused. ' When G. wants a baronetcy he is very rich, and when he wants a place he is very poor. I think we may fairly turn the tables on him, and when he asks to be made a baronet make his poverty the objection, and his wealth when he asks for an office.' [1]

Wherever he could, he tried to select candidates for office for character and capacity ; and new offices, he determined, should be awarded on no other grounds. He fought hard to save the new police force, which he set up in 1814, from the clutches of the ghouls.

' If the present or any other Government make a job of it,' he wrote to the Attorney-General, ' they will most grossly betray the confidence which Parliament has placed in them, and shame-fully sacrifice the best interests of the country to the worst ; ' and later, to another Irish official, ' We ought to be crucified if we make the measure a job, and select our constables from the servants of our parliamentary friends.' [2] The reward of virtue was a violent and public attack from an Irish judge, who, in charging the jury at Quarter Sessions, considered it his province at the same time to charge Mr. Peel with instituting the police force solely in order to extend Government patronage.

The longer that Peel remained in office, the more strictly did he enforce economy. The Irish estimates were scandalously extra-vagant. In 1816 the military department sent over an estimate for an army of 63,474 men, which was cut down to 25,000. The reduced estimates Peel defended in a brilliant speech to a rather hostile House, and carried them with the loud applause of both parties.[3] ' Set your face steadily against all increases of salary, all extra allowance, all plausible claims for additional emolument,' he instructed his subordinates. ' Economy must be the order of the day, rigid economy, or—— But I need not allude to the alter-native.' [4]

He had not long been in Ireland when an attempt was made to place the Irish Exchequer in direct communication with that of the United Kingdom, removing it altogether from the influence of the Chief Secretary. Peel was not likely to surrender financial control, and strongly opposed the arrangement, even though the Chancellor threatened resignation. In the end, with his approval,

[1] Parker, i. p. 271.   [2] *Ib.* pp. 151-2.
[3] *Speeches,* i. p. 49.   [4] Parker, *Peel,* i. p. 218.

the two Exchequers were united, and a single Vice-Treasurer in Ireland replaced six highly-paid officials : even then the House of Commons reduced the Vice-Treasurer's salary from £3000 to £2000.

The office of Clerk of the Pleas to the Court of Exchequer had long been a public scandal, and its regulation had been determined on, whenever the then holder should die. In 1816 the office fell vacant—and the Chief Baron of the Irish Exchequer without a moment's hesitation appointed his son. The Crown claimed the right to appoint, and the case went before the Courts. Every effort was made to delay it there, in order that the temporary incumbent might continue to enjoy his fees, which amounted to at least £30,000 a year. Peel countered this by hurrying a bill through Parliament, securing all profits to the Crown until the case should be decided, and forcing the officers concerned to account for the whole of the fees, from the death of the late holder. In the end the emoluments were reduced to £3000 a year, and the office made an effective one.

Besides this general tightening of the reins, Peel carried a series of administrative reforms. One of the earliest was the introduction of measures to check what he once called ' that grievous bane to Ireland—illicit distillation.' [1] The secret manufacture of spirits was enormous, and the whole population, of every class, connived at it, so that detection was almost impossible, and the loss to the revenue and the demoralisation of the people increasingly great. Peel gave the House of Commons an instance where a gentleman had ' actually imported mantraps, with the avowed intention of catching any revenue officer that might come near them.' [2] According to the recommendation of a Committee which sat in 1812, he introduced the system of imposing fines upon the townland, which interested the whole population directly in the suppression of the practice.

One of the great difficulties in governing Ireland was the character of the local authorities, which contrasted very unfavourably with that of the active and conscientious country gentlemen who filled the Commission of the Peace in England. Financial affairs in particular were administered in an extraordinary manner.

' Grand Juries in Ireland,' Peel told the House, ' could dispose

[1] *Speeches*, i. p. 50.   [2] *Ib.* p. 106.

of the money of landowners to an almost unlimited amount, by means of . . . presentments . . . so that when the direct taxes of Ireland did not exceed £4,000,000, the indirect taxes imposed by grand juries were scarcely less than one-fourth of that sum. . . . The sums required by grand juries were demanded with scarcely any inquiry, upon the mere representation of two individuals,'[1] and the funds thus granted were frequently squandered. Peel's amendment subjected both the grants and their application to the scrutiny of the magistrates.

The appointment of sheriffs he removed from the control of the local M.P., and placed it under that of the judges. The difficulty about such reforms, however, was that the judges and the magistrates themselves were urgently in need of improvement. The judges were often bitter political partisans : the magistrates in too many cases were incapable and corrupt. It was beyond the power of Government to deal with such matters as these. Peel, indeed, for a moment, dallied with the notion of a ' general revision ' of the magistracy, ' dissolving the present Commission and forming a new one,'[2] but in the end he abandoned the scheme, the difficulties of which were insuperable. How could the Government acquire the necessary information of the character of the gentlemen to be selected ? And if the new magistracy proved to have the faults of the old one, the situation would be worse than before.

In the last year of his term of office, events occurred which made a lasting impression on Peel's mind, and which gave an opportunity for him to show his ability as a practical administrator and organiser. There was a partial failure of the potato crop, and certain districts found themselves in immediate danger of famine. The Government was urged to suspend distillation and to prohibit the export of potatoes. Peel refused to do either. In a speech, which admirably displayed his unequalled power of clear and convincing argument, he proved to the House of Commons that the suspension of distillation could only lead to the increase of illicit spirit manufacture, and by depriving the small farmer of a market for his inferior grain unfit for human consumption[3] would merely add to the general distress. He remarked afterwards, with justifiable pride, that he ' had convinced every man who

---

[1] *Speeches*, i. p. 110.   [2] Parker, *Peel*, i. p. 219.
[3] The grain harvest was deficient in quality, not quantity.

heard him.'[1] As to potatoes, he investigated the question, and discovered that for some months past the imports into Ireland had exceeded the exports by three to one, and that his timely scruples had saved the Government from ridicule. He was well aware of the peculiar nature of Irish famines, which were due to lack of money more than to scarcity of food ; he had the prejudices of a convinced individualist against State assistance in any form ; but he was ready to abandon his principles in case of necessity. If any of the remote districts were in danger of starvation, he wrote, ' I would overleap every difficulty and buy food for them at the public expense,' but ' I would do this only under circumstances of extreme necessity, and with every effort to prevent its being known that the relief came from the hands of Government.'[2] In the end, he adopted the plan of making Government grants of money to all districts where local subscriptions were opened in aid of the poor, enlisted the aid of the Catholic priests as agents, and advised the establishment of soup kitchens as the best form of relief, as this would increase the consumption of meat and lessen that of grain and potatoes. More than £37,000 was granted in this manner for relief, and when the famine produced its usual result in an infectious fever, an additional £15,000 was expended on the provision of medical aid in the districts affected. The famine was not a very severe one, but the impression which it made upon Peel's mind was great and lasting. He learned from personal experience how narrow a line divided the Irish peasant from sheer starvation, and he never forgot it.

During his six years of office in Ireland, Peel seems to have immersed himself entirely in his work. His speeches in the House of Commons deal almost exclusively with Irish affairs, except that he spoke, in 1818, repeatedly in favour of his father's bill for the protection of factory children. Nothing was too small for his attention. As an example of his care for details, it may be mentioned that he introduced a bill to limit to a certain season the period in which the Foundling Hospital in Dublin might receive children, on the ground that the health of the foundlings suffered from their being brought there in inclement weather, and he gravely informed the House that no less than 180 of the infants had suffered, last year, from acute sore throat. It is interesting to note how closely throughout the period his private letters tally with his public

---

[1] Parker, *Peel*, i. p. 240.　　　　[2] *Ib.* p. 244.

speeches. Sometimes the letters are expressed more strongly, but again and again the same ideas, the same line of thought, even the same phrases, occur in both. Not all the private letters of statesmen could so well bear inspection.

His devotion to his work and his strict integrity won him a high reputation in political circles in Ireland. With Lord Whitworth, who was Lord Lieutenant for four years of his Secretaryship, he was on terms of close confidence, and he originally intended to resign when Whitworth left : but he was dissuaded by a letter signed by fifty-nine Irish members, who, while stating that they disagreed with his views on the Catholic Question, entreated him to remain and watch over the improvements which he had introduced. The letters printed in his collected papers show that he was not only respected, but liked, by his colleagues.[1] Wharncliffe, no very warm friend of his, said of him long after, ' no man was ever more easy to act with, more candid and conciliatory, and less alarming than Peel in the Cabinet.' [2] With those he liked and trusted, he could always be very engaging ; and as yet his manners were not quite so cold and repellent as they became in later life. He still had the attraction of youth and high spirits. Those who knew him then said of him that he had a ' radiant ' look. Some reflection of that look has been caught in Lawrence's fine portrait, which seems always on the point of breaking into an arch smile. It was the look of a young man who was very happy : absorbed in work which he enjoyed ; exhilarated by the consciousness of his own expanding powers ; ignorant, perhaps, of some of the feverish pleasures of youth, but ignorant also of the bitter taste these pleasures leave behind ; full of confidence and ambition for the great career which he saw opening before him.

His greatest advantage in dealing with the Irish Administration had been the entire orthodoxy of his views. The Tory Cabinet which he represented could rely without the least uneasiness on his stanchness, and were therefore not afraid of giving him a free hand. Any ideas of a notably liberal character would have set against him the greater part of his colleagues in Dublin, and the whole force of organised corruption would have been employed to thwart his efforts. As it was, he had their entire confidence :

[1] See also letters in *Mr. Gregory's Letter Box* from Whitworth, Saurin, Gregory, etc., where Peel is always mentioned with great affection and admiration.

[2] *Greville*, iii. p. 257.

he had not the least desire to tamper with the principles on which the Irish Government was founded, but only to amend the details. His instinct was for administrative, not organic, reform.

All this, however, which had strengthened his position with the Government, had made him bitterly hated by the Catholic leaders and the Catholic population of Ireland. To them he had become the archtype of intolerance and oppression, the representative of all they detested in the Union with England.

Mr. Peel had, in fact, got himself into the Catholics' black books before ever he set foot in Ireland. In February, 1812, he had spoken against Lord Morpeth's motion for a committee on the state of Ireland, and had expressed himself strongly against any concession to the Catholic claims. His first important speech after entering his new office, in March, 1813, was a yet more spirited defence of the Protestant supremacy. It attracted much attention,[1] and very soon the extreme Protestant party, both in England and in Ireland, adopted Mr. Peel as their chosen champion. The Government had declared Catholic Emancipation an open question ; and with the exception of Peel, those Ministers who took the Protestant side were almost all in the Upper House. Many a time he was the only speaker of reputation or capacity who rose to defend the Protestant cause in the House of Commons against the eloquence of Grattan and Plunket, Canning and Pole. In 1817 he was elected member of Parliament for the University of Oxford, then the centre of Anglican intolerance, because of his attitude to the Catholic Question ; and thereby came, for the first time, into personal rivalry with Canning, who had long desired to represent the University.

All this served to make Peel both popular and conspicuous in England, but it made him detested in Ireland. He was at once nicknamed Orange Peel, and wild tales were circulated of his inciting Orange societies to violence, and toasting ' The Glorious Memory of King William III,' with one foot on his chair and one on the table.[2] He had no arts to cultivate a personal popularity

---

[1] Peel himself was dissatisfied with the speech, because he remarked, ' I was so wholly unprepared . . . that I did what I believe many of those do who are so young in debate as I am—totally forgot while I was speaking that which before I rose and after I sat down occurred to me as the most material thing that I had to say.' (Parker, *Peel*, i. p. 78.)

[2] ' I have,' he wrote to Croker shortly after his arrival in 1812, ' survived the hospitality of Ireland hitherto, contrary to my expectation. . . . I fancy I see some who think the Government of England have a strange notion of Ireland

that might have lessened political hostility. Lord Melbourne, a few years later, won all hearts by himself interviewing everyone who called at his office in Dublin ; but Peel was too busy to be so accessible, and had none of Melbourne's charm and gaiety. He did not know how to say ' No ' both gracefully and convincingly.[1] One would indeed conclude from Lady Morgan's caricature that the Irish disliked their Secretary as much because he was a bore as because he was a bigot.[2]

' Bigot,' however, is not the right word. Peel's attitude was not due to religious prejudice.

It is true that he considered the Roman Catholic religion inferior to the form practised by the Anglican Church, and believed its effects in Ireland to be pernicious. Writing to Croker, he agreed that ' Papal superstition is the cause of one-half the evils of this country,'[3] and to the Speaker, Abbot, he declared, ' It is quite impossible for anyone to witness the remorselessness with which crimes are committed here, the almost total annihilation of the agency of conscience as a preventive of crime, and the universal contempt in which the obligation of any but an illegal oath is held by the mass of the people, without being satisfied that the prevailing religion of Ireland operates as an impediment rather than as an aid to the ends of Civil Government.'[4] Moreover, he considered that the Irish Catholics made claims which it was impossible to concede to any sect in their attitude towards papal supremacy. ' They are excluded,' he wrote, ' from privileges for which they will not pay the price that all other subjects pay, and that all other Catholics in Europe feel themselves bound to pay.'[5] But it is most unlikely that these opinions would have made him persist in opposing Catholic Emancipation for sixteen years. He was too strong an individualist ever to be a religious persecutor. Gladstone later remarked that Peel, though he was ' a religious man, was wholly anti-church, and unclerical, and largely undogmatic,'[6] and Peel's old tutor, Bishop Lloyd, told him that he

when they put a man here who drinks port, and as little of that as he can. The Governor of the Bank remarked with horror that I was not fully impressed with the necessity of toasting the Glorious Memory.' (*Croker*, i. p. 47.)

[1] ' I plead guilty to the charge of coldness ; particularly in reference to Irish candidates for office. I had early experience in that country of the danger of saying a civil word.' (Parker, *Peel*, ii. p. 13.)

[2] Peel is the original of ' Mr. Vandaleur ' in *O'Donnel*.   [3] *Croker*, i. p. 89.

[4] Parker, *Peel*, i. p. 236.   [5] *Ib*. i. p. 76.   [6] Morley, *Gladstone*, i. p. 177.

was 'little better than a heretic.'[1] The truth was that Peel
resisted Catholic Emancipation because he believed it would be
the first step to the repeal of the Union, and the separation of
Ireland from the United Kingdom.

The success of the Catholic movement must in the end cause
the disestablishment, or at the very least the partial spoliation, of
the Established Church of Ireland. It has been seen that this
Church was regarded as a great pillar of the English domination
in Ireland : but apart from that, Peel was a strong believer in a
State Church. The Church, he held, was a most important
influence in the education and moral training of the people. A
wealthy and well-organised national Church derives its strength
from one of two sources : the especial care of the State, or the
spontaneous support of the people. To the latter alternative
Peel would have seen great objections : in the first place, such a
movement must be highly democratic, and he disliked and distrusted democracy ; in the second place, a wealthy and well-
organised Church, independent of the State, would be a dangerous
rival for the State to tolerate within itself. Any institution so
influential ought, he believed, to be under the control of the State.
He was not particular about the exact nature of the Church : it
might be the Episcopal Church of England or the Presbyterian
Church of Scotland—though the latter was even then just a little
too independent for his taste.[2] A Roman Catholic Established
Church he objected to, because such a Church, acknowledging the
authority of the Pope, could not really be in the control of the
State. In Ireland the alternative was such a semi-independent
Roman Catholic Church or an Anglican Church, supported by the
whole weight of the Government, and in close alliance with it.
The Irish Church, he always maintained, was an integral part of
the English Church, and he feared that a blow struck at the one
must inevitably damage the other.

Peel believed that the union with Ireland was a necessary condition of the safety of Great Britain, and that its maintenance was
one of the first duties of a British statesman. His whole policy
towards Ireland was based on this assumption. By this it stands
or falls.

This has always been the chief justification of the English occupation of Ireland. How far it holds good—how far the advantages

[1] Parker, *Peel*, i. p. 386. [2] Parker, *Peel*, ii. p. 99.

of holding Ireland counterbalanced the disadvantages of holding Ireland by force—is questionable.

From an external point of view, moreover, this justification can only be accepted if Ireland were not sacrificed to English interests. It might be a necessary condition for England's security to have control of Ireland ; but she had no moral right to enforce that claim unless she were able to give Ireland a Government as good as, or better than, Ireland would have had as an independent State. It will not be disputed by anyone that in the eighteenth century England had failed to fulfil this condition. The Union of the Parliaments, however, had, it was hoped, been the commencement of better times. The policy of commercial exclusion had been entirely abandoned, that of religious exclusion almost entirely ; Ireland paid less than her share of taxation. There was, in fact, a general disposition to do well by Ireland, and a general wish for her prosperity. The question was now, not of the intentions, but of the intelligence of British statesmen. Were they capable of real understanding and sympathy in dealing with Irish problems ? Could they detach themselves sufficiently from their English surroundings to give Ireland what her peculiar circumstances demanded, not merely what worked well in England ?

It was not likely that Peel, with his character and upbringing, would set himself to think out the rights and wrongs of the Irish Question. He simply assumed that the Union must be preserved, and that the Established Church must be preserved. He had been educated in these beliefs, and they were, in fact, the opinions of the vast majority of his fellow countrymen. There is no hint, in his speeches or letters, that he ever examined the advantages and disadvantages of the Union. On the other hand, there is a very definite indication that for many years he entirely failed to realise all that was implied by the position of the Established Church in Ireland. In 1828, discussing in a private letter the question of the payment of the Irish Catholic priests by the State, he remarked, ' Will there not be among the religious classes of the community a very great repugnance, founded on higher motives than the unwillingness to be taxed, against contributing in any manner to the propagation or maintenance of the doctrines of the Church of Rome ? ' [1] The simplicity with which this plea is advanced, the entire failure to notice the deadly indictment which it implied

[1] Peel to Wellington, 11th August, 1828. (Parker, *Peel*, ii. p. 60.)

against the Irish Church, are very remarkable ; especially remarkable in one so naturally sincere, so anxious to be just.

If we ask, then, what Peel offered to Ireland to justify the English occupation, which he assumed to be right and necessary, we must first reply that the two most striking points in his policy—the refusal of Catholic Emancipation and the maintenance of the Established Church—in themselves involved the blackest injustice to Ireland. The existence of the Irish Church was a scandal that could only exist in a conquered country, held by force : and when Peel defended it, he by the very act condemned English rule, and weakened what he wished to strengthen. His attitude to the Irish Church is, in fact, the greatest blot on his career. Whatever his motives, he defended a gross and cruel injustice, and for many years delayed its redress. How much this embittered Irish feeling, discredited English rule in Ireland, and degraded the character of the Anglican Church, can only be guessed at.

As Lord Melbourne remarked, on the question of Catholic Emancipation all the wise men proved to be wrong, and all the damned fools right. It did, in point of fact, prove to be the first step to the repeal of the Union. But this does not prove that Peel was right in principle when he opposed the grant of emancipation. Had the concession come in 1801 it might have been successful in conciliating Irish feeling : in 1829 it came too late. For the fact that it was delayed too long Peel, perhaps more than any other individual except George III., was responsible, and it is a heavy responsibility.

Apart from this, Peel was sincerely anxious to secure the interests of Ireland. He was eager to encourage trade, and, being at this time a high Protectionist, he advocated protection for Irish industries and preference for Irish goods in British markets. But the most important objects of his policy, the chief advantages which he offered Ireland to compensate for subjection, were the maintenance of good order and the encouragement of education. It is difficult to say which of these aims was the more difficult to attain.

The century-long attempt to conquer Ireland ; the bloody civil wars which marked her history ; the repeated insurrections so ruthlessly put down ; the repression that was never wholly effectual : all these had roused or preserved, in the mind of the Irish peasant, a savagery and lawlessness now unparalleled in any other State of Western Europe. It is to this inborn savagery that

Irish disorder during the nineteenth century is to be attributed, more than to the actual misgovernment and suffering of the moment. Crime was attributed, first, to the laws against the Catholics, then to tithes, to land laws, to the existence of the Union itself : but the Catholics were emancipated, tithes were abolished, land laws reformed, the Union repealed, and Irish lawlessness remained, tamed perhaps, but not eradicated.

The crofters of the Scottish Highlands were in a condition very similar to that of the Irish peasants. They, too, existed on the very margin of subsistence, almost entirely dependent on the potato crop, liable to be reduced to starvation when it failed, and with no legal security against the landlord. They, too, were evicted by hundreds—to make place for sheep-runs or deer forests. They, too, were a bold and spirited people. When legal protection was given to the Irish peasant, it was found equally necessary to extend it to the Highland crofter. Yet the Highlander did not resort to violence, and the burnings and shootings that were everyday occurrences in Tipperary would have roused as much horror and revulsion in Strathnaver or Glen Ey as they did in Parliament House.

Peel at least had no doubt on the subject. The immediate causes of crime he had some understanding of. In the House of Commons, discussing the subject, he divided Irish crime into three classes : that caused by religious animosity, that caused by political agitation, and that—much the largest—which was caused by the land laws. But the fact that crime was so prevalent he roundly said was due to ' sheer wickedness and depravity.' These atrocities, he said, ' were the acts of a set of human beings very little advanced from barbarism, unaccustomed to regard the law either as the protector from or as the avenger of outrage.' [1] In one of his speeches he paid a fine tribute to the Irish people—to their courage, their fidelity, their chastity, their freedom from vice, their great honesty (' in their dealings with each other,' he cautiously added).[2] But these are savage virtues ; and one cannot help concluding that Peel in his own mind thought the Irish a people but little removed from savagery, whom it was the task of the British Government to civilise.[3]

[1] To Mr. Beckett, 5th December, 1816. To the Speaker, 25th December, 1816. (Parker, Peel, i. pp. 235-6.)

[2] 26th April, 1816. Speeches, i. p. 58.   [3] Parker, Peel, ii. p. 120.

Over a great part of Ireland at this time the law was a dead letter. Order could only be enforced, and that very imperfectly, by the employment of troops. There was no police force. The magistrates were helpless, sometimes incapable, sometimes intimidated. Bands of armed men, calling themselves Threshers, Carders, Whiteboys, and so forth—that brigandage which has reappeared under one name or another throughout the history of Ireland—ranged the countryside at night and terrorised the inhabitants. Those who for one reason or another offended them were shot at in the roads, or burned in their houses, or were haled from their beds at night and punished by means of the carding-combs used in the woollen industry, by which the flesh was literally torn from the victim's bones. The perpetrators of these outrages were scarcely ever brought to justice. If they were arrested, no one would testify against them—frequently the victims even perjured themselves rather than give evidence. If the evidence was forthcoming, juries in the face of it refused to convict. It was partly due to the national horror of an ' informer,' but more to the fact that if a conviction were obtained, prosecutors, witnesses, jurymen, and even the magistrates themselves were exposed to the vengeance of the prisoner's comrades. The outrages in the large majority of cases were directed against those who had paid a higher rent than their neighbours could afford, or who had consented to occupy farms from which the last tenant had been evicted.

The tales of misery and horror that came to Peel daily had a lasting effect on his mind. Years after he told the House of Commons, ' I am still haunted by the recollection of the scenes of atrocity and suffering with which I was once familiar.' [1] His letters testify to the revulsion that he felt.

' What must be the state of morals in a country where thirteen men, after having killed the husband, and when all apprehension of danger was at an end, could kill a woman with an infant in her arms, and where the orphan child of that woman could be told by " all the people in the neighbourhood," to whom she appealed for protection, that " *she might go to the devil* ? " All comment would but weaken the unparalleled atrocity of this transaction. The Dillons were Catholics.' [2]

' On the night of Tuesday last,' he reported to the Home Secre-

[1] March 1, 1833. *Speeches*, ii. p. 641.   [2] *Croker*, i. p. 91.   Italics Peel's.

tary, ' the house of a person, who had prosecuted capitally to conviction three persons at the last Louth Assizes, was set on fire by
a number of armed men, who prevented the escape of the inmates
of it, and actually consigned to the flames a family of eight persons,
five of whom were children. This abominable outrage . . . is
but one of many proofs of the wretched depravity and sanguinary
disposition of the lower orders of this country.' [1]

One tale in particular seems to have impressed him. In 1833 he
related it, from memory, in all its details to the House of Commons,
and with great effect. It was that of a man whose evidence had
led to the conviction of several criminals, and who, in spite of
warning, insisted on returning to his home. His house was surrounded by nine men, and he was dragged out and murdered with
pitchforks. While this was going on, his wife concealed her
daughter of nine years old, and bade her mark the faces of the
murderers. When they returned to seize the woman, she flung a
handful of fuel on the fire that it might burn brightly and reveal
their faces ; and she in her turn was dragged out and killed. The
little girl did as she was bid ; ' and by the artless evidence of that
child, which nothing could shake, five of those assassins were convicted and hanged.' [2]

Personal courage and independence were qualities which always
attracted Peel's admiration, and throughout his career his sympathies were engaged on behalf of the individual oppressed by the
tyranny of the majority.[3] Not only the wish to enforce good
order, but a warm desire to help such individuals, who had the
courage to defy the Whiteboys, inspired his policy in Ireland. He
would make the law not only the avenger of crime, but the protector of the innocent.

In 1829, when Peel was for the first time in a position to initiate
and control British policy in Ireland, he formulated his ideas distinctly. He wished to establish a ' thoroughly efficient police,'
and institute a system by which every case of outrage should be
investigated and prosecuted by the Crown ; in fine, to try fairly
' the experiment of, at any cost, compelling for ten years to come
obedience to the law. Ten years' experience of the advantage
of obedience,' he added, ' will induce a country to be obedient

[1] Parker, *Peel*, i. p. 231.

[2] *Speeches*, ii. p. 641.   For the effect of the story see *Hobhouse*, iv. p. 279.   See
also the *Diary of Lady Shelley*, ii. p. 18.

[3] See also his action on the Combination Laws, below, ch. v.

without much extraordinary compulsion.' The expense of all
this should be borne by Ireland. 'Why should an absentee Irish
landlord draw ten thousand a year from Ireland, contribute
nothing by personal exertion towards the maintenance of the peace
in Ireland, and throw . . . on the Treasury the charge of protecting his property and ensuring the receipt of his rent ? ' This
unflinching enforcement of order by the strong hand should be
accompanied by measures for the education of Irish children of all
religions in common, one day a week to be devoted to the separate
religious instruction of the child by the priest of its own Church,
but the Government to provide and control secular education
without reference to the prejudices of any Church, Catholic or
Protestant.[1]

It is clear that during his Irish Secretaryship he was actuated by
these principles ; but he was a subordinate, without even a seat in
the Cabinet, and he could not carry them to their logical conclusion.

In July, 1814, he introduced into Parliament a ' Bill for the
Execution of the Laws in Ireland.' This bill gave the Lord
Lieutenant power to proclaim any district to be in a disturbed
state, to appoint a salaried superintending magistrate, and a
limited number of special constables with salaries. The magistrate had no extraordinary powers. He was responsible immediately to Government, and removable at its discretion. The
constables were under his control. Such was the first incon-
spicuous beginning of the famous Royal Irish Constabulary Force.
The temporary and local measures were gradually developed and
extended into a national system. In substituting a civil force for
the military one hitherto made use of, its value was incalculable.
In point of practical utility, it proved one of the most successful
of Peel's administrative measures. The magistrates were carefully
selected for their ability and high character. The constables were
mainly drawn from the ranks of discharged non-commissioned
officers of the army, only those being chosen who could show
certificates of good character and capacity : and Peel urged that
Catholics and Protestants should be employed without distinction.

For cases of extreme need, Peel introduced and maintained for
several years a Coercion Act, which might supplement the Execution of the Laws Act. As long as the war with France lasted the
Government had the fear of rebellion continually before their

[1] Parker, *Peel*, ii. pp. 122-129 incl.

eyes. It was barely ten years since Emmet's rising : any fine
morning they might be wakened with :

> Boney's on the say,
> He'll be here by break of day,
> And the Orange will decay,
> Says the Shan Van Vocht.

But Peel, though he carried his Coercion Act as a temporary war
measure, privately wished that it might be a permanent part of
the law of the land, to be enforced very rarely, but always to be
held in reserve. The Act was the revival of one passed in 1807.
It provided that an extraordinary meeting of not less than seven
magistrates might report to the Lord Lieutenant that the civil
force of the district was insufficient to keep the peace, and the
Lord Lieutenant, with the consent of the Privy Council, might
then proclaim the following : All public-houses must be closed
by nine o'clock ; all persons must keep within doors from sunset
to sunrise, unless they could show good reason for being out ;
magistrates might pay domiciliary visits, and if necessary enter by
force ; and for breaking the ' curfew ' regulations, the offender
might be liable for seven years' transportation ; while, if necessary,
trial by jury might be dispensed with. The last regulation was,
of course, directed as much by a desire to protect the juryman as
to secure convictions. This Act remained on the Statute Book
for several years, but was very rarely put in force : and in 1817
Peel was delighted to find the state of Ireland so quiet as not to
warrant the introduction of measures suppressing the Habeas
Corpus Act and prohibiting public meetings, which the Government had considered it necessary to enforce in England.

He wished, however, to do more than enforce order. He
wished to encourage the Irish people to look to the law for protection. In July, 1814, therefore, he introduced a bill simplifying
the procedure of obtaining redress for assaults, enabling the
victims to procure relief and protection immediately and without expense.[1] The judge was allowed to award the plaintiff
compensation and expenses, and Peel accepted a suggestion from
a private member that the compensation should be levied on
the district where the assault took place. In the following year
he carried another law, to pay the costs of witnesses and prosecutions in cases of felony from Government funds.

[1] *Hansard*, 1st Series, vol. xviii. p. 502.

The second means upon which Peel relied for the improvement of Ireland was the progress of education; but the conflict of creeds made the promotion of Irish education an uncommonly difficult question. In 1793 all restrictions upon Catholic education had been removed, but the endowments were chiefly in the hands of Protestant bodies, and Trinity College, Dublin, still excluded Catholic students. Any attempt to remove education from the exclusive control of the Established Church at once aroused that institution to fury. Any grant of funds to the Established Church schools maddened the Protestant Dissenters. Any attempt at a purely secular education offended conscientious persons of every sect. The Catholic Church wanted to have complete control of the education of Catholic children, and though they would have liked their share of Government funds, distrusted every attempt of Government to foster general education as a plot to proselytise.

For these reasons Peel avoided introducing legislative measures. The Government confined their efforts to aiding and encouraging the Kildare Street Society, which had been founded in 1811, to establish schools by State aid, where, in order to avoid giving any-one offence, the only religious instruction was to be the reading of the Bible without explanation or comment. The Catholics objected strongly to this system, but still, for a time, they accepted it. A grant of £30,000 a year was made by the State, and many schools were founded.

For the agrarian problem, which lay at the bottom of so much of Ireland's misery, Peel as yet offered no remedy. It is possible that he hardly realised its importance at this time. Few persons did so; O'Connell himself did not.[1] Peel once or twice, it is true, hinted at the desirability of a law against absentees; but he never proposed any such measure, and it is in the highest degree unlikely that he could have carried one through Parliament.[2] For

[1] Sir W. Gregory, a great admirer of O'Connell, remarks that O'Connell's ' own estate was a model of all that ought not to be.' (Gregory, *Autobiography*, pp. 72-3.)

[2] Lord Eversley, in his *Peel and O'Connell*, declares that Peel passed two measures facilitating eviction. One of these measures was introduced, not by Peel, but by an Irish member, his persistent opponent, Sir John Newport, and the only reference that Peel made to it was to recommend that it should be submitted to the criticism of Irish lawyers. It was directed equally to ' the protection of the tenant from undue distress,' as well as to facilitating the landlord's procedure. I cannot discover that Peel had any connection with any other bill dealing with evictions.

the rest, he fully realised that the country was over-populated in proportion to its resources, and he thought the emigration of the southern Irish might be encouraged, and that Government, even at ' considerable expense,' should settle the emigrants in Canada, rather than allow them to be lost in the United States.

None of these measures were calculated to endear Peel to the Irish people. His Coercion Act—a high-handed piece of work, to say the least of it—was called English tyranny. His police force was represented as a Government job : it was hated by the disorderly elements in the country, and the people were openly incited to murder policemen.[1] In matters of education and of famine relief, as has been seen, he tried to make the Government's share in the work as unobtrusive as possible ; and his system of secular education was unpopular. His efforts to purify the administration were unknown, and probably would not have commanded the admiration of a party, many of whom did not desire to abolish patronage, but to share it.

Even had his measures been much more conciliatory, however, they would probably have been overlooked in the storm of hatred aroused by his opposition to Catholic Emancipation.

In 1810 Daniel O'Connell had revived the almost defunct Catholic Board, and had made it an effective organ for agitation. His policy and methods were not altogether approved by the Catholic leaders of the old school—neither by the Irish Protestants who favoured emancipation, such as Grattan and Plunket, nor by many of the Irish Catholics of high position, nor by their English allies. In 1813 there was a split in the Catholic party. Grattan's relief bill of that year proposed, as a Protestant security, a royal veto on the appointment of Catholic bishops. The Catholic Board quarrelled over the scheme ; Lord Fingall and his followers supported the veto ; O'Connell passionately opposed it ; and Fingall seceded from the Board. Henceforth the parliamentary leaders lost their hold upon the popular movement, and O'Connell became its real leader. In 1814—the moment the fall of Napoleon made such action safe—the Government suppressed the Catholic Board, but the movement continued, with no definite organisation that might lay it open to attack, but centring in the personality of O'Connell.

At the time when Peel first arrived in Ireland, O'Connell was

[1] In 1821 the chief police magistrate in Limerick was murdered.

thirty-seven years old. He had been destined for the priesthood and educated at Douay, but had taken to the law instead, and rapidly risen as high as a Catholic could rise in his profession. As an advocate he was greatly in demand, for unless the dice were loaded against him he was sure to win his case. He was such a man as people turn in the streets to look at—six feet tall, with a head of fox-red curls, and a face thoroughly Irish in type, irregular in feature, ugly perhaps, but glowing with spirit and intelligence. He was an incomparable speaker, his voice peerless in power and melody : ' You'd hear it a mile off, and it sounded as if it was coming through honey,' said an Irish peasant. His headlong eloquence ranged through all the gradations of pathetic appeal, savage denunciation, cutting sarcasm, playful humour, and sublime declamation. He could impress a hostile English audience ; but an Irish audience was a plaything in his hands, with which he could do as he willed. In later days, someone sneered at him as ' a broguing Irish fellow,' and Peel replied, ' My own opinion is, that if I wanted an efficient and eloquent advocate, I would readily give up all the other orators of whom we have been talking, provided I had with me this same " broguing Irish fellow." ' [1] He was the first great agitator. The English reformers a few years later, and afterwards Cobden and Bright more effectively, copied his methods. With all his magnificent gifts, however, O'Connell's character was so undisciplined that he was continually running himself and his cause into danger. He had many of the qualities of a statesman : he was both broad-minded and keen-sighted, fit to plan a campaign and to carry it into action ; but his violent temper, his hasty enthusiasms, and his uncontrolled impulses led him to folly, and worse than folly. He was full of contradictions— capable of absurd vanity and of the noblest self-sacrifice, at once cunning and reckless, generous and vindictive. He had a sincere horror of bloodshed, and always urged his followers to confine themselves to peaceable methods and avoid violence ; but his habitual language was such as to rouse not only the patriotic spirit of his hearers, but all the impulses of hatred and revenge.

It was impossible that such a man could accept Peel and his policy. Not only was Peel to him the embodiment of the English domination that had been the curse of Ireland, but there was a natural personal antipathy between them. To O'Connell, Peel

[1] Eversley, *Peel and O'Connell*, p. 310.

was a cold-blooded, affected prig; to Peel, O'Connell seemed a foul-mouthed, notoriety-seeking scoundrel.

'A raw youth, squeezed out of the workings of I know not what factory in England!'—thus O'Connell had greeted the Chief Secretary on his first arrival in Ireland—'who began his parliamentary career by vindicating the gratuitous destruction of our brave soldiers in the murderous expedition to Walcheren, and was sent over here before he got rid of the foppery of perfumed handkerchiefs and thin shoes. . . . a lad ready to vindicate anything—everything!'[1]

In 1815 O'Connell was challenged by one d'Esterre for a violent attack upon the Corporation of Dublin. A duel was fought, and d'Esterre was killed. O'Connell was overwhelmed by remorse. He paid an annuity to d'Esterre's daughter as long as he lived, and solemnly resolved never to fight again. He was incapable, however, of modifying his habitual language in public speaking; he continued to attack his opponents with savage and scurrilous abuse. Within two months of the duel he made a personal attack upon Peel so fierce that the latter was advised to prosecute him, but refused.

Soon after, a motion in favour of Catholic Emancipation came before Parliament, and Peel succeeded in getting it rejected by a large majority. In his speech he quoted some remarks of O'Connell's on Grattan's Bill of 1813, adding that 'such language augured the impossibility of any conciliatory arrangement.'[2] At the close of the session—Waterloo having in the meantime been fought and peace made—he went off to Paris for a holiday, in company with Croker and Vesey Fitzgerald. It seems to have been Peel's only holiday during his service in Ireland, and he and Fitzgerald evidently spent most of it in sleeping.[3] Returning to Ireland, he learned that during his absence O'Connell had publicly declared his late speech an insult to himself; and a week or two later the agitator repeated with more emphasis, 'Mr. Peel would not *dare*, in my presence, or in any place where he was liable to personal account, use a single expression derogatory to my interest

---

[1] Speech to the Catholic Board, 29th May, 1813.

[2] See *Speeches*, i. p. 45. O'Connell had called Grattan's emancipation scheme 'that absurd and mischievous bill.'

[3] 'What good boys we are! We are all in bed by twelve. Fitzgerald does nothing but sleep; he goes to bed at eleven, and makes his appearance twelve hours after. Peel also is tolerably lazy. I rise at half-past six, but have to wait for breakfast till after ten,' etc., etc. See *Croker*, i. p. 63 f.

or my honour.' Peel then sent Sir Charles Saxton with a message that he was ready to repeat every word he had uttered whenever or wherever Mr. O'Connell desired. O'Connell consulted a friend, who frankly told him that he would not act as his second against Peel, since his (O'Connell's) language had been ' grossly offensive.' O'Connell did not want to be involved in another, possibly fatal, duel, and told Saxton he would take no steps. Unfortunately the affair was generally known, and Saxton thought it necessary to publish in the newspapers a statement of what had passed. This brought a protest from O'Connell, who accused Peel and Saxton of resorting to ' a paltry trick,' and added that he had ' retracted nothing . . . and only regretted that they had ultimately preferred a paper war.' Peel then challenged O'Connell.[1]

O'Connell being arrested and bound over to keep the peace in Ireland, the four duellists set out separately for Ostend. Peel reached his destination safely, where, according to the Irish press, he spent a week ' swaggering on the battlefield and practising at an ace of hearts.' O'Connell was again arrested in London, owing to information secretly sent by his wife. The whole affair became ridiculous, and both the would-be combatants were exposed to a good deal of mockery. It hung in the air until 1825, when O'Connell apologised, and Peel warmly accepted the amends. Soon after, however, O'Connell publicly stated that he had apologised only in the hope of propitiating Peel in the matter of the Catholic Relief Bill then before Parliament. Peel resented the imputation ; and to the end of their lives the two were never upon friendly terms.

It is impossible to avoid the conclusion that Peel was very much to blame in this affair. It was, no doubt, trying to a hot-tempered young man of twenty-seven to have imputations cast upon his personal courage, but Peel was not in the position of a private individual. He was responsible for far more than his own honour. That his colleagues approved his conduct might condone, but not excuse it.[2] It is only necessary to consider what

---

[1] The whole correspondence may be found in the *Life and Speeches* of O'Connell, by his son, vol. ii. p. 217 ff.

[2] ' It is, my dear Peel, with great satisfaction that I assure you that your conduct in this unfortunate business is entirely approved by Lord Liverpool and Lord Sidmouth. They both consider it is truly unfortunate, but unavoidable, and both speak of you in terms of the greatest affection.' (Lord Whitworth to Peel. Parker, *Peel*, i. p. 196.)

would have been the effect on Irish politics had Peel killed O'Connell, or even had O'Connell killed Peel, to see how unjustifiable was his conduct. Even as things went, the introduction of personal feeling into a delicate political situation—the known enmity between the two great men who at a later time seemed to be almost the embodiment of English and Irish feeling—had a most unhappy effect.

In 1818 Peel resigned the Irish Secretaryship. For his motives it is not necessary to look further than the reason he gave to Robert Plumer Ward, that ' he was tired of it.' [1] He was now thirty, and he had been in office without a break since he was twenty-two. He wanted a holiday.

' I am for the abolition of slavery,' he wrote to Croker, ' and no men have a right to condemn another to worse than Egyptian bondage, to require him, not to make bricks without straw, which a man of straw might have some chance of doing (as Lord Norbury would certainly say), but to raise money and abolish taxes in the same breath. "Night cometh when no man can work," said one who could not have foreseen the fate of a man in office and the House of Commons. A fortnight later I shall be free as air.' [2]

[1] Plumer Ward, *Memoirs*, ii. p. 48.   [2] *Croker*, i. p. 116.

CHAPTER IV

INDUSTRIAL DISTRESS AND FINANCIAL CRISIS
1815-1822

THE six years that Peel spent in Ireland were eventful years in British history. The first three saw the long war end in an unparalleled triumph for Great Britain, but the years that followed brought a violent reaction. The waste of capital, the uncompensated destruction caused by the war, were now for the first time fully felt.

> There *was* a time for borrowing,
> But now it's time to pay . . .
> A Budget is a serious thing . . .

Peace brought no prosperity. The country was saddled with a vast national debt that necessitated heavy taxation. Trade languished; unemployment was general. The poorest were threatened with starvation, and, in Cobbett's forcible words, the working-men with one voice exclaimed, ' Curse the victories and curse the peace ! '

For twenty years the war had given an accidental protection to industry and agriculture. Britain had been the only European State free from invasion, and, moreover, the inventions that had revolutionised economic conditions were almost all British inventions. Now, however, the continental States were at last at liberty to develop their own trade and industry. They turned to repair their heavy losses, and they could not afford to purchase much from abroad. Britain at the same time lost her customers and found new rivals. The demand for supplies for the army ceased. Prices fell rapidly, and wages fell with them. Workshops and factories closed down, throwing their hands upon the rates. The natural compensation for the workman would have been a similar fall in the price of bread, but even of this they were deprived.

Agriculture had received an unnatural stimulus from the war and from the extraordinarily rapid growth of population. No foreign imports came in, and the new millions must be fed from home sources. The margin of cultivation was pushed further and further, and inferior land was laid down under corn. When peace was signed, farmers and landlords feared a sudden fall in the price of wheat would make much of their production unprofitable. The landed interest was supreme in Parliament, and they demanded and obtained a measure of high protection. The import of foreign wheat was prohibited until the home price should have reached 84s. the quarter. When a bad harvest came this meant something like starvation for the poor.

No sooner had peace been signed than a cry arose for the disbanding of the army and the reduction of taxation. The army was demobilised, and thousands of discharged soldiers swelled the numbers of the unemployed. The House of Commons triumphantly carried the repeal of the property tax, against the strenuous opposition of the Government, who were thus not merely reduced to great financial straits, but deprived of the means of lessening other taxes which pressed more heavily on the poor.

The fiscal system was thoroughly bad. It was cumbrous, confused, expensive, and very unjust. The great bulk of the revenue was raised from customs and excise duties, many of which were levied on the necessaries of life, and pressed far more heavily on the poor than on the rich. Sugar, tea, coffee, spirits, beer, tobacco were loaded with taxes. Corn and meat were not taxed for revenue, but the prohibitive duties on their import, levied in the interest of the landowners and farmers, were equivalent to a tax on the food of the poor. The duties on timber and coal, and a multitude of duties on raw materials, were a drag on industry. The land tax, the house and window taxes, the luxury taxes, and the stamp duties fell on the rich, but they constituted little more than a quarter of the total revenue. Half the expenditure consisted of the interest due on the National Debt ; but an extravagant pension fund of £90,000 a year, used chiefly for bribery, offered demagogues an excuse to say that the money extorted from the poor was squandered for despicable objects.

In the meantime population was increasing rapidly. In 1750 the population of England and Wales had been estimated at 6,039,684 ; in 1801 it had risen to 9,187,176, and was growing steadily. The increase was a healthy sign, for it was due less to a rise in the birth-rate than to a fall in the death-rate—due to the higher standard of life, the greater cleanliness of all classes, improved medical knowledge, and the conquest of the old scourges, smallpox and scurvy, that had ravaged the country in the past. The growing population was provided for by a great expansion of trade and industry, but this involved a change in the domestic economy of Great Britain. The country had ceased to be agricultural, and was becoming industrial; sooner or later this fact must be recognised, and with it the fact that she could no longer feed her own population economically. As yet the governing classes had not recognised this fact, and the Corn Law of 1815 was the proof of their blindness.

At the same time industry itself was changing form under the influence of mechanical inventions; it was passing from the domestic to the factory system. These structural changes offered opportunities to capitalists to exploit the working classes, and equal opportunities to ignorance to blunder and destroy and waste. The introduction of labour-saving machinery commonly means an immediate fall in the demand for labour and a subsequent great increase. The temporary fall, especially among a growing population, must result in great suffering if not carefully regulated.

In the period 1815-1830 such a fall in the demand for labour was taking place in the textile industries, or at least in the most important of them, the cotton trade. The improvement in spinning machinery, which had come first, had caused a great demand for handloom weavers to cope with the increased output. When the handloom itself began to be replaced by the powerloom, the weaver was faced with ruin. His wages fell steadily, and he had long and frequent periods of unemployment. The handloom weaver, bent and twisted with toiling at his loom, haggard with starvation, was one of the great problems of the day—a figure which statesman and philanthropist alike contemplated with helpless despair.

The increase of population during the Industrial Revolution had been accompanied by a movement of population: the weight shifted from the south to the north, and new towns grew up, and old towns extended themselves on all sides. The question of the housing of the poor was added to other difficulties: the factory hand must live near his work, and there was no accommodation ready for him. The condition of the great industrial towns, many of which had no municipal authorities, was indescribable. In

Birmingham more than half the inhabitants lived in cellars.   In
Manchester the unofficial Board of Health had improved things
a little, but even in Manchester there were streets along the river-
side where the houses were several feet below the level of the river,
and where there was no water supply save from the polluted stream
itself.

In the 'twenties the country worker also began to suffer from
the introduction of machinery—the threshing machine.   Agricultural wages were sometimes as low as 6s. or 7s. a week.   In 1795
the Justices of the Peace, realising that men could not live on such
a sum, began to supplement wages out of the poor-rates.   The
practice spread through most of the agricultural counties, and in
some semi-industrial districts it was resorted to also in the case of
the handloom weaver.   Widespread demoralisation among the
poor was the result, and the poor-rates rose to be a crushing
burden on the ratepayer.

Both in town and country the rate of wages was lowered by
the immigration of hordes of half-starved Irish, accustomed to live
on potatoes, and ready to take whatever work offered.

Both in town and in country, in mine and farmstead, factory
and workshop, and in its own home, the child was exploited, working longer hours than its parents, never seeing its pitiful wages, and
helping to lower the standard of life for others.

If such were the conditions in which the labourer worked, no
better provision was made for his hours of leisure.   Notwithstanding his low wages, he contrived not infrequently to get drunk ; he
enjoyed an occasional bull-baiting or bear-baiting, or, if he were a
Londoner, the even more disgusting sport of ox-driving.   Schools
were few and bad, though they were now improving, and even the
religious teaching of the workman was often poorly provided for.
The Church was in crying need of reform.   Pluralism, and consequent neglect, were frequent.   In one large parish Trinity
College, Cambridge, drew £2000 a year in tithes, and paid the
officiating clergyman £24 a year.   W. H. Hudson mentions a case
of later date than this, where there were only four religious services
in the year.[1]   In one notorious instance, the vicar, Dr. Free, lived
in open immorality, only entering the pulpit occasionally to
blaspheme and insult such of his parishioners as appeared, and it
took more than ten years' work, appeals to indifferent bishops and

[1] *A Shepherd's Life*, p. 109.

procedure in the ecclesiastical courts, to turn him out.[1] The hunting, swearing parson was still a too frequent apparition, and the tithe system created ill-feeling against the Church. In many cases the failure of the Church was the opportunity of the Dissenting minister. But, devoted and high-minded as the Dissenters often were, they were sometimes very ignorant. In some of the growing industrial towns the population of individual parishes had increased so enormously that it was impossible for the most devoted pastor to perform the necessary duties.

Such was the problem that confronted the Government; but the economic problem was complicated by the effects of the war. In normal times, the process of emendation would have gone on alongside that of evolution; there would probably have been no attempt to grasp the problem as a whole, but there would have been a continual tinkering at details. As it was, the clock had stopped at 1793 : there was nearly a quarter-century's arrears of reform to make up.

Yet it was difficult to know what the Government was to do. The problem could not be solved by legislation. The whole machinery of State control necessary to the working of modern industrialism had still to be created, and the evolution of industry itself had not yet reached a stage that facilitated interference. The cotton trade was the first to be touched by Government, not because it was the worst, for it was not, but because it was the only trade sufficiently organised on a large scale to make State control practically possible. Most of the other great industries were still organised—or rather unorganised—in numberless small, often domestic, workshops. Birmingham, a centre of misery, was one vast collection of such small businesses. It was literally impossible to bring these under any adequate control. In an age when the principles of hygiene were little known, and the science of town-planning in its infancy, what could be done as to the housing question? No government on earth could have arrested the substitution of machinery for hand-labour, one of the main causes of distress at the moment, or even greatly mitigated the suffering caused by the transition. To the present day neither theorist nor practical statesman has devised a real remedy for unemployment

---

[1] This scandal seems to have inspired Peel with his first desire to reform the Ecclesiastical Law. See a letter to the Law Officers of the Crown, 26th March, 1827. H.O. 49, 7, p. 319.

arising—as much of the unemployment at that time did—out of the natural course of trade. The fumbling attempt to relieve the underpaid and under-employed resulted in the miseries and degradation of the Poor Law allowance system. The very facts of the situation were not known : since then the work of a hundred great Parliamentary Commissions has made them more familiar to the twentieth-century student than they could have been to the statesman of that day. The railway, the telegraph, and the newspaper press had all to be developed before the knowledge and rapid free communication necessary for efficient control could exist.

Moreover, all this vast work of sweeping away abuses and outworn laws, and building a new system in the ruins, had to be done by the Central Government with what feeble aid they could get from the magistracy. The municipalities were rotten or non-existent ; the mechanism of the parish and the county was out-of-date ; there was practically no local government to aid the central power.

A sick child turns to its mother and says, ' Make the pain go away ; ' and nations have a pathetic faith in the power of their government to set all wrongs right. The British people looked to Parliament for help in their distress, and when no help seemed to be forthcoming, when it seemed no one cared for their suffering or their appeals, the Government was blamed for all their distress.

' There is a limit, very soon reached, to the amount of workmanlike creative legislation or administration of which any government is capable in a given time. There was no limit to the call on creative ability in a nation barely recovered from twenty-two years of war, shaken by ill-comprehended economic change, and bewildered by a growth in its own numbers without precedent in history.' [1] But, if the Government could not do much, for a time they did less than they could. They were still hag-ridden by the ghost of the French Revolution. They did not understand the economic problems before them, and could offer no remedy but force. ' They thought they were imitating Mr. Pitt, because they mistook disorganisation for sedition.' [2] But one thing they did : they brought the country through a period of sudden and intense suffering, without a serious outbreak of revolt, and at the cost of only a handful of lives, and they did this when all the means at

[1] Clapham, *Economic History of Modern Britain*, i. p. 316.
[2] Disraeli, *Coningsby*, p. 70.

their disposal were some 12,000 soldiers and a few hundred very inefficient police.

Two threads, twisted together, run through the history of a great nation. It is continually moving, upwards and downwards : one generation after another adds its contribution to civilisation— to the national fund of wealth, culture, and morality : but while this process goes on, another accompanies it, in the submerged portion of the people, piling up a fund of poverty, ignorance, misery and crime, which dwindles or contracts with circumstances, but in the long run increases with the increase of the total population. In every great modern State there is a reptile element, fed on such ignorance and misery and degradation, which, at moments when the bonds of society are loosened, creeps from its den and preys upon what it can seize.

In the Britain of that day it was strong : thirty years before, in the Gordon Riots, it had broken loose and terrorised London ; twenty years before, it had broken loose, and Birmingham lay for four days at the mercy of an anti-Jacobin mob ; in 1831 it broke out again and burned Bristol and sacked Nottingham Castle.

Those of the working classes who hung upon the edge of subsistence, driven to desperation by prolonged and hopeless suffering, were the potential allies of this reptile element. The labourer who fired ricks and stables, the spinner who flung vitriol in a blackleg's face and fired shots in at his window, the miner who beat his child assistant almost to death—all these might be the victims of social injustice, innocent in the sight of heaven, but they were nevertheless a threat to the life of the State. The first act of political rioters was often to open the gaols ; the first result of industrial riots was that professional thieves flocked out from the haunts where the police dared not penetrate, and joined in plunder.

In the early nineteenth century Britain faced the alternative : Reform or Revolution. Revolution is a lottery : it may destroy more than it creates. Unless the national need calls forth great men to control and guide the forces let loose, the remedy may be worse than the disease. It is a desperate remedy, only to be desired where no organ for peaceful reform is to be found. But Britain did possess such an organ in her Parliament—dormant for the moment, perhaps, but still workable.

Reform, however, also has its disadvantages. It must be

gradual. If it is hasty and reckless, it may be ineffective or even damaging ; but if it is very slow, it may drive the sufferer to premature revolt. In the days following 1815, there was a great and crying need for reform, but there was also the need for a strong hand to hold the forces of disintegration in bounds while reform was prepared and carried out. The Tory Government at least did this last : they held disorder in check until the paralysis of exhaustion following the war was past, and the reformers could begin their work.

The working man, however, felt nothing of this. He saw only that the governing class was callous, and tyrannical, and selfish. He saw in the Corn Laws, the Combination Laws, the Game Laws, the savage Criminal Law, the fiscal system, the selfish legislation of a privileged class. He was told by agitators that he could hope for nothing from the legislature in its present form, and that the cure for all his distresses lay in parliamentary reform.

The poorer classes wanted less taxation, cheaper bread, higher wages, protection from exploitation, insurance against want, and they believed that a reformed Parliament would give them all this. This agitation was in reality economic in its character ; it was transformed into a political movement by the teaching of a few demagogues. It obtained the support of the Whigs in Parliament partly because reform was a tradition of the party, and their leader, Lord Grey, was pledged to it ; partly because they were in opposition, and adopted any popular cry ; partly because conditions in the unreformed Parliament operated more in favour of the Tories than of themselves ; and partly—especially among the younger Whigs and the Radicals—out of sincere conviction of its necessity and justice.

The agitation for reform was accompanied by economic disorder ; and the Government failed to distinguish between the two. The weavers rose, and destroyed the power-looms ; the agricultural labourers burned ricks and broke reaping-machines ; the Radical agitators summoned monster meetings, and talked wildly of revolution—one such assembly, held upon the outskirts of London, marched into the town, attacked the gunsmiths' shops, and raised a dangerous riot ; one of the leaders shot a bystander who remonstrated with him ; unemployed weavers shot at their masters from behind hedges ; a plot to sack and burn Manchester was formed in the surrounding districts. The Government took it all for part of the same movement. They suspended the Habeas Corpus Act, prohibited public meetings, arrested the agitators, and transported or hanged the rioters when they could catch them. The Whigs took up the popular cause, and eloquently protested against these infringements of personal liberty.

By this time several changes had taken place in the Government. Canning had seen himself shelved for four years, and watched his once despised rival, Castlereagh, conduct the national cause to an unparalleled triumph, and move, the central figure, in the Congress of the Powers. His pride was tamed, and in 1816 he accepted the Presidency of the Board of Control for India. Two years later, the Duke of Wellington, in all the prestige of his victories, took the Ordnance Board. The Ministers who were specially associated, in the public eye, with repression and reaction were those three personified by Shelley as Force, Fraud, and Hypocrisy :

> I met Murder on my way :
> He had a mask like Castlereagh.
> Very smooth was his face, yet grim.
> Seven bloodhounds followed him.
>
> Next came Fraud, and he had on,
> Like Eldon, an ermine gown ;
> His big tears, for he wept well,
> Turned to millstones as they fell.
>
> Clothed with the Bible, as with light,
> And the shadows of the night,
> Like Sidmouth next, Hypocrisy
> On a crocodile rode by.

Peel had had no responsibility for the repressive policy of the Government. His work lay entirely in Ireland, and he was not a member of the Cabinet, nor had he spoken on the subject in Parliament. He had not long been out of office, however, before he publicly identified himself with their policy.

In 1819 fresh disorder broke out. A monster meeting to petition for reform was summoned in Manchester. The people determined to appear in an orderly and impressive manner, but unfortunately they acted with great imprudence. For some weeks beforehand they were drilled by discharged soldiers, performing various military evolutions, and all clapping their hands when the order ' Fire ! ' was given. A man who chanced to approach one of these drilling parties was taken for a spy and beaten almost to death. These proceedings were reported to the magistracy, and great alarm was caused.

On the morning of August 16, 1819, a vast crowd of nearly 60,000 persons, including several hundred women, approached the open space called St. Peter's Fields, on the outskirts of Manchester. They marched in orderly companies, each with its leader distinguished by a rosette in his coat, and they carried large banners inscribed with such legends as ' Liberty or Death ! ' ' We will Conquer Our Enemies ! ' ' No Corn Laws ! ' At the head rode ' Orator Hunt,' the agitator, in an open carriage.

The magistrates were waiting in a house near by, and a company of yeomanry and a troop of regular horse were at hand, also what police the town could boast. The police were ordered to arrest Hunt, but could not approach him. One of the magistrates read the Riot Act, but in a voice inaudible with fear. The magistrates next ordered the yeomanry to disperse the crowd ; they advanced at a walking pace, in single file, and were in a moment swallowed up in the tossing sea of heads ; some were pulled from their saddles. In a panic, the magistrates ordered the Hussars to the rescue. The troops instantly formed up and charged the crowd, who fled in terror, but owing to the pressure could not escape. Numbers were trodden down, or struck down by the swords of the cavalry, and about six persons, including a constable and a woman, were killed. The news was hurried to London, and the Government, without waiting to learn the details, expressed public and full approval of the conduct of the magistrates.

This tragic and disgraceful affair, of course, aroused violent indignation throughout the country. Public meetings were everywhere held to censure the conduct of the magistrates, and the Whigs took up the question in Parliament, and fiercely attacked the Government. The Ministers stuck to their guns. They dismissed a Whig Lord Lieutenant for convening a meeting of protest in his county, and they introduced a series of measures, known as the Six Acts. The first, which is still in force, forbade the unauthorised training of the people in arms. Another was to prevent delay in the trial of persons indicted for misdemeanours. The remaining Acts were more objectionable : they authorised the seizure of seditious libels, and made transportation the punishment for a second offence ; imposed a stamp duty on pamphlets and leaflets ; authorised the issue of warrants to search for arms in

some specified counties ; and restricted the right of public meeting within very narrow limits. They were emergency regulations,
and most of them were only in force for a few years ; but they
involved a dangerous encroachment on popular liberty, and were
fiercely denounced by the Whigs. In the midst of the storm Peel
had the boldness to rise and to declare his full approval of the
conduct of the Manchester magistrates, and to defend the most
objectionable of the repressive measures—the Seditious Meetings
Prevention Bill.

Peel was, however, engaged upon work of a more constructive
nature.

The difficulties of the economic situation were intensified by
the fact that the national finances were in confusion. In 1797
there had been a financial crisis, produced partly by over-specula-
tion, partly by the scare of a French invasion, but chiefly by the
reckless borrowing of the Government. Pitt had rushed through
legislation which authorised the Bank of England to suspend payments in cash. These measures were intended to be temporary,
but they were continued from time to time for the whole duration
of the war. They led to the almost complete disappearance of
gold from circulation, part of it being hoarded by private persons,
but the greater part, of course, exported. In place of gold, there
was a currency of inconvertible paper. The Bank of England,
with the example of the French Assignats before it, was anxious
to avoid over-issue, and for some years there was no evil result.
The Governors of the Bank, however, had not sufficient knowledge
and experience to understand the abnormal financial conditions
of the times : about 1808 they began to issue their notes too
freely, the price of gold rose, and the foreign exchanges showed
an unfavourable balance against the pound sterling. The first
person to draw attention to the state of affairs was the economist,
Ricardo, and in 1810 the House of Commons appointed a Committee of Inquiry. This Committee, under the leadership of
Francis Horner, drew up the famous *Bullion Report* : it pointed
out that the system of inconvertible paper must inevitably lead
to over-issue and consequent depreciation, unless it was strictly
limited in accordance with the price of gold bullion and the state
of the foreign exchanges. The result of over-issue was a general
fall in the value of paper currency : prices measured in paper
rose, debtors gained, and creditors suffered ; all those with fixed

incomes lost. The country labourer in especial suffered, for his
wages accommodated themselves to values ' more slowly than
the price of any other species of labour or commodity.' [1] The
Committee therefore recommended that cash payments should
be restored within two years, whether the war were ended
or not.

The *Report* had a very hostile reception. Vansittart, then
Chancellor of the Exchequer, moved a series of contrary resolutions, the most important of which affirmed that Bank of England
notes were held ' in public estimation to be equivalent to the legal
coin of the realm, and generally accepted as such.' This flagrant
contradiction of fact was passed by the House of Commons by a
large majority : one of that majority was Mr. Peel.

The unreality of the proceeding was shown by the fact that immediately afterwards Parliament was obliged to make banknotes
legal tender, as an attempt had been made by a landlord to get
his rents paid in gold, which his tenants could neither afford nor
procure.

In 1816, however, the Bank of England, which had evidently
pondered the *Report* in its heart, began to restore gold payments
by slow degrees. They did not, however, restrict their issue of
notes any the more, and as gold was still at a premium, they soon
found themselves in an awkward position. In September, 1817,
they had held gold reserves for nearly £12,000,000, but by
February, 1819, £7,500,000 of this had been drawn out, while the
notes in circulation had only been reduced by £4,500,000. As a
result of this situation, both Houses of Parliament appointed
secret Committees to consider the return to cash payments. The
House of Commons Committee appointed Peel to the chair—a
high compliment to one who was still a young man, with little
financial experience. It may have been due to the hope that,
having voted for Vansittart's ridiculous resolutions in 1811, he
would take the same ground in 1819.

If so, these hopes were disappointed. Peel read the *Bullion
Report* for the first time, and was completely converted. The
evidence laid before the Committee all tended to the same effect.
In May, 1819, he presented its Report, largely drawn up by himself, to the House. He began by acknowledging that he had
entirely changed his views, and adverted to the pain with which

[1] *Bullion Report*, p. 67.

he found himself forced to oppose his father, who was one of the leaders of the anti-bullionists. He then proceeded to a lucid exposition of the state of the finances and the evils to which over-issue of notes had led—increased speculation, fluctuating values, and over-production—ending with the declaration that 'every consideration of sound policy, and every obligation of strict justice, should induce them to restore the ancient and permanent standard of value.' He then proposed a series of resolutions founded on the Report, by which the resumption of cash payments was to begin in February, 1820, and be completed by May, 1823, while at the same time the circulation of notes should be periodically reduced—the reduction being made possible by the Government's repaying to the Bank the sum of £10,000,000 borrowed by means of Exchequer bills.[1] These resolutions passed without a division. As a matter of fact, the Bank was able to resume cash payment in full by May, 1821, instead of May, 1823.

Peel's Act, as it was called, was the object of violent attacks in the next few years, and he was repeatedly called upon to defend it in the House. The restoration of the currency to its real value did, in fact, press hardly on the producing classes for a short time by lowering prices. It was particularly hard on the farmer and landlord, for two fine harvests lowered the price of corn at the same time, and poor soil could only be cultivated at a loss. But all this was a small price to pay for the restoration of the currency to its just value, and the establishment of an honest and reliable financial system. A small minority, however—some of the land-owners in the House of Commons, led by 'Squire' Western, and some Radical agitators outside it, of whom Cobbett was the chief—represented Peel's Act to be the cause of much of the distress of the country, and as being responsible for the financial crisis of 1825.

It was in December, 1819, that Peel spoke in defence of 'Peterloo' and the Six Acts. After that, for the space of fourteen months, the pages of *Hansard* know him no more. Mr. Peel was engaged upon urgent private affairs.

In 1820 he married Miss Julia Floyd, daughter of a general in the Indian Army, and a celebrated beauty. History preserves no record of the courtship save a tradition that he gravely told the lady of his choice that 'he feared she was too fond of the world,'

[1] *Speeches*, i. p. 127.

and that she disarmed all criticism by replying, ' You are my world.' [1]

This marriage had the most important influence upon Peel's later career. The Duke of Wellington told an inquisitive lady that ' Peel had no wish to marry a clever woman,' and that his wife had no influence with him.[2] This means no more than that Peel would have been miserable married to a woman who kept a salon. What he wanted from his wife was sympathy, and this he got. Peel's nervous organisation was, in truth, much too fine-strung for comfort. Physically, he was abnormally sensitive : his physician in later life said that ' he never saw any human frame so susceptible of pain ; ' [3] on one occasion when he accidentally pinched his finger in a door he fainted on the spot. This physical peculiarity was accompanied by a mental sensibility equally extraordinary. He was ridiculously thin-skinned in public life : other statesmen might ignore or laugh at attack ; with Peel, every arrow, from however mean a hand, struck home and rankled. In his private relations he was just as easily wounded. One example may be given. He was occasionally the guest of Lord Hertford [4] at his shooting-lodge ; Mrs. Peel could not visit such a house, and she may have disliked his doing so, for when he complained of home-sickness, she seems to have indulged in a mild sarcasm. It elicited this remarkable reply : ' I should have but little satisfaction in the thought that anyone but myself had seen a letter from you to me, during my separation from you, in which there is such a sentence as this : " How will you bear to think of *one*, compared to fifteen ? I know it is nothing in the scale." I will only remark upon this that I would suffer much rather than write such a sentence to you, at a time when I was absent from you. Is the repetition of the word *fashion* meant to be *severe* ? I only feel its injustice and un-kindness if it is. Kiss my children for me. I hope *they* will always

[1] *Peel Private Letters*, p. 28.

[2] Maxwell, *Wellington*, vol. ii. p. 260. Having heard Wellington on Peel's marriage, it is interesting to hear Peel on Wellington's. ' She (the Duchess of Wellington) burst out a-crying, and such things make me still more hate the sight of those who can find it in their heart, even if they have no sense of virtue, to usurp her place. . . . It really seems something to her to have me to talk to. What wickedness and what folly to undervalue and to be insensible to the affec-tion of a wife ! ' Peel to Mrs. Peel, 1827. *Private Letters*, p. 96.

[3] *Greville*, vi. p. 368.

[4] Lord Hertford was the original from which were drawn Thackeray's Lord Steyne and Disraeli's Lord Monmouth.

justly estimate my affection for them.'[1] Poor Julia must have been a little startled by the effect of her teasing. A susceptibility so extreme as this was all the more dangerous because Peel's excessive shyness and pride usually led him to conceal the hurt he had received. To his friends he showed offence only by cold avoidance. In public life his self-control gradually became so complete and so habitual that in his later years he was regarded as cold-blooded and unfeeling; and when on rare occasions he lost his temper, those who did not know him well believed that his passion was affected. Neither in public nor in private did he complain or blame those who attacked him. Few public men have encountered such storms of obloquy and reproach as he had to face; they would have been insupportable if it had not been for the perfect ease and happiness of his domestic life.

Most of his contemporaries had the habit of carrying on long correspondences, bristling with important Cabinet secrets, with the ladies of their acquaintance. It is a habit most convenient for posterity. Peel had no such feminine correspondent, nor did he find one in his wife. His letters to her consist largely of such interesting items of information as, that little Julia had gone to sleep with her feet on the pillow and her head at the bed-foot; that he lay awake all night planning a house at the seaside where they might enjoy themselves 'with our little ones, and not an earwig to molest us;' that 'no one shall prepare my dinner for me in *my own way* but my own, my dearest Julia;' that 'I kiss the little locket every time I take it off or put it on;' and, in fine, that he is her 'own, own, own R. P.' References to politics are comparatively casual; the House of Commons is 'that infernal place, which I wish I need never enter again.'[2] He liked to live two lives: one political, where he worked, when in office, harder than any factory slave in the country; and one in his quiet country home, growing his early peas and strawberries, shooting his coverts, making that great collection of pictures, which later passed to the nation, choosing his Julia's cloaks and bracelets, and making original drawings for his little boys and girls—absorbing himself as completely in trifles as at other times he did in the routine work of government or the excitement of debate. From the quiet

[1] *Peel Private Letters*, p. 65.
[2] *Peel Private Letters*, pp. 47, 57, 81, 98.

happiness of this life, from the perfect understanding of his wife, he derived the strength for his arduous political career.[1]

While Peel was going a-courting, the Government were wooing him as eagerly to return to office. They were involved in ever greater difficulties, and knew not where to turn for help. In the spring of 1820 George III., the ' old, mad, blind, despised, and dying King,' did at last die, and the first action of his successor was to instruct the Ministry to institute proceedings for his own divorce. After a sitting of thirteen hours, the Cabinet refused to comply. The King had threatened to dismiss them if they refused, but he did not dare to carry out his threat, and for a moment it seemed that Ministers had saved both their characters and their places. At the same time their position was improved by the discovery of a Radical plot to murder the entire Cabinet and establish a provisional government; while a revolt actually broke out near Glasgow, and was put down by troops. These events horrified the more respectable classes, and produced a reaction in favour of the Government, but it did not last long.

The Queen refused the provision of £50,000 a year offered to her, and came to England to enforce her claims in person; and the Ministry reluctantly began proceedings against her. The Whigs and Radicals took up her cause, as a convenient stick to beat the Government with : the people, indignant that a person of character so degraded as George IV. should have the impudence to demand a divorce on the ground of his wife's immorality, rallied round her, and the Ministry was almost overwhelmed by the storm which their proceedings aroused. Their majority in the House of Commons dwindled steadily, and they were forced to withdraw the Bill of Pains and Penalties which they had introduced. They lost one of their ablest men, Canning, who resigned as a protest against the treatment of the Queen. Their prestige sank to the lowest ebb, and they were universally despised.

Conscious of their weakness, they looked round for help. They might bring back Canning, they might bring back Peel, or they might obtain the services of the little group known as the

---

[1] There were seven children of this marriage: 1, Julia, b. 1821, afterwards Countess of Jersey; 2, Robert, b. 1822, afterwards 3rd baronet; 3, Sir Frederick Peel, b. 1823, President of the Railway Commission, etc.; 4, Sir William Peel, b. 1824, sailor and explorer, the first naval V.C.; 5, John, b. 1827; 6, Arthur, b. 1829, afterwards Viscount Peel, Speaker of the House of Commons, 1884-1895, and temperance reformer; 7, Eliza, afterwards Mrs. Stonor.

Grenville Party. The King, however, was furious with Canning, and would not hear of his return ; and for the rest, as Lord Grenville remarked, ' It would be little short of an act of direct insanity for any man not involved in this mass of difficulty to go voluntarily and implicate himself in it.' [1]

In December, 1820, they offered Canning's vacant post to Peel, who unhesitatingly refused it. All the next year they continued to woo him, and he coyly to refuse. He suspected that Liverpool really wanted Canning, and was keeping him (Peel) as a second string, and he was a little piqued. He thought, too, he had a claim for something better than the India Board. The King, however, continued obdurate, and Canning in despair at last accepted the Governor-Generalship of India. The unfortunate Queen was now dead, and the Ministry, in spite of all their weakness, seemed to have weathered the storm. The Grenvilles consented to come in ; and the Government made Peel a more tempting offer : Lord Sidmouth would vacate his post in his favour. Peel accepted, and the opening of 1822 saw him installed at the Home Office.

[1] *Buckingham Papers*, 2nd Series, i. p. 95.
[2] *Croker*, i. p. 187 ff.

CHAPTER V

THE HOME OFFICE, 1822-1830

Poor Lord Sidmouth, who had been Home Secretary for ten years past, was a benevolent gentleman with an anxious face and bulging forehead, full of good intentions : but he was less eminent for wit than for piety, and as one studies the records of his administration, there arises before the mind's eye a strange picture of the Home Office as a place of dust and cobwebs, midst of which sits the Secretary of State tranced in his chair, while now and then ' shadow shapes that come and go ' bear to his side letters from spies, letters from lunatics, letters from murderers threatening death. . . . When, one day in January, 1822, Mr. Peel walked into the Home Office, it was as if a door opened on the outer world, and a fresh wind blew through the dim corridors, dispersing the enchanted mists—a wind that was the breath of the opening nineteenth century.

The spies vanished : the *agent-provocateur* disappeared for good and all from British history.[1] The threatening letters stopped as if by magic. Even the lunatics seemed to feel that they no longer addressed a kindred spirit, and almost ceased from troubling : those who were so misguided as to continue found themselves

[1] During Sidmouth's administration *agents-provocateurs* were certainly employed by the Home Office, though, his biographer contends, not with his knowledge, which would merely serve to indicate the laxness of his control. Peel made a clean sweep of all Sidmouth's spies, and for four years Government spies ceased to exist. During the disorders of 1826-7, however, Peel connived at the employment of spies by the military authorities in the north. Sir John Byng employed two, Buckley and Bradbury or Bradley, the latter of whom seems to have been specially selected by Peel, when Byng complained that he could not himself find an honest and reliable man. No doubt, choosing a spy is a delicate task, and Peel does not seem to have been so successful in this department of his work as in some others : Bradley drank, and was an ex-convict. Colonel Fletcher, another commander in the north, employed a private spy named Alpha, to whom he clung with pathetic faith, but who was detected by the Home Office as an impostor and dismissed. In 1830, for about six weeks, the Home Office itself seems to have employed a spy to report on the state of London. All these four individuals were employed to procure information only : they performed a function which would to-day be performed by a news-

speedily and effectively suppressed. Instead, came letters of a new kind—full of grateful amaze, from persons who had found their communications answered, their grievances investigated, their business quickly and effectively put through.

The hour of blind reaction, of repression without reform, was ended. Peel had supported the coercive measures of the Government, but he did not mean to imitate them. He wished to rely on the law of the land, without encroaching upon the liberties of the people ; and all that was objectionable in the Six Acts was quietly and unobtrusively allowed to lapse.

For the first three years of his administration all was plain sailing. Financial and commercial reform went on apace, and partly owing to this, partly to the natural course of trade, there was a revival of prosperity. Profits, prices, and wages were all low ; wheat went down to 40s. the quarter, the lowest level it touched between 1815 and 1835 ; but demand was good, there was no unemployment, and rioting and disorder ceased.

Peel secured a valuable ally in his defence of the currency when William Huskisson joined the Cabinet as President of the Board of Trade. They united in opposing the measures brought forward by Western for the depreciation of the currency, and Huskisson proposed and carried a counter resolution, reaffirming Montague's famous declaration of 1691, ' That this House will not alter the standard of gold or silver, in fineness, weight, or denomination.'

In 1818 Joseph Hume had re-entered the House of Commons, and constituted himself unofficial auditor of the national accounts. Hume and Vansittart, the incompetent Chancellor of the Exchequer, were nicknamed ' Penny Wise and Pound Foolish ; ' but paper reporter : they attended Radical meetings and reported the speeches made. The formation of the new police ultimately did away with the necessity of these methods : to-day our anarchists spout with a blue-coated bobby listening benevolently at the door ; but in 1826 a policeman attending a Radical meeting would have done so at the risk of his life. The utmost precautions were taken to prevent any of the spies acting as *agents-provocateurs*, and no prosecution was based on information communicated by them. No one, in fact, seems to have attached the slightest credit to any of their statements. ' Pray see this man,' says a note (7th March, 1827, H.O. 40, 22) on the back of one of Byng's reports, ' when he arrives in town. I do not believe one word of his story. Tell him to be on his guard and to state nothing but the truth. Ask him particularly about the map he talks of—whether he actually saw it—and if he did—where ? With whom ? Where is it now ? By whom the map was prepared ? Make him put down his answers in writing. I disbelieve the whole tale about the map. R.P.' (The Byng-Bradbury-Buckley correspondence is in H.O. 40, 20-22. Alpha's letters are in H.O. 40, 22. The 1830 spy's in H.O. 40, 25.)

even Vansittart could not resist the growing demand for economy, and in 1823 he was replaced by Robinson.

From 1820 onwards the estimates were steadily reduced. Vansittart carried two wise measures, one instituting a tax of 5 per cent. on civil service salaries and 10 per cent. on those of all other Government officials, the other converting a part of the funded debt, with a considerable saving. Robinson conferred a boon on the nation by quietly dropping Pitt's absurd sinking fund, and thereby converting an annual deficit into a surplus. Taxation was reduced: the poor were exempted from the house tax and the window tax; the duties on coal, iron, wool, silk, coffee, sugar, were lowered. The navigation laws were slightly relaxed, which allowed the expansion of overseas trade.

Meanwhile Peel had turned his attention to legal reform. He was Secretary of State for Home Affairs for two periods, comprising together a little over eight years, with an interval of eight months between them. When he finally left office in 1830 he had reformed and consolidated practically the whole of the Criminal Law of England.

The English Criminal Code was incomparably savage. In France, the only capital crimes were now murder, armed robbery and housebreaking. In England, they were without number: men could be hanged for cutting down a tree, sending threatening letters, impersonating a Greenwich pensioner, cutting down the banks of rivers, stealing in a shop or on a navigable river, stealing 40s. from a dwelling-house, and a hundred more or less serious offences. Naturally juries refused to convict for petty offences, and where conviction was secured, the death penalty was frequently commuted to transportation. The death sentence lost its awful effect when it was pronounced so often, and when the hearers knew that as likely as not it would not be carried out.

Moreover, the law was as confused as it was sanguinary. It depended upon hundreds of obscure and conflicting statutes, some modern, some hundreds of years old, many of them involved with regulations of a quite unconnected nature. The preservation of trees depended upon no less than twenty different statutes, one of which was entitled, ' An Act for the better securing the duties of customs upon certain goods removed from the outports and other places to London; for regulating the fees of his Majesty's customs in the province of Senegambia . . ; for allowing to the receivers-general of the duties on offices and employments in Scotland a proper compensation ; for the better preservation of hollies, thorns, and quicksets in forests ; and for authorising the exportation of a limited quantity of an inferior sort of barley called bigg from the port of Kirkwall.'

' Now, Sir,' said Mr. Peel, introducing his bills, ' what I propose is . . . not to throw open the holly or thorn to wanton depredation, but merely to transplant them to a more congenial soil than the province of Senegambia.' [1]

While consolidating the Criminal Law, Peel also mitigated its severity and simplified its procedure.

He cannot claim to have been the first to point out the deficiencies of the law. The credit of that belongs to Jeremy Bentham, to Sir Samuel Romilly, and to Sir James Mackintosh. All these, however, laboured in vain for years, until a member of the Government was found ready to take up their work. Romilly introduced bill after bill, only to see them thrown out either by the Lords or by the Commons : he died without doing more than securing the abolition of the death penalty for two petty offences.[2] His successor, Mackintosh, was a more effective politician. He was a retired Indian judge, and during his long service he had kept perfect order in his district while only once inflicting the death penalty, and that upon a British soldier who had murdered a Hindu. In 1819 he secured the appointment of a Committee upon capital punishment, and carried three bills founded upon its report, abolishing the death penalty for a considerable number of offences.[3] In 1823 he introduced a series of resolutions upon the subject of the Criminal Law, but Peel, objecting to his method of proceeding, proposed to take up the matter himself, and Mackintosh agreed.

Peel took first the laws relating to theft and the malicious injury of property and consolidated them into a single statute. Next he did the same for those dealing with offences against the person ; and, lastly, he undertook the forgery laws. There had, for example, been 130 statutes relating to larceny : they were all condensed into one Act, comprised in a small book of thirteen pages. [4]

---

[1] *Speeches,* i. p. 400.

[2] For picking pockets, and for stealing from bleaching grounds.

[3] Mostly offences which were at that date never committed.

[4] The consolidation of the offences against the person laws was partly carried out by Lord Lansdowne during Peel's absence from office in 1827, but it was begun and concluded by Peel, and introduced by him.

The death penalty was abolished for over a hundred offences, leaving only the more serious felonies liable to capital punishment. A similar mitigation was made in less severe punishments : the penalty for fishing in another person's waters, for example, Peel reduced from seven years' transportation to an obligation to pay three times the value of the fish caught.

At the same time the Home Secretary undertook the consolidation of several branches of the civil law. The laws relating to the licensing system, to the regulation of juries, and to the jurisdiction of magistrates were all condensed each into a single Act ; while at the same time a whole series of reforms in legal procedure were introduced.

By abolishing patent offices and substituting fixed salaries for fees, Peel removed the great obstacle to the reform of the law courts, for hitherto every holder of a patent office had strenuously resisted such reforms as might, by simplifying and cheapening proceedings, lessen his fees. He abolished Benefit of Clergy. Up to this time a clergyman could still escape with impunity for a first offence in several kinds of felony, and the term ' Benefit of Clergy ' was used to create unnecessary confusion where the culprit was a layman. He put an end to the practice of suing out frivolous writs of error, by which a trial could be postponed for twelve months upon a mere pretext, and he ended also the absurd rule by which a guilty party might be acquitted because of a small technical error in the indictment—as, for instance, the misspelling of his name. He simplified the legal terminology to be used. He lessened the expense of obtaining a pardon from the Crown. By abolishing the necessity for certain proofs, he made it easier for the victims of sexual offences to obtain justice. Most important of all, he empowered the judges to award expenses to the prosecutor in cases of misdemeanour.[1] England, alone of civilised States, had no public prosecutor.

Peel also increased the number of judges, and instituted a Third Assize, which lessened the delay in bringing prisoners to trial.

The convict system seems to have been one of his chief cares. He consolidated all the laws dealing with prison discipline and with transportation, and he exercised continual care to prevent abuses in their administration. Every complaint was at once investigated, and more than one official convicted of harshness

[1] They already had the power in cases of felony.

or dishonesty was dismissed. No detail was too small for Mr. Secretary Peel's attention : we find him writing to order, on his own responsibility, that two pairs of woollen drawers, not one as heretofore, shall be provided for every convict on the voyage to Australia ; that the keeping of pigs by officers on transport ships, though not contrary to the letter of the law, is an offence against its spirit, and must cease ; demanding information as to why such-and-such a surgeon was paid without his giving the formal certificate as to the health of his convicts ; or whether it is true that such-and-such a prison doctor neglects the gaol for paying patients in the town ?

As the process of legal reform goes on, one can see the reformer's mind develop. In 1822 he spoke of the English law as ' the most perfect system of jurisprudence in the world.' [1] As time went on he ceased to refer to its perfection, and dwelt rather on the points in Scottish law which might with advantage be imitated.[2]

It might be thought that the reform of the Poor Law would be particularly congenial to Peel, with his intense individualism and his horror of pauperisation ; and he probably considered the subject, for immediately on entering office he circularised the local authorities of eight large towns for accounts of the poor-rates assessed, levied, and expended in the past year.[3] In 1824 he sup-

---

[1] *Speeches*, i. p. 181.

[2] In concluding this account of Peel's legal reforms it may be well to refer to his connection with the Chancery Commission. Peel had, as Home Secretary, the disagreeable task of defending Lord Eldon against the attacks made on him as Chancellor—the work of the Court of Chancery was then twenty years in arrears. It may be noted that he confined his defence to Eldon's acknowledged honesty and ability, and left his dilatoriness alone. He finally announced that the Government would appoint a Commission of Inquiry. Many historians refer to this as a sham, to put reformers off the scent—apparently forgetting that the ultimate reform of the Court of Chancery was founded on the report of this Commission. It is clear, however, that Peel meant the Commission to be no sham. On 15th December, 1825, he writes to Canning that he has been pressing the Commissioners hard : ' The truth is that I consider myself personally committed to the production of the report on the meeting of Parliament. . . . I have every assurance that the report will be forthcoming at the opening of the session. Secondly, I am promised that the *whole of the evidence* without a single omission shall be attached. . . ., and, thirdly, I have made arrangements for the immediate printing of the mass of the evidence, so that the evidence can be generally read at the meeting of Parliament.' (Italics Peel's. *Peel Papers*, British Museum, 40311, p. 163.)

[3] H.O. 43, 31, 11th April, 1822. The towns selected were Manchester, Birmingham, Glasgow, Leeds, Sheffield, Coventry, Liverpool, Stockport, so that the inquiry may have been intended to throw light on unemployment, not on Poor Law administration.

ported Lord John Russell's motion for a Committee to inquire into the practice of supplementing wages from the rates ; and in 1828 he spoke very strongly against this practice.[1] But he proposed no measures of his own, and he would probably have hesitated to introduce such stringent remedies as the Whigs ultimately did in the great Act of 1834. He was always inclined to underrate the effects of legislation in economic questions ; in 1829, while referring to the evils of supplementing wages from rates, he added, that ' there was a necessity in the present condition of the poor that would paralyse any Act of Parliament.'[2] He approved of the Act of 1834, but he did not approve all its provisions. He objected to the separation of families ; he thought the change should be introduced gradually and cautiously.[3] Perhaps he had not quite that cool courage, a little like callousness, which made the Poor Law Commissioners ready to contemplate great present suffering for the sake of greater future gain.

' What struck me most of all,' wrote Guizot long after, ' in the conversation of Sir Robert Peel, was his constant and earnest solicitude with regard to the condition of the labouring classes in England.'[4] That solicitude was slowly growing to be the dominating passion of Peel's life. In his happy and sheltered boyhood he had thought as little as any other of his class about such things : his life in Ireland had first accustomed him to the knowledge of misery and crime. Now he was learning the same lesson with regard to England, and with him the continual contemplation of the problem did not lead, as it does with some, to apathy or callousness. Inexperienced in the study of social problems, cautious, and never too hopeful, he could as yet devise no remedy for the evil as a whole : but in the meantime he did what he could with the materials ready to his hand.

In February, 1823, he wrote to the clerks of the peace for the counties in which the cotton trade was chiefly located, demanding the names of all persons appointed as visiting magistrates to cotton mills under the Health and Morals of Apprentices Act. The inquiry revealed, as he probably expected, that the Act was very imperfectly enforced ; in some cases visitors had not been ap-

---

[1] *Speeches*, i. p. 560.   [2] *Ib.* ii. p. 11.

[3] *Ib.* ii. p. 105. Peel did not speak on the bill of 1834, though he voted for it. The references are to earlier speeches on the same subject.

[4] Guizot, *Peel*, p. 83.

pointed for many years, in others never. The Secretary ordered
that they should be appointed immediately, and the Act strictly
observed in future. When the list of visiting magistrates was completed, Peel wrote to each individually, requesting them to report
'whether you have any reason to believe that the provisions of
the 59 Geo. III. c. 66' (*i.e.*, the Factory Act of 1819) ' are materially transgressed with respect to the hours of work, hours of
meals, and the age of the children employed.' It will be noted
that Peel made use of the machinery of the Act of 1802, which set
up visiting magistrates, to enforce the Act of 1819, which provided
no means of inspection.

The replies are interesting, showing the disadvantages of the
system of local inspection. Some visitors did excellent work,
while other reports were of the most perfunctory nature. One
magistrate was three months late in sending his report, as he had
'had a painful sensation in his head.' Another had not inspected
at all, as he was not now resident in the district to which he had
been appointed. The visitors for the Hundred of Leyland contented themselves with succinctly stating that no one factory had
observed the Acts in any one respect. It is satisfactory to note
that Peel & Co., Radcliffe Bridge, had a clean bill; while Jacob
Bright, Rochdale, had transgressed to the extent of employing
one child under nine.[1]

When the reports came, strict orders were sent that prosecutions
should at once be undertaken in all cases where the law had been
broken.[2]

[1] John Bright's father.

[2] The instructions and reports are in H.O. 43, 31 and 32 ; and H.O. 44, 14.
Peel paid special attention to the Factory Acts. In 1823 he ordered an investigation into a case which had occurred in 1819, where the masters were reported to have deterred their workmen from giving evidence in a prosecution.
(Peel to the Mayor of Macclesfield, 29th March, 1823, H.O. 43, 31.) In 1828
he wrote personally to two mill-owners of Wigan who had worked illegal
hours. (Peel to W. Wood and Thomas Darwell, 14th March, 1828, H.O. 43,
35.) Next year John Doherty, the trade union leader, informed him that the
two masters were again working over-hours, and that it was impossible to
prosecute them as all the magistrates were cotton spinners, and would not act.
Peel then wrote to the magistrates stating that if the practice did not stop at
once he ' would introduce a bill into Parliament for the purpose of giving to
the magistrates of the county a concurrent jurisdiction with those of Wigan.'
(To the magistrates of Wigan, 17th February, 1829, H.O. 43, 37.) Mr. and
Mrs. Hammond, in *The Town Labourer*, discuss the inefficiency of the Factory
Laws, and give these reports as evidence, but omit all reference to Peel's
attempts to enforce the law, and call him ' the opponent of factory reform.'
(See *The Town Labourer*, p. 64.)

This method of using the authority of the Secretary of State to enforce an ineffective law is open to objection, but it was thoroughly characteristic of Peel, whose instinct was for administrative reform rather than fresh legislation. He gave full support, however, to John Cam Hobhouse's two Acts of 1826 and 1831, extending and supplementing the earlier Factory Acts.[1]

There was another branch of the law which was but little more effectively enforced than the Factory Acts. In the stress of the war with France, the formation of trade unions for the purpose of regulating the conditions of labour and rate of wages had appeared to the Government equally dangerous with the formation of political Jacobin clubs; and both had been forbidden. In 1799-1800 Pitt had passed the Combination Laws, which made trade unions illegal, and a strike a criminal offence. It also forbade combinations of masters, but obviously the workman was not in a position to prosecute his master, so that the law was not only unwise, but unfair. It entirely failed to prevent combinations of workmen, but it roused ill-feeling, and drove the men to acts of violence and crime. Secret societies, bound by illegal oaths, were formed, or trade unions masqueraded as benefit societies. Strikes were frequent, and were usually accompanied by violence and intimidation. Blacklegs were beaten, attacked with vitriol, or shot at, mills were set on fire and machinery destroyed, and occasional attempts were made to assassinate unpopular masters.

The new individualism, which found its chief expression in the writings of Bentham and the political economists, had now gone far to alter popular feeling as to the Combination Laws. It taught that any legislative interference with the natural course of trade was mischievous, and this point of view was obtaining an increasing hold on the minds of the educated classes. Many of the master manufacturers were themselves in favour of repeal, and most leading politicians, including Mr. Secretary Peel, shared this opinion.

The leading spirit in the attack upon the Combination Laws was Francis Place, a master tailor, who by dint of his powerful intellect, strong will, and unrivalled capacity for organisation, had

---

[1] Mr. and Mrs. Hammond, *The Town Labourer*, p. 170, state that Peel 'gave a lukewarm support' to Hobhouse's Act. This is contrary to the account given by Hobhouse himself, who states that Peel supported him, and that reports which represent him as against the bill are not correct. (*Hobhouse*, iii. p. 93, 98.)

obtained a great though secret political influence. His tool, through whom he managed his parliamentary business, was Joseph Hume. Place was a bitter, solitary man, who despised and distrusted his fellow-beings, even while he laboured to help them. A hanger-on at the fringes of the parliamentary system, he saw politics at their worst, and could not comprehend the best. In all his letters there is scarcely a word of kindness, or admiration, or gratitude for those who worked with him : he used them and abandoned them as unscrupulously as Bismarck. There is never a word of appreciation for a good enemy : only hatred, contempt, and vilification. He was a man of great ability, but unfortunately his days were passed among men smaller than himself, and this produced a dangerous pride of intellect, an overweening egotism : of all the great reformers, he was the most inhuman.

Place disliked combinations : he believed they were due only to the oppressive laws in force. ' These being repealed,' he wrote, ' combinations will lose the matter which cements them into masses, and they will fall to pieces. . . . He knows nothing of the working people who can suppose that, when left at liberty to act for themselves . . . they will continue to contribute money for distant and doubtful experiments, for uncertain and precarious benefits. . . . If left alone, combinations, excepting now and then for particular purposes, under peculiar circumstances, will cease to exist.' [1] Never was there a falser prophecy.

For years Place had been working for the repeal of the laws, and at last, in 1824, Hume secured the appointment of a House of Commons Committee to consider the subject. The management of this Committee was a masterpiece of organisation on Place's part : he collected witnesses from all over the country, arranged the whole case for repeal, and supplied Hume with summaries of the evidence for each day. He drilled the working men who were to appear as witnesses, teaching them what to say. They all expected that repeal would produce a great and sudden rise in wages, and they were full of notions that machinery and taxation were the causes of distress : if they had expressed these guileless opinions it would not have produced at all the effect which Place desired.

A Parliamentary Committee, after taking evidence, usually

---

[1] Wallas, *Place*, p. 217-8. The passage raises doubt of the author's sincerity (he was writing to Sir Francis Burdett to get his support for repeal), but Mr. Wallas appears to accept it as genuine.

discusses it, and then draws up one or more reports.   Place wished
to prevent this, lest, as he said, ' some sinister interest ' should
prevail.   He prepared a number of short resolutions, each con-
taining a statement of fact which it was very difficult to dispute ;
and, when the Committee was tired out, Hume produced these
and proposed that they should be presented instead of a report.
It was so agreed, and Hume succeeded in smuggling through
Parliament a bill founded on the resolutions, without a debate.
The bill, however, differed from the resolutions in one very important respect.   The last resolution ran : ' That it is absolutely
necessary, when repealing the Combination Laws, to enact such a
law as may efficiently, and by summary process, punish either
workmen or masters, who by threats, intimidation, or acts of
violence, should interfere with that perfect freedom which ought
to be allowed to each party of employing his labour or capital
in the manner which he may deem most advantageous.'   This
resolution was absolutely ignored in Hume's bill, and no such
legislation was passed.   Now Place had got hold of the bill after
it left the hands of the law officers, and altered it to his own satisfaction.[1]   It may be guessed that this remarkable omission was due
to his manipulations.

But though it is quite possible to manage the House of Commons,
it is not always wise to do so.   During 1824-5 there was a great
expansion of trade and general prosperity.   This, coinciding with
the repeal of the Combination Laws, led to trade unions being
formed everywhere, and such an epidemic of strikes as startled
everyone.   In Dublin a series of murders were committed.   In
Glasgow [2] an unpopular master was boycotted, a general lock-out
followed, and a plot to assassinate several masters came to light.
The shipwrights and sailors struck, the disturbance centring in
London and Newcastle ; and the coasting trade, and even to some
extent foreign trade, were held up.   Attempts were made, not
merely to raise wages, which would have roused less feeling, but
to interfere with the conduct of the business, limit the number
of apprentices, and prevent the introduction of labour-saving
machinery.   The Government became alarmed ; the masters were

---

[1] Wallas, *Place*, pp. 209-16.

[2] There had been a regular reign of terror in Glasgow since the formation of
the cotton spinners' union about 1820, with repeated cases of vitriol-throwing
and attempted murder. (See *Quarterly Review*, March, 1927, for details.)

in a panic. Attention was drawn to the late repeal of the Combination Laws, and for the first time it became generally known that the Committee had made no report, and that the subsequent legislation had been rushed through without discussion : it was also whispered that the evidence had been tampered with. Place had made the mistake, natural to one of his temperament, of underrating the men with whom he had to deal.

On the 29th of March, 1825, Huskisson, acting in concert with Peel, moved for a new Committee to inquire into the effect of Hume's Act. There is only one complete account of the doings of this Committee—the manuscript narrative left by Place. It may be roughly summarised as follows :

' The Committee was prejudiced from the beginning, and its proceedings were throughout grossly unfair. Huskisson determined beforehand that new and stringent laws must be enacted against trade unions, and the committeemen were carefully chosen to be his tools. He was, however, forced to include Hume. The Committee refused to examine the workmen themselves or to hear any evidence except in favour of the masters : only in a few cases, owing to the efforts of Place and Hume, the men were able to force themselves on the Committee and insist on being heard. The evidence offered by the masters was largely false. Accusations were brought against working men : these men wrote and demanded to be heard : the Committee refused to hear them, and " the stigma affixed to individuals and bodies of men remained unexplained and uncontradicted."

' Peel and Huskisson introduced a plan for a bill, drawn up by the shipowners, which made it necessary for workmen subscribing funds for any purpose to have the approval of a magistrate, who was also to act as treasurer. They ordered Sir John Copley to draw up a bill to this effect, but he, under the influence of Place, refused to do so, on the grounds that it was impracticable. The evidence forced on the Committee by Place compelled them to reject this bill, and to adopt more moderate measures. The reason for this moderation was that Peel and Huskisson had behaved " so shamefully . . . and with such scandalous injustice " that their own Committee revolted against them and showed them that " they dared not encounter an open opposition on the bill." Hume's Act of 1824 had repealed both the Statute and the Common Law against Combinations : the new bill restored the

Common Law, but exempted from its scope combinations of men
or masters to regulate the hours of labour or the rate of wages ;
and it also prohibited the use of threats or violence in picketing,
and introduced summary methods of conviction.

' As soon as the second reading had passed, however, Peel noti-
fied Hume that " unless the shipwrights of the River Thames
went to their work on Saturday " (June 25th) " two clauses would
be introduced when the bill should be in Committee . . . to put
the people under the fangs of the Common Law." ' [1]

Such is Place's story ; and as it is the only narrative in existence,
it seems to have been generally accepted.   I hope, however, to be
able to show that it is not altogether trustworthy.

There is no evidence beyond Place's word that Peel ever contemplated legislation on the lines of the shipowners' bill.   As a
matter of fact, on March 24th, before Huskisson moved for his
Committee, Peel wrote to the Law Officers of the Crown, to ask
' what power would exist of punishing combinations among
artisans if a repeal were to take place of so much of that Act '
(Hume's Act—5 Geo. IV. c. 95) ' as prevents prosecutions at
Common Law.' [2]   Copley replied, on March 27th, that the old
Common Law procedure was very defective, owing to delay and
expense.[3]   Now the Act of 1825 *did* restore the procedure at
Common Law, but with new provisions for cheap and summary
conviction.   It is therefore clear that before the Committee ever
met Peel was contemplating legislation on exactly the same lines as
were ultimately adopted.[4]   There is no letter in the Home Office
Records, to Copley or to any of the other Law Officers of the
Crown, ordering them to draw up a bill on the lines proposed by
the shipwrights.

Next we may consider the alleged refusal of the Committee to
hear evidence on behalf of the workmen.   Peel certainly did not take
up this attitude.   On March 31st he wrote to Goulburn, the Irish

---

[1] The manuscript narrative, from which I have worked, is in the British
Museum (27,798), as is also a letter from Place to Sir Francis Burdett, from
which some quotations are made.   The manuscript narrative is also printed in
full by Wallas in his *Life of Place.*

[2] H.O. 49, 7, p. 267.   [3] British Museum, 40,375, p. 218.

[4] Huskisson may have leaned more towards the shipowners' proposals.   In
1824 he wrote to the Mayor of Liverpool as to the desirability of preventing
benefit society funds from being diverted to trade disputes.   (*Huskisson Papers*,
British Museum, 38,745, p. 215.)

Secretary, requesting him to collect information and send over witnesses about the Dublin trade unions, adding that it would be specially desirable to get copies of the rules of the unions, and that 'I think the chief agents in forming the combinations ought to be summoned.'[1] Peel himself replied to Hume's criticisms by saying, 'If the Committee had heard all the evidence offered by workmen to prove that their combinations were less improper than the combinations of other classes, not seven years would have been sufficient to get through the business.'[2] No less than ninety petitions from workmen's associations had come in. Place was particularly indignant that the Glasgow cotton spinners were not given a hearing : no one would gather from his account that these individuals had been tried in a court of justice for the offences of which they were accused. In these circumstances it would have been very improper for the Committee to examine them on the subject.

It is highly probable that the Committee were inclined to look with suspicion and hostility upon any witnesses brought forward by Place : but if this was so, it was Place's own fault. His methods of drilling the witnesses for last year's Committee were talked of, and it was not unnaturally suspected that he might have tampered with the evidence. Huskisson in the House of Commons told Hume that some of the letters he had received, purporting to be from workmen, used precisely the same words and phrases as Hume employed in his speeches—'he could not even give the honourable member credit for originality on this occasion.'[2] This remark was received with loud applause, showing how strong was the feeling which Place's unwise proceeding had aroused.

There remains the statement that Peel approached Hume and threatened to introduce two new clauses into the bill in Committee, ' putting the people under the fangs of the Common Law,' if the shipwrights on strike did not go back to work at once. Now, the bill had before this restored the operation of the Common Law. Moreover, though the shipwrights, on being approached

---

[1] *Peel Papers*, British Museum, 40,331, p. 73. A hasty note from Henry Hobhouse, the Under-Secretary at the Home Office, seems to refer to the same question. He says that he has seen Mr. Money Wigram and ' instilled into him ' Peel's orders, and that ' he appeared to imbibe the notion of examining the men more readily than that of examining the masters.' *Ib.* p. 367.

[2] *Morning Chronicle*, 30th June, 1825.

by Place, refused to go back to work, no new clauses whatever were introduced into the bill in Committee. The only alteration made was the addition of the words 'molest or obstruct' to the clause prohibiting violence in picketing. Let us assume, however, that this is what Place meant by 'two clauses putting the people under the fangs of the Common Law.' No doubt Peel had the ordinary courtesy to tell Hume beforehand that this amendment would be proposed : but that he tried to make the absurd and disgraceful bargain described by Place is quite inconsistent with anything we know of Peel's character. If he had thought that such an amendment should be made, he would have proposed it, whether or no an individual strike had ended.

. It seems likely that Place was in a state of acute excitement in 1825. His language is exaggerated and hysterical throughout. 'So atrocious a proposition,' he says, 'was never made by any Government against any people who could be called civilised, however cursed the Government which ruled over them. . . . A more atrocious proposition could hardly be conceived. . . .'[1] Does this refer to Philip of Spain's warrant condemning to death the whole population of the Netherlands for heresy ? No ; it refers to the shipowners' bill of 1825.[2]

Place always credited the Government with the worst intentions, and now he was convinced from the first that they were bent on evil. Of Peel he says that he 'stuck at nothing ; he lied so openly, so grossly, so repeatedly, so shamelessly, as even to astonish me, who . . . always thought him a pitiful, shuffling fellow.'[3] 'Anything more utterly mean and disgraceful than (Peel's and Huskisson's) conduct has hardly ever been exercised by ministers of State.' The report of the Committee—which seems to the reader of to-day an inoffensive document—is described by Place as 'a vile performance—studiously false, and directly contradicts the evidence—silly gabble—downright nonsense—infamous lies,' while the Committeemen are 'silly sheep—old women—fools—a

---

[1] Letter to Sir Francis Burdett. (*Place Papers*, British Museum, 27,798, p. 45.)

[2] Most persons will agree that the shipowners' bill would not have worked fairly in the circumstances ; but it would at least have protected trade unions from the evil to which they were particularly liable—the secretary or treasurer's bolting with the funds.

[3] Wallas, *Place*, p. 236. Place adds that Peel was 'repeatedly detected and exposed' by Hume. The *Morning Chronicle* was, according to Place himself,

perfect Inquisition.' [1] All this hardly reads like the language of a sane man.

Peel and Huskisson publicly disclaimed any idea of class legislation. The strongest proof of this is that their new legislation was actually founded on the recommendations of Hume's Committee—on that 11th Resolution which the Act of 1824 had ignored. Peel regarded the Act of 1825 as closely connected with the extension of Lord Ellenborough's Act to Scotland, which he carried at the same time. This extension was made to protect Scottish workmen from the acts of violence which had become terribly frequent in the Glasgow district, and a special clause was added to it, making the throwing of vitriol with the intent to maim or murder punishable by death—vitriol being the favourite weapon of the Glasgow men, though not unknown elsewhere.[2]

The difference between Peel and Place was one of temperament, not of opinion. Both wished well to the workmen : but Place's sympathy was given to them as a class, oppressed by bad masters and forbidden to combine for self-defence ; while Peel, the individualist, felt a peculiar interest in the solitary workman, who,

the only paper which gave an accurate report of these debates. It does not record a single instance where Hume corrected an assertion made by Peel. It does record that Hume repeatedly accused Peel of saying that the disorders of 1825 were caused by Hume's Act, while Peel repeatedly denied that he had ever said or thought any such thing, at last declaring that ' the honourable member's misrepresentations were so gross that he really must rise to correct. He had stated over and over again, till he was tired of stating it, that he did not attribute combinations to the honourable member's bill, and still the honourable member persisted in throwing the imputation on him.' (*Morning Chronicle*, June 30, 1825.)

[1] These quotations are partly from the letter to Sir Francis Burdett (see above), and partly from Hume's copy of the report, with marginal notes in Place's hand. (*Place Papers*, British Museum, 27,802.) That Place did not stick at false statements can be shown out of his own mouth. In his account of the doings of the Committee, he refers to the Dublin murders, admitting that the facts were correct, but calling them ' transient and worthy of little notice.' In his letter to Sir Francis Burdett, however, he refers to the Dublin evidence as ' false accusations,' and says that he ' sincerely believes ' that not a single case against the workmen would have ' remained unrefuted, had the persons accused been heard in their defence.' The first statement shows that Place knew the Dublin murders to be indisputable facts ; the second shows that he deliberately tried to make Burdett believe that they were not. (Wallas, *Place*, p. 226, British Museum, 27,798, pp. 43-7.)

[2] See Peel to the Solicitor-General for Scotland (J. Hope), 21st July, 1825. (*Peel Papers*, British Museum, 40,379, p. 132.) The vitriol clause was limited to five years, but was renewed in 1830. The Act allowed the Public Prosecutor to restrict the pains of the law, and is probably the only case where Peel introduced a new death penalty.

R.P.

through independence, poverty, or loyalty to his master, refused
to join the unions, and was persecuted by his fellows. ' Sufficient
precautions,' he wrote to Leonard Horner, ' had not been taken
under the Act of 1823 ' (sic : 1824) ' to prevent that species of
annoyance which numbers can exercise towards individuals, short
of personal violence and actual threat, but nearly as effectual for
its object. . . . Men who . . . have no property except their
manual skill and strength ought to be allowed to confer together,
if they think fit, for the purpose of determining at what rate they
will sell that property. But the possession of such a privilege
justifies, while it renders more necessary, the severe punishment
of any attempt to control the free will of others.' [1]

Scarcely had the regulation of the Trade Union Law been completed, when a great disaster destroyed for the time being the
hopes of the workmen. In the summer of 1825 the general
prosperity had risen to its height. Prices were high, demand
great, money easy. A trade had begun with the revolted Spanish-
American colonies, which opened a new field for British enterprise. A great outburst of speculation, both in home and foreign
trade, followed, and the Bank of England, which should have controlled the movement, encouraged it, and continued to advance
money freely when it should have been restricting its issues.

The summer went merrily ; with autumn came the turn of the
tide. Over-production led to a fall in prices, which continued to
drop steadily. Many speculators were ruined. At this time the
Bank of England was the only joint-stock bank in that country.
The smaller banks were limited by law to six partners, and had no
limited liability : consequently they were often weak and badly
managed, for prudent persons shrank from embarking upon such
uncertain enterprises. The country banks had made large issues
upon securities realisable at distant dates, and now, as the demand
upon them grew, they turned to the Bank of England for help.
But the great Bank itself was in difficulties : it had more than
£19,000,000 of notes in circulation, and only £3,600,000 in its
reserve fund. The rate of discount rose ; a run upon the banks
followed ; and the result was a panic and disaster such as had not
been seen since the South Sea Bubble broke. Seven London
banks and some eighty country banks failed.

In Scotland only one bank closed down, and it ultimately paid

[1] Parker, *Peel*, i. p. 379.

in full.[1] The contrast was striking, and while the crisis was still raging, Peel urged the legalisation of joint-stock banks in England, upon the Scottish model. The Government was thoroughly alarmed by the crisis, and, after an inquiry, Peel's suggestion was carried out in 1826. As a concession to the Bank of England, however, the joint-stock banks were only permitted outside a radius of sixty-five miles from London. In order to check the issue of worthless paper by the smaller banks notes of less than £5 were prohibited.

These measures, however, were too late to prevent disaster. Everywhere demand failed, employers were on the verge of ruin, mills and workshops were closing down, wages dropping like a stone. Unemployment spread, and the country was plunged into distress as universal and severe as in the years following the war. In such conditions a successful strike was impossible : but strikes there were sure to be, and disorder and disaffection must follow. Mr. Secretary Peel had had an easy time of it as yet ; now he had to face the same problem as Lord Sidmouth before him.

History has little to say of the industrial depression of 1826-1829, compared with that of 1816-1819. No startling events were associated with it—no Peterloo, no Oliver the spy, no Cato Street Conspiracy, no repressive legislation. Nevertheless it was bad enough. The handloom-weaving industry was now in its last agony, and the districts where it centred were sunk in misery almost unbelievable. The Spitalfields silk weavers were in a state of almost chronic semi-starvation ; by the end of January, 1826, 10,000 of them were out of work. Later in the year it was officially reported that in Manchester 46,000 were unemployed out of a total population of 203,000, and that in other districts things were worse. At Entwhistle 1353 persons out of a population of 1611 were receiving relief. Padisham was going to try the obsolete Poor Law provision of applying to the rates of neighbouring townships, as it could not maintain its own poor. In Blackburn, where there were no resident gentry, the handloom weavers were all on the rates and the farmers paying more in rates than in rent.[2] By 1829 the position at Blackburn had grown worse. Out of a total

[1] The Stirling Banking Company. The Caithness Banking Company failed, but its liabilities were taken over by the Commercial Bank. The Fife Banking Company stopped payment, but did not actually fail until 1829. All these three were creations of the late speculative wave.

[2] *Report of the Grand Jury of the County of Lancaster*, H.O. 40, 21.

population of 19,869, more than half were living on an average of
1s. 3¾d. per week, which represented wages supplemented by poor
relief.[1]   Outside the textile trades the situation was almost as bad.
The coalfields were in a state of chronic disorder, owing chiefly
to the practice of paying wages in truck,[2] a practice which neither
the law nor the action of the more respectable coalowners availed
to prevent.   Everywhere strikes against the reduction of wages
broke out, and were frequently accompanied by violence against
non-union men and blacklegs.

Serious rioting followed : machinery was destroyed and mills
were burned.   In Blackburn Hundred alone it was estimated that
£13,625 worth of property was destroyed.   At Rochdale the town
was papered with placards reading : 'Bread or Blood ; ' ' Bread or
No King ; ' ' Down with the Rag Rookeries ' (i.e., the banks of
issue) ; and only the efforts of an able and sympathetic magistrate,
Mr. Crossley, prevented a serious outbreak.   At Macclesfield unemployed weavers rose and sacked the provision shops, and later
there were similar but more serious riots at Manchester.   At Bury
a mob armed with clubs attacked the mills and stoned the troops
sent against them, who in return fired, killing several persons.   The
jury which sat on one of these returned a verdict of murder against
an unknown soldier.   In West Yorkshire large bands of destitute
people wandered here and there, begging for relief.[3]

Peel did not mistake these disturbances for signs of political unrest.   'The great cause of apprehension,' he wrote to Goulburn,
' is not in the disaffection, but in the real distress of the manufacturing districts.   There is as much forbearance as it is possible
to expect from so much suffering.' [4]   But how was this suffering

---

[1] Memorial of the Cotton Manufacturers of Blackburn, 1829, H.O. 40, 23.

[2] The practice of paying to the employee a certain percentage of his wages
in money, the rest in the form of a printed paper, known as a Tommy Ticket,
which gave him credit for so much goods at local shops.   It originally arose
from shortage of small currency, but was greatly abused : the employer or
one of his relatives frequently kept the shop, and sold inferior goods at unfairly
high prices ; or in other cases an unfairly large proportion of wages was paid
in food, leaving insufficient for other necessaries.

[3] Report of the Grand Jury of the County of Lancaster, H.O. 40, 21.   From Mr.
Crossley, 1st March, 1826, H.O. 40, 19.   Ib. 7th and 9th December, 1826, H.O. 40,
21.   From Major Eckersley, 20th February, 1826, H.O. 40, 19.   From Mr.
Watkins, 1st May, 1826, H.O. 40, 19.   From Lord Harewood, 1st August,
H.O. 40, 20.

[4] Peel to Goulburn, 2nd July, 1826, Peel Papers, British Museum, 40,332,
p. 57.

to be relieved ?   An unsigned note among the Home Office papers discusses the advisability of giving State aid : ' I know all the objections, and all the danger of the precedent,' but the necessity must be considered.[1]   Peel disliked the principle of State assistance, which he bluntly called ' quackery ' ; [2] but he was ready to sacrifice principle to the needs of the moment.   In the end the means adopted was to give grants to the local subscriptions which were opened everywhere for the relief of the poor.   A special central committee on the distressed manufacturers was set up to administer the funds.   In 1829, when the distress again became severe, Peel sent secret agents into the country to make inquiries, and to relieve the worst cases, instructing them ' to be careful not to allow it to be known that they were the agents of Government.' [3]   It is possible that he may have followed this plan also in 1826.   Certainly the greatest precautions were taken to conceal the fact that the grants of money came from the Government : they were given in the King's name, and it was popularly believed that they came from the Privy Purse, George IV. thus getting the credit for a generosity quite foreign to his nature.

The need of these precautions is obvious, when the contemporary exploitation of the Poor Law is considered : it is made clear by a letter from J. C. Herries to Peel in October, 1826.   There was still, Herries wrote, £40,000 available for relief, and ' the two manufacturers on the Committee are strongly of opinion that any new ostensible measure for increasing the funds of the Committee at this time would have the effect of encouraging the masters in their systematic endeavour to keep down the price of labour, and thereby to prolong the evil with which we are contending.' [4]

Another letter from Peel to Goulburn gives some idea of the Home Secretary's methods of administering relief.[5]   He is making every effort, he says, to tide over the next two months, in hopes that there will then be a slight revival of trade, for stocks must be getting low, and a new demand is to be expected.[6]   Goulburn

---

[1] H.O. 40, 19.   No date, probably early in 1826.

[2] Peel to Goulburn, 21st July, 1826, *Peel Papers*, British Museum, 40,332, p. 74.

[3] *Speeches*, ii. p. 791.   [4] Herries to Peel, 25th October, 1826, H.O. 40, 21.

[5] Peel to Goulburn, 21st July, 1826, *Peel Papers*, British Museum, 40,332, p. 74.

[6] Compare Herries to Peel, 11th August, 1826 : Rothschild foretells an improvement shortly, and he has hitherto been ' only too accurate ' in his forecasts, H.O. 40, 21.

may have £4000 from the Treasury for fever relief, ' which may be fairly charged as Civil Contingencies in next year's Estimates. I mean that the advance of this year may be covered in the next. Of course, absolute necessity must over-ride any minor consideration, and if fever spreads, and more money is indispensably necessary, you must inform us and we must contrive to send you more. You may take £2000 on account of distressed manufacturers. Take what you absolutely want from time to time, and if you can do with less than the sum I name, do not call for it, for we are poor. Do not give it in the King's name, for we have given so much in the King's name, that if we give more one of two inferences will be drawn—either that these advances do not come from the Privy Purse, or that the Privy Purse is vastly too large. . . . (It) had better be advanced as you may find it absolutely necessary without publicly adverting that it is derived from any public fund. In fact, it must be squeezed out of Droits.' [1] This is indeed ' doing good by stealth.'

Such ' quackery,' however, was merely a temporary expedient. The state of the country had convinced the Government that more stringent measures for the relief of the poor were necessary. In September, 1826, they opened the ports by Order in Council,[2] and summoned Parliament to approve their action. It was a dangerous proceeding, for their power, their very political existence, depended on the landed interest, whose support was given for the price of high protection for agriculture. The need, however, was desperate, and the squires agreed to admit foreign corn, then in bond, and the importation of 500,000 quarters more. Even this was only carried after a hard fight ; but the Government was determined to persevere. In the following year Canning, supported by Peel, proposed a general reduction of the corn duties. The measure was defeated in the Lords, but in 1828 a very similar bill was carried by the Peel-Wellington Government. The new Corn Law still gave a very high protection, but it did allow the import of foreign corn when the home price had risen to 60s., and so conferred some benefit on the consumer.[3]

[1] I.e., the revenue accruing from the Admiralty Droits.

[2] A report of the failure of the oat and potato crops in Ireland and Scotland decided them upon this measure. See Peel to Goulburn, 1st September, 1826, Peel Papers, British Museum, 40,332, p. 115.

[3] The old Corn Law practically prohibited import, as the price scarcely ever rose to 84s. Canning's bill was slightly more generous than Wellington's, but was said to have technical defects.

Such were the measures adopted for the relief of distress ; but the problem of maintaining order and protecting property was equally pressing. The Government had to rely entirely on military aid, and the functions of the general commanding in the Northern area were remarkably varied. Besides his military duties, he was called upon to advise the magistrates, soothe and restrain the master manufacturers, investigate the causes of disorder, and occasionally even to aid in administering relief. In this state of affairs Peel's mind naturally turned to the creation of an adequate police force.

The country had long outgrown its police system. There were only two bodies of police in Great Britain which could be called efficient—the Manchester police, and the small force under the authority of the Bow Street magistrates. Even these were by no means faultless : the Manchester police were corrupt, and only shone by contrast with their contemporaries, and the function of the Bow Street runner was to detect crime, not to prevent it. In the other great towns there was practically no protection for life and property. Whatever police existed often connived with thieves to pillage the public. Carlisle in particular was a scandal to the country, its entire force consisting of two constables, so that it was said to be impossible to execute a warrant there without calling in military aid.

The state of London, however, was still worse. Each parish managed its own affairs independently of the others or of any central authority, and the state of the ' watch,' as it was still called, varied from one to the other. Even within the parish itself there might be many independent districts. In St. Pancras there were no less than eighteen ' different, irresponsible, isolated police establishments.' [1] One side of a street might be in a different parish from the other, and a policeman on the left-hand pavement might have to watch helpless while a burglar robbed a house upon the right. In twelve parishes, including that of Deptford with 20,000 inhabitants, there was not a single policeman on duty at night. Where night watchmen did exist, they were commonly aged paupers, whose keep was thus saved to the rates. It was little wonder that crime was steadily increasing in London, and that in 1828 one person in every 383 was a criminal : little wonder

[1] *Speeches,* ii. p. 5.

that all over the country the populace showed themselves ever more ready to resort to mob violence to enforce their desires.

Peel, with his usual caution, brooded for years over the problem before he undertook to solve it. In 1826 he began to collect evidence for the purpose of comparing crime with population.[1] In 1828 he secured the appointment of a Parliamentary Committee to investigate the subject—the last of four successive Committees in the past twenty-five years, but the first to do valuable work. He had at first intended a measure which should create a police force throughout the kingdom : he ended with a modest scheme, whose operation was confined to London, and at first to a limited number of parishes.

By this plan the old parish authorities were abolished. The new police was to be under no local authority, but directly responsible to the Home Office. It was placed under two magistrates, later called commissioners, and its headquarters were at Scotland Yard. It was composed of carefully selected men of powerful physique and good character : Peel thought non-commissioned officers retired from the army with certificates of good conduct would be suitable recruits. The force was carefully weeded out—during the first three years more than 3000 men were dismissed. The same care was exercised in selecting the commissioners, and the two first of them, Colonel Rowan, a retired soldier, and Richard Mayne, a lawyer, were men of the highest capacity and character. Peel was anxious that the moral character of his police should be above suspicion.

He was also anxious, however, that it should be cheap, so that Radical ranters might have no reason to attack it for extravagance. The estimates were calculated to the last halfpenny. The whole cost of clothing the force, for example, came to £5 3s. 6d. for each man the first year, and £3 17s. 6d. the second, which was paid by the stoppage of 2s. out of the man's pay of one guinea weekly.[2] The upkeep of the force was paid by a police tax, which was not to exceed 8d. in the £1, and which was levied in place of the old watch tax. In many districts the new force proved to be actually cheaper than the old night watchmen had been.

The system was rapidly extended, and within less than a year practically the whole of London and the suburbs were under the new police. It was, however, received with violent opposition.

[1] See H.O. 43, 33.   [2] H.O. 61, 1, No. 29.

The old, corrupt parish authorities were jealous, and the City of London was always roused by any hint of interference with its privileges. A large body of the nation, moreover, regarded the establishment of an efficient police force as an attack upon English liberty. The whole of the press was hostile, and, above all, the lower-class Radicals were furious. 'Peel's police, raw lobsters, Blue Devils, or by whatever other appropriate name they may be known . . .', 'Swing' described them.[1]

'Unite in removing such a powerful force from the hands of the Government, and let us institute a Police System in the hands of the PEOPLE under *parochial* appointments!' said a handbill distributed from door to door in London (by 'a person who professed himself a political reformer . . . of gentlemanly aspect but smoking a cigar'); 'UNITY IS STRENGTH! . . . Join your brother Londoners in one heart, one hand, for the ABOLITION OF THE NEW POLICE!'[2]

As late as 1833, the jury, in a case where a policeman had been killed by rioters, returned a verdict of 'justifiable homicide!' But soon the benefits of the reform began to be felt, and within a few years all criticism ceased. The London police were gradually imitated by local authorities throughout the country. To-day it is difficult even to imagine the days before 1830, so entirely is the comfort and security of modern life based upon the existence of an efficient police : the protection of the 'Bobbies,' as they were nicknamed from their founder, is a condition as natural as the shelter of a roof or the provision of daily bread.

The new police were intended for the purpose of preventing, not merely detecting, crime. The evil old system of granting 'blood-money' for the arrest of every criminal was abolished, and with it the temptation of the policeman to connive at crime. In the old days Government had relied upon a bloody Criminal Code to terrify lawbreakers, and it had proved useless. Peel comprehended the principle, that certainty of detection is a far greater deterrent from crime than severity of punishment. Viewed from this point of view, the establishment of his police force is the necessary correlative of his reform of the Criminal Law. Between

[1] A seditious placard received by post from 'Swing' (the gentleman who burned ricks in the agricultural counties), and forwarded by the recipient to the Home Office. H.O. 44, 21.

[2] See an anonymous letter, October, 1830, H.O. 61, 2.

them they went far to make the Government of Great Britain what a Government should be—swift and effective in preventing and detecting crime, just and merciful in punishing it.

The Police Bill was not introduced until 1829. In dealing with the earlier disorders, therefore, the Home Secretary had no such assistance as this ; and it was with some pride that he reflected that he had conducted the country through troubles as severe as those of 1819, without applying to Parliament for extraordinary powers, without a single prosecution for sedition, and with scarcely any loss of life.

' Every law found in the Statute-Book when I entered office,' he said, on his resignation in 1827, ' which imposed any temporary or extraordinary restriction on the liberty of the subject, has either been repealed or allowed to expire. I may be a Tory—I may be an illiberal—but the fact is undeniable . . . that those laws have been effaced. Tory as I am, I have the further satis-faction of knowing that there is not a single law connected with my name which has not had for its object some mitigation of the severity of the criminal law ; some prevention of abuse in the exercise of it ; or some security for its impartial administration.' [1]

[1] *Speeches*, i. p. 507.

CHAPTER VI

PEEL, CANNING, AND THE CATHOLIC
QUESTION, 1822-1829

IT has been seen that when Peel joined the Government in 1821 he did not do so alone : the Grenville Party joined at almost the same moment. Lord Grenville himself had now retired from political life, and left the leadership of his followers to his nephew, the Marquis of Buckingham. The 'Party' included no person of first-rate ability, but it had the weight of the Grenville name, and as Buckingham controlled no less than six pocket boroughs, his support was of some value. Nobody wanted the Marquis himself in the Cabinet, and he was bought off with a dukedom : but his cousin, Mr. Charles Williams Wynn, got a seat in the Cabinet, and his other cousin, Mr. Henry Williams Wynn, a mission to the Swiss Cantons ; and his friend, Colonel Fremantle, and his other friend, Dr. Phillimore, got seats at the Board of Trade. Now, the Grenvilles favoured Catholic Emancipation, and they did not make their bargain without some stipulation on this subject. Lord Liverpool assured Wynn that he should have full liberty ' to support, to advocate, and even to originate' measures for Catholic relief, and to adopt ' any line of conduct which . . . a consideration of what is due to this question . . . may appear to you to require. . . .' [1] Moreover, the Government entered upon a course of conciliation in Ireland. Lord Sidmouth, to be sure, told a friend that it was ' conciliation, not concession ; ' [2] but Lord Wellesley, Wellington's brother, a strong ' Catholic,' was sent over as Lord Lieutenant ; Saurin, the old Orange Attorney-General, was dismissed, and the ' Catholic' Plunket was given his place ; and Liverpool assured Wynn that ' the opinion of any individual ' on the Catholic Question would not be ' a bar to his appointment to office in Ireland.' To balance the administration, Peel and

[1] Liverpool to Wynn, 12th December, 1821, *Buckingham Papers*, 2nd Series, vol. i. p. 251 ff.

[2] Pellew, *Sidmouth*, vol. iii. p. 295.

Goulburn, the new Secretary for Ireland, were both 'Protestants.' Peel was highly disgusted at the summary dismissal of Saurin and Talbot ; but he knew nothing of the bargain that had been made with the Grenvilles, and when he discovered it next year was hurt and offended at the manner in which Liverpool had treated him.

Before two months had passed, the Cabinet took on a complexion still more favourable to the Catholics. Castlereagh, worn out with hard work and responsibility, and shaken by the hatred with which he was regarded, committed suicide ; and with him died the system of the Congresses, which, imperfect though it might be, was still the first movement towards a European league of nations. The foreign policy of Britain now entered upon another phase, glorious for British prestige and power, happy indeed for popular liberty abroad, but making no further advance in the direction of international arbitration, so that the impulse left by the French wars died away, until a hundred years later another European war revived it.

There could be but one successor to Castlereagh. Canning had not yet sailed to take up his Indian Governorship. He now returned in triumph, to find himself, after an interval of thirteen years, once more Secretary of State for Foreign Affairs.

It was not without difficulty that this was effected. The King hated Canning for his attitude to Queen Caroline ; and the King's mistress, Lady Conyngham, hated him more. He had no personal popularity with either political party, and the Ultra-Tories in particular disliked him. Only the difficulty of finding a champion to set up in opposition to his claims prevented them from trying to keep him out.

The only possible candidate for this position was Peel. To be sure, Peel had no experience of foreign affairs, could not speak French, was twenty years younger than Canning, and in delicate health ; but all that would not have deterred the Ultras if they could have persuaded him. Nothing, however, would induce him to move.[1] He was with the King in Scotland when the news of Castlereagh's death arrived, and George at once attempted to draw him into a plot against Canning. He, however, maintained an impenetrable reserve against the royal blandishments, and con-

[1] ' To Peel especially I feel it quite impossible to do justice,' Canning wrote to Croker, ' for a frankness and straightforwardness beyond example, and for feelings for which I own I did not before give him credit, but which I hope I know how to value and to return.' (Parker, *Peel*, i. p. 331.)

tented himself with reporting the whole transaction to Liverpool.
On returning to London, instead of lending himself to the schemes
of the Ultras, his first action was to call on Canning and assure him
of his friendship and full support.

The Ultras, burning with rage and spite, were obliged to keep
quiet, and Liverpool, after a long struggle with the King, was able
to bring Canning in.

Two years later, the final resignation of Lord Sidmouth still
further diminished the Orange element in the Cabinet. Liverpool, Eldon, and Wellington, in the House of Lords, were ' Protestants,' but in the Commons Peel stood alone ; as he said himself,
' in no enviable situation . . . , opposed by all my colleagues, and
daily seeing those very colleagues . . . actively concerting measures with my political opponents.' [1]

These changes should have afforded great encouragement to the
Irish Catholics, and for a short time they may have done so, but
not for long. Time passed, and nothing was done. The King was
obstinate, and Liverpool, though willing to conciliate, was as
resolutely opposed to emancipation as ever. In 1823 Wynn remarked that ' the Catholic Question has gone back to such an
incredible degree, and its supporters are now so little in earnest,'
that the Government might soon be able to dispense with Eldon [2]
—whose deficiencies as a Chancellor they had hitherto tolerated
owing to his influence over the King. It was, in fact, seen that
even the presence of the chief ' Catholic ' leaders in the Cabinet
could do nothing to effect legislation ; and those Irishmen who
had hitherto been the most faithful supporters of constitutional
methods now lost heart. Many flung themselves into the arms of
the agitators ; and the popular movement headed by O'Connell
received a tremendous impetus.

At the same time, the Wellesley experiment had not been a
success. Charles Grant, Peel's immediate successor, had found
Ireland quiet, and left it in a tumult ; and Wellesley, despite his
good intentions, did not succeed in making much improvement.
He was full of self-confidence, and would listen to no advice.
' The Irish Government, sir ? I am the Irish Government ! ' he

---

[1] *Speeches*, i. p. 506. On one occasion Canning and Plunket, finding Peel
alone in the writing room of the House of Commons, turned and went out,
Canning remarking, ' We are going to talk treason, and you are the last man
to hear us.' (Parker, *Peel*, i. p. 296.)

[2] *Buckingham Papers*, 2nd Series, vol. ii. p. 9.

exclaimed on one occasion to a critic. He lay in bed all day, would see no one, not even the Under-Secretary, and refused to write letters home. The *Buckingham Papers* are full of references to the impossibility of getting any information out of him and to Peel's consequent annoyance. Wellesley had failed to carry out the plan of equal promotion for Catholics and Protestants, while at the same time he had favoured the Catholics sufficiently to give bitter offence to the Orangemen. The Orange Lodges projected a riot, and when Wellesley visited the theatre one night he was received with groans and hisses, and a bottle was thrown at him, which crashed on the drop-scene. No one was able to take this affair very seriously, except Lord Wellesley himself. He was deeply moved, and told all the world of his horror during that ' awful moment.' He and Plunket, without consulting the Government, decided to prosecute the ringleaders for conspiracy to murder. It was soon found that the facts gave no ground for this, and the indictment had to be altered to conspiracy to riot ; and, as popular opinion had veered to the side of the rioters when so unjustly accused, even this was not successful. In the following year Wellesley and Plunket decided to prosecute O'Connell for seditious language—again without consulting the Home Secretary. The words selected for prosecution were very unfortunately chosen : O'Connell had expressed the hope that ' another Bolivar ' might arise for the deliverance of Ireland, and Plunket declared this to be an exhortation to revolt. At this moment, however, Canning was at his task of ' calling in the New World to redress the balance of the Old,' and was therefore extending the moral support of Great Britain to Bolivar. The evidence was insufficient, and the jury threw out the bill. The prestige of the Irish Government sank to a low ebb ; but for these and other independent actions the Home Secretary was obliged to assume public responsibility.

To check disorder a new Insurrection Act was passed, and to conciliate the Catholics a measure making the commutation of tithes permissible : but these had little effect. In 1823 O'Connell had founded the Catholic Association, and in the following year the Catholic Rent was begun. It was a weekly subscription, which might be as low as $\frac{1}{4}$d. per head, and soon practically every Catholic peasant in Ireland was a member. The village priests were the collectors of the rent ; the proceeds were to be devoted to preparing petitions to Parliament, subsidising the English press in

Catholic interests, defending Catholics in the courts against acts of violence by Orangemen, and encouraging Catholic educational establishments. All classes joined the association, high and low, rich and poor, Catholic and Protestant. O'Connell was soon at the head of a national movement such as had never been seen before.

By the end of 1824 the British Government were discussing how the association could be suppressed. All were united in disapproval, none more eager for action than Canning, who abhorred democratic movements. O'Connell had organised his society so skilfully that it did not come within the operation of the Convention Act of 1793, and it was therefore necessary to enact new legislation. Peel urged that the new law should be a general one, which could be enforced against Orange societies as well as against the association, and on such lines the Act was framed; but O'Connell boasted that he could ' drive a coach-and-six through any Act ' they might pass. There was no difficulty in carrying the bill through Parliament, for by far the greater part of English opinion favoured it; but Peel, whose speeches on the Catholic Question were always his poorest, made a bad blunder, and laid himself open to an attack from Brougham so telling and so ferocious that it seems almost to have stunned him.[1] O'Connell easily made good his boast: the association was continued without a definite organisation, but as powerful as ever.

In the meantime, however, Catholic feeling in the House of Commons was growing steadily stronger. In March, 1825, Sir Francis Burdett's resolution to go into Committee on the Catholic Question was carried by a majority of 13; in April the second reading of his relief bill was carried by 27; and in May it was passed by 21 votes. The bill was carried on two ' wings,' one providing for the payment of the Catholic clergy, the other for the disfranchisement of the 40s. freeholders. Peel had strenuously opposed all three measures, and now he went to Liverpool and offered his resignation. Liverpool replied that his own feelings

---

[1] He referred to a distinguished Irish member of the association, Colonel Hamilton Rowan, who had been one of the heroes of '98, as ' an attainted traitor.' Brougham pointed out that Rowan was fully pardoned, had been received by the King and by several Lord Lieutenants, and was a member of the bench of magistrates. So impressive was Brougham that Peel was entirely overborne, and only discovered the following week that Rowan was not, and never had been, a magistrate. *Speeches*, i. pp. 333, 337. *Hobhouse*, iii. pp. 89-90.

were equally strong, and that if Peel resigned he would do the same
and break up the Ministry. He urged that a general election was
now near, and begged Peel to remain until a new House of Commons should pronounce upon the question. Peel still hesitated,
when the situation was unexpectedly altered. The Duke of York
rose when the Relief Bill came before the House of Lords, and
solemnly declared that he would always oppose the Catholic
claims, ' whatever may be my situation in life, so help me God.'
This declaration from the heir to the throne, and from the only
one of the sons of George III. who was at all respected by the
nation, made a great impression. The Lords threw out the bill :
under the same influence the constituencies in the succeeding
election returned a majority unfavourable to the Catholic claims.
It was not until March, 1827, that Burdett again ventured to introduce his Relief Bill, and then, after a long and acrimonious debate,
the House of Commons, dividing at five o'clock in the morning,
reversed, by a majority of four, and in a full House, the decision
they had given in 1825. Peel had expected to be beaten, and had
intended in that case to resign. There was now no immediate
necessity for this step ; but his resignation was not to be long
deferred.

Their long tenure of power, however gratifying to the rank and
file of the Tory party, was very trying to the strength of the
leaders : the whole Cabinet, judging from contemporary descrip-
tions, appeared but a cluster of fading flowers. The Prime
Minister was exhausted after twelve years of office, and only
struggled on from day to day—' damned ill and damned cross,' as
Eldon remarked. Eldon himself was growing very old. Peel
seems to have suffered from almost chronic ill-health at this
period ; Lord Maryborough remarked that he ' would not long
be an object of speculation,' and Plumer Ward describes him as
' a scarecrow,' going about with a bad black eye, really due to an
operation, but giving him the look of having been ' in a row in
St. Giles'.' [1] Canning, always delicate, was rapidly failing, and
did not improve matters by doctoring himself with opium. Even
the Iron Duke was in poor health and as thin as a spectre.

Liverpool's final collapse came in February, 1827, shortly before
the debate on the Catholic Question. He was struck with
apoplexy, and though he lived for some time afterwards, it was in

[1] *Buckingham Papers*, 2nd Series, vol. ii. p. 99.

a condition of imbecility. Only his personal influence had held together the incongruous elements composing the Cabinet. Moreover, there was now so strong a ' Catholic ' interest in the Government that only Liverpool's own views had made it a ' Protestant ' Government at all. When the Prime Minister was gone, Eldon and Peel—Old Bags and the Orange Lily, as disrespectful colleagues called them—would be left practically alone.[1] So, while the business of the House continued as usual, behind the scenes feverish negotiations were going on for the appointment of a new Prime Minister. Already the loosening of control was obvious to the enemy. ' I never saw such a scene as the Treasury Bench presented,' wrote John Cam Hobhouse, on the night of the Catholic debate—' Mr. Secretary Peel accusing his own Irish Attorney-General of encouraging rebellion, and Mr. Secretary Canning tearing to pieces the Master of the Rolls and the Under-Secretary of State.' [2]

Peel and Canning had always been on good terms in the Cabinet ; their correspondence, preserved in the *Peel Papers*, gives a remarkable impression of complete and intimate confidence. On questions where the Cabinet was divided, Peel supported Canning's foreign policy and the commercial policy of Canning's friend, Huskisson. They worked together, Canning regularly showing Peel the despatches and private letters from the ambassadors, while Peel sent him the important Irish papers.[3] Peel said that it repeatedly happened that in council, before he had time to speak, Canning would say all that he had intended, only ' clothed in much better language than any into which I could have put ' it.[4] It was only on the Catholic Question that they differed, and even here Canning praised Peel's conduct, saying that when he opposed him, he always did it ' in a fair, open, manly manner.' [5] He was fiercely and unscrupulously opposed by some of his Tory colleagues, and he knew that Peel could, if he had given any counten-

---

[1] Wellington was not nearly so hostile to the Catholic claims, and had in 1825 even considered a very large measure of relief. See Maxwell, *Wellington*, ii. pp. 178-9.

[2] *Hobhouse*, iii. p. 175.

[3] ' My Dear Peel,—Could you call here for five minutes to look at some despatches just received from Lamb. Ever yrs., G. C.' This is a typical note. 5th December, 1825. *Peel Papers*, British Museum, 40,311, p. 209.

[4] Lawrence, Peel, p. 152.

[5] *Buckingham Papers*, 2nd Series, vol. ii. p. 125 ff.

R.P.

ance to these, have made his position much more difficult. On
one occasion, Peel, forwarding a despatch from Goulburn, remarked that he had not troubled to suppress the lament over the
progress of the Catholic Question with which it commenced ; and
this brought a warm reply. ' There could be no reason for with-
holding from me the prefatory part of the letter. It is a great and
constant source of regret to me that there is any subject on which
we cannot communicate freely with each other. Happily there is
but that one, not only on which we are unable to communicate,
but on which, I believe, we do not cordially agree.' [1]

The two statesmen, therefore, would gladly have come to an
understanding : but the Catholic Question stood between them.
Canning knew he had a right to the Premiership, and he was determined to enforce it. He had before this overcome the King's dislike. By making Lord Conyngham a Chamberlain, and Lord
Francis Conyngham an Under-Secretary, and hinting at a bishopric
for Lord Francis' tutor, he was able to gain over ' The Lady.' His
chief, indeed his only, difficulty now lay with the Ultra-Tories.
He knew he had not long to live, and he would not resign the fair
prize for which he had so long striven, and which was now within
his grasp—not even to retain Peel.

Peel, however, felt he could not serve under Canning. He was
willing that they should retain their present positions, and that
some inoffensive peer should be appointed to succeed Liverpool.
He had long felt himself alone in his opposition to the Catholic
claims. The support of Eldon was not of much value : only the
close and intimate sympathy of Liverpool had made his position
bearable. Now all the prestige and influence attaching to the
office of Prime Minister would be transferred from Liverpool to
Canning, from the Protestant to the Catholic side of the balance.

He was in a particularly difficult position owing to the office
he held. As Home Secretary, he was responsible for Ireland,
and it would be his duty to defend the Government's Irish policy.
Then, though the Prime Minister had absolute disposal of the
patronage, every appointment had to be countersigned by the
Home Secretary, and if there were a continual difference of opinion
the situation would be very painful. To exchange the Home
Office for another would be a mean attempt to avoid a difficulty

[1] Peel to Canning, 25th November, 1825. Canning to Peel, same date.
Peel Papers, British Museum, 40,311, pp. 154, 156.

which must be faced in the end ; for whenever Canning introduced measures of Catholic relief, he would have to choose between resignation or supporting legislation which he had throughout eighteen years of political life consistently opposed. ' The proposal of office to me,' he wrote afterwards, rather bitterly, ' was in effect saying to me, " Govern Ireland without support, discountenanced by all that is influential in the Government, and when we have discredited you, we will remove you." ' [1]

Pressure was exerted upon him from both sides. The Ultras, with the blind recklessness of their kind, would have put forward Peel, or Eldon with Peel's support, as a possible Prime Minister, if he had been foolish enough to have lent himself to any such schemes. On the other hand, Croker, who had always been a ' Catholic,' and who had an odd sort of vicarious ambition for Peel, like the stepmother hen that leads her ducklings to the pond, was passionately anxious that his friend should follow Canning. Interpreting some remarks of Peel's according to his own wishes, he entered into secret negotiations with Canning, apparently with the object of bringing about an understanding between the two. The only result was that Peel suspected Croker of betraying him, in some unexplained manner ; was bitterly offended ; and required repeated and humble apologies before he finally condescended to forgive the unhappy go-between. The King, who was very anxious to retain Peel, privately offered to guarantee him that he would never consent to any measure for Catholic relief ; but Peel thought it unfair to Canning to enter into any such understanding ; nor would he in any case have relied upon the King's promises.[2] Peel himself suggested that the Duke of Wellington should be Prime Minister, he and Canning keeping their places. It was an extraordinarily tactless proposal, for Wellington and Canning had a mutual antipathy that could not easily have been overcome. Naturally Canning refused.

On April 10, Canning was at last definitely commissioned by the King to form a Ministry. Peel saw him that day, and told him

---

[1] Peel to Bishop Lloyd (he is usually at his worst in writing to the bishop), 26th August, 1827.   Parker, *Peel*, ii. p. 17.

[2] On a later occasion he wrote, ' I should think it not improbable that the King had made my exclusion from office a *sine qua non*, on the appointment of Goderich. It is very natural in a man, and particularly when that man is a King, to hate another who declines to trust him ' (to Arbuthnot, 17th August, 1827). Parker, *Peel*, ii. p. 9.

(as he had already done a fortnight before) that he felt it his duty to resign. They finally parted with great regret, and on the best of terms.[1] On the following day, however, the Duke of Wellington, Lord Eldon, and Lords Bathurst, Melville, and Westmoreland all sent in their resignations. The Duke acted on his own responsibility, the four other lords probably in concert. Wellington, unfortunately, contrived, in some incomprehensible manner, to convince himself that Canning had insulted him, and he not only resigned his office, but also the command of the Army. This most improper manner of dragging political feeling into a question that should have been altogether free from it was generally and justly condemned ; and the six retiring Ministers were accused of an intrigue against Canning and the King.

It was unlucky for Peel that for many years past his own friends and admirers had endeavoured to force him into a position of rivalry and hostility to Canning. In reality, the two statesmen had always been in full agreement, except upon the Catholic Question : but, as has been seen, both in 1822 and 1827 the Ultra-Tories had tried to make Peel their catspaw to keep Canning out. They had used the Catholic Question as a means of annoying and opposing Canning, and on this point Peel, owing to his views on the subject, had to some extent worked with them and given them invaluable assistance. Long ago Peel had defeated Canning's long-cherished hopes of representing the University of Oxford. It was not altogether unnatural, then, that Peel's enemies should now put the worst construction upon his attitude. Events in the near future were to make things look even blacker. Before two years had passed, Peel had completely changed his views on the Catholic Question, and had himself proposed a measure of emancipation in Parliament ; and what is more, he did what Canning had never been able to do—he carried it.

Had it not been for his later action, the accusations brought against him, that he had acted out of jealousy and personal enmity, would soon have been forgotten. No one could expect him to remain and make himself responsible for legislation which he really disapproved. The only thing that could in any way have justified his remaining in office would have been a belief that Canning did

[1] ' Adieu, my dear Peel. I will relieve you as soon as I can from the labours of your office, which is the one that I find it most difficult to fill—no wonder, after such a predecessor.' Canning to Peel, 15th April, 1827. Parker, *Peel*, i. p. 465.

not intend to press emancipation at present.   He had, however,
no such belief.   Canning's chief biographer says that ' he assumed
the premierhip on the express understanding that an early
measure of relief should be carried,' [1] and Peel himself declared,
' I had watched throughout the splendid career which my right
honourable friend had pursued with regard to the Catholic
Question, and each hour of my deliberation confirmed the opinion
I had formed, that he would employ the influence of his new office
to promote the success of that question. . . . I am perfectly
satisfied, I say, with his honesty, sincerity, and zeal ; and I declare
that it will be as much his duty, as I believe it always was his intention . . . to promote, by every fair means . . . the success of the
Catholic Question.' [2]

Canning set to work to fill the vacant places in the Cabinet.
He had still the support of Wynn, Huskisson, Palmerston, Wellesley, Vansittart, Harrowby, and Robinson.   The last, who eighteen
years before had been classed with Peel as one of the two most promising young men in the Tory party, was now sent to the Upper
House, where the Government was very weak, as Lord Goderich.
The King had demanded a ' Protestant ' Chancellor, and Copley,
the Master of the Rolls, had hastily qualified for the place by making a strong speech against Burdett's relief motion in March.
Copley had started life with very revolutionary principles, and had
by a brilliant speech defeated the Government prosecution of the
Radical Watson in 1817.   Castlereagh then thought it necessary
to secure his talents for the Government service, and a seat in
Parliament, a Chief-Justiceship, and later the Attorney-Generalship, had worked a complete change in Copley's opinions.   He
had hitherto abstained from committing himself on the Catholic
Question, and now his speech consisted of an almost word-for-
word repetition of a pamphlet lately published on the subject by
Dr. Philpotts, Prebendary of Exeter.   Canning, as he listened,
whispered to his neighbour the old song :

> ' Dear Tom, this brown jug which now foams with mild ale,
>   Out of which I now drink to sweet Nan of the vale,
>   Was once Toby Philpotts'. . . .'

The witticism went round the House, and Copley's speech was
received with uncontrollable giggles ; but it fulfilled its object of

---

[1] Temperley, *Canning*, p. 107.   [2] *Speeches*, i. p. 502.

catching the King, and the orator was now raised to the peerage as Lord Lyndhurst.

All this, however, could not make the Government a strong one, and Canning sought a coalition with the Whigs. The offer led to another split in that party, never very closely united. Grey, Althorp, and Bedford refused; but Bedford's two sons—Lord Tavistock and Lord John Russell—supported the Ministry, as did a number of the younger Whigs and Radicals, and Lansdowne joined the Cabinet, and became Peel's successor at the Home Office. Peel, when he came to the House and saw Brougham and company ranged behind the Treasury Bench, attacked the coalition in those terms of cold criticism and polite but wounding insinuation which with him took the place of the vituperative personalities frequently indulged in by his contemporaries. This speech roused wild hopes among the Ultras that he would yet head an Opposition : but they were doomed to disappointment. Peel's attack was directed against the Whigs, not against Canning : as soon as he discovered that no guarantees had been made to the Whigs on the subject of reform—that they had compromised their principles and joined the Government without obtaining a single concession to their own views—he withdrew from the position he had momentarily occupied, and took up one of general support of the Government, speaking in their favour both on the shipping question and on Canning's Corn Law bill.

Ministers, however, were exposed to far more unscrupulous attacks from another quarter. Grey, in the House of Lords, led a ferocious and factious opposition, and Goderich, who had been put there to represent the Government, proved himself wholly incapable. A clever financier, and originally a promising debater, he was now for the first time placed in a position of real difficulty, and the essential weakness of his character came out. Before the violent assaults of the Whigs he could do nothing but weep and stammer; and Canning, deeply hurt by Grey's accusations, actually meditated taking a peerage that he might answer in person. Nor were the Tory peers behindhand, though their attacks were marked by more sense of decency. Wellington carried an amendment to Canning's Corn Law, which, though meant to guard against unfair profits being made by speculators on bonded corn, had the practical effect of raising the minimum price at which foreign corn might be admitted. Wellington took this step without giving any warning whatever to Peel, and Peel, though he defended the Duke's motives, continued to support Canning's measure.   It was the first occasion on which a divergence was seen in the policy of the two Tory leaders ; but not by any means the last.

In the House of Commons the scene was less disgraceful.   A few, however, of the smaller fry among the Tories, including Peel's brother-in-law, Dawson (a gentleman renowned for his indiscretion), attacked the Government in a tone as factious and unscrupulous as Grey's own ; but they were of little importance, and were discountenanced by their leaders.

Just before the end of the session Canning and Peel encountered one day by chance in Westminster Hall.   Canning knew that Peel had been blamed for his resignation, and perhaps guessed that he would be exposed to further attacks.   He took the younger man's arm (for he was by now very near his end), and walked with him several times up and down the long hall in talk, that all might see that they were friends.

In January, 1827, the Duke of York had died ; and it was said that at his funeral, standing in the damp and icy cold for hours, more than one got his death.   Peel had made old Eldon stand on his silk hat to keep his feet warm.   Canning contracted a chill there ; overwhelmed with work, and intolerably vexed by the spiteful and irritating opposition, he could not throw off the effects. Not six weeks after the meeting in Westminster Hall he was dead. This premature end to a career that had been so glorious for Britain shook even his enemies.   The Whigs began to feel they might go from bad to worse. ' He was no friend of mine,' wrote Hobhouse, ' but I felt his death would probably give a triumph to our bigots, and that we should see that cold-blooded apprentice . . . take the seat from which the great orator had lately poured forth his thunders, and shaken the thrones of superstition and despotism.' [1]   The ' cold-blooded apprentice ' was Peel, but Hobhouse was not yet to be vexed by his triumph.   The King, as has been seen, had not been pleased by Peel's conduct, and he now approved an attempt to carry on with Canning's Cabinet under Goderich. ' Poor Goody,' as Lyndhurst called him, was, however, unable even to concoct a King's Speech for the opening of the next session. After struggling on, bullied by his Whig colleagues, for three

[1] *Hobhouse*, iii. p. 212.

months during the recess, he finally appeared one night in Lyndhurst's house, moaning and wringing his hands. The Chancellor
kindly offered to accompany him to Windsor, where Goderich
presented his resignation and burst into tears. The King offered
him his pocket handkerchief, and, by the advice of Lyndhurst,
sent for Wellington. Wellington wrote at once to Peel.

' I have declined to make myself the head of the Government,'
he said, ' unless upon discussion with my friends it should appear
desirable, and excepting Lord Lyndhurst, who, it must be understood, is in office, everything else is open to all mankind except one
person, Lord Grey. I have sent for nobody else, nor shall I see
anybody till you come.' [1]

This was an offer of the leadership, but Peel thought that the
Duke should be Prime Minister, and preferred to return to his old
Secretaryship. Thus, after eight months, he found himself again
at the Home Office ; but now in a far different position. Under
the Liverpool Government, Canning had led the House of Commons, and Canning and the Prime Minister, on every point save
one, had directed the policy of the State. Now Peel himself was
leader of the House, and it was he and Wellington who must
determine the Government's policy. For the first time Peel had
his hands entirely free : he had little doubt that a long period of
office lay before him, and his head was teeming with plans.

The first symptom of a change was seen in the construction of
the new Government. Poor Lord Eldon waited for a fortnight,
expecting every moment a summons, and finally read in the newspapers that he was superseded. Peel, it is true, liked Eldon
personally, and did not like Lyndhurst, whom he thought unscrupulous and untrustworthy ; but if the choice lay between
retaining Lyndhurst and restoring Eldon to hang like a dead
weight upon every project of reform or innovation, he could not
doubt which was the lesser evil. He urged, too, that overtures
should be made to the Canningites ; and Huskisson, Palmerston,
Grant, and half a dozen others consented to join the administration.

The session opened badly for the new Government. During
the recess the battle of Navarino had been fought, and the King's
speech referred to it as ' this untoward event '—a grotesque
blunder that brought a shower of mockery and reproach upon the

---

[1] Parker, *Peel*, ii. p. 27.

heads of the Ministers. Nearly all the advantage gained by Canning's Eastern policy was thrown away, in a fashion very discreditable to the Government, but fully in accordance with the traditional British policy of ' bolstering up Turkey.' [1] Before three weeks had passed they were beaten on a question of first-rate importance. Lord John Russell introduced a motion for the repeal of the Test and Corporation Acts, and carried it against them.

These laws, which a century before had degraded the Sacrament of the Anglican Church to a political test and debarred many conscientious Dissenters from public office, had for long ceased to be of much practical importance. An annual Indemnity Act was regularly passed for the benefit of those who violated the law—a characteristically English method of avoiding a difficulty. The mere existence of the laws, however, was an insult to the Dissenters, and a concession to Anglican intolerance.

Peel opposed the motion, on the ground that the laws now involved little or no practical injustice. It was carried over his head, and he then tried to induce Russell to accept a short delay for the Government to consider their action, and suggested, as a compromise, an annual Act *suspending* the law. Lord Milton accused the Government of ' idle pretences,' and of seeking by delay ' to obtain the vantage ground they had lost.' Peel lost his temper completely, denied the accusation, passionately declared that he now ' would not only not propose suspension, but would not even accept delay,' and walked out of the House. While foes and friends joined in solemn condemnation of this shocking behaviour, the sinner walked upstairs, and, having had nothing to eat since nine o'clock breakfast, sat down to a good meal. He then returned in high spirits, said he was sorry to be informed that one of his followers was about to withdraw his support from the Government on the grounds of his leaving the House, for he was just about to repeat the offence, and leave it again ; and he did so. No one can read this little incident, even in the unexpressive pages of *Hansard*, without realising the intense nervousness that underlay Peel's outward frigidity.

In the next debate he admitted frankly that he had thought over his own proposal for suspension, and concluded that it was

[1] It is fair to state that it was Peel, however, who took steps for the restoration of the Greek Christians kidnapped by Ibrahim Pasha.

quite impossible, and that the Government would withdraw their opposition. The Acts were therefore repealed, and the whole affair naturally gave great encouragement to the hopes of the Irish Catholics.

The session ran its stormy course, and the union with the Canningites came to an abrupt end. Lord John Russell was again the source of the trouble. The small boroughs of Penryn and East Retford had each been proved guilty of gross corruption, and Lord John introduced bills for disfranchising them. Peel agreed to the disfranchisement, and consented that Penryn's seats should be transferred to Manchester, which was at this time entirely without representation in Parliament. In the case of East Retford, however, he insisted that the franchise should be merged in the surrounding hundreds. Penryn was a Cornish borough, and Cornwall already returned no less than forty-two members, being the most over-represented county in England; but East Retford was in Nottingham, which sent only eight members in all, and if the two seats were transferred to some distant industrial town— Birmingham was proposed—Nottingham would have only six seats in the House, and this, he contended, was an unfairly small proportion. The Lords agreed to the disfranchisement measure, but amended the bill for Penryn, throwing in this case also the seats into the adjoining district. The East Retford bill was still before the Commons, and the Whigs now claimed that Peel had promised that in one case at least the franchise should go to a great town, and that he should now support the transfer of East Retford's seat to Birmingham. Peel denied that he had ever made such a promise, reiterated his objections, and refused to allow the East Retford seats to go out of the county. Huskisson, Palmerston, and Lamb, however, considered themselves obliged to vote against their colleague and in favour of the Whigs. They gave no warning of what they intended to do, Peel believing to the last moment that Huskisson at least intended to vote with the Government. Peel, however, thought the matter not one of first-rate importance, and would have taken no notice of what had occurred; but Huskisson was apparently not perfectly satisfied with his own conduct,[1] and he wrote to Wellington, offering to resign if the

---

[1] The truth seems to have been that in Cabinet beforehand Peel favoured giving *both* the vacant franchises to large towns, while Huskisson objected. In discussion Peel was overruled, and agreed to his colleagues' views as to East

Prime Minister considered it necessary. Wellington disliked finesse ; he waited for a few hours to give Huskisson the chance to withdraw his letter, then took him at his word, and accepted the resignation. Poor Huskisson, who had conceived himself to be making a polite apology merely, suddenly found himself out in the cold. Palmerston, Lamb, Charles Grant, and Lord Dudley all resigned as a protest against the way in which Huskisson had been treated. The Duke can hardly be acquitted of a little malice, for he certainly did not like Huskisson ; but he had been exceedingly imprudent, and he soon regretted his hastiness. Huskisson on his side was furious. ' Nothing could be more factious,' noted Hobhouse of his ' explanation ' in the House. Peel's reply was admirable, defending the Duke's conduct without condemning that of Huskisson. He read Huskisson's letter, which certainly appeared to be a definite tender of resignation, and he pointed out that had anything else been meant the customary course would have been for Huskisson to call upon Wellington for a personal discussion.

The loss of five of their ablest members was a serious matter for the Government ; but the event had another and unexpected result. It led to the final solution of the Catholic Question.

Vesey Fitzgerald was selected to succeed Charles Grant at the Board of Trade, and his accession to office necessitated his re-election to his seat for Clare. No difficulty was anticipated. Not only was Fitzgerald a member of the family which ruled supreme in the district, but he was also a warm and consistent champion of the Catholic cause, and was very popular personally.

The Catholic Association had lately had to overcome a double disappointment—first, the unfavourable vote of the House of Commons in 1827, and, later, the death of Canning before he could accomplish anything for the cause. O'Connell had before this given up the hope that emancipation could ever be obtained, in the way he thought it should be obtained, as ' a kind concession ' to be received ' in the spirit of affectionate gratitude.' Now, he thought, a display of force was the only remedy, though there

Retford. In the House of Commons Huskisson became alarmed at the strength of the opposition, and voted against his colleagues, while Peel thought himself bound to adhere to the agreement they had come to. This sudden change on Huskisson's part explains Wellington's annoyance. See *Greville*, vi. pp. 222, 432. The story seems to have been generally current, but as Greville heard it from Graham, Peel's most intimate friend, it is probably true.

should be no actual violence. ' One may as well endeavour to coax a pound of flesh from a hungry wolf as to conciliate the (Established) Church,' he wrote. ' From our numbers, our combination, and the continued expression of our discontent . . . there would appear such a union of physical force with moral sentiment that Mr. Peel would be insane if he continued his opposition. We *never never never* got anything by conciliation.' This was in 1826 : when the Wellington Ministry followed Goderich's, O'Connell was almost in despair. The Duke was credited with a much more intense hostility to the Catholics than he really felt. ' We are here in great affright at the idea of the Duke of Wellington being made Prime Minister,' wrote the Liberator to a friend. ' If so, all the horrors of actual massacre threaten us.' [1] The Clare election offered an opportunity for an effectual protest.

In the previous year, in Waterford, the Association had made its first experiment in electioneering, running a candidate of its own against the Government's. They had won the day, with the assistance of the 40s. freeholders, who revolted against their overlords, the Beresfords—and had since been evicted by hundreds. Now the Association took a more daring step. They needed, to oppose the popular Fitzgerald, a candidate whose attractions would brook no rivalry : they put up O'Connell himself. He was a Catholic, and so not eligible in the eyes of the law : but what was the law, weighed in the balance with the enthusiasm which, in Peel's words, ' inspired the serf of Clare with the resolution and energy of a freeman, which . . . in the twinkling of an eye made all consideration of personal gratitude, ancient family connection, local preferences, the fear of worldly injury, the hope of worldly advantage, subordinate to one absorbing sense of religious obligation and public duty ? ' All the Fitzgerald influence was swept away in the storm. The whole countryside was up. Thirty thousand people camped in the streets of Ennis, and the Catholic priests led their flocks by orderly companies to the polling-booths. The demonstration was all the more impressive for the perfect order and quiet which prevailed. ' I wish you had been present,' wrote Peel to Sir Walter Scott, ' for no pen but yours could have

---

[1] (i.) To F. W. Conway, 17th June, 1820. (ii.) To the Knight of Kerry, 31st December, 1826. (iii.) To the same, 22nd February, 1827. Fitzpatrick, *O'Connell*, pp. 69, 135, 140.

done justice to that fearful exhibition of sobered and desperate enthusiasm.' [1]

On the fourth day Fitzgerald in despair abandoned the hopeless contest. The securities upon which the Government had so long relied had failed them ; the mockery of a democratic franchise had suddenly become an awful and threatening reality.

Peel and Wellington, confronted by this unexpected news, were not long in making up their minds. Both were men of action, not given to hesitate or procrastinate in a crisis. The agitation which they had believed to be that of a section had become the movement of a nation, and to both it appeared that the alternative before them was concession or revolution. Both were too clear-sighted to doubt the reality of the danger that threatened or to listen to the outcry of smaller men, that there must be no concession to agitation, that the authority of Government must be vindicated by force. Peel did not doubt that they had the power to put down all resistance : but he thought that force offered no solution—' the question would remain precisely what it was, but with all animosities . . . doubly infuriated, and with all the relations of society, and all the connections between man and man, poisoned to an infinitely greater extent than they were before that collision took place.' [2] As for Wellington, he said afterwards in the House of Lords that he would lay down his life to avoid one month of civil war ; and the effect of these words, from one who could so well measure their weight, was noticeable even in that somewhat case-hardened assembly.

Though, however, the Ministers might have made up their minds, this was only the first part of the difficulty. There still remained to persuade the King, whose solitary scruple (which he naturally valued) was upon this subject. When the King had been cajoled or threatened into giving his consent, there was the task of piloting a bill through Parliament in the face of outraged Tories, infuriated bishops, and strong-minded individuals of all ranks and parties, who demanded that there should be no concession to illegal force. Then the details of the measure must be decided, and securities established to conciliate the English Church. The session was on the point of ending, and nothing could be done until after the recess.

Peel's first decision had been, to state his opinion that con-

[1] Parker, *Peel*, vol. ii. p. 99.   [2] *Speeches*, i. p. 695.

cession must be made to the Catholics, and then to resign ; he retained his office for the moment to help Wellington in tackling the King and the bishops. 'It would not conduce to the satis-factory adjustment of the question,' he wrote to the Duke, ' that the charge of it in the House of Commons should be committed to my hands. . . . I am quite ready to commit myself to the support of the principle of a measure of ample concession and relief, and to use every effort to promote the final arrangement of it. But my support will be more useful if I give it . . . out of office.' [1]

As the days went by, however, his mind altered. He saw more and more clearly the difficulties which their policy would have to encounter. The King stormed and prayed, threatened to abdi-cate and retire for good and all to Hanover ; the feeling of the Tories, and probably of the greater part of the nation, was still anti-Catholic ; it proved impossible to conciliate the Church. Finally the Archbishop of Canterbury and the Bishops of London and Durham saw the Duke, and told him that they must oppose any concession with all their strength.

' I could not but perceive . . . that the Duke of Wellington began to despair of success. . . . I was firmly convinced that if the Duke of Wellington should fail, no other public man could succeed in procuring the King's consent and in prevailing over the opposition to be encountered in the House of Lords. Being convinced that the Catholic Question must be settled, and without delay ; being resolved that no act of mine should obstruct or retard its settlement . . . I determined not to insist upon retire-ment from office, but to make to the Duke the voluntary offer of that official co-operation which he scrupled, from the influence of kind and considerate feeling, to require from me.' [2]

On the 12th of January, 1829, Peel wrote to the Duke and offered to withdraw his resignation. Wellington accepted the offer, saying, ' I tell you fairly that I do not see the smallest chance of getting the better of these difficulties if you should not continue in office.' [3]

To some men the struggle might have been between a desire to retain office, and a sense that duty called them to retire, rather than support a measure they had until now opposed. To Peel the question appeared in a different light. The Government needed all its strength for the fight ahead : was he at such a

[1] Parker, *Peel*, i. pp. 56-7.   [2] *Memoirs*, i. p. 298.   [3] Parker, *Peel*, ii. p. 80.

moment to desert it, in order to vindicate his own consistency—
to save his own face ? Would he allow the measure which he
believed was wise and necessary to risk disaster because he was
afraid to hear himself accused of betraying his cause for selfish
ambition ? There was, moreover, for such a man, so proud, so
self-confident, so imperious, a sort of exultation in overriding
ordinary scruples and defying public opinion. ' It may be,' he
wrote long after, ' that I was unconsciously influenced by motives
less perfectly pure and disinterested, by the secret satisfaction of
being,

> When the waves ran high,
> A daring pilot in extremity ;

but at any rate it was no ignoble ambition that prompted me to
bear the brunt of a desperate conflict, and at the same time to
submit to the sacrifice of everything dear to a public man, excepting the approval of his own conscience, and the hope of ultimate
justice.' [1]

Probably no action in Peel's career has been so generally condemned as his failure to resign in 1829. Even many of those who
fully admit the purity of his motives—notably Lord Rosebery—
hold that he deceived himself, and that he could have done all he
did in office fully as well by giving his unofficial support to the
Government. Such critics seem to forget that the problem is not
one of addition—What is the value of the Wellington Government
plus Peel's unofficial support ? but of subtraction—Take Peel
from the Wellington Government, and what is left ? Anyone
who troubles to read the list of Cabinet Ministers will readily
reply—Nothing. The Ministry could not have stood for a week'
without him. ' His single speech,' wrote Croker a year later,
' has every night supported the whole debate upon our side.' [2]
Who was to take his place at the Home Office and in the leadership of the House—Goulburn ? J. C. Herries ? Vesey Fitzgerald ?
There was not another man of first-rate reputation in the Government's party in the House of Commons. But even if the Government had been stronger, it is ridiculous to pretend that Peel's
influence as a private member could have equalled his influence as
a Minister of the Crown. There are always men who will vote
for a Minister simply *because* he is in office.

[1] *Memoirs*, i. p. 366.
[2] Croker to Vesey Fitzgerald, 3rd May, 1830. *Croker*, ii. p. 59.

The truth is that Peel's resignation would have meant the fall of the Wellington Government, and that a prolonged and disastrous political crisis must have followed. The Whigs would have come in, and found themselves unable to persuade the King, and unable to handle the House of Lords. The relief measure might or might not have passed in the end ; but it could only have been after a protracted struggle, and in the meantime what would have been the state of Ireland ? The question demanded an instant solution. It could not wait for the English party system to adjust itself.

Parliament met again upon February 5th, 1829. During the recess there had been great excitement and much speculation as to what would be done. In 1828, immediately before the prorogation, Wellington and Lyndhurst, by Peel's advice, had both hinted at conciliation : but since then the signs had been contradictory. The impulsive Mr. Dawson had made another indiscreet speech in Ulster, of which his exasperated brother-in-law wrote, ' Did you ever read anything like Dawson's speech, except, perhaps, his former ones on the other side ? The time, the place, the topics, the tone ! It is very singular that a man could blunder in everything with such sinister dexterity.' [1] The expectations aroused by this, however, were dashed by the dismissal of the Lord Lieutenant, Lord Anglesey, who had been behaving in a fashion rather insubordinate, and likely to rouse ill-feeling on all sides. It was thought that he had been removed because of his Catholic sympathies, and as his successor, Lord Northumberland, had the reputation of being a bigoted anti-Catholic,[2] it was generally held that the whole affair indicated an inclination on the part of the Government towards a strong and high-handed ' Protestant ' policy. The secret, therefore, was well kept, and up to the very meeting of Parliament the Tories cherished hopes of resistance.

The King's Speech dispelled their illusions, and the rage of the Ultras passed all bounds. They assailed the Government with unbridled fury. Peel had considered it necessary to make one concession to popular opinion ; he had resigned his seat for the University of Oxford. The University threw him out, and

[1] Parker, *Peel*, ii. p. 53. Peel to Goulburn, July (?) 1828.

[2] He was, as a matter of fact, in the confidence of the Government, and was prepared for conciliation.

elected that stanch Protestant, Sir Robert Inglis. Peel found a temporary shelter in Westbury, a pocket borough of Sir Manasseh Lopes, and even there was received with groans, hisses, and missiles, and was only elected because the rival candidate was delayed, and did not appear upon the scene in time. In Cambridge the Rev. Mr. Maberley attempted to raise a riot, demanding that Wellington and Peel should be impeached. The old Duchess of Richmond exhibited in her drawing-room a case of stuffed rats, labelled with the names of the various Ministers. The Duke of Newcastle filled his diary with frantic invective, calling Peel 'Judas,' and Wellington a 'villain' and worse.[1] Peel's Protestant friends were horrified. 'Your letter has overwhelmed me with surprise and dismay,' wrote his old lieutenant, Gregory. 'That you have been influenced by the purest motives is impossible for me to doubt. . . . Yet . . . I do not think this is the time you should yield to the demands of menacing rebels.'[2] 'I fear your last concession will only embolden resistance,' said his own father, and considered it necessary to sign himself 'with unabated attachment.'[2] 'I should not like to write to you how folks talk of his supposed conversion,' wrote Croker to Lord Hertford.[3] A younger brother, Jonathan Peel, M.P., opposed the Emancipation Bill. In the House of Commons, treason—apostasy—base connivance—selfish ambition—cowardly truckling to violence, were the accusations hurled at him by the angry Tories. He took all the attacks with perfect self-control. He was not the least surprised at their opinion, he said ; 'he could well understand why he was reproached . . . by his honourable friends, who thought his present conduct inconsistent with his former views and declarations. He did not blame them. He would only say, that if they were in possession of the information which he was in possession of, with respect to Ireland, he firmly believed, that they would come to the same conclusion with himself.'[4] The weapons he employed against them were temperate argument, and a little sarcastic raillery ; the worst he did was to prove from their own utterances that his two most virulent assailants, Mr. Bankes and Sir Charles Wetherell, had themselves been guilty of similar

[1] Martineau, *Newcastle*, pp. 8, 25.

[2] Parker, *Peel*, ii. pp. 88, 93-4. See also *Mr. Gregory's Letter Box*, p. 308 ff., for the disappointment of Peel's friends.

[3] *Croker*, ii. p. 8.   [4] *Speeches*, i. p. 676.

inconsistency on the Catholic Question. But he warmly defended
his own integrity.

' However painful it may be to me to dissever party connections
—and I have this night received a formal menace that all such connections shall be dissevered—still those are consequences which
ought not to weigh with one who has undertaken the responsibility to the Crown and to the country. . . . I cannot purchase their
support by promising to adhere at all times, and at all hazards, as
Minister of the Crown, to arguments and opinions which I may
have heretofore propounded in this House. I reserve to myself,
distinctly and unequivocally, the right of adapting my conduct to
the exigency of the moment, and to the wants of the country.' [1]

A hard fight was exhilarating to Peel, and his intimates noticed
that he was always bubbling over with high spirits at such a time.
Croker notes in his diary how Peel at a dinner made a joke about
a certain stanch old Tory, who, ' not knowing Peel's conversion,
had written to him to say that he was hastening up to support
the good old Protestant cause ; ' but the next moment he recollected that he was hardly the person to joke on the subject,
' looked very grave and almost discomposed at his own mirth, and
sat silent and frowning the rest of the evening.' [2] But, though he
could not restrain his sense of humour, Peel was at the same time
deeply wounded by the conduct of his old followers ; and, when
the excitement of the struggle was past, the wound remained and
festered. He never quite forgave the Ultras ; several years passed
before he could bring himself to even the most superficial reconciliation with them. He never forgot the accusations that had
been made. He, who was so reserved and shy, thought it necessary, years after, to write his short *Memoirs*, justifying himself
against accusations which by that time no one dreamed of believing.

On the 6th of March Peel introduced the Emancipation Bill
itself in one of his finest speeches, lasting for four hours, and
received with cheering so loud as to be heard in Westminster Hall.
' The University of Oxford,' remarked Greville, ' should have been
there to hear the member they have rejected, and him whom they
have chosen in his place.' The Whigs were in high delight, Lord
Sefton throughout whispering to his neighbour, Hobhouse, ' My
God, did you ever hear anything like that ? There he goes, bowl-
ing them all down, one after another ! ' But the Canningites were

---

[1] *Speeches*, i. p. 767-8.   [2] *Croker*, ii. p. 8.

downcast; the Government's change of front had destroyed all their hopes of a return to office.[1]

He opened by saying he knew that the majority of the House were prepared to vote for the measure 'upon higher grounds than those on which I desire to rest my arguments.' These he would not address, but only those who, like himself, required to be convinced. ' Sir, the outline of my argument is this : We are placed in a position in which we cannot remain. We cannot continue stationary. There is an evil in divided cabinets and distracted councils which can be no longer tolerated.'

He then related that it had at first been his own intention to resign ; but that he came to believe that this would mean the shipwreck of the measures he advocated. ' I resolved, therefore, and without doubt or hesitation, not to abandon my post, but to take all the personal consequences of originating and enforcing as a Minister the very measures which I had heretofore opposed. I was called upon to make those sacrifices of private feeling, which are inseparable from apparent inconsistency of conduct. . . . Sir, I have done so ; and the events of the last six weeks must have proved that it is painful in the extreme to prefer, to such considerations, even the most urgent sense of public duty.

> 'Tis said with ease, but, oh, how hardly tried
> By haughty souls to human honour tied—
> Oh ! sharp convulsive pangs of agonising pride.

Sir, I return to objects of more public concern. . . . A dreadful commotion had distracted the public mind in Ireland . . . a feverish and unnatural excitement prevailed, to a degree scarcely credible, throughout the entire country. . . . Social intercourse was poisoned there at its very springs . . . . family was divided against family, and man against his neighbour . . . the bonds of social life were almost dissevered . . . the fountains of public justice were corrupted . . . the spirit of discord walked openly abroad. . . . Perhaps I shall be told . . . that " this is the old story ; that all this has been so for the last twenty years, and that therefore there is no reason for a change." Why, Sir, this is the very reason for the change. It is because the evil is not casual and temporary, but permanent and inveterate—it is because the detail of misery and of outrage is nothing but " the old story," that I am contented to run the hazard of a change.'

[1] *Greville*, i. p. 189. *Hobhouse*, iii. p. 308. *Speeches*, i. p. 698 ff.

He went into a full description of the deplorable situation in Ireland, and of the influence obtained by the Catholic Association ; and then, in reply to those who cried out for forcible repression, he asked, ' Will the issue, the successful issue, of civil war leave us in a better condition now than it left us in the year 1800 ? Or shall we not, at its close, have to discuss this same question of concession—with embittered animosities—with a more imperious necessity for the adjustment of this question—and with a diminished chance of effecting that adjustment on safe and satisfactory principles ? '

Next he described the measures which he intended to introduce. There was to be a complete concession of equality of privilege to the Catholics of the three kingdoms ; they were to be excluded only from four offices—that of Regent, and those of Lord Lieutenant of Ireland and of British and Irish Chancellors, because these three had the duty of distributing the patronage of the Anglican Church. Two other measures were to accompany the relief bill. The first was the disfranchisement of the 40s. freeholders, which he defended on two grounds, ' First, as an indispensable security, a necessary concomitant, of the complete extension of privilege ; and, secondly, as a measure politic, if considered abstractedly, being calculated to improve the civil and moral condition of Ireland, by discouraging the subdivision of land for mere political objects, by diminishing the temptation to perjury, and by giving weight to enlightened and independent opinion.' The second measure was the exclusion of the Jesuits and the limitation of monastic orders. The Catholic Association was also to be suppressed.

' What return,' he asked, ' is to be made to the . . . freeholder, whose franchise is to be abolished ? . . . I would say to the Roman Catholic, " The stigma is about to be removed, of which you have so loudly complained . . . the avenues of honour, and power, and distinction, are about to be opened to you and your descendants ; you will stand erect on the footing of perfect equality. Compared with this, what is the miserable privilege which you are asked to relinquish, which has made you the instrument, at one time of your landlord—at another of your priest— and has distracted you between the conflicting claims of gratitude and temporal interest on the one hand, and of spiritual obedience on the other ? " To the Protestant I would say, " We restore to you your just weight in the representation . . . you are now over-borne by a herd of voters . . . you are foremost in that indus-trious, honest, and independent class, whose influence will be mainly increased by the disfranchisement of poverty and ignor-ance." To both—to the Protestant and Roman Catholic, I would say, " Look for a still higher compensation. Cherish the hope that the sources of civil discord may be dried up ; that you may be freed from mutual fears and jealousies ; that a new field may be opened for the enterprise and capital of England ; and that you may find, in the gradual spreading of tranquillity and improvement, your own individual conditions elevated, and ample compensation made to you for any privilege you now relinquish, in the increased value and secure enjoyment of whatever you possess."

' Perhaps,' he ended, ' I am not so sanguine as others in my expectations of the future ; but . . . Sir, I will hope for the best. God grant that the moral storm may be appeased, that the turbid waters of strife may be settled and composed, and that, having found their just level, they may be mingled with equal flow in one clear and common stream. But, if these expectations are dis-appointed . . . still, I am content to run the hazard of the change. The contest, if inevitable, will be fought for other objects and with other arms. The struggle will be, not for the abolition of civil distinctions, but for the predominance of an intolerant religion. Sir, I contemplate that struggle with pain, but I look forward to its issue with perfect composure and confidence. . . . The rally-ing cry of " Civil Liberty " will then be all our own. We shall enter the field with the full assurance of victory.'

The ' Wings ' passed with comparatively little difficulty. All the English members approved them, and even O'Connell did not oppose them very strenuously. ' Peel's bill . . . is good, very good—frank, direct, complete ; no veto, no control, no payment of the clergy,' he wrote ; and later, ' The freehold wing is as little objectionable in its details as such a bill can possibly be. It will make the right of voting clear and distinct.'[1] The Catholic Association, its work done, dissolved itself without waiting to be suppressed.

It was over the Emancipation Bill itself that the struggle was

[1] Fitzpatrick, *O'Connell*, vol. i. pp. 174-178. In 1825, O'Connell, bargain-ing with the Government, declared himself ready to agree to the disfranchise-ment of the 40s. freeholders and the payment of the clergy.

fought.   The greatest sensation was the conduct of the Attorney-
General, Sir Charles Wetherell, who suddenly threw over his colleagues, and attacked them with unparalleled violence, even letting
out some communications that he had received from them in
confidence.   Wellington dismissed him for his conduct.   It was
said that Wetherell was drunk when he made his speech, and, as he
had the habit of undoing his braces when he rose to address the
House, the Speaker remarked that 'Wetherell's only lucid interval
was between his waistcoat and his breeches.'   Behind the scenes
the battle raged almost as fiercely.   The King had withdrawn his
consent on learning the details of the bill, and, though no one
knew it, the whole Cabinet had actually resigned one day ; but
George's courage failed him, and he sent a note to Wellington
during the night, recalling him.   At last, after three weeks' angry
debate, the bill passed the Commons upon March 30, and the
Home Secretary, with some hundred gleeful members at his heels,
carried it to the House of Lords, where the Chancellor received it
with his celebrated Mephistophelian smile—no doubt highly
entertained to see priggish Mr. Peel for once in the same boat
as his unprincipled self.[1]

Old Sir Robert, as the fight went on, had forgotten disapproval
in paternal pride.   'Robin's the lad after all !' he would cry as
he read his papers.   'The Duke could do nothing without him !'
And now he sent a warm invitation to come and recuperate at
Drayton, with 'dear Julia and the children.'[2]

The carrying of Catholic emancipation was the turning-point
in Peel's life.   It is this, rather than, as Gladstone said, the passing
of the Reform Bill, that marks the division between the 'two
Peels.'   It was a definite breakaway from tradition, a conscious
and deliberate setting of his own personal judgment against the
creed in which he had been brought up.

The act was not quite so sudden or so strange as it appeared.
His mind had been developing, slowly but steadily, for a long time
past.   His conduct on the financial committee of 1819 had been
the first sign of rebellion.   Then he had dared to change his mind,
and, what was perhaps more important, had freed himself from

---

[1] 'Who would have guessed that I should be the bearer of the Roman
Catholic Relief Bill to the House of Lords ?   However, it was necessary.'   Peel
to Sir Walter Scott, 3rd April, 1829.   Parker, *Peel,* ii. p. 99.

[2] Parker, *Peel,* ii. pp. 109, 110.

the influence of the father whose docile pupil he had been for so long. Since that time new ideas had been—perhaps half unknown to himself—fermenting in his brain. His marriage had helped him to break away from home influences. His long preoccupation with legal reforms, even though they had been reforms of detail rather than of principle, had stimulated his critical faculties : no one could study the imbecile fictions of English legal procedure without contracting a wholesome disrespect for precedent. He began to dally with wild and romantic projects. It is amusing to note how, in his speeches on law reform, he recurs to the plan of instituting a public prosecutor in imitation of Scottish law, and then, after toying with it lovingly for a while, sighs and sets it aside as too Utopian a dream to be realised in this workaday world. He seems half delighted, half afraid at the boldness of his own speculations.

This growth of intellectual independence could not but have its influence upon his Irish policy. It is not without significance that his speeches against Catholic emancipation are the poorest he ever made. There is not another subject that he touches that he cannot make seem reasonable and just. The reader to-day, even though disagreeing heartily, is for the moment convinced against his will, so plausible are his arguments. Delivered in the House, enforced by the magic of his persuasive and beguiling voice, the effect must have been far greater : but the speeches against Catholic emancipation would convince no one who was not already an obstinate ' Protestant.' It is as if a devil of dullness possessed the orator, and blinded him to his own weakness and inconsistencies ; as if his innate good sense refused to be prostituted to the cause of injustice and bigotry. This is the more remarkable, because his speeches *in favour* of emancipation were the finest he had yet made. The first, it is true, was lame enough ; but, once the struggle had actually begun, from the day when he introduced his bill, there was a change, and he came down to the House, night after night, to give one magnificent display after another— speeches that had all his old power of close reasoning, good sense, sly humour, and clear exposition, but with a driving force of passion behind them that was new. Peel's oratory never touched the sublime, but his speeches on Catholic emancipation came nearer to it, perhaps, than any others. It seemed that the national crisis had awakened powers hitherto dormant, or as if his genius, free at last from the trammels of outworn prejudice, sprang suddenly erect, to its full height. He fought the battle alone, not caring to make use of what assistance he might have had : exulting, it seemed, in his new-found strength.

It is probable that for some time before 1828 Peel's convictions on the Catholic Question were shaken. He did not for an instant admit this to himself, nor even realise that it was so. He was going on for forty, a time when most men are settling into fixed opinions, not beginning to criticise and to rebel against the traditions of their youth. To lose a life-long conviction is a painful process ; for one of his temperament it was especially difficult. Even as it feels its foothold giving way, the mind seems to cling so much the more desperately to its cherished beliefs, and to oppose the more passionately the arguments that so insidiously lay hold upon it. Even as Peel ostentatiously nailed his colours to the mast—trying to resign in 1825, actually resigning in 1827—his speeches seem to carry less and less conviction, he himself, probably, became more and more distressed. He saw his cause losing ground ; he felt himself all the more pledged to it. But when the supreme crisis came, he could no longer deceive himself as to where his duty lay. All that was best and most honest in his nature rose to meet the danger, he flung aside regrets, scruples, and fears, and, outraging all political conventions and party obligations, did what needed to be done. Long after, referring to the attacks that were made upon him for having betrayed his cause, he defended his own honourable motives, but added :

' If it had been alleged against me that the sudden adoption of a different policy had proved the want of early sagacity and forethought on my part—if the charge had been that I had adhered with too much pertinacity to a hopeless cause, that I had permitted for too long a period the engagements of party, or undue deference to the wishes of constituents, to outweigh the accumulating evidence of an approaching necessity—if this had been the accusation against me, I might find it more difficult to give it a complete and decisive refutation.' [1]

He won, by this action, his own moral and intellectual independence. For the rest, he took no credit for the successful conduct of the measure which he had long opposed. ' If it fail, the responsibility will devolve upon me,' he told the House of Com-

---

[1] *Memoirs*, i. 365.

mons, in thanking and complimenting them for their behaviour.
' If it succeed, the credit will belong to others. . . . It belongs to
Mr. Fox, to Mr. Grattan, to Mr. Plunket, to the gentlemen
opposite, and to an illustrious and right honourable friend of mine
who is now no more. By their efforts, in spite of my opposition,
it has proved victorious. I will not conceal from the House that,
in the course of this debate, allusions have been made to the
memory of my right honourable friend, now no more, which have
been most painful to my feelings. An honourable baronet has
spoken of the cruel manner in which my right honourable friend
was hunted down. Whether the right honourable baronet were
one of those who hunted him down, I know not ; but this I do
know, that whoever did join in the inhuman cry that was raised
against him, I was not one. I was on terms of the most friendly
intimacy with my right honourable friend down even to the day
of his death ; and I say with as much sincerity of heart as man can
speak, that I wish he were now alive to reap the harvest which he
sowed, and to enjoy the triumph which his exertions gained. I
would say of him, as he said of the late Mr. Perceval, " Would he
were here to enjoy the fruits of his victory ! "

Tuque tuis armis : nos te poteremur, Achille.'[1]

[1] *Speeches*, i. p. 742.

CHAPTER VII

THE COMING STORM, 1829-1830

In 1830 the Peel-Wellington Government found itself much weaker than it had been at its establishment two years before. It had lost first the services of the Canningites, next the support of the Ultra-Tories. Its change of front on the Catholic Question had made it very unpopular in the country. The Ministry, however, did not anticipate any immediate disaster. Since 1807 Cabinets had come and Cabinets had gone, but they had all been Tory Cabinets. Confident Tories said that the Whigs, with neither experience nor unity, could not form a Government even if they had the chance.

Moreover, Peel's head was full of plans for reforms, and throughout his career he preserved a touching faith that his political opponents would be mollified by his good intentions. He hoped that crime and disorder would decrease with the extension of the new police, and that the condition of the poor would improve with the reduction of the duties on corn, which they had carried in 1828.[1] He was still working at the codification and amelioration of the Criminal Law. He was dreaming, as we have seen before, of what might be done for Ireland by ten years' strong government and the progress of education. In Scotland he had made an excellent impression by filling four legal appointments in succession with Whigs—for the unheard-of reason that they were the best men. ' Those whose memory went back a few years ' felt ' they had got into a new world,' says Lord Cockburn. [2] Under Peel's leadership, too, waste was being checked and sinecures abolished, and the Budget of 1830 introduced economies and remitted taxation to the extent of £3,400,000.[3] Hume was so

---

[1] The measure was of the same nature as Canning's defeated bill, but not quite so extensive.

[2] Cockburn, *Memorials of his Time*, p. 430.

[3] It is perhaps not unjust to assume that Wellington had little to do with these reductions. The Duke was quite of the old school in his dealings with public funds. In 1823 Huskisson, after becoming President of the Board of

agitated by this unexpected sign of grace that he lost his head and challenged the Government to reduce their estimates below those of 1822. As the estimates were in fact considerably below the level of 1822, Peel did not fail to take advantage of this lapse.

The Whigs, however, felt their growing strength, and were not disposed to be satisfied with Peel's reforms. The split in 1827 had weakened the party, and Tiernay had never been able to hold it together effectively : but in 1830 Tiernay died, and the two sections were reconciled. The leading members met, and elected a chief of a different type. The first public intimation of this was given when Lord Althorp rose in the House of Commons to say, ' *We* intend to take the sense of the House upon such and such a question,' and Peel was seen to start as he heard.

Althorp had already distinguished himself as a leader of the opposition to the suspension of the Corn Laws in 1826, and as an advocate of the reform of the Debtors' Law. He was a man of forty-eight, the heir of Earl Spencer. He had been a neglected child, growing up in the company of servants and stableboys, and taught to read by a Swiss footman, and though he had since taken a first at Oxford, firsts at Oxford were not in those days the infallible indication of intellectual eminence which (one assumes) they are now. Those who wished to praise Lord Althorp praised his honesty, his good sense, his good temper (all of which were superlative)—but not his intellect. His leading passion, as he himself said, was ' to see sporting dogs hunt.' Bagehot remarks that he had ' extreme sensibility to the sufferings of animals and man. . . . To hear of cruelty or injustice pained him like a blow,' and goes on to describe how he would ride down from London by night to hunt next morning, galloping one hack after another till they fell beneath him on the road.[1] In addition to his other virtues, he was so modest that his lady had had to propose to him. Under his leadership the Whigs were not likely to fall into their old fault of

Trade, thought it his duty to resign the Ceylon Agency, value £1,200 a year, which had been given him twenty years before as a reward of service. He did so under the belief that the Government, which was then being attacked for extravagance, meant to reduce the office and make it non-political. Liverpool and Wellington at once transferred the agency, untouched, to Mr. Arbuthnot. Mrs. Arbuthnot had received a pension of £1,200 a year not three months before. The relations of the Duke with the Arbuthnots are well known Canning and Huskisson finally succeeded in reducing the office to £800 and giving it to someone else. See *Huskisson Papers*, British Museum, 38,745.

[1] Bagehot, *Biographical Studies*, p. 313.

factious opposition ; he was far too honest for that.   His views also
were very liberal, and the party was now committed to a policy of
Parliamentary Reform on advanced lines.   Under the influence of
Althorp, Brougham, Russell, and others of the younger generation in politics, the old Whig reformers, with their sentimental,
aristocratic liberalism, found themselves hurried into courses
which they did not altogether like.

The question of Parliamentary Reform was now the most pressing problem of the day.   The distress of 1829 had been a hotbed
for political agitation, which took a new form.   Inspired by
O'Connell's success in Ireland, the lower and middle classes began
to form associations for the expression of their opinions.   For the
first time the popular movement for Reform was effectively
organised.

In January, 1830, Thomas Attwood—' the most influential man
in England,' as Francis Place called him—started the Birmingham
Political Union of the Lower and Middle Classes, with the tempting programme of ' manhood suffrage and paper money.' [1]   Attwood was a fanatic on the subject of Currency Reform, and was
therefore inspired with a strong personal hostility to Peel,[2] but
under the influence of his colleagues the agitation for inflating the
currency was subordinated to the agitation for Parliamentary
Reform.   Before this a society, ultimately called the National
Union of the Working Classes, had been formed in London.
These two associations were soon to be imitated all over the
country.

The same tendency to organisation was visible in economic
affairs.   The failure of the great spinners' strike at Hyde in 1829
had made John Doherty, the trade union leader, decide that
movements which were merely local had no chance of success.   In
the winter of 1829-30 he organised the National Union of Opera-
tive Spinners, which held its first meeting in the Isle of Man, and
which, he hoped, would include the whole United Kingdom.   In
February, 1830, Doherty launched a more ambitious project—the
National Association for the Protection of Labour, the first
attempt at a general trades union : it was to include all trades,

[1] Wallas, *Place*, p. 251.

[2] This personal hostility was so noticeable as to make Peel seriously alarmed,
in 1831-2, for the safety of his family, Drayton being within easy reach of
Birmingham.   See Mr. Nicholls to Peel, 21st November, 1831.   *Peel Papers*,
British Museum, 40,402, p. 123, etc.

and was to organise strikes against reduction of wages. Both
societies spread with ominous rapidity ('short summers lightly
have a forward spring'), and there was a fresh outbreak of strikes.
The spinners came out at Bolton and Ashton-under-Lyne, and
strikes in the coalfields added to the disorder in the cotton trade :
the price of coals rose, the mills had to close down, and the poor of
Manchester could get no fuel. The strikers threatened to obstruct the canals if coals were brought from a distance.[1]

About the same time—May, 1830—the first reports of the
grand Cotton Spinners' Union reached the Home Office. Peel's
first action was to apply to the Law Officers of the Crown, informing them of the existence of ' a general and dangerous combination
. . . for the control of the wages of labour, and respecting the
measures resorted to under the name of " picquetting," with a
view to promote the success of this combination, by deterring
parties, who are not members of it, from working at a rate of wages
not sanctioned by the combination.' Did the Statute or Common
Law, he asked, afford any remedy against ' the constitution and
acts of a Confederacy calculated in its immediate effects to disturb the peace of the manufacturing districts, and capable, if
allowed to gain strength and consistency, of being converted at
once into an instrument of sedition and open resistance to the
law.'[2] It appeared, however, that the only legal remedy, as
matters stood, was to prosecute the pickets for molestation under
the Act of 1825, and this was very difficult, as the system had been
brought to great perfection : crowds dispersed at the first approach of the police, and pickets were brought from a distance so
that they might not be recognised and identified.[3] Nothing was
done for the present beyond keeping a careful watch on the Union
and its proceedings.

In the midst of all this, a great impetus was given to the movement for Parliamentary Reform by two events. George IV. died,
and the whole nation drew breath with relief. There was a general
feeling that something old and evil and hideous was gone, that a
deadweight of reaction and bigotry had dropped away. The new
King, although he had few personal attractions, shone by contrast

[1] From Mr. Foster, 23rd October, 1830, H.O. 40, 27.

[2] From the Borough-Reeves of Manchester, 26th May, 1830, H.O. 40, 27.
To the Law Officers, June, 1830, H.O. 49, 7, p. 393.

[3] From the Borough-Reeves of Manchester, 26th May, 1830. From Mr.
Foster, 26th December, 1828, H.O. 40, 22, etc., etc.

with his brother. He was a vulgar, eccentric, weak-minded old man, but good-natured, comparatively respectable, and amenable. Above all, he had not acquired the Tory habit : he had no prejudice against the Whigs—no broken pledges and friendships dishonoured to brood over.

The demise of the Crown necessitated the dissolution of Parliament : and at the very opening of the general election news arrived that gave the reformers their opportunity. For three days no word had got through from France ; now it was announced that the people had risen, had deposed the King, who was trying to subvert the constitution, and set his cousin in his place. Soon after came news from Belgium, where the country rose against the detested union with Holland. The speed, order, and efficiency with which the French rising had been carried out had a great effect upon public opinion ; it was seen that bloodshed and anarchy were not the necessary accompaniments of revolution. The result of the elections was a great infusion of liberalism into the House of Commons. It was clear that when the new Parliament met the Government must be prepared to deal with the question of Reform.

At the same time the excitement of the working classes was greatly increased, and a new and alarming element made its appearance in the general disorder. The harvest was no sooner over, when agricultural riots, the most dangerous yet known, broke out in Kent. They were caused not by disaffection to the Government, nor by sudden and unusual distress ; it was the slow, grinding, protracted misery of their lot that had at length driven the labourers to desperation. The immediate cause was the introduction of threshing machines. Threatening letters, signed by an unknown and ubiquitous person named ' Swing,' with subsequent incendiarism, were the first signs ; but soon the labourers began to parade the country in bands, armed with pitch-forks, presented themselves at the better class houses, and with threats extorted money, food, and written promises to raise wages and remit tithes. They were occasionally joined by farmers, who took this opportunity to attack the hated tithe system.[1] Timely severity might have nipped the trouble in the bud ; unfortunately a mistaken sympathy led magistrates to sentence the first of those who were

[1] From Mr. Maule, 30th November, 1830. From Mr. Tallents, 20th November, 1830, H.O. 40, 27.

arrested very leniently, and made agitators like Cobbett and
Carlile applaud and encourage the rioters.   The outbreak spread
through Hampshire, Wiltshire, Buckinghamshire, Surrey, and
Sussex, and ricks, barns, private houses, and stables with the live
stock in them were burned by secret incendiaries or angry mobs.
Here and there a spirited landlord armed his servants and dispersed the rioters easily, but in general the better class inhabitants
were terrorised, and refused even to act as special constables.

In the meantime the troubles in the north continued, and the
Home Secretary could not but speculate as to the causes that lay
at the root of this chronic disorder.   Clearly one of them was the
system of paying wages in truck; but he did not find it easy to
invent a remedy for this.   For years past the most intelligent
magistrates, the respectable master manufacturers, and the
middle class residents of the districts affected had urged that new
enactments should be passed :[1] but none of them could suggest
a remedy for the systematic evasion of the existing Acts against
truck, the latest of which was as recent as 1821 ; and Peel was
thoroughly awake to the disadvantage of continually repeating
legislation that could not be effectively enforced.[2] Another
possible remedy was State-aided emigration ; and Peel seems to
have contemplated a measure of this sort,[3] together with others,
for the session of 1830-31 ; but his habitual reticence makes it
difficult to know exactly what or how much he intended.   At the
opening of the session Mr. Wilmot Horton wrote to Peel in some
distress, as to a report which he had seen in the press, that Peel had
declared he could offer no remedy for the distress of the country.
He received this characteristic reply :

' My Dear Horton,—This is the third time within a month that
you have called upon me to relieve you from the anxieties and
astonishment to which unfounded rumours have given rise.   I was

[1] From Mr. Haden, 22nd May, 1822, H.O. 40, 17.   From Frome Magistrates, 15th July, 1823, H.O. 40, 18.   Petition from the Inhabitants of Industrial Staffordshire, H.O. 40, 27.   Petition from Master Manufacturers,
28th April, 1829, H.O. 40, 23.   Peel to the Duke of Beaufort, 6th May, 1829,
H.O. 40, 23, etc., etc.

[2] He spoke very strongly in favour of Littleton's Truck Bill in December,
1830, declaring himself ready to 'throw aside the principles of political economy'
in order to protect the workman's right to the product of his labour. Speeches,
ii. p. 255.

[3] To Mr. Wilmot Horton, declaring he will support such a scheme, 21st
September, 1831, British Museum, 40,401, p. 171.

asked by Mr. Portman a few days since what measures for the relief of the labouring poor the Government meant to propose during the present session. I protested against the right of any man to ask such a question, said it was very difficult to adopt any measure of internal policy that had not a bearing on the condition of the poor, that the remission of taxes [1] . . . that every measure connected with the employment of the unemployed in Ireland, with the prevention of the immigration of Irish labourers,[2] with the amendment of the Poor Laws, all affected the condition of the English poor, and that I would not enter into such questions in answer to a casual remark made without previous notice to me, and when the House was quite unprepared for the discussion. If I had in my desk the most perfect measures ready for introduction in a week on all the points above referred to, I should have returned precisely the same answer.' [3]

Peel did not, however, attribute disorder entirely to the sufferings of the poor. Some of it he attributed to the lawlessness and violence deliberately excited by agitators, and especially by the trade union leaders. He wished, however, to understand clearly the rights and wrongs of the question, and for nearly two years past he had been trying to get information about the rates of wages in the disaffected districts. In May, 1829, he had written to Mr. Foster and Mr. Humphreys, the magistrates of Manchester and Stockport, asking for reports on the rate of wages in the cotton trade, and Sir Henry Bouverie had been asked for information about the coal trade.[4]

The results appear to have been rather misleading. Though Foster examined the books of many of the manufacturers in Manchester, the rates of wages which he reports are in general higher than those given by the Factory Commission of 1833, which, of course, must be considered more reliable. The information sub-

---

[1] Apparently the taxes on soap and candles were to be abolished. To Wilmot Horton, 21st September, 1830. *Peel Papers*, British Museum, 40,401, p. 171.

[2] At this time there was a large immigration of Irish labourers every harvest, which of course both lowered the wages of the English country labourer, and deprived him of employment.

[3] To Wilmot Horton, 16th November, 1830. *Peel Papers*, British Museum, 40,401, p. 281. Horton's letter, to which this is a reply, seems to imply that Peel had given Horton to understand he was going to take action both on the Poor Laws and on the question of emigration. From Mr. Horton, 15th November, 1830. *Peel Papers*, British Museum, 40,401, p. 279.

[4] H.O. 41, 7.

mitted as to the coal trade seems to have been very inaccurate too. The Home Secretary was led to believe that a young male spinner could earn from 25s. a week, and that there were cases where an experienced spinner could earn up to £4 a week ; and that a collier earned from 5s. to 5s. 6d. for an eight hours' shift. These rates may have been correct in a few cases, as far as the colliers were concerned, though in general wages were lower (ranging from 15s. a week to 25s. in a few cases) and hours longer ; [1] but as to the cotton trade, they seem to have been grossly exaggerated. As a matter of fact, spinners rarely earned more than 30s. a week ; [2] 35s. 9d. was the figure for a first class spinner in 1833, and in the same year a third rate man made 22s. 6d.

In the previous year Peel had very fully and carefully investigated the cost of living, when calculating the wages of his new police ; and he had come to the conclusion that they could live very comfortably, and at the same time save 10s. a week, out of their wage of one guinea a week. It was not unnatural that he should consider that the rates of wages reported to him from the north were very liberal. [3]

He probably selected the cotton trade for his investigations because it was unusually well organised : strikes were many, were often successful, and were sometimes accompanied by great disorder and violence. Everywhere, however, strikes were maintained by objectionable methods. Place's hope, that with the legalisation of the trade unions violence would disappear, had not been fulfilled as yet. The weavers' union sent its emissaries to take the shuttles out of the looms so that they could not be worked, and if blacklegs contrived to work in spite of this, the ' flying angels,' as they were called, came by night and destroyed the webs.

---

[1] Many miners, however, had a house and free coal in addition to these regular wages.

[2] I cannot account for these discrepancies. It seems incredible that even the masters of the period, those much-abused men, deliberately gave false information. Sir Henry Bouverie and Mr. Foster are, of course, above suspicion, and that they were neither incompetent nor prejudiced against the workmen anyone who reads their letters may be satisfied. The reports submitted to Peel were mostly of net wages, so that the deduction of piecers' pay will not account for the difference. Possibly some individual firms were at this time giving unusually high rates as a result of successful strikes. The reports to the Home Secretary are in H.O. 40, 23, 24, 26, 27. Compare the *Supplementary Report of the Factory Commission of* 1833, Appendix ; also Porter, *Progress of the Nation*, chap. ix. *Clapham*, i. pp. 550-1 and 558-9.

[3] H.O. 61, 1, No. 29.

R.P.

In some districts strikers would march through the villages, halting outside the houses of blacklegs, and chanting in sing-song tones the punishment which would be inflicted by ' the Man in the Moon ' on those who disobeyed the union : the hint was understood. If blacklegging persisted, assault, shooting, or throwing explosives in at the window might be resorted to. Secret and illegal oaths were still imposed, and it was even suggested that the old spinner's oath, of the days before Combination Law Repeal, which pledged men to the assassination of ' oppressive and tyrannical masters ' at the unions' orders, might be still in use. Looms were still smashed, and mills sacked and burned. The victims of the outrages against workmen were usually the poorest of the poor, those who could not afford to join the unions or to prosecute their tormentors.[1]

It must be admitted that on the question of strikes Peel was *not* on the side of the angels. According to the modern point of view, he was here thoroughly reactionary. He disliked strikes, and in May, 1830, told an inquiring magistrate that he thought strikers had no claim to poor relief. The picketing system he detested. ' An abominable tyranny has been established (in Lancashire),' he wrote to his brother Edmund, ' by means of the Union of Trade.' [2] He was indignant with the middle classes for the lack of spirit they showed in this dangerous crisis. They would not act as special constables, they were terrified by threats of violence, they would not combine as the men combined—they would not lift a finger to help themselves, in fact, and did nothing but cry for military aid and repressive laws. The Home Office Records of this year are full of indignant and reproachful letters from Peel to individuals who have surrendered to force or threats.

In October, after receiving new reports of disorders and of the high wages current in the trade, the Home Secretary's anger suddenly broke out in a startling manner.

' Dear Sir,' he wrote to Mr. Foster, ' I am deeply impressed with the importance of your communication. . . . Under ordinary

[1] From E. P. Burnell, 31st January, 1826, H.O. 40, 19. From Mr. Midgly, etc., January, 1827. From J. S. Mills, 23rd February, 1829. From Worship Street Police Office, 4th May, 1829. From Mr. Foster, 5th May, 1829. Do., 12th May, 1829, H.O. 40, 22. From the Mayor of Norwich, 24th December, 1827, H.O. 40, 24, etc. The spinner's oath is also printed in the *Report of the Committee on the Combination Laws.*

[2] *Peel Papers*, British Museum, 40,401. To Edmund Peel, 29th October, 1830, p. 253.

circumstances no doubt could be entertained that the best policy would be for the masters to resist the demands of their workmen, to close their collieries, to stop their cotton mills, and abide the consequences. It is clear that the wages received by the men are ample, that the men have no just cause of complaint. To whatever distress the workmen might be subject, they would only have themselves to blame. It is equally clear that nothing permanent will be gained by the concession to unjust demands, and that the time must come when there will be no alternative but the positive and decided refusal of the masters to advance the wages of their men. We must look forward, however, to all the consequences of this refusal, and we must take every possible precaution for the preservation of the Peace and the protection of Property. . . .' He goes on to say that he has asked General Bouverie to go to Manchester, and confer with Mr. Foster and Mr. Hulton, and decide ' what will be the probable consequence of the total stoppage of the collieries and the cotton mills dependent upon them for their supply of coal. The " turn-out " of some thousand persons in the present state of feeling so easily excited, would probably soon lead to a breach of the peace, to a conflict between the civil power and the adherents of the union, to the employment of the military in aid of the local power. The first conflict might be the signal for many others, and the manufacturing district might suddenly be involved in very general confusion. I am anxious to know, after you have conferred . . . what is your opinion as to the probability of any extensive disturbances, supposing that there should be a serious conflict on any one point between either the civil or military force and the populace ? Whether you think any steps can now be taken, or could be taken on the instant in case of necessity, for organising some sort of volunteer force in aid of the military ? The upper classes possessed of property must be willing to exert themselves for the defence of property in case it should be seriously threatened ; but the upper classes alone could not exhibit numbers sufficient to overawe and overpower the populace. Their organisation alone might establish a marked line between property and physical force ranged on opposite sides, and might serve as a pretext for the organisation and arming of those opposed to property. Are there among the workmen, servants, and adherents of the masters, and among the lower classes of shopkeepers and householders a sufficient number of persons entirely to be depended upon, who would unite with the upper classes, and form themselves into volunteer associations for the defence of property in case it should be threatened ? . . . If you . . . are of the opinion that the civil power, the military, and the aid that can be derived from the well-affected, would prevail practically over the combined efforts of the union, would either compel the men to submit for want of means of subsistence, or would suppress and effectually put down any open attempt at violence, I think there can be little doubt that the true policy for the owners of collieries and the masters of mills to pursue is peremptorily and decidedly to refuse concessions which they feel to be unjustly demanded. But this step once taken, there ought to be no retreating, and therefore it is of importance to consider the probable result of it, and the means of successfully maintaining resistance. (Signed) Robert Peel.' [1]

Peel cannot be blamed for accepting the statements as to wages, which apparently came from authentic sources. Opinions may differ as to his refusing, in the previous year, to see John Doherty, on the grounds that such an interview would be misrepresented.[2] His warmest admirers, however, will agree that the writer of this letter was using his influence as a Minister of the Crown to support one party to an industrial dispute in a very improper manner.

Fortunately Mr. Foster saw things more clearly. He deprecated any interference for the purpose of assisting the millowners or encouraging them to put in blacklegs. 'The greatest good has arisen,' he wrote, ' from the conviction in the minds of the men, that whilst the magistrates were determined to preserve the peace, they were equally determined not to become parties against the men in their disputes with the masters. In the disputes also . . . the merits are not always so clear. Things are often quite different in different mills, and the public opinion would be divided.' In this case he thought the masters were clearly in the right, and should not give in, but it was quite impossible to induce them to work together. ' This seems to be the one great reason why combinations of masters cannot effectually resist combinations among

---

[1] To Mr. Foster, 25th October, 1830, H.O. 41, 8.

[2] Doherty called at the Home Office in September 1829. See Peel to Mr. Foster, 11th September, 1829, H.O. 41, 7. ' I was unwilling to have any personal communication with him on the particular subject on which he wished to see me, the difference between the master manufacturers and the spinners . . . fearing the misrepresentation to which such a communication would be liable when reported by him in Manchester.' He invited Doherty to write to him instead, but Doherty did not do so.

the men.' One coalowner had already given in. The press was all on the side of the men. A volunteer force in aid of the military could not be raised in sufficient numbers. He thought a collision in the end inevitable, and that only a legislative enactment could protect the masters.[1]

Peel seems to have given way at once : we hear no more of the grand scheme for organising the middle classes against the unions, and it may be conjectured that the indiscreet letter was written in a moment of excitement and then repented. That Peel was in a state of considerable nervous tension at this time is indicated by the tone of asperity which appears in his letters. The situation in the country was daily becoming more alarming, and Sir Denis le Marchant was told by clerks in the Home Office that Peel at the last could sometimes hardly bring himself to open his letters for fear of the news they might contain.[2]

The Home Secretary returned to the idea of new legislation, which he had been considering for some time past. He had been pressed to legislate against the unions, but he was himself more inclined to attack the picketing system only. ' I doubt whether Parliament would pass a law directed against unions of workmen,' he wrote, ' without very clear proof not only of their mischievous tendency, but of their unjustifiable acts.' To take such action and fail would make matters worse : and it might be impossible to get witnesses in the state of terrorism which prevailed.[3] The picketing system, however, offered a much better opportunity. Peel had long considered that the protection given to the independent workman was insufficient, and here a remedy seemed easier to apply. The local Police Act in force at Ashton-under-Lyne, which had been found exceedingly useful in dispersing pickets, seemed a possible model.[4] There is little doubt that Peel contemplated legislation on such lines. Before he could take action he left the Home Office for the last time ; but he took the some-

[1] From Mr. Foster, 26th October, 28th October, 1830, H.O. 40, 27.

[2] Le Marchant, *Althorp*, p. 255.

[3] To Mr. Foster, 26th October, 1827, H.O. 40, 27. Trade unions.

[4] This Act authorised the arrest and punishment by fine or imprisonment of persons ' disturbing the public peace and wilfully obstructing the free passage of any street, standing, loitering, or remaining on any footway without some reasonable, good or sufficient excuse, or in any manner . . . hindering the free passage of such footway, or prejudicing, insulting, jostling or annoying any person thereon.' The whole correspondence about picketing is in H.O. 40, 27.

what unusual step of leaving a note behind him, attached to Foster's letter on the Ashton Act. ' I take the liberty of recommending the subject of this letter, and the whole of my recent confidential communications with Mr. Foster respecting the Trades Union at Manchester, to the immediate and serious consideration of my successor in the Home Department. (Signed) Robert Peel.' [1] As a matter of fact, for a moment his successors contemplated action far more drastic than any that he seems to have thought possible : but it was unnecessary : before the end of the year both the Cotton Spinners' and the grand Trades Union had unobtrusively faded away.

In the midst of all this disorder Parliament met at the end of October. The whole country was waiting with intense eagerness for a declaration of the policy of the Government : What would they offer for the relief of the distress ? What, above all, would be their attitude on the burning question of Parliamentary Reform ?

It was obvious to all—except, perhaps, to the Prime Minister— that a dangerous crisis was at hand ; and one would have imagined that the Cabinet would have discussed this most important question in full, and decided upon the policy which they meant to pursue. In fact, it seems that not only had they come to no decision, but that they had not discussed the matter at all. Future events made it clear that Peel and Wellington held directly contrary opinions ; but it is by no means so clear that either of them as yet knew how far they differed. There was at no time close intimacy or real confidence between the two. Each admired the other deeply, but the less they saw of each other the better they liked it. Wellington, blunt and open in his own manners, disliked Peel's cold and cautious reserve. ' All the Duke's little Cabinet (the women and the toadeaters) hate Peel,' Greville remarked.[2] Peel, one is almost inclined to think, was a little afraid of the Duke. Lord Francis Egerton, who had been Irish Secretary in 1828-9, said that ' Peel, who was the man who might naturally be expected to put himself forward, never would, and that repeatedly he had got him (Francis) to go to or write to the Duke about some matter or other on which it was necessary to refer to him.' [3] Peel seems to

[1] This is the complete version of the letter, of which an oddly inaccurate summary is printed by Hammond, *The Town Labourer*, p. 313.

[2] *Greville*, ii. p. 96.   [3] *Greville*, ii. p. 45.

have been thoroughly dissatisfied with his colleagues. Aberdeen
and Goulburn were his confidential friends, and he was becoming
very intimate with Sir Henry Hardinge, newly appointed Irish
Secretary; but with the others he was not much in sympathy.
He had no one competent to assist him in the management of the
House of Commons, and the strain of eight years of almost unbroken toil was beginning to tell upon him. 'I personally could
not long have continued to discharge the rapidly increasing duties
of the Home Office and the business of the House of Commons,' he
wrote to Henry Hobhouse a month later.[1] He felt that the Government could not go on without new support; but the Duke did
not see this at all, and they had just come into collision on the
subject. Peel carried his point, but the Duke was much annoyed.[2]

The matter in dispute was this. In August a great gathering
had been invited to celebrate the opening of the Manchester and
Liverpool railway, and Huskisson, as member for Liverpool, was
of course present. 'The Great Captain is to be there with all
his tail,' he wrote bitterly to Sir James Graham. 'Of course, one
object is to throw me into the background.'[3] Poor Huskisson!
not even Wellington's presence kept him from being the central
figure at the ceremony: he was knocked down by one of the
engines, at the Duke's very feet, and died in a few hours. Peel at
once saw a chance of recovering the support of the Canningites,
and insisted on making overtures to Palmerston and his friends.
They, however, refused his offers, and presently joined the
Whigs.

Peel was therefore left alone to face the new House of Commons
—'full of boys and all sorts of strange men,' Greville described it,[4]
of new members pledged to Reform, Whigs and Radicals full of hope
and confidence, and Ultra-Tories thirsting for revenge on their
apostate leaders. At the last moment, however, an offer of support came from an unexpected quarter. Sir James Graham and
Mr. Stanley secretly approached the Government, through
Wellington's tame cat, Mr. Arbuthnot, and offered their alliance,
if they were assured that a moderate Reform bill should be part
of the official programme. They did not ask for much—the

---

[1] Peel to Hobhouse, 24th November, 1830. *Peel Papers*, British Museum,
40,401, p. 290.

[2] Maxwell, *Wellington*, ii. p. 252.   [3] Parker, *Graham*, i. p. 86.

[4] *Greville*, ii. p. 30.

immediate grant of representatives to Manchester, Leeds, and Birmingham, and the admission of the principle that in future, when a borough was disfranchised for corruption, its seat or seats should be given to a large unrepresented town. Peel would probably have been only too glad to accept this offer; but the matter was taken out of his hands.

The Government had begun very badly: the Ministers had shown little understanding of the urgent need to allay the excitement under which the country was labouring. The King's Speech struck a wrong note: a reference to foreign affairs was interpreted as meaning that war with France was contemplated, and wild rumours were circulated that the hated Dutch connection was to be restored in Belgium by British arms. As a matter of fact, Peel thought the French revolution not merely justifiable, but necessary; and the views of the Ministers regarding Belgium were probably very much the same as those of Palmerston—though it is very unlikely that they could have carried them out as successfully as he did. In the excited state of opinion, however, the mere suspicion was enough. The greatest disappointment, moreover, had been caused by the failure of the Speech to suggest any remedy for economic distress. Peel believed that the promise —even the vaguest hope—of State assistance always had evil effects in relaxing individual effort: but his habitual caution was very much out of place at this moment. To the nation, shaken with wild hopes and fears, the frigid platitudes of the Speech seemed an insult. Worse, however, was to come.

The offer from Stanley and Graham was made on November 1: on the following day, apparently without the slightest warning to his colleagues, Wellington rose in the House of Lords and announced that in his opinion the Constitution was perfect, and that he would not consent to the smallest measure of Reform—would indeed oppose it to the last. Sitting down, His Grace seemed to feel a little doubtful, and whispered to his neighbour, ' I have not said too much, have I?' Lord Aberdeen stuck out his chin, according to his habit, and answered briefly, ' You'll hear of it.' Leaving the House, Aberdeen met a friend, who inquired what the Duke had said. ' He said that we are going out,' replied the taciturn Scot.

Peel, on the following day, spoke on the same subject so moderately that Graham and Stanley renewed their offer to him individually; but he felt himself bound to Wellington, and it was refused.[1]

In the meantime, the Duke's imbecile declaration had thrown the whole country into agitation. Seditious leaflets were distributed everywhere, some calling upon Englishmen to rise against the new police, while another, headed 'Nice Pickings,' pretended to give an authentic account of the enormous sums of public money distributed to bishops and peers. The King's entry into the City to open Parliament had caused a riot, and it was now rumoured that his visit to the Lord Mayor's Dinner, on November 9th, would be the signal for a more dangerous disturbance. The streets were strewn with placards of a lurid description.

'To Arms!' ran one of these. 'London meets on Tuesday next!... Come armed, be firm, and victory must be ours!' while another declared, 'We assure you from ocular demonstration that 6,000 cutlasses have been removed from the Tower for the use of Peel's bloody gang. Remember the cursed Speech from the Throne! These damned Police are now to be armed. Englishmen, will you put up with this?'

Threatening letters and warnings of conspiracy began to pour into the Home Office in a manner reminiscent of 1820. The Government were told that 10,000 rioters were coming up from Kent to join the mob on Tuesday;[2] that the army could not be depended on, that seditious meetings were being held everywhere;[3] that a 'desperate character... who wears a butcher's knife,' had returned to town. Swing himself sent his compliments to Peel.[4] Wellington had many warnings of a plot to assassinate him as he rode into the City. 'A Lover of Order' wrote to suggest that all loyal householders should be instructed to collect 100 bricks to drop from their windows upon the heads of the rioters below.[5] It was said that the gas-pipes would be cut to facilitate plundering.[6] Every night a crowd assembled at the Rotunda, Blackfriars, to hear inflammatory

[1] Parker, *Peel*, ii, p. 165 ff.

[2] From Lieutenant-Colonel Fairman, 6th November, 1830, H.O. 40, 25.

[3] From Mr. Bayley, 5th November, H.O. 40, 25.

[4] H.O. 40, 25. 'Parliamentary Reform in a full and fair representation of the People or Death!!! Mark this, thou contemptible Cad. Swing to Robert Peel.'

[5] Two anonymous letters, also from J. Williams, 4th November, and from Miss Lowe, 5th November, H.O. 40, 25.

[6] From the Duke of Wellington, 5th November, H.O. 40, 25.

speeches from Cobbett, Taylor, the apostate clergyman, and other Radical leaders; and then, roused to a fine frenzy of Liberal enthusiasm, would break the neighbouring windows and assault the passers-by before going home to bed.[1] Francis Place, in his quiet room, was spinning his threads like a spider in its hole, and brooding on revolution. Joseph Hume himself came to call on Peel with a letter informing him (Hume) that a rising was planned for the 9th, and inviting him to head the populace. 'Penny Wise,' who had no desire to figure as a Desmoulins, came to warn the Government instead.[2] Finally, on the 7th, the Lord Mayor-elect, Key, with another alderman, informed the Government that they could not be responsible for the maintenance of the peace on Tuesday, and demanded military aid. The Cabinet was in a quandary. If there was a dangerous riot, they would be blamed for allowing the King to visit the City; if, on the other hand, they postponed the visit—well, they did postpone the visit, and the results were startling enough.

The funds, which had dropped four points since Parliament

---

[1] Magistrate's Report, 10th November, H.O. 40, 25.

[2] H.O. 40. 25. This letter is such a curious example of the mentality of the lowest type of Radical that I print it below. ' Joseph Hume, Esq. Honble. Sir, Your being the representative of the Metropolitan County which will no doubt take the lead in the forthcoming events and you have already proved yourself the uncompromising friend of the people, and against Wm. and his Government by telling Peel to his face and before the whole world that you and your friends (the people) were ready to " overwhelm in utter destruction the whole government" it has been deemed right to furnish you with the enclosed ' (no enclosure) ' in order that you may be aware the people are ready to follow you when you call for their services—for who can but be ready to sacrifice his life in exterminating those Tyrants, after having read the Nice Pickings, and I can assure you they have been circulated through every City Town and Hamlet in the United Kingdom and read by almost every poor man who is capable of reading, and for the benefit of those who cannot we have established a mutual instruction society which meets at No. 30 Wilderness Row St. Luke's. We thought at first of inviting Mr. O'Connell or Mr. Brougham but we cannot but be mistrustful of lawyers although both have used very appropriate language this Session—perhaps you would have the kindness to let them know what we are doing—at least we shall leave that entirely to you—Our Committee the Union Society meet every evening and have called a public meeting for Monday evening at the Rotunda Blackfriars Bridge Mr. Hunt has promised to take the chair—it is in order that our friends may know their strength for the following Evening when the King comes to the City Feast. We hope you will be ready to take the lead—we intend attacking St. James as soon as the soldiers are in their barracks—our friends at Manchester will furnish pikes and we expect assistance from Kent to the amount of 8 or 10 thousand—Cobbett's lectures on the French Revolution are attended by thousands and they have enlightened the people very much. I am Honble. Sir your most sincere friend William Chubb. 18 Holywell St, Strand.'

met, fell three more. The Ministry was violently attacked by Whigs and Radicals. Peel, when he came down to the House, was very ill received. His announcement of the threats to assassinate Wellington was greeted with incredulous laughter and sarcastic cheers. Alderman Waithman announced that the action of Key and his friend had not been authorised by the Court of Aldermen. Hume did not scruple to join in the attack. ' I might have risen and crushed him, the impudent dog,' said Peel afterwards.[1] It was generally declared that the King could have gone with perfect safety, and that Ministers had only shrunk from exhibiting their own unpopularity : to these accusations Peel replied, ' I will submit to any taunt founded on the obloquy or objectionable character of the Ministry among the people, rather than give them any cause for excitement which I can possibly avoid.' Ministers had not anticipated any personal danger to the King : but the presence of enormous crowds, including women and children, in the streets, on a dark November evening, offered the chance of a tragedy which they would not risk.[2]

The action of the Ministry has generally been considered a grotesque blunder—' The boldest piece of cowardice I ever heard of,' Lord Wellesley called it. As a matter of fact, whatever they had done would probably have led to disaster for themselves. There was certainly some sort of absurd scheme afoot among the lowest class of Radical : the letter to Hume indicates this, and so do the papers found on a young man, William Knight, who led a riot in London on the night of the 8th.[3] If the King had gone, there would probably have been rioting, not perhaps dangerous, but still sufficient to give an excuse for blaming the Government for having allowed the procession to take place.

As it was, the action had made their position hopeless, and their fate was only a question of time. On the 15th they were defeated by a considerable majority, partly composed of the revolted Ultras,

---

[1] Peel told the story to Disraeli some time afterwards. Monypenny, *Disraeli*, i. p. 202. Dizzy thought he ought to have denounced Hume and produced the letter. In regard to his own later relations with Peel, this opinion is interesting.

[2] *Speeches*, ii. p. 238.

[3] These papers included various incendiary placards of the ' Liberty or Death ' type ; a will, leaving his pistols to his father, his body to make a barricade, etc., an original effusion beginning ' Oh, Anti-Christian ! How my heart glows when I hear thy name,' etc. ; and a new tricolour cockade wrapped in tissue paper.

on the Civil List. On the following day Peel came in, 'looking very pale indeed,'[1] and announced the resignation of the Government. There was no cheering : the House was almost awed at the thought that the long Tory domination was ended at last.

Peel himself left office without regret. 'Whatever may be the result of Tuesday next,' he wrote to his brother on the eve of the Civil List debate, 'I think it is better for the country and better for ourselves that *we* should not undertake the question of reform.'[2] But he seems to have felt bitterly enough both towards his enemies and towards his friends. 'I certainly do not envy,' he wrote to Lord Egremont, ' the situation of those who have excited public expectation and public discontent, by complaining of the amount of the military establishment, by urging the necessity and the easy duty of making great additional reductions, if they intend, on undertaking the administration of public affairs, to fulfil the expectations they have raised.'[3] The whole of this passage, which is dated ' 2 a.m.,' was cancelled by the writer : we are all apt to be a little indiscreet at 2 a.m.

To Henry Hobhouse he said frankly what he thought of his party. ' It was better that this should happen than that we should continue to administer the Government in difficult times without the requisite support. . . . Our own party saw no injustice in requiring that the same persons who did the effective business of the Government should also do the mere drudgery of attendance in the House of Commons, and remain there three or four hours every night with a miserable attendance. Four Cabinet Ministers have sons in the House of Commons—the Duke of Wellington, Lord Rosslyn, Lord Bathurst, Lord Melville—not one of these sons ever opened his lips, and they could only serve us by attendance and a silent vote. But on the night which determined the fate of the Government—and terminated the official existence of their fathers, *NOT ONE* (*sic*) of those sons—though all were in town—voted on that night. Can I personally regret the end of such a Government ? '[4]

[1] *Hobhouse*, iv. p. 67.

[2] To William Peel, 12th November, 1830. *Peel Papers*, British Museum, 40,401, p. 267.

[3] To Lord Egremont, 18th November, 1830. *Peel Papers*, British Museum, 40,401, p. 287. As it proved, the Whigs, who had persistently urged military reductions, largely increased the army in their first budget.

[4] To Henry Hobhouse, 24th November, 1830. *Peel Papers*, British Museum, 40,401, p. 290.

CHAPTER VIII

THE STRUGGLE FOR REFORM, 1830-1832.

THE Ministry formed by Lord Grey in November, 1830, was the most aristocratic of the nineteenth century. At first only four Cabinet Ministers sat in the House of Commons, though two more were eventually added. Of these, Althorp and Stanley were heirs of earldoms ; John Russell was the younger son of a Duke ; Palmerston an Irish peer ; and Grant and Graham wealthy land-owners of old family. There was one exception, however, to the prevailing tone. Henry Brougham's father had been a north country squireen ; his mother was the daughter of an Edinburgh lodging-house keeper. In the gallery of contemporary portraits, among the high-bred, cultured, bland—and, alas, frequently vacant—faces of his colleagues, the strange and fierce face of Brougham burns like a torch—the man of the people, the man of genius. He was the great Radical, Old Wicked-Shifts, the head and front of the Reform Movement : his aristocratic colleagues hated and feared him, but they dared not do without him. Grey, indeed, ventured to offer him the Attorney-Generalship ; but a hardly-veiled threat soon brought his lordship to heel, and next day—' Brougham Lord Chancellor,' wrote John Cam Hobhouse in his diary, ' Reform of Parliament, Anti-Slavery, Law Reform, Useful Knowledge Society, *Edinburgh Review*, Hail and fare-well ! ! ! ' [1] For Hobhouse, no more than anyone else, guessed how far the new Government meant to go in the way of Reform.

The system whose reform was so loudly demanded was, like most English institutions at this time, out of date. Like them, it had grown up in a somewhat haphazard fashion and was full of confusions and anomalies.

The representation of the English counties was the healthiest part of it. Each county returned two members, save Yorkshire, which since 1821 returned four. The general franchise was that of the 40s. freeholder, which in England had not been exploited

---

[1] *Hobhouse*, iv. p. 71.

as in Ireland. The electorate was too large and scattered for bribery. The county voters, who numbered some 130,000, were generally free from corruption, and the 92 members whom they returned were the most independent in the House.

Very different was the state of the borough membership, which had been untouched for centuries past—for Cromwell's reforms had been swept away with the Restoration. Towns called upon by the Plantagenets and the Tudors to send representatives had dwindled and vanished ; but they still returned their two members apiece. New towns, great and thriving, had grown up ; but they had no voice in Parliament. The franchise varied from town to town : there was no general qualification as in the counties.

In 43 boroughs the members were returned by a close corporation, sometimes self-elected, frequently existing for this purpose alone, and having allowed all its other functions to lapse.

Then there were the burgage boroughs, where a tenement held in the town qualified the holder to vote. In one case the burgages were seven or eight black stones in a nobleman's park wall. In the classic instance of Old Sarum, there was no house left in the town, and the seven burgage holders came from a distance to vote in a tent put up in an open field.

In 62 boroughs all freemen voted. Freedom could be acquired by inheritance, apprenticeship, marriage with a freeman's daughter, or by election of the corporation. Such a franchise might be democratic in a large town ; in a small one it offered special facilities for corruption.

In the scot-and-lot and potwalloper boroughs generally every resident not a pauper voted. The great democratic constituencies, such as Westminster, generally belonged to this order. There were 59 in all.

The small decayed boroughs had fallen entirely into the control of local potentates. In 1827 Croker estimated for Canning that 33 Tory landowners between them returned 116 members, at the head being Lord Lonsdale, who controlled no less than 9 seats ; while about 30 Tories returned one member each. Whig landlords controlled about 73 seats. The influence of the patron of course varied from place to place. In such a case as Old Sarum he had little to do but nominate his candidate. The nursing of the larger pocket-boroughs, however, might be an expensive business. The patron must do all his shopping there, encourage local industries, grab whatever places he could for his constituents, and be prepared to bribe if necessary in a cruder manner.[1]

Both patrons and corporations sold their boroughs. In 1811 Joseph Hume bought a pocket-borough for £3,000 : the patron broke the contract, and turned him out at the next election, whereon Hume sued him for damages and won his case, getting back his money.

Corruption, however, was not confined to the pocket-boroughs. In most cases of contested elections, both parties bribed freely, and also used intimidation. In 1822 an election candidate at Lynn hired a hundred navvies, armed them with clubs, and set them to drive his opponent's supporters from the hustings. Westminster, not long before this, was said to be the largest democratic constituency in England, and the most easily bribed.

These evils were partly due to the unequal distribution of seats throughout the country. The industrial revolution had altered the balance of population in England, shifting it from the south to the north ; but the south still returned the majority of representatives to Parliament. The County of Cornwall returned 44 members and the whole of Scotland 45.

In Scotland the representative system was a farce. The county members were returned by a handful of electors, the town members by corporations. There was no vulgar bribery in Scotland, because it was unnecessary : the members were managed by patronage. Scottish affairs were left entirely to the Lord Advocate ; in general, the members voted at his nod. On Scottish questions, however, they combined in a solid phalanx that often carried the day. In this manner, while the people of Scotland were powerless to express their opinions in the imperial Parliament, they contrived to get much more than their share of the imperial patronage. The representation of Wales, on the other hand, was very largely independent and the electorate uncorrupt.

How was it, then, that such a man as Peel could defend this system warmly to the last, and wished to concede only the most moderate reform to public opinion ?

It has been seen that a threefold reform was necessary : public opinion demanded that corruption should be ended, that the

[1] A number of these pocket-boroughs belonged to no individual, but were in the control of the Treasury.

pocket-boroughs should be swept away, and that there should be a redistribution of seats upon fair principles. How did these three questions appear to Peel in 1830 ?

Political corruption, though increased by the condition of the unreformed Parliament, was not entirely caused by it. The proof of this is that corruption did not end with the Reform Act of 1832. At the first election under the new system corruption was widespread. Direct bribery of electors is said to have continued until the passing of the Corrupt Practices Act of 1883. Even at the present day political corruption is not dead, though it may have taken other and less conspicuous forms. Even the improvement which has undoubtedly taken place is not due to the reform of Parliament only. It is due to the spread of education, to the gradual elevation of public opinion, to the institution of a cheap press and rapid internal communication, to the great increase of population, and even to the influence of individual statesmen, including Peel himself, who stood out against corrupt practices in high places. In the old days it was only on questions of extreme national importance that the ordinary elector could or did take any interest in politics. There were no cheap newspapers to bring him the daily news, he rarely saw reports of the proceedings of Parliament, he knew little or nothing of what was going on in the world beyond his own country town. Under these circumstances, what should he do but sell his vote to the highest bidder, or vote at the orders of the great man of the neighbourhood ? But, in a great national crisis, when the issues were set clearly and simply before him, the elector often did vote as his opinions dictated, and even the rotten borough might revolt against its patron. Peel saw this : and he believed that legal enactments could do little to check corruption, and that only the progress of education and of a higher morality could remove it. No doubt he underrated, as he often did, the power of legislation in aiding and forming public opinion : it is difficult to judge of this impartially, for the tendency of the present day is probably to overrate the influence of such legislation as much as he underrated it.

Peel, as has been seen, loathed political corruption, and used all his influence against it. In the various cases that had come before the House of Commons in his time he had voted for the disfranchisement of boroughs convicted of corruption, and in the case of Penryn he had showed himself satisfied with much less evidence than was required by others.[1] But he thought it highly unjust to disfranchise by Act of Parliament any borough, however small, that had not actually been convicted of corrupt practices.

To the pocket-borough as such Peel had no objection—in fact, he thought it most necessary. The pocket-boroughs may be roughly divided into two classes—those where the patron nominated the members, and those where the seats were for sale. The first class constituted the means by which the great landlords maintained their influence : and Peel thought that the aristocracy ought to have a decisive vote in the councils of the nation. He saw the relation between landlord and tenant in a romantic light— kind protection and guidance on the one hand, affectionate gratitude and loyalty on the other.[2] It is possible that this relationship may have existed more frequently than some critics of the unreformed Parliament would have us believe.

The marketable pocket-borough and the treasury borough were almost indispensable elements in the political system as Peel saw it. By means of these boroughs (and through the action of private patrons also) young men of promise were brought into Parliament at a very early age, and were thus enabled to receive a long professional training, both in office and in parliamentary tactics.[3] To these boroughs the worn and exhausted Minister of State turned for relief, when he could not undertake the labour of representing a popular constituency and the excitement of an election fight : to these turned for aid the Minister unseated at a bye-election. Peel himself owed a great deal to the borough-mongering system. He had entered Parliament for the pocket-borough of Cashel, exchanged it a few years later for a similar seat in England, and, when the University of Oxford threw him out in 1829, the close borough of Westbury had received him [4] (with a shower of missiles, it is true, but any port in a storm !). A whole string of eminent names were associated with the close boroughs : Fox, Pitt, Burke, Perceval,

---

[1] *Speeches*, ii. p. 257. [2] *Speeches*, ii. p. 278-9.

[3] E. and A. Porritt, *The Unreformed House of Commons*, p. 313 ff., have collected a good deal of evidence to show that the part played by the pocket-borough in bringing clever young men into politics has been much exaggerated. I am not concerned with the correctness of this reasoning (though it does not seem to me entirely conclusive), but am trying to present the subject from Peel's point of view.

[4] *Speeches*, ii. p. 279. In 1830 Peel was invited to represent the great popular constituency of Liverpool, in succession to Huskisson, and refused it, as the work entailed would have been too much for him.

Canning, Wellesley, Plunket, Huskisson, Brougham, Horner, Romilly, Liverpool, Hume, Macaulay entered political life by this means. Canning, when his health began to fail, sought refuge in such a borough. Sheridan, Wyndham, Tiernay, Castlereagh, and Grey, entering the House of Commons originally for great constituencies, had exchanged them for pocket-boroughs.

Besides this, the pocket-borough brought into Parliament a type of man almost unknown to-day—the independent member. Anyone who had enough money could buy a seat and hold it unfettered by party or patron. By this means a remarkable infusion of bold and original opinion was brought into the House. The reformed Parliament offered less opportunity to such men : what independent member of to-day ever had a hundredth part of the influence and reputation of Hume or Romilly, Mackintosh or Brougham ? Such men were usually critics, often adversaries, of the Tory Government ; but Peel was capable of seeing that their presence was both a sign and a cause of a healthy political life.

Upon the third point—the redistribution of seats—there was less disagreement between Peel and the Reform party. He thought the great unrepresented towns ought to be enfranchised— only he did not wish to acknowledge, as a universal principle, that population should be the basis of representation. Wealth and intelligence, and not mere numbers, he thought, should be the decisive influence in politics. He hardly realised, perhaps, how, in the eyes of the nation, the landed aristocracy had failed to justify the exclusive power that had been placed in their hands, and how selfishness and class legislation had alienated the minds of the people from them : he was to realise it later.

Yet it must always be remembered that the old system, if it gave an unduly large share of influence to the landlord, did not exclude any class, except the agricultural labourer, from representation. Under it there were democratic constituencies such as did not exist again until the very end of the nineteenth century. It had a crudely practical way of securing minority representation, more effective than any of the elaborate systems since devised by theorists. The farmer, the mercantile interest, and the town labourer all returned their own members, and could make their voices heard. Even women were not entirely disfranchised : a woman could hold the freedom of a city, and often did, and in the freeman boroughs women could transfer their vote to a male relative. Peel saw the old system as a national council where every class could make its voice heard and its grievances known, but where the casting vote was in the hands of the educated and wealthy classes.

Deep as was his attachment to the old constitution, however, he fully realised that some reform was necessary. He had never pledged himself against Reform as he had against Catholic Emancipation. As early as 1819 he seems to have felt that Reform must come some day.[1] Later, he had been willing to transfer Penryn's seats to Manchester, and to disfranchise East Retford. As soon as he left office, and was no longer pledged to Wellington, he publicly declared himself not unfavourable to Reform. ' He had always contended,' he said, ' that the franchise was given for a public purpose, and that the House had a right to dispose of it when that would benefit the public. He had taken no part in any former debate that should preclude him . . . from transferring a franchise from a corrupt borough to Birmingham or any other large unrepresented town. . . . He had reserved himself full liberty to give the franchise to great towns on any fitting occasion.'[2] These words were but little pleasing to his Tory friends ; but, indeed, his whole course of conduct at this time puzzled and angered them.

The Whigs found themselves faced with the usual difficulties that beset a party coming into power after long opposition. They had attributed the disorders of the country to the misgovernment of their predecessors ; but the disorders continued, and they were soon forced to use such measures as would have exposed any Tory Government to virulent attack. Troops were rushed from every side into the revolted agricultural provinces, a special commission was appointed to try the rioters, and they were punished with a relentless savagery, a hundredth part of which, if exercised by the local magistrates at the beginning, might have nipped the insurrection in the bud. The Whigs had repeatedly accused their predecessors of extravagance, but on investigation they found that Peel's late economies had been so drastic that it was only with great trouble that something under £1,000,000 could be pared off the estimates. The late Government had fallen on the Civil List : Peel had saved £85,000 on it,[3] and the Whigs only managed

---

[1] Plumer Ward, *Memoirs*, ii. p. 25. [2] *Speeches*, ii. p. 257.
[3] He saved £135,000 nominally, but £50,000 was to go to the Queen.

to scrape off £11,000 more. Althorp felt himself obliged to do something sensational with the budget to satisfy the expectations that had been aroused, but it was very difficult with so small a margin. He reduced a number of duties—on coals, glass, tobacco, newspapers, land auctions, and so forth ; and he replaced the losses with taxes on the transfer of real and funded property, on raw cotton, on passengers in steamboats, on the export of coal, and by removing the preference on Canadian timber, and levelling up the duties on wine. All these proposals were simply asking for criticism. The protectionists objected to the alteration of the timber duties, the wine duties were denounced as an infringement of the Methuen Treaty with Portugal, the steamboat duty was almost prohibitive to poorer passengers, the duty on raw cotton was contrary to all the principles of sound commercial policy and infuriated the cotton masters ; but it was the tax on funded property that had aroused most opposition. The City was at once in an uproar, and the tax was warmly assailed in Parliament. Peel, in an able and moderate speech, pointed out that the duty on landed property would fall, in practice, on bad land and not on good, and that the duty on funded property was a violation of public faith : [1] also he did not fail to point out what would have been said had the Tories proposed to increase the army by 10,000 men, though he supported the proposal to do so. Goulburn drew attention to the fact that a little trifle of £350,000 had been lost to the Government owing to some mistake in calculation. In the end Althorp was obliged to withdraw both his property tax and his timber duties : the honest man's budget had been a lamentable failure.

All Peel's criticisms, however, were moderate, and even friendly in tone. The Tories were much displeased by his conduct. They would have liked to press home the attack against a Government whose weakness offered so many opportunities ; but they could do nothing without Peel, and Peel would have nothing to do with them.

On the day of his resignation he had called a meeting of influential Tories at his house, and informed them that he meant to

[1] Peel has been blamed for this attack, as he later introduced an income tax himself. The income tax, however, was no violation of public faith, for it fell on all sorts of wealth ; while, as the duty on landed property was negligible, Althorp's proposal was practically penalising the fund-holder, who had been definitely promised exemption from taxation. See *Speeches*, ii. p. 264 ff.

retire into private life—' to give no opposition, and not to lead the party—in short, to be his own unfettered man. We did not like that,' said Croker.[1] But like it or not, they had to put up with it. Peel and Wellington had both refused overtures from the Ultras, who were now beginning to be alarmed at the mischief they had done, and who, thus repelled, began to talk wildly of forming a ' Moderate Tory party ' (save the mark !) without either of the leaders.[2] But Peel seems to have been equally estranged from his own followers. He was disgusted and impatient with them, and weary with the strain of the last three years. He was furious with Wellington : [3] who could work with such a colleague ? He had broken up the Government with his insane and uncalled-for declaration on Reform, and the man had not even known what he had done, but went about saying brightly to his friends, ' Lord, I shall not go out ! ' [4] Peel had had enough of such doings : he had stuck to Wellington loyally while they were still in office, but now he meant to have his hands free. He refused to meet the other Tory chiefs when they gathered at Strathfieldsaye to plan their campaign, ' alleging his wife's illness and business with his architect and gardener.' [5]

' I feel a want of many essential qualifications which are requisite in party leaders,' he told Goulburn. ' Among the rest, personal gratification in the game of politics, and patience to listen to the sentiments of individuals whom it is equally imprudent to neglect and an intolerable bore to consult.' [6]

There is little doubt that he intended to break away from his party politically also, and, if the Whig Ministry brought in a moderate Reform Bill, to support it.

' I wanted him,' wrote Croker to Hertford, ' to pledge himself, like the Duke, against all Parliamentary reform, but . . . he will pledge to nothing. He said good-humouredly that he was sick with eating pledges, and would take care to avoid them for the future.' [7]

Peel himself said later, ' I was prepared to make a compromise on the subject, and support a measure of moderate Reform, if

---

[1] *Croker*, ii. p. 77.

[2] *Buckingham Papers*, 3rd series, i. p. 197.

[3] *Greville*, ii. p. 306. Mr. George Peel also told me he had always understood his grandfather was very angry with Wellington on this occasion.

[4] *Greville*, ii. p. 57.   [5] *Croker*, ii. p. 105.

[6] No date except 1830. Parker, *Peel*, ii. p. 170.   [7] *Croker*, ii. p. 101.

such had been introduced.' If this involved a final break with the
Tories, and the temporary shipwreck of his career, he was no doubt
prepared to risk it. ' Oh, believe me, my own dearest life, my
heart is set upon home, and not upon ambition,' he had written
to his wife on taking office three years before.[1] During the
summer of 1830 his father had died, leaving him heir to a baronetcy
and £30,000 a year.[2] He had no temptation to political life, save
love of power or sense of duty.

He cannot, however, have had much fear of disaster. It must
be remembered that Stanley and Graham were influential members
of the new Government, and he had good reason to think that the
proposed reform would be on the lines which they had traced for
him. Even if it went too far for his taste, he probably thought
that he would be well able to control and modify it. He had always
great confidence in himself, and his position and influence in the
House were at this time almost unparalleled. ' All agree that the
Government holds its seat at the mercy of Sir Robert Peel,' Croker
wrote ; and Greville remarked, ' Peel plays with his power in the
House, only not putting it forth because it does not suit his convenience ; but he does what he likes, and it is evident that the
very existence of the Government depends on his pleasure. His
game, however, is to display candour and moderation, and rather
to protect them than not, so he defends many of their measures,
and restrains the fierce animosity of his friends, but with a sort of
sarcastic civility, which, while it is put forth in their defence, is
always done in such a manner as shall best exhibit his own authority and his contempt for their persons individually.' [3] He may
have dreamed of finding himself at the head of a party of moderate
Liberal-Conservatives, such as the Canningites, Stanley, Graham,
and his own immediate followers and friends, Goulburn, Aberdeen,
and a few others—freed at last from the necessity of conciliating
the Ultras, whom he despised, and whom he could not forgive for
their treatment of him in 1829.

Such a combination was not impossible. The Whig Ministers

---

[1] *Private Letters,* p. 103. 4th January, 1828.

[2] Sir Robert Peel died on May 3rd, 1830. ' We saw him this morning
separately,' Peel writes to his wife. ' He was a good deal affected when I went
in to him, cried, and kissed me two or three times. . . . There was an immense concourse of people at the funeral. The whole Corporation of Tamworth attended, 60 tenants on horseback.' *Private Letters,* pp. 119, 122.

[3] *Greville,* ii. p. 119.

were united only upon the subject of Parliamentary Reform ; and
even here they differed as to details. They appointed a small
committee to draw up a scheme of reform—Sir James Graham,
Lord Durham, Lord Duncannon, and Lord John Russell. The
association of these four minds appeared to have a stimulating
influence. The little committee drew up a bill of much wider
scope than any member of the Government, perhaps, had originally contemplated. It disfranchised completely all boroughs of
less than 2,000 inhabitants ; deprived of one member all those of
less than 4,000 ; introduced vote by ballot and five-year Parliaments ; gave five new members to Scotland, five to Ireland, and
one to Wales, and added 55 to the English counties and 44 to
great unrepresented English towns, out of the 167 seats available
by disfranchisement ; finally, it levelled up the franchise all over
the country—in the counties, 40s. freeholders, £50 leaseholders,
and £10 copyholders were the voters; in the towns, the £20 householders only. When the bill was laid before the Cabinet, two
important alterations were made—Grey objected to the ballot,
and it was struck out ; Brougham succeeded in reducing the town
voter's qualification to £10, and would have introduced household
suffrage if he could.

The bill was a curious mixture of Radical reform and reaction.
As it originally stood, it was as much a measure of disfranchisement
as of enfranchisement ; and even after Brougham's amendment,
it totally disfranchised the working man. It also offered no real
remedy against corruption : the only security, the ballot, was
removed by Grey's intervention. On the other hand, it went far
further than anyone had imagined possible in its reorganisation
of the representative system. By increasing the county voters
and the county members, it secured the influence of the landed
interest as a whole ; but by sweeping away the close boroughs
almost entirely, it broke the power of the landed aristocracy ; and
by the enfranchisement of new towns, it gave the commercial
middle class at least an equal voice with the land.

The very daring of the scheme silenced opposition in the
Cabinet : a less sweeping measure would probably have been more
freely criticised and amended. The Ministers were startled, yet
allured. When Althorp told Stanley the details of the measure,
he burst into an incredulous laugh.[1]

[1] *Hobhouse*, iv. p. 93.

On the 1st of March, 1831, Lord John Russell introduced the bill in the House of Commons. He was not a Cabinet Minister, but he had been chosen for this important task because for ten years past he had identified himself with the cause of Reform, introducing resolution on resolution, and bill after bill. He was the younger son of the Duke of Bedford, a delicate child, who had had to be removed from his public school and educated by a private tutor. He was now thirty-nine years old, a slight, pale, stunted little man, who looked as if he had been starved in the cradle. No one, however, could look at John Russell without seeing that here was a remarkable man : the eyes sparkling with intelligence and pugnacity ; the thin, close-shut lips hinting of resolution, even of obstinacy ; the whole outline of face and head, so keen, alert and vivacious, like that of a high-bred hound—all gave promise of a great career.

The secret had been well kept, and the House was on tenterhooks to hear the bill. As Russell outlined the great scheme, his audience sat at first sunk in mute astonishment. The Whigs themselves were startled ; one turned to his neighbour, repeating in an agitated whisper, ' They're mad ! They're mad ! ' Amazement gave place to anger and mockery, and finally, when the speaker, pausing with a smile at his gaping adversaries to say, ' More yet ! ' read aloud the list of boroughs to be disfranchised, the Tories burst into yells of derisive laughter, drowning the halfhearted cheers of the bewildered Whigs. There was one Tory, however, who did not laugh. Peel had listened almost with stupefaction : his opponents, watching him curiously, saw him turn slowly crimson ; until at last, as if unable to control himself, he bent forward and hid his face in his hands.[1]

He was overwhelmed at the magnitude of the disaster, the more so as his keen mind at once realised the bold bid for success that the Whigs had made. Probably he had never given them credit for half the unscrupulous daring (as he thought it) or for half the statesmanship that they had displayed. By making their reform so radical, they had carried it beyond all reach of his power to modify it. They had made a bid for popular support that would rally all the lower and middle classes round them and must carry them to success by sheer weight of numbers. He could not support such a reform—he was thrown back into the clutch of the

[1] *Hobhouse*, iv. p. 87. Le Marchant, *Althorp*, p. 299, note.

party from which he had been striving to escape ; but he could not oppose it, either, with any hope of success. He saw the old Constitution, the old England of his younger years, go down, as it seemed to him, to red ruin, and his own hopes with it.

Two days of hot debate passed before Peel spoke, and ' the whole House of Commons looked with unutterable anxiety to his opinions and conduct.' [1] When at last he rose, his speech was moderate in tone, but uncompromisingly hostile to the bill. He attacked it at its weakest point—the disfranchisement clauses. What right, he contended, had the Government to disfranchise boroughs that had not been convicted of corruption ? More, what right had they to sever all connection between the working man and the representation ? Did they think the workman would tamely acquiesce in his disfranchisement ? If so, they were much mistaken. He would claim the rights of which he had been deprived, and, once the principle of equal representation had been admitted, there would be no grounds for refusal, and the progressive advance of democracy would be irresistible. ' If you were establishing a perfectly new system of representation, would it be wise to exclude altogether the sympathies of this class ? How much more unwise, when you find it possessed from time immemorial of the privilege, to take the privilege away, and to subject a great, powerful, jealous, and intelligent mass of your population to the injury, ay, and to the stigma, of entire uncompensated exclusion ? ' He admitted that if he had to choose between the £10 qualification and the potwallopers' franchise, he would prefer the former— but he had not to choose : under the present system he could have both. He taunted the Ministers with having deliberately raised the storm of public agitation which they now declared to be irresistible ; and again denied that he was opposed to reform, and declared his willingness to support a moderate measure.[2]

He had by now rallied from the first shock and begun to hope that a successful resistance was after all possible. What he hoped for was a reaction of public opinion, when the nation began to realise that the great bill meant the disfranchisement of the poor man. If only time could be gained, this reaction might come. ' Give us another month,' he wrote to Croker on April 15, ' and there is an end to the bill, positively an end to it. . . . One month hence, if the bill is still in suspense, there will be an enforced

[1] *Greville*, ii. p. 125.   [2] *Speeches*, ii. p. 276.

natural union between aristocracy and disfranchised population.' [1] But he did not get his month.

In these hopes he spoke out boldly in the House for a moderate
reform, wishing to strengthen the moderate men of all parties—
but infuriating the Tories. He had refused another offer from the
Ultras, who in their agony were appealing to the political dead—
Eldon and Sidmouth—for the help they could not get from the
living.[2] He still held aloof from his party. Wellington knew
nothing of his plans or opinions. ' My belief is, that he wishes to
defeat the bill. He may think some reform desirable, but of that
I am not certain,' [3] the Duke wrote.

On March 22 the bill had passed its second reading by a majority
of one, at four in the morning, the Whigs in hysterics of delight,
laughing, weeping, yelling, waving their hats, the Tories in a cold
fury—' and the jaw of Peel fell, and the face of Twiss was as the
face of a damned soul, and Herries looked like Judas taking off his
necktie for the last operation,' while passage, stair, and street were
thronged with people, waiting till the news was out. ' Is the bill
carried, sir ? ' said the driver of the cab hailed by young Mr. Macaulay, the member for Calne, who was making such a brilliant
reputation. ' Yes, by one.' ' Thank God for it, sir ! ' [4]

The real struggle, however, would be fought in committee ;
and the Tories were resolute not to be beaten again. On
April 18th a resolution proposed by a Tory member, that the
number of representatives for England and Wales be not reduced,
was carried against the Government by a majority of eight. Three
days later Lord Althorp announced the dissolution of Parliament.

A dissolution was what Peel ultimately desired—but not too
soon ; not before the hoped-for reaction had taken place and the
enthusiasm for Reform had died down. ' Peel looked exceedingly
foolish,' Hobhouse notes.[5] Once again he was taken aback by the
boldness and determination of the Government. He was accustomed to be an unpopular Minister, and he did not realise what.
men might dare who knew that they had the nation at their back.
There was still, however, a faint hope. The House of Lords was
preparing an address to the Crown, protesting against the dissolution. The Government learned this on the following day

[1] *Croker*, ii. p. 114.   [2] *Buckingham Papers*, 3rd series, i. pp. 272-3.
[3] *Buckingham Papers*, 3rd series, i. p. 275.
[4] Trevelyan, *Macaulay*, p. 147.   [5] *Hobhouse*, iv. p. 103.

(April 22), and determined to strike before the address could be carried. They asked the King to come and dissolve Parliament in person, which could be done without a moment's delay. William was annoyed at the attempt of the Lords to interfere with his prerogative, and, moreover, he thoroughly enjoyed such an escapade as this. It is said that an attempt was made to delay his arrival by pretending that the State carriage was out of order, whereon he declared he would go in a hackney coach.

The two Houses met early in the afternoon, having just learned their fate. Such a scene followed as had not been paralleled since that wild day in 1629 when Denzil Holles and the rest held the Speaker in his Chair, with Black Rod hammering at the door. Sir Richard Vyvyan, an old Tory and an intolerable bore, had got the floor, and denounced the bill. He was called to order by the Whigs at every sentence, and every other moment the discharge of the cannon announcing the King's progress interrupted him. Still he struggled on, till the yells and groans and cheers and laughter, and the continual booming of the guns, became too much, and he sat down suddenly. Peel, Althorp, and Burdett were all on their feet together : each party yelled for its champion : cries of ' Bar ! Order ! Shame, shame ! ' drowned the voices of the orators. Peel stormed, Althorp, according to his admirers, stood in haughty calm ; though by the less partisan testimony of *Hansard* he gesticulated wildly. The Speaker, crimson with rage, at last shouted down the uproar, and called on Peel, who had now lost all self-control. ' His speech was such as completely unmasked him,' wrote Hobhouse. ' All his candour, all his moderation, all his trimming, shifty policy disappeared. . . .' [1]

He was not, like some, afraid of dissolution, he said. ' He had better hopes for England. He did not advise his countrymen to sit with their hands before them, patiently expecting the confiscation of their funded property. He had a proper confidence in the good sense, and intelligence, and just appreciation of character of the people of England ; and he was satisfied, that if they united religiously in a just cause, and unite he knew they would, that there were no fears of a successful issue to that struggle into which they were about to enter. . . . If they carried that bill . . . they would introduce the very worst and vilest species of despotism—the despotism of demagogues. . . .' He denounced

[1] *Hobhouse*, iv. p. 106.

the dissolution. 'Ministers had adopted this course to protect their places ; and they held them with the established character, in the eyes of the country, of having . . . exhibited more incapacity—more unfitness for the conduct of public business than was ever shown by any Ministry that attempted to hold power in England. . . . Not a single measure had emanated from them, from the day they took office till that moment, for the benefit of the country. . . . They had tossed on the table some bills—a Game bill and an Emigration bill—and after having established, with respect to them and other measures, what they called liberal principles, they abandoned them to their fate. What, then, was to be——' [1] At this moment the speaker's voice was drowned in a general cry of 'Bar !' John Cam Hobhouse, from across the House, was signalling to him to stop and not make a fool of himself,[2] but he was still speaking when Black Rod appeared and summoned the Commons to the King's presence. The scene in the upper House was even wilder, various eminent peers having almost come to blows when the King's arrival separated them. Lyndhurst had rushed from the bench of the Court of Exchequer to join in the row. Sidmouth, meeting Lord Grey, said to him, " I hope God will forgive you for this bill, for I cannot ! "

That night London was illuminated, and the mob marched through the streets and broke the windows of the Tory chiefs. The election took place in the midst of a frenzy of excitement. The result was not for a moment in doubt : Peel, in spite of his boasts, seems to have abandoned hope from the moment the dissolution was announced. 'I never doubted . . . that royalty and physical strength combined must carry all before them,' he wrote to Henry Hobhouse ; and he advised him and other Tory candidates to withdraw from a hopeless contest, and save their money for another occasion.[3] Peel himself came in for Tamworth (he had fled from Westbury at the first opportunity) unopposed, but elsewhere the party fared ill. Vyvyan, Knatchbull, Gascoyne, Bankes, and most of the Ultras were turned out. Peel's two brothers and his brother-in-law lost their seats. Tory candidates were hooted and pelted, Tory voters assaulted and driven

---

[1] *Speeches*, ii. p. 309.

[2] ' I waved, and shook my head, as if to show him, in no unfriendly manner, that he was doing harm to himself and injuring the character of the country.' *Hobhouse*, iv. p. 105.

[3] 9th May, 1831, *Peel Papers*, British Museum, 40,402, p. 43.

from the polls, pocket-boroughs revolted against their patrons. Under the influence of the general excitement, Peel sent a challenge to John Cam Hobhouse for expressions used in a public speech. Hobhouse, who seems to have regarded his own remarks as the usual small change of electioneering, and was in general friendly enough to Peel, was much astonished, but apologised and withdrew sufficient for the affair to be ended peacefully.

When the new House of Commons met, on June 21, it was at once obvious that the Reformers had a large majority. The Tories did not yet despair : they had no real chance of destroying the bill, but they could at least delay it. They had, too, a faint hope that on some isolated point it might be possible to combine with the Radicals against the moderate Whigs and turn out the Government—what was to come after, they cared not. They wasted the time of the House, and exasperated the country, with aimless and malignant discussion ; and the passage of the bill was protracted for weeks.

With these proceedings Peel had little concern. He knew the bill must pass. He thought it a bad bill, and he thought it his duty to speak against its various stages ; but he would not associate himself with the spiteful and factious tactics of the Tories. He refused to attend the party's political dinner.[1] He had, before Parliament met, made up his mind not to countenance the Tories in their schemes for coalition with the Radicals, and also to refuse to propose a measure of moderate reform himself as an alternative to the bill.

' I will not play that game,' he wrote to Croker, ' which, played by the Ultra-Tories against us, is the main cause of the present evils.' [2] And to Henry Hobhouse he had written, ' At present I am a private man, and, as I am sure I differ as to Reform from the House of Commons . . . I am likely to enjoy the real luxury in public life of acting on my own opinions. There may be no alternative, after the hopes excited, but some Reform, greater than I can approve of ; but the hopes were not excited by me, and I do not therefore feel myself called upon to realise them.' [3] The tone of these letters would lead us to conclude that his momentary

[1] *Herries*, p. 121.

[2] To Croker, 28th May, 1831. Parker, *Peel*, ii. p. 187. Of course he means the combination with the Whigs by which the Ultras turned out the Wellington Government.

[3] 29th May, 1831, *Peel Papers*, British Museum, 40,402, p. 81.

panic had a little abated. Croker remarks, in an undated letter of this year, ' I do not feel, *like Peel*, that the fright goes off by habit.' [1]

The Tories were much disgusted with their leader. They would have thrown him over if there had been anyone whom they could set up in his place. Greville's journal is full of the complaints of these sheep without a shepherd : they did not know what Peel meant ; he would not give them a civil word ; in the midst of one of their most spirited attacks on the Government, he got up and walked out of the House, ' and was heard of no more that night.' [2] Even Croker began to complain presently that Peel's opposition was ' somehow not hearty.' [3] In truth, Peel was tired of the struggle, lonely, and depressed : he had sent his family to the country, and was homesick. ' I have hinted to the committee that I cannot go on staying here to fight the tedious battle, and that they must choose some other leader if the House is to go on sitting much longer,' he wrote to his wife ; and later, ' I went this morning to Charles Street, and told the persons assembled there that I could not undertake to continue in town—that in my opinion there is very little use in protracting the debates on the Reform bill, and that I could not remain here to conduct the battle. . . . We parted not in very good humour.' ' I cannot much longer bear this separation from you ; I get a sort of lassitude and languor here which quite depresses me. The coming home at 2 or 3 in the morning to a desolate house with the prospect of the same thing the next night, the bedroom with your tables and glass, and all the outward marks of habitation, the lonely nursery and the drawing-rooms all silent and unoccupied—are sometimes too much for me.' [4]

At last, at the end of September, the bill passed the Commons. A fortnight later the Lords threw it out on the second reading, and in a few hours the country was in a blaze. The lower House carried, by a great majority, a resolution of confidence in the Government, and of regret for the conduct of the Lords. The leading newspapers came out in mourning. Loyal addresses poured in, urging the Government to proceed with the bill, and they decided to prorogue immediately, that it might be reintro-

---

[1] *Croker*, ii. p. 140.   Italics mine.   [2] *Greville*, ii. p. 164.
[3] *Croker*, ii. pp. 150-3.
[4] *Private Letters*, pp. 133-4-5, August 22, 23, 24, 1831.

duced without delay. Attwood summoned a mass meeting at Birmingham, which passed a resolution to pay no taxes, and votes of thanks to Althorp and Russell. Althorp returned a discreet answer, but the same could not be said of Russell, who made his well-known declaration that ' the whisper of a faction could not prevail over the voice of a nation.' The political unions began to arm themselves with cudgels. Lord Milton told the tax-collector to ' call again.' The mob at Nottingham rose and burned the castle—the property of that arch-Tory, the Duke of Newcastle— and fired the mills and attacked a mansion-house in the neighbourhood, where the lady of the house (it was Byron's old love, Mary Chaworth) was forced to spend the night hiding in the garden, and died as a result of the exposure. Newcastle himself was mobbed in Parliament Street, Londonderry was pulled from his horse and nearly lynched, and Wellington was only saved from a like fate by two old Peninsular veterans, who guarded him through the crowd.

The worst news, however, came from Bristol. Sir Charles Wetherell, the foremost champion of the Ultra-Tories, went to pay his official visit as Recorder of the city. His arrival was the signal for a riot, and he barely escaped in time. The citizens and the corporation looked with complacency on the mob : they were well pleased to give Wetherell a fright. One respectable householder, when asked to act as special constable, violently declared he would not lift a finger to keep Sir Charles from being thrown over the bridge. Thus countenanced, the mob grew bolder : they besieged the Mansion-House. The mayor and magistrates began to be frightened, but they were more frightened of the Government than of the mob. The whole city, in fact, believed that the Whig Ministers secretly approved the political riots, and that whoever took action against the mob would get small thanks for it. They feared to be held responsible for another Peterloo. One magistrate declared that arms must on no account be used against the rioters—if anyone were killed they might be hanged for murder ! Gentlemen who called to offer their services were told that ' every man must act on his own responsibility and defend his own property,' and withdrew in disgust. The officer commanding the handful of troops in the city was of the same mind as the mayor : under his leadership the dragoons fraternised with the rioters, and the few special constables were left unsupported.

On Saturday night the mob sacked the Mansion-House, and such a Sunday as had never been seen in Bristol followed. The gaols were attacked one after the other, and the prisoners swelled the numbers of the mob. No sooner had darkness fallen than they streamed up the hill and fired the Bishop's Palace. The Custom-House, too, was set aflame, and then the rioters began the systematic destruction of the large houses in Queen's Square, gutting and firing each in turn. Not a magistrate was to be found : the mayor had concealed himself in a private house far from the scene of destruction. The householders who had cheered for Reform yesterday trembled through a night of terror. It seemed as if half the town were in flames ; thirty miles away in the surrounding countryside they saw the fire reflected in the midnight sky, and thought the English revolution had begun. Fortunately, there was in Bristol one man who was not afraid of responsibility. Major Mackworth, who happened to be present on leave, went out on Monday morning and joined the troops, who were watching the destruction in a strange apathy. He saw the fire was about to seize upon the shipping in the basin, and he took upon himself to order the dragoons to charge. They obeyed him and he dispersed the mob, set the townsfolk to quench the fire, and galloped into the country for the troops whom the authorities' insane fears had banished on Saturday. Returning, he found that reinforcements had arrived, and the danger was over. Thirty dragoons, led by one resolute man, had crushed the revolt that in another few hours might have destroyed the town and set all England ablaze.[1] The Tories had had their lesson—but so had the Whigs.

The Government were forced to realise the danger of the methods they had adopted, and when Wellington, in his capacity of commander-in-chief, wrote to the King and thoroughly alarmed ' Our Billy,' they at last issued a proclamation against the political unions. The mayor of Bristol was prosecuted : the wretched soldier who had forgotten his military duty in political scruples committed suicide.

Peel had dashed off to Drayton on the first alarm (' to the great disgust of his party, whom he never scruples to leave in the lurch ' [2]), scared at the thought of his little flock within ten miles of revolutionary Birmingham. Thence he wrote to Henry Hob-

[1] See *State Trials*, iii. (new series) Rex *v*. Pinney, for the details given.

[2] *Greville*, iii. p. 211.

house, ' How you must be disgusted at seeing the influence which is now exercised on the councils and destinies of Old England by the whole reptile tribe of spouters at public meetings, newspaper editors, Attwoods, O'Connells, Edmonds, and Lord Durhams. It is quite sickening. . . . I wish you would come and see us here, and watch the tardy progress of my new house. I am just import- ing carbines—I mean to defend the old one as long as I can.' [1] He, like other Tories, dallied for a little with a scheme of forming counter-unions for defence against Radical rioters, but Wellington nipped the project in the bud as unconstitutional.

A small group of Tory peers, led by Harrowby and Wharncliffe, were frightened by the events at Bristol and Nottingham into an attempt at compromise. Peel gave no support to the negotiation —he did not believe the Government meant to compromise : he thought they were playing with Wharncliffe and Harrowby. There was a faint chance of carrying some small amendments to the new bill, and, if this could not be done, he thought there should be a fight to the bitter end and no surrender. ' I am determined to die hard,' he wrote to Hobhouse.[2] The Waverers, as the com- promising peers were called, were afraid that if the Lords threw out the bill opposition would be swamped by the creation of a crowd of Liberal peers, and they were anxious to avoid this at least. Others clung desperately to the hope that the King would refuse to create peers when the time came. Peel did not share this illusion. ' As the King repeatedly said to me—perhaps being the only poetry he ever made—

> I consider dissolution
> Tantamount to revolution,

I have no belief that when the hour of trial comes he will resist the making of peers.' [3] But he thought that this was the lesser evil, and that the dignity of the Lords would be better preserved by their rejecting the bill, and forcing the Government to make the new creation, than by surrendering to avoid it.

In the meantime the Whigs themselves were divided on the subject. The more daring of the Ministers urged a creation of peers sufficient to overwhelm all opposition. The older members

---

[1] 30th November, 1831, *Peel Papers*, British Museum, 40,402, p. 140.
[2] 21st December, 1831, *Ib.* p. 149.
[3] To Croker, 19th November, 1831. Parker, *Peel,* ii. p. 192.

R.P.

did not like this, and the Prime Minister himself was specially averse to it. 'Damn Reform! I wish I had never touched it!' said he : he had been dragged into proceedings that he had never anticipated. He had not had the resolution at first to resist the ardent enthusiasm of his younger colleagues, and now he had not the resolution to take the steps logically necessary to complete the task he had begun. He talked of resigning. 'He did not seem aware that he could not do so without losing his character and risking the ruin of the country,' as his own son, Howick, told John Cam Hobhouse. Palmerston, Melbourne, Richmond, supported Grey. Althorp, Brougham, Durham, were on the other side, and threatened resignation. Althorp was miserable, and talked of shooting himself : 'For God's sake shoot anybody else you like,' said Hobhouse.[1]

The work went steadily on, and, contrary to all expectation, the bill passed its second reading in the Lords : but, on the first evening after the Easter recess, Lyndhurst proposed and carried an amendment against the Government. Grey surrendered to the demands of his colleagues, and proposed to the King the creation of fifty peers. The King refused, Grey resigned, and the King sent for Lord Lyndhurst, who went at once to Wellington.

In the state of public opinion it was absolutely necessary that a Reform bill similar to and extensive as the Whig bill must be carried ; and the King thought his honour pledged to such a measure. If the Tories accepted, they must be prepared to carry such a bill. Wellington, who thought the greatest possible disaster for the country was a Whig Ministry, undertook the Government on these conditions.

This was on May 9. On the following day a meeting of the Tory leaders was held at Lord Stormont's house ; when it was over Peel and Croker met Wellington and Lyndhurst at Apsley House. Croker asked who was to be Prime Minister, and the Duke, with a gesture of the hand, replied, 'That Peel must answer.' Peel said, 'in a tone of concentrated resolution,' that he would have nothing to do with the affair ; he would neither be Prime Minister nor anything else to pass the Reform bill. It was as a moral protest that he had wished the Lords to reject the bill, not because he had had any hope of overturning the Government. Croker next day wrote to beseech him to alter his mind, and, on

[1] *Hobhouse*, iv. p. 190.

the 12th, called at his house, and pled with him for hours ; he tried his friend's temper nearly beyond endurance, but did not shake his resolve.[1]

' I foresee,' was Peel's answer, ' that a Bill of Reform, including everything that is really important, really dangerous in the present bill, must pass.   For me individually to take the conduct of such a bill, to assume the responsibility of the consequences which I have predicted as the inevitable result of such a bill, would be, in my opinion, personal degradation to myself. . . . It is *not* a repetition of the Catholic Question.   I was then in office.   I had advised the concession as a Minister.   I should now assume office for the purpose of carrying the measure to which up to the last moment I have been inveterately opposed.' [2]

Peel being obdurate, the Tories decided to do without him. They offered the Premiership to Harrowby, who refused it ; at last Wellington took it himself, and attempted to form a Government.   Meanwhile London was in a frenzy, and the excitement was rapidly spreading to the provinces.   The King was mobbed on Constitution Hill ; the Queen, who was believed to be at the bottom of his resistance, was abused and vilified.   The *Times* in a leading article urged the people to revolt.   Private houses began to hang out cards with ' No Taxes Paid Here.'   Francis Place, who was under the impression that the Duke would refuse any reform, was planning a revolution : he calculated that even a small band of men could hold up the supplies for London, and that in three days starvation would bring out the whole of the lower classes, ready for any excesses ; the army would be required in London, and meanwhile the Midlands would rise.   As a preliminary he organised a run on the Bank of England, and papered the town with placards that read, ' To Stop the Duke—Go for Gold ! '   The run actually began, and John Cam Hobhouse got a letter from Place to frighten Lord Grey with.[3]

Wellington's mouthpiece in the Commons, Alexander Baring, was shouted down by the infuriated Whigs ; but the decisive moment came when Sir Robert Inglis, an Ultra-Tory respected by all parties for his stainless honour, rose and condemned the Duke's

[1] *Croker*, ii. pp. 154-159.

[2] Peel wrote his answer and handed it to Croker, who read it in his presence. Parker, *Peel*, ii. p. 205.

[3] Wallas, *Place*, pp. 297-313.

attempt as disgraceful and ignoble. Baring hurried to the Duke and threw up his place. The Speaker, when the House broke up, took Peel and Croker in his carriage to Apsley House, where a meeting was hastily convened to consider a hopeless situation. Peel proposed that the Duke should inform the King that he could not form a Government, and that the Tory Peers would withdraw their opposition. All agreed to this, and next morning the Whigs were again in power.

Wellington and Lyndhurst, after bitter and violent speeches of farewell, left the House of Lords, followed by their supporters. Even now, however, the Ministers were not satisfied of their security, and they extorted a definite promise from the King to create whatever number of peers should be necessary. On the following day Althorp announced it to the Commons. But it was not necessary to resort to these extreme measures : the dissentient peers continued to absent themselves, and the great bill passed quietly.

Peel had meantime made his own statement. He spoke in the most complimentary terms of Wellington, but he could not defend his own conduct without condemning that of his friends. His speech was not long, and was confined chiefly to the statement that ' It would not be for my honour, or for the advantage of the country, that I should accept office, on the condition of introducing an extensive measure of reform.' But he repelled with great indignation the accusations, current among his enemies, that ' I was a party to the formation of a phantom Government which should carry the Reform Bill, in the belief that, when that was done, I should step in and build my authority and power upon the ruins of that administration. If there is any gentleman in the House who thinks my conduct open to the slightest suspicion in this respect, I will satisfy him that that was not the motive of the course which I pursued. . . . As, however, some person has stated, that on this subject he defies contradiction, and that I was a party to an understanding such as I have mentioned, I beg leave . . . to declare that it is an infamous falsehood. I look at the circumstances in which the country is placed with much deeper interest than any I can have in my return to office, and I can with truth assert, that this is the last consideration to which I have adverted in any advice I have given in reference to recent events.' [1]

[1] *Speeches*, ii. p. 541.

Althorp in reply, with his usual felicity, declared that ' he thought as highly of the honourable baronet as ever.' This left-handed compliment ' made poor Peel look very foolish and sulky. He did not acknowledge Althorp's civility, but blushed and fidgeted, and was silent.' [1] He was once more in the rather uncomfortable situation of being praised by his adversaries and attacked by his friends. The Tories were furious with him, attributing Wellington's failure entirely to his conduct. As a matter of fact, he had saved the party from irremediable disaster. Whatever the result of the formation of a Tory Government at this moment, it must have been fatal to the welfare of the country. No doubt the master tailor's pocket revolution could have been put down by the army under the leadership of the Duke of Wellington, but it would have roused all the evil passions of civil strife and have left a legacy far more bitter than Peterloo. Moreover, wild though Place's schemes were, it is always possible that his misguided hand might have let loose social revolution upon the country—the great mass of the suffering people might have been sufficient to sweep all before it, and a period of anarchy might have followed. But, even if Wellington had been successful—if Place's rising had fizzled out, and an extensive Reform bill had been forced through the indignant House of Commons—the Tory party would have been ruined in the eyes of the nation. They would have met at the next election a disaster greater than that which overwhelmed the Liberals in 1924. Their reputation would have been in the dirt, and not theirs only ; the whole tone of political life would have been lowered by such a gross disregard of honour and consistency. Wellington had deceived himself. He was not, as Peel clearly saw, in the same position as in 1828. Then he was in office, and a pressing danger called for instant remedy : now he had turned out the Government, against the declared will of the House of Commons. Then the Tories were the only party strong enough to carry the legislation that was needed : now they proposed to take office to carry the very measure which they had so bitterly opposed, and which could have been carried more easily, and with far greater benefit, by their opponents. The Duke's motives were honourable, but he had wilfully blinded himself. It was well for the Tories, and well for Britain, that Peel was not afraid to face the truth.

[1] *Hobhouse*, iv. p. 233.

CHAPTER IX

THE NEW CONSERVATISM, 1833-1835

IT is difficult to-day to realise the sincere horror and dread with which the Tories regarded the great Reform bill and the disastrous results which they anticipated from it : general confiscation of property, the abolition of the House of Lords, and probably that of the Monarchy, the uncontrolled reign of demagogues, were confidently predicted, and some even believed in a Red Terror. Croker, who had sworn a solemn vow never to sit in the degenerate House of Commons (and, for a wonder, kept it), expected to see ' Hume Chancellor of the Exchequer and O'Connell Attorney-General for Ireland ' at once, and wrote plaintively, ' I for one believe that this day twelve months I shall be either in my grave or the workhouse, and hope it may be the former.' [1] Ninety-five years have passed and these predictions are as yet only imperfectly fulfilled : the Tories underrated the conservative instincts of their fellow-countrymen.

Moreover, the bill was a much less democratic measure than its enemies—and indeed many of its supporters—realised. It contained within itself, it is true, the seeds of democratic revolution : it admitted the principle of majority representation, while at the same time it disfranchised the working man, and so far it was pregnant with the threat of further change. But as it stood, it worked no very violent transformation. There was still a very small electorate, and it was now composed almost entirely of the propertied classes—the shopkeeper, the smallholder, and the master tradesman were not likely to promote any very revolutionary measures. It was the methods employed to secure the passage of the bill that had produced an alarming situation and not the bill itself. When gentlemen of position and great lords openly talked of refusing to pay taxes, or of armed resistance, it was small wonder that a disrespect for law and a disposition to threaten and defy authority should spread among the lower classes.

---

[1] Croker to Peel, 11th October, *Peel Papers*, British Museum, 40,320, p. 218.

The Whigs were now a little scared by the devil they had raised, and even some of the old Radicals were undergoing a reaction. The Duke of Bedford was heard to say that the country was faced with anarchy : on this being reported to Wellington, he said with a grin, ' I can tell Johnny Bedford that if we have anarchy, I'll have Woburn ! '   John Cam Hobhouse, at the election, refused to pledge himself to press for further reform, saying that ' only knaves gave pledges, and only fools asked for them.'   Croker met Sir Francis Burdett, and wrote to Peel : ' Talk of you and me as Conservatives ! Why, he beats us both. We ran the whole round of affairs, and we did not find one point to differ on, unless indeed that he would carry everything with a higher and more aristocratical hand than you and I would venture, or perhaps wish to do. . . . I wish I could sketch the utter contempt with which he spoke of " *Mr. Tailor Place*." ' [1]

The Whigs had played a dangerous game, and they knew it. They had deliberately used, and even roused, a spirit of unrest and lawlessness to further their ends.   The wildest and most un-bounded expectations had been awakened—expectations which could not be entirely fulfilled by any Government, and which the Whig Cabinet, for the most part, had no intention of trying to realise.   They had got what they wanted, and now they thought it time to pull up.   But this was easier said than done.   They had to deal, in Parliament, with a strong Radical opposition, hot to try all sorts of experiments, and full of dislike and distrust for the lukewarmness of the Whigs.   Outside Parliament the spirit of unrest was still abroad.   The men in the mines and the potteries, in the spinning mills of Manchester, the forges and furnaces of Sheffield and Carron, the weaving rooms of Coventry and Spital-fields—they whose word, in the last resort, had been decisive—they had not carried the bill only to set the middle classes in the seat whence the landed aristocracy had been hurled.   They had called for parliamentary reform as the means to an end only. They wanted what the Whig Government could not and would not give them—cheap bread and high wages and short working hours—economic freedom, protection from exploitation ; and they had been taught what to do if their wishes were refused them.

At this critical moment what was wanted was time—time to breathe—time for the nation to recover its balance, and for the

[1] 3rd March, 1833, *Peel Papers*, British Museum, 40,320, p. 233.

new House of Commons to gain experience and stability, time for
Government to settle itself once more firmly in the seat. Calm
must be restored before the course of reform could go quietly
forward. At such a moment an unscrupulous adversary could have
added greatly to the embarrassment of the Government, could
perhaps, with so many weapons ready to his hand, have paralysed
their action and even driven them from office. At this moment,
however, the Ministry gained the support they needed from their
late opponent, Sir Robert Peel. His conduct, as Lord John
Russell afterwards admitted, brought the country safely through
a dangerous passage : ' for recourse to faction,' as Peel said proudly,
' or temporary alliances with extreme opinions for the purposes of
faction, is not reconcilable with *Conservative* Opposition.' [1]

' What are we doing ? ' he wrote to Croker a few weeks after the
opening of Parliament. ' We are making the Reform Bill work ;
we are falsifying our own predictions . . . we are protecting the
authors of the evil from the work of their own hands.' [2]

Though they were saved from the worst disaster, the Tories
had met with an awful retribution at the polls. When the new
Parliament met, a poor 149 of them was all that was left, and there
was talk of their abandoning the Opposition Bench to the Radicals :
Cobbett came and plumped himself down there beside Peel, to
the latter's exceeding annoyance.

In this difficult and disagreeable situation Peel at once displayed his statesmanship. ' He went down to the House,' notes
a contemporary diarist, ' that night with the public feeling certainly against him ; he returned home with the tide of popularity
running full in his favour.' [3]

He was aware, he said, of his changed position in the House.
He had stood there before as the leader of a powerful party ; he
was now one of a small minority, and his party, some said, was
destroyed for ever. But, though he still held to his old opinions, he
was sure the House would listen to him with indulgence. He
stated frankly that he had no great confidence in Ministers, but
declared that he would support their policy wherever he conscientiously could—this was no time for party tactics of annoyance
and delay ; he would support them in maintaining the Union
with Ireland, in putting down agrarian disorder there—that
' tyranny more oppressive to the poor than the rich '—and, while

---

[1] Parker, *Peel*, ii. p. 338.   [2] *Ib.* p. 216.   [3] Raikes, *Journal*, i. p. 160.

he would always defend the lawful rights of the Church, he would approve any redistribution of its property in the interests of religion. He had opposed their Reform bill, though he had never been an enemy to gradual and temperate reform : but that struggle was now past and done with, and he would look to the future only. He would consider the Reform Act as final, and as the basis of the political system from now on. He was not against reform, as his record when in office proved. He was for reforming every institution that required it, but he was for doing it gradually, dispassionately, and deliberately, that the reform might be lasting. What the country now needed was order and tranquillity, and he would take his stand in defence of law and order, enforced through the medium of the reformed House of Commons.[1]

'The Government were extremely pleased at his speech,' says Greville, ' though I think not without a secret misgiving that they are likely to be more in his power than is pleasant.' That wise critic believed that this ' frank address, and politesse, are all finesse ; ' he thought Peel was playing a deep and crooked game. ' Under that placid exterior he conceals, I believe, a boundless ambition, and hatred and jealousy lurk under his professions of esteem and political attachment.'[2] Upon the general public, however, the effect of this speech was very different. Peel had once for all escaped from the false position in which his opposition to the great bill had placed him, and stood forth as the champion of orderly government and moderate reform. He had taken the first step towards the reorganisation of a great new party on the ruins of the old—a party to which Croker gave the name Conservative. It was by his conduct as a leader of Opposition that he slowly gathered about himself the trust and admiration of that large section of the nation that desired a policy of peace, security, and gradual reform, and that looked for a leader who could, in time of crisis, set the welfare of the nation above the interests of his party ; while at the same time he gathered a little band of men, of great ability and high character, who were attached to their chief by personal affection as well as political loyalty. With these more liberal elements he hoped to swamp the Tory reactionaries, who must still form a section of his party.[3] He hoped, also,

---

[1] *Speeches*, ii. p. 604.   [2] *Greville*, ii. pp. 352, 363.

[3] If we are to believe Croker, Peel for a time expected a new division of party on the subject of currency reform, and a coalition of Radicals and Ultras

to educate that party, as he was continually educating himself, to keep the violence of the extremists within bounds, and gradually to lead them to a more conciliatory attitude and a more unprejudiced outlook. Whether he would succeed in fusing these diverse elements into one organic whole remained to be seen.

At present things looked a little black. The Tories were not so dainty about their methods, and many of them considered that a factious opposition was quite compatible with Conservatism. They had to learn that they must take their leader as they found him, and pardon his liberalism for the sake of his talents, and that, hanker as they might for a reactionary policy, they were helpless to carry it out without his assistance : that, in fact, the only chance for the party was to group themselves once more round this most unsatisfactory chief. As yet, however, this process had only begun, and Peel stood alone, as never before. Not only was he divided from the Ultras, but he was on bad terms with Wellington. All through the Reform struggle they had been very cool : ' There's that fellow in the Commons,' said the Duke. ' One can't go on without him, but he is so vacillating and crotchety that there's no getting on with him. I did pretty well with him when we were in office, but I can't manage him at all now. He is a wonderful fellow—has a most correct judgment—talents almost equal to those of Pitt, but he spoils all by his timidity and indecision.' [1] (May one hazard a guess that this ' timidity ' means Peel's unwillingness to commit himself to an indiscriminate opposition to all Parliamentary reform ?) Since then, however, the breach had become much wider. When the Duke explained, in the House of Lords, his motives for accepting the King's commission to form a Government in May, 1832, he had used the expression, that if *he* had refused to assist the King, he ' could not have shown his face in the streets for shame.' Peel had taken this to refer to his own conduct, and contrasted it with the generous praise which he himself, in his explanation to the House of Commons, had given to the Duke's honourable motives. He showed his hurt in his usual manner—by sulky silence ; and it was not

against moderates of all parties. Such a coalition was actually suggested at this time by Mr. Disraeli, a ' Tory-democrat ' candidate at the general election. Peel, however, must soon have been disabused of this idea. Only financiers like himself and fanatics like Attwood were really interested in currency reform, and it could never have become a party test.

[1] Maxwell, *Wellington*, ii. p. 257.

until the spring of 1834 that the two chiefs were at last reconciled, by the efforts of Peel's friend, Aberdeen, and Wellington's devoted ' Gosh.' [1]

The new House of Commons was strange and excitable—a good House to speak to. Many of the members, new to Parliamentary life, heard for the first time speeches of a high quality, and when the great orators rose—Stanley, with his fiery and reckless eloquence ; Peel, with his finished reasoning and seductive voice ; Macaulay, with his unequalled knowledge and power of denunciation—they were swept off their feet at the start. ' I could have moved them just the other way,' said Peel to Croker, when his own and Stanley's speeches had saved the day for the Government, ' I could have trampled the bill to dust.' [2] This little outburst of arrogance seems to show him glorying in his own power : nor had he long to wait before a public demonstration was given of the feeling in his favour. Cobbett proposed a resolution, to pray the King to remove Sir Robert Peel from his Privy Council—the most severe punishment, short of impeachment, that could fall on a public man. Cobbett's attack, which was distinguished both for ferocity and misrepresentation,[3] was based on Peel's reform of the currency. It was seconded by Mr Fielden, on the grounds that in 1826 Fielden and his friends had sent Peel a memorial on the distress in Lancashire, and received no answer but an offer of troops to suppress disorder. Peel replied to the accusation in a speech whose restrained passion made its reasoning all the more telling.[4] He tore Cobbett's arguments to shreds ; showed that he was guilty of repeated misstatements, and pointed out that the letter quoted by Fielden was not written to him and his fellow-memorialists at all, but was an answer to an application from the Lord Lieutenant of the county for military aid, of which fact Fielden must have been well aware. Having concluded his

[1] Mr. Arbuthnot was usually known by this engaging nickname.

[2] Peel to Croker, 5th March, 1833, *Croker*, ii. p. 203.

[3] He accused Peel of wishing to raise the value of money in 1819 in order to increase the value of his own salary : Peel was not then in office, and had no salary. He accused him of introducing the finance bills of 1822 and 1826, which were not introduced by Peel at all, etc., etc.

[4] ' What struck me as singular was this, that . . . Sir R. Peel was greatly excited in dealing with . . . a contemptible antagonist. At that period shirt-collars were made with " gills " which came up upon the cheek ; and Peel's gills were so soaked with perspiration that they actually lay down upon his neck-cloth.' Thus Gladstone, who was sitting just behind him. Morley, *Gladstone*, i. p. 114.

speech, he walked out of the House in a storm of cheers, without waiting for the result.   Cobbett, rising, was refused a hearing ; and when he pressed his motion to a division, found himself in a minority of 4 to 298 ; and Althorp then proposed that Cobbett's resolution should not be entered on the minutes of the House.[1]

The reformed Parliament had great promises to fulfil, and it set itself to its task without delay.   The achievements of its first two years make a notable list.   The Abolition of Slavery, the Factory Act of 1833, and the Poor Law Act of 1834 would have given any Government a title to the undying gratitude of their country. They were not due only to the victory of the Whigs, but to the general spirit of humanitarian and reforming zeal which had been growing steadily for the last twenty years : the chief promoters of the Factory Act—Michael Sadler and the young Lord Ashley [2]— were both Tories, and Peel himself approved all three measures : [3] but the reconstruction of Parliament had undoubtedly given that humanitarian spirit more free scope.   An extraordinary number of lesser reforms accompanied these.

All this, however, did not greatly increase the popularity of the Government with the lower classes.   The working man might feel a moral exultation in the emancipation of the slaves, but it could make little difference to his material comfort.   The Factory Act was not altogether satisfactory.   The men who had petitioned for it had wanted a general restriction of hours : the restriction of children's hours, without a limitation on adult labour, was not enough, and the cotton spinners in particular objected to the Act, believing that it would raise the wages they paid to their little piecers : [4]   and this was a consideration to persons who had found it worth while to work their six-year-old children thirteen hours a day for sixpence a week.   Most of all, however, the Poor Law Act was detested by the working classes.   No Tory Government, probably, would have dared to introduce so stringent a measure. It swept away the whole system of supplementing wages from the

[1] *Speeches*, ii. p. 694.

[2] Sadler had been defeated by the Whig Macaulay at the last election, and Ashley had taken his place as leader.

[3] He spoke in favour of the apprenticeship system rather than the immediate complete abolition of slavery.   On the other bills he did not speak, but he generally approved them.

[4] Appendix to the *Report of the Factory Commission of* 1833.

poor rates, practically abolished outdoor relief, and made the conditions on which indoor relief could be granted very severe.

In other respects the conduct of the Whig Ministers had given offence, both to the Radicals and to the lower classes. Now that they no longer depended on popular support, the political unions were discountenanced. A Radical paper, which urged its readers to pay no taxes until certain reforms were adopted, was prosecuted and convicted, although the counsel for the defence quoted Lord Milton and Lord Althorp in justification. A rigid censorship was exercised over the press by means of the newspaper stamp duty, and it was noticed that Government prosecutions discriminated between Radical and educational publications—the latter being allowed to escape. In a word—

> ' The Nation ! ' roared in '32,
> Is just ' the mob ' in '33.

All this caused a certain reaction against the Government. Next year the savage punishment of the Dorsetshire labourers drew further denunciations upon them.[1] Critics were not now wanting to point out that the Reform Bill had been so drawn up as to spare Lord Lansdowne's pocket-borough of Calne and Lord Bedford's Tavistock, and to note the frequency with which the names of Lord Grey's relatives appeared in the lists of places and promotions.[2] Sir John Cam Hobhouse lost his seat at Westminster by the influence of Place. Lord Durham being entertained at Birmingham by the city, Mr. Attwood (' The most influential man in England ') forced his way into the hall and insisted on reading him a condemnatory address : poor Lord Durham had to appeal to the city authorities for protection, saying piteously, ' Mr. Attwood, I have not deserved this of you ! ' Mass meetings passed resolutions in favour of the ballot and other objectionable

[1] Six country labourers who led a strike were prosecuted for administering illegal oaths, and received the atrocious punishment of seven years' transportation. The Government, anticipating demonstrations against this judgment, hurried them off to Australia without the usual delay. They received a free pardon two years later.

[2] ' That Lord Grey of all men in the world—with his eighteen relatives quartered in a few months on the public (not one of them having done anything) —should lop off your hard-earned remuneration for years of zealous service— and such service !—is too bad.' Peel to Henry Hobhouse, 21st December, 1831, written when the Government suppressed a small office, value £200 a year, which he had given to Hobhouse as a pension for his service at the Home Office. *Peel Papers*, British Museum, 40,402, p. 122.

things. To make matters worse, the Cabinet, while thus assailed from without, began to show signs of weakness within. Only the Reform Question had held it together so long: now the essential divergence of opinion which existed among its members began to appear.

It was on the Irish Question, that never-failing source of dissension, that the trouble began. As yet the Whigs had not been very successful in governing Ireland. For some time past it had been impossible for the Protestant clergy in many districts to collect their tithes at all. Stanley, the Irish Secretary, had passed a measure making the commutation of tithes, hitherto voluntary, compulsory, and the Government was authorised to advance money for the relief of the clergy (some of whom were almost destitute), and to reimburse itself by levying on the tithe-payers for the money due. In spite of the use of the army, they had only succeeded in collecting a tenth part of the sum ; and Ireland was in a state of distraction. The temporary alliance with O'Connell, for the purpose of passing the Reform Bill, had been broken up when the Liberator saw that the Irish Reform Bill did not restore the 40s. franchise, and when Stanley early in 1833 introduced the most stringent Coercion Act that had been passed for thirty years. It was certainly needed : murder, robbery, cattle-houghing and assault were of daily occurrence, and trial by jury had been perforce suspended, for it was impossible to get men to serve on juries. Only Stanley's extraordinary eloquence and determination, however, carried the Act, for a great part of the Cabinet disapproved its stringency ; and Peel could easily have thrown it out by combining with the Radicals and the Irish had he so chosen.[1] To sweeten the dose [2] the Government introduced a scheme of reform for the Irish Church ; 10 of its 22 bishoprics were to be suppressed, and all benefices over £200 a year were to be taxed. The estimated profit was to be employed instead of Church rates, which were to be abolished. The £60,000 saved on the bishops' salaries was to be at the disposal of the Government. In the House of Commons Peel, while supporting Church reform and the abolition of the rates, objected to the Appropriation Clause, as it was termed, and Stanley was authorised to omit it. In the

[1] It was on this occasion that he said, ' I could have moved them just the other way.' See above, p. 171.

[2] The Church Bill was introduced before the Coercion Bill, but Stanley had prepared both during the recess.

Lords, Lyndhurst and Wellington succeeded in deleting the clause which suspended benefices where no duties had been performed for three years : and thus, stripped of much of its value, the measure became law.

Stanley had by now made himself more detested than probably any Irish Secretary before or since. He was also much disliked by the Radicals, and not too popular with his colleagues. At the opening of the session he had been roundly attacked for his Irish policy : not one of the Ministers rose to defend him, and Peel was the only person who spoke in his favour. This was not altogether just ; for his reorganisation of Irish education, founded on the report of the committee of 1827, had been highly beneficial. He was naturally disgusted and eager to leave Ireland. No one, however, was anxious to go to Dublin to ' break a lance with Doctor Doyle and change a cuff with Dan,' and no one wanted to give up a comfortable post to oblige Stanley. At last poor Lord Goderich, at the Colonial Office, was fastened on as the victim, and bribed with an earldom [1] to accept the Privy Seal : even then the King had to beg it of him as a personal favour, and before he could back out Grey and Durham crammed the seals into his pocket, ' poor Goody ' wailing the while, ' Why should Stanley have my place ? Why shouldn't he have Melbourne's ? ' [2] Ultimately Mr. Littleton consented to take Ireland ; he was a self-confident gentleman, and when they told him he might have trouble with O'Connell, he replied airily, ' Oh, leave me to manage Dan ! ' [3] One of his first steps was to extend the imprudent proceedings relative to tithes. These were now £1,200,000 in arrears. Littleton induced the Government to advance £1,000,000 to the clergy and undertake the whole collection of tithes itself.

These various Tithe Acts had partly relieved the poorest Irish peasantry from the payment : but they had not relieved the Roman Catholic population from the grievance of a tax in support of the Protestant Church ; and not the whole military force in Ireland availed to collect the tithes. Accordingly, in the session of 1834, Littleton introduced yet another bill to commute the tithe into a land tax. In the ensuing debate, Russell rose and made a positive declaration that it was the duty of the State to appropriate the surplus revenues of the Church to the purpose of

---

[1] He became Lord Ripon.   [2] *Hobhouse*, iv. p. 298.
[3] *Greville*, iii. p. 105.

education. The speech was received with Radical cheers, but it was wholly unexpected by the Minister's colleagues. Stanley scribbled a note and passed it to Sir James Graham : ' John Russell has upset the coach.' [1] Any chance of tiding over the difficulty was ended by a private member, Mr. Ward, proposing a resolution on the same lines as Russell's declaration.

Neither Stanley nor Graham could agree to the alienation of the revenues of the Irish Church. They resigned, and were followed immediately by Goderich (now Lord Ripon) and the Duke of Richmond. Though long debated, the decision was in the end very sudden : Grey hesitated until the last moment as to whether he should stand by Stanley and his friends or by Russell and Althorp. ' They will be forced to put peers in the vacant places,' remarked Greville, ' because nobody can get re-elected. The rotten boroughs now seem not quite such abominations.' [2]

The troubles of the Cabinet, however, were not at an end with the loss of their most brilliant debater and their ablest administrator. The Coercion Act of 1833 was now at the point of expiring. Littleton, Brougham, and Althorp all thought that the clauses which suspended the right of public meeting and set up courts-martial should not be renewed ; and it was known that O'Connell objected to the Act on account of these clauses particularly. Grey, however, approved of them, and the Lord Lieutenant, Lord Wellesley, had declared that the state of the country made their re-enactment absolutely necessary. Brougham and Littleton, both writing privately to Wellesley, induced him to send a second despatch, withdrawing what he had said in the first, and advising that the two clauses be dropped.[3] Littleton then suggested to Althorp that he should approach O'Connell privately, and let him know that the obnoxious clauses would probably not be renewed. Althorp agreed, though caution-

---

[1] Parker, *Graham*, i. p. 187.   [2] *Greville*, iii. p. 90.

[3] Wellesley's first letter was in April, and he repeated his advice on June 10. His letter contradicting the first, and advising the dropping of the two clauses, was dated June 21. Littleton contended that Wellesley was perfectly justified in what he did, as he had written to Melbourne to ask advice, and Melbourne had not answered his letter. This is new light on the position of the Irish Viceroy—he is to regulate the advice he gives to Government by the instructions of the Home Secretary in London, not by his own knowledge of Irish affairs !

ing Littleton not to commit himself,[1] and he assured Littleton that he himself would ' resign rather than allow them to be renewed, and Lord Grey could not risk that result.' Littleton sent for O'Connell, and the result of the interview was that O'Connell withdrew the candidate he was running in the Wexford election against the Government's nominee.

Lord Wellesley's *volte-face*, however, was too much for the Cabinet : such a change of opinion within ten days was too startling. Grey was determined to reintroduce the Act entire, and persuaded all to agree with him. Althorp told Littleton of the decision, saying ' nothing of his intention to resign.' Littleton, however, ' did not feel embarrassed ' in introducing the Act—courts-martial, prohibition of meetings and all—for, he said, ' Mr. O'Connell had given me the strongest assurance that he should consider my conversation with him as strictly confidential.' The Irish Secretary, therefore, rushed light-heartedly on his doom. On July 3 the bill was brought in, and next day O'Connell rose and denounced the Government, revealing the whole transaction, and declaring that he had been betrayed. ' The pig's killed,' said Althorp expressively to John Russell.[2]

In the House of Lords, Grey, introducing the bill, had relied on Lord Wellesley's letter of April ; and had simply suppressed the later and contradictory despatch. Now he refused to produce it, alleging that it was a private letter.

All the world now knew that the Irish Secretary, with the connivance of the Chancellor of the Exchequer, had entered into an intrigue with a leader of opposition, without the consent of the Prime Minister, and which he knew the Prime Minister would strongly disapprove : that the Viceroy of Ireland had flatly contradicted himself on a point of vital importance in the space of ten days by the secret advice of the Irish Secretary and the Lord Chancellor : and that the Prime Minister had based important legislation upon the report of the Viceroy, without informing his hearers that the Viceroy had since contradicted this advice.

Lord Althorp was, as we know, honest as the day. His conduct, though it may appear for a moment a little questionable, is no doubt susceptible of the most honourable explanation. The

[1] The only object in approaching O'Connell, however, can have been to induce him to modify his conduct by holding out this hope.

[2] Russell, *Recollections and Suggestions*, p. 125.

House of Commons in general was quite convinced of this : to them the culprit was O'Connell, who had basely betrayed a confidential communication. There was one exception to this, however : Peel had supported the Coercion Bill : but he said that O'Connell had good reason to think himself unfairly used, and warmly expressed his sympathy.[1]

No Government, however, could stand after such revelations. Althorp eventually decided to resign. Grey declared he could not go on without Althorp and resigned also, complaining, not unreasonably, of the way his colleagues had treated him.[2] The King sent for Melbourne, and requested him to form a coalition with Peel ; but Melbourne, and Peel himself, told His Majesty that it was impossible : the divergence in their respective opinions was too deep. Melbourne at last formed a new Ministry out of much the same material as the old, but with Grey left out. Littleton came back, for Althorp refused to come without him. The last moderate element was gone, and the Liberal Ministers were set free for a grand career of Reform : but, somehow, the virtue was gone out of them. They had touched pitch, and were defiled. For the next seven years—for the next sixteen years, it might be said—the course of the Whig party was very slowly but very surely downward. A gradual loss of power, a gradual degradation of character, was theirs.

Stanley, shortly after his resignation, had made an attack upon his late colleagues so reckless and violent that he had greatly discredited himself : and while all his rivals were thus sinking in public estimation, Peel's position became more and more favourable. ' It is remarkable how men's minds are gradually turning to Peel . . . ' Greville notes. ' No matter how unruly the House, how impatient or fatigued, the moment he rises all is silence, and he is sure of being heard with profound attention and respect.' [3]

Peel was himself well aware that the tide was now running in his favour, and that the hoped-for conservative reaction was coming at last : but impatience was not one of his faults—he had no desire to rush into premature action. He did not think the

[1] *Speeches*, ii. p. 857.

[2] I have followed throughout the account of these transactions given by Littleton in his *Memoir of Lord Hatherton*, which prints the whole of the correspondence involved, and from which all quotations are made.

[3] *Greville*, iii. pp. 66, 77.

pear was ripe yet, and so little did he look forward to any sudden and favourable change in the situation, that he went off with his wife and his eldest girl, 'little Julia,' to spend the winter in Italy. He had not long been gone when Earl Spencer died, and Lord Althorp was suddenly translated to the upper House. The Whigs had told themselves so often that they could not stand without Althorp that they hardly knew what to do. His successor as leader of the Commons must be Lord John Russell. Now Russell's abilities were still regarded as a little doubtful ; were the qualities that had made him the darling of the people in '31 those which would fit him for this most difficult task ? He was an ardent reformer, too, and it would be necessary to make some concession to his views—perhaps to identify the party with the principle of appropriation of Irish Church revenues. Melbourne laid all this before the King, offering in a somewhat half-hearted manner to go on. William, however, was tired of Reform, tired of his Ministers, alarmed for the Irish Church, and thought he saw the chance for a brilliant *coup d'état*. He informed the Prime Minister that he could not sanction the Government's entering upon a new career of Reform, that he did not think Lord John capable of acting as leader of the Commons, and that the Ministry was not strong enough to go on without Althorp. He would accept Melbourne's resignation, and send for the Duke of Wellington.

The Duke declared that Peel must be Prime Minister : but he accepted in his own person all the chief offices of Government, pending Peel's return, and despatched a messenger post haste to Italy to summon him home. His Grace, as we know, was not bashful in such circumstances ; and he does not seem to have quite realised what he was taking in hand, for he wrote to Peel that the Whigs ' are all, particularly Lord Melbourne, delighted to be relieved.' [1] There was, however, something so spirited in the old man's taking the whole work of Government thus on his own shoulders, that his three-weeks' Premiership was popular enough with the country.

Peel's reception of the messenger was characteristically ungracious ; he listened in silence to Hudson's account of his hurried journey, and then remarked that by choosing another route he might have saved a day. He himself started for home immediately, accompanied by wife and daughter, and, travelling day and

---

[1] Peel, *Memoirs*, ii. p. 23.

night, reached London in a fortnight. He went straight to the King, without seeing anyone, and accepted his commission to form a Government.

The new Prime Minister's position was a very unpleasant one. He had not been called to power by a vote of the House of Commons, but by the individual action of the King exercising a prerogative that had not been used for fifty years. His party were in a small minority in the House of Commons, and it was very uncertain whether the Conservative feeling in the country was yet strong enough to turn this into a majority. His enemies, so summarily ejected from office, were furious, and were likely to give him no quarter : Wellington had been much mistaken in judging the feelings of the others from those of the easy, flippant, good-natured Melbourne.

The very fact that Peel had gone abroad for the winter showed that he had never contemplated such an event as this. If a change of Government were at this moment desirable at all, he said later, he thought it would have more chance of leading ' to a satisfactory and permanent result if it should take place in consequence of dissensions among members of Lord Melbourne's Government, or quarrels between the Government and its supporters, or, in short, from any cause rather than the direct intervention of the King. . . . Had it been possible that I should have been consulted previously, I might have dissuaded the act of dismissal as premature and impolitic.' He would, in fact, have allowed time to do its inevitable work with the unstable Melbourne Government, which no one expected to last more than a year or two ; and at the same time allowed the Conservative revival in the country to gather strength. The impatience of the King, and the imprudence of his Tory friends, had wrecked these hopes. But it was too late now to undo the mischief. As things stood, he could do nothing but accept office. ' I could not reconcile it with my feelings,' he said, ' or, indeed, with my sense of duty, to subject the King and the Monarchy to the humiliation . . . of inviting his dismissed servants to resume their appointments.' [1] He could not pretend that in Italy he had had such opportunities of judging the situation as those at home : to refuse now would appear a mere act of cowardice, and must have been the final abdication of his position as leader of the Conservative party : the Tories had forgiven him

[1] Peel, *Memoirs*, ii. pp. 30-1.

much, but they would not forgive this. He had not made the situation, but he must make the best of it.

He had no difficulty in deciding on his first steps. He found all prepared for an immediate dissolution of Parliament, and these preparations he fully approved. Critics afterwards declared—including one whose opinion is worthy of attention, Lord John Russell [1]—that Peel should have met the House, and dissolved after he had been defeated there, as Pitt had done in 1784. Peel's own reasoning seems conclusive against this. He had not Pitt's advantage—his opponents had not discredited themselves as Fox and North had done in 1784 ; a skilful opposition might lessen the chances of a successful appeal to the country ; but, most of all, to meet the House of Commons in the present state of affairs would inevitably lead to a bitter conflict between that House and the Lords, and give to his Ministry ' the decided character of a Government supported by the Crown and the Lords against the House of Commons,' which would almost certainly have ranged the mass of the people once more on the side of the Whigs.[2]

Peel had little or no hope that he could maintain himself in power ; but he did hope to be able to attain two objects : he would show the nation that the new Conservatism would identify itself with economy and reform, while it still took its stand for Crown and Church ; and by dissolving now he was sure of a considerable accession to the numbers of his party. He might not —probably would not—get a majority of votes in the House of Commons ; but at least he would get an accession of strength that would enable him to offer an effective opposition when he was once more out of office : the Tory party would no longer be a despised remnant in the legislature. He did not look forward to difficulties with his party on this point : Reform bears a very different aspect when you introduce it yourself and when the other fellow does it. Wellington reported that the Tories were ' very well disposed to go all reasonable lengths in the way of reform of institutions. . . . I have been astonished at their being so docile.' [3]

The best chance of success, frail though it was, was by a coalition with Stanley and Graham, and Peel, eager to obtain colleagues whose outlook would be more sympathetic with his own than that of Wellington and Goulburn, at once made overtures. The

[1] See *Recollections and Suggestions*, p. 132.
[2] Peel, *Memoirs*, ii. p. 46.   [3] *Ib.* p. 29.

ci-devant Whigs, however, felt that the time was not yet ripe for
a coalition. They felt that they could not with decency so soon
set themselves in opposition to their late friends ; and, though they
assured Peel that their confidence in himself was complete, they
hesitated to unite themselves with one who had shown himself so
reactionary, and so hostile to their late chief (Grey), as Wellington.
These were the reasons given : but it is probable that they also
felt averse to entering upon a struggle that must be hopeless ;
while Stanley was nursing daring hopes of constituting himself the
leader of a ' Middle Party,' [1] and would not consent to serve under
Peel while this seemed possible. Peel certainly seemed to think
Stanley's motives not too creditable, for he spoke of him in a tone
that is distinctly one of contempt.[2] Graham, however, came up
to town and had the matter out in a personal interview, and thus
laid the foundation of a warm and close friendship, which was to
last till death. Graham was delighted, telling Greville that Peel
was ' cordial and obliging to the greatest degree, and without any
appearance of that coldness and reserve of which he had been so
often accused.' [3]

Peel was deeply disappointed. Croker remarked that he said
several times, ' in a querulous tone, that it " would only be the
Duke's old Cabinet." ' [4] A Tory Cabinet was the last thing he
wanted at the moment, and he grudged the distribution of offices
among the Rosslyns, Knatchbulls, Murrays and so forth, who had
to be raked in to fill up the list : the names of such a Cabinet were
bound to make a bad impression on the country.

With the subordinate appointments he was free to please himself. Contemporary opinion blamed him for not giving the
younger men of the party a chance, but to-day it is instructive to
note the number of famous names that found place in that short-
lived Government. Lord Ashley as philanthropist, Winthrop

---

[1] Parker, *Graham*, i. p. 213 ff.

[2] ' I should have thought that in such a crisis as that in which we are almost
unconsciously living, a man might have made up his mind to some definite
course of action . . . that, if he left his colleagues because they were " destruc-
tives," to use his own word ; if he did what he could to ruin them in public
estimation by the grossest . . . abuse . . . I should have thought, having
been one of the main causes of the King's embarrassment, he might, òn the
highest courageous principles, have assisted in the King's defence.' Peel to
Croker, 10th January, 1835. Parker, *Peel*, ii. p. 278. ' I envy not Stanley's
" visions " of my place. I would not exchange my position for his.'

[3] *Greville*, iii. p. 255.　　　　[4] *Croker*, ii. p. 248.

Mackworth Praed as poet and journalist, had already gained some fame, and Lord Mahon had already begun his work as a historian : but Peel selected also a number of very young men, the eldest only twenty-five, whose career he had noted at the University : William Ewart Gladstone ; James, Lord Ramsay ; Sidney Herbert ; and Henry Pelham, Earl of Lincoln.[1] Of these only Gladstone had as yet distinguished himself in any degree, and he by voting consistently, throughout his first session, against every measure of reform proposed.[2] But Peel made no mistake : these four young men, with Lord Canning, Edward Cardwell, and others of lesser fame, were one of the great legacies that he left to his country : a statesman of the first rank, one of the greatest of Indian Viceroys, and a group of great administrative reformers. They were trained by Peel : from him they received their ideal of public service ; and they were closely attached to him by personal affection. It was curious that the Minister, so cold and unapproachable with his equals, was remarkably happy in his dealings with young men. He treated them with an easy, cordial, open friendliness that was very flattering and very attractive. Aberdeen remarked that when Peel once laid aside his reserve he was ' the most confiding of men.' Some of his young friends—Herbert, Lincoln, William Gregory—were like sons of his house,[3] and went in and out at Whitehall Gardens as they pleased, dropping into their chief's study for a chat ; but with all of them he would discuss affairs of State with the most entire frankness, treating them as his equals, and often ending a political talk with one of those risky stories, of which he had a great store, and ' which he told extremely well and with fits of laughter.' [4]

Peel had five boys of his own, of whom he was intensely fond

[1] He also offered a place to Canning's young son, afterwards Earl Canning, the Indian Viceroy.

[2] With one exception—he voted for Ashley's Factory Act. See Morley, *Gladstone*, i. p. 106.

[3] Peel, not a demonstrative man, writes to Herbert in 1834 as ' My very dear Sidney.'

[4] Gregory, *Autobiography*, p. 80. The testimony to Peel's popularity with young men is abundant. See, for example, Stanmore, *Herbert*, and Martineau, *Newcastle*, also Young's *Poems of Winthorp Mackworth Praed*, xviii. ; Morley, *Gladstone*, i. p. 123, etc. ; and Playfair's *Memoirs*, pp. 60-1, etc. : ' The impression he made on me is very different from that which is usually entertained of the great Prime Minister. . . . He was the most genial of hosts and the most delightful of companions.'

and proud : but probably all this was not merely due to the liking
for boys, which he shared with Pitt, as he shared Pitt's haughty
reserve. It was due also to the fact that Peel was in many ways
more in sympathy with the younger generation than with his own.
A new type of young man had begun to appear in political life, not
confined to one party or class, but common to all, because it was
produced by a spiritual change that was passing over the whole
nation. These young men were very serious, deeply imbued with
religious feeling, and with high moral principles.[1] For them
politics was not a game, but a high calling. The outlook of Macaulay and Morpeth, Gladstone and Lincoln, was far more congenial to Peel than that of Croker and Hertford, Melbourne and
Holland.

The new Prime Minister opened the campaign with an address
to his constituents, known as the Tamworth Manifesto, and constituting the charter of the new Conservatism. He pledged
himself to maintain the Reform Act as the settlement of the constitutional question and the basis of political life ; and he declared
his adherence to a policy of moderate and steady reform. This
manifesto was approved by the Cabinet : but it must have been
a disagreeable dose for some of the Ministers to swallow, however
deeply they were convinced of the need for it. It created an
extraordinary sensation in the country : it did for the general
public much the same as his first speech in the reformed Parliament had done for the House of Commons, and placed him in a
high position in the minds of moderate men of every party. In the
general election the Conservative party almost doubled its numbers : it carried nearly every one of the counties, and, best of all,
Lancashire ; while one of the leading Whigs, Lord Palmerston,
found himself unexpectedly unseated. With all these gains,
however, the party did not even now secure a majority in the
House of Commons.

From the first moment, Peel took a high tone in his dealings
with the House. He boldly justified the King's action by an
appeal to the state of the country, to the break-up of the

---

[1] Gladstone and Herbert at this time were members of a secret society, of
which the main rule was that each member should subscribe a considerable
proportion of his income to charity. Only the secretary knew the sums subscribed, but they were very large. Stanmore, *Herbert*, i. p. 95. Lord Holland
told John Cam Hobhouse that he was afraid to talk before Morpeth and Howick,
for fear of shocking them. *Hobhouse*, iv. p. 360.

Whig party, and to the history of the prerogative : but he appealed with equal frankness to the generosity and justice of his adversaries.

After they had availed themselves of his services, and after he had co-operated with them in re-establishing the character of the first Reform Parliament for decorum, it would be unfair to take the first opportunity to subject him to disgrace, he said. ' I make you great offers, which should not lightly be rejected. I offer you the prospect of continued peace—the restored confidence of powerful States that are willing to seize the opportunity of reducing great armies. . . . I offer you reduced estimates, improvements in civil jurisprudence, reform of ecclesiastical law, the settlement of the tithe question in Ireland, the commutation of tithe in England, the removal of any real abuse in the Church, the redress of those grievances of which the Dissenters have any just ground to complain. I offer also the best chance that these things cán be effected in willing concert with the other authorities of the State, thus restoring harmony, ensuring the maintenance, but not excluding the reform . . . of ancient institutions. You may reject my offers . . . you may prefer to do the same thing by more violent means ; but if you do, the time is not far distant when you will find that the popular feeling on which you rely has deserted you, and that you will have no alternative but either again to invoke our aid—to replace the Government in the hands from which you would now forcibly withdraw it—or to resort to that " pressure from without," to those measures of compulsion and violence, which, at the same time as they render your reforms useless and inoperative, will seal the fate of the British Constitution.' [1]

The appeal was made in vain. A considerable number of the Whigs were impressed by Peel's liberal declarations, and urged that he should have a ' fair trial : ' but they were not all of this mind ; and John Russell in particular was determined to wage a relentless and unceasing warfare with the supplanter. He was obliged to agree to his followers' demands for ' a fair trial,' but he interpreted the words in a different sense : they meant that Peel should be allowed a breathing space, in which to bring forward his measures and show what he could do ; Russell regarded ' a fair trial ' as meaning a trial of strength on some legitimate point of

[1] *Speeches*, iii. pp. 4, 19.

difference.[1] His first wish was to limit the supplies to three months—an almost unheard-of measure in modern times : but his party overruled him, pointing out the danger to public credit.

The first piece of business of the session was the choice of a Speaker. The Government proposed to re-elect Manners Sutton, who had been Speaker since 1817 ; the Whigs proposed one of their own leaders, Abercromby, member for Edinburgh, and carried his election in the teeth of the Ministry by a majority of ten. On this occasion the two leaders came for a moment into personal conflict : Peel accused Russell of opposing Manners Sutton on the grounds that he had instigated the King's action : Russell contradicted this. Peel had in his hand at the moment a letter written by Russell, in which the statement was made, but he did not produce it.[2]

Three days later the Whigs carried an amendment to the Address, lamenting that ' the progress of reform had been interrupted and endangered by the unnecessary dissolution of Parliament : ' and so the process went on. The Government made one serious mistake—they appointed Lord Londonderry Ambassador to Russia. It has been suggested that Londonderry, an influential person, had to get *something*, and that his friends could not endure his company at home. He had, however, so closely identified himself with a reactionary policy both at home and abroad, and particularly in relation to Poland, that the appointment was a very unwise one, and the Whigs did not fail to take advantage of the blunder. Condemnation was general, and Londonderry was obliged to resign.

In the midst of the storm, Peel introduced his measures for reform : the establishment of an efficient ecclesiastical court ; the institution of civil marriages for Dissenters, who had hitherto been obliged to go through the marriage ceremony of the Anglican Church ; the conversion of Irish tithes into a rent-charge at a reduced rate ; and the commutation of tithes for England. These measures were all admirable in themselves, and in full accordance with Whig principles. How, then, could they be opposed ?

[1] Russell's biographer says that he ' was probably himself aware that . . . he attached a very different sense to the words.' Walpole, *Russell*, i. pp. 244-5.

[2] Goulburn was handed the letter, he did not know by whom, and passed it to Peel. See *Greville*, iii. pp. 223-4. *Speeches*, iii. p. 3. Russell, an impulsive man, had, of course, forgotten the letter.

Many of the Whigs were well inclined to support them, and Russell found himself obliged to have recourse to a new expedient.

If the Whigs could not be relied on, it was necessary to go to the Radicals. Lord John met O'Connell at the house of a friend, and a bargain, more or less vague, was concluded : the Irish were to unite with the Whigs to turn out the Government, and in return Russell pledged himself to promote legislation favourable to Ireland—probably the appropriation of tithes, corporation reform, and an amendment of the Irish Reform Act were hinted at. This arrangement, known as the Lichfield House Compact, was soon public, for on March 31 O'Connell acknowledged Russell as his leader, but its details were not known.[1]

The Whig leaders cannot be blamed for snatching at every means to turn Peel out of office. A great constitutional principle was at stake : it was necessary to decide whether the King had or had not the power to dismiss his Ministers at his own will. The fate of Peel's Government definitely established the principle that the King had no such power, and the Crown never again attempted anything similar. Undoubtedly this decision was the one in accordance with the spirit of the English Constitution and of the new age. Peel's action, however, could not be called ' unconstitutional,' for the case was only now being tried—the decision still uncertain : and certain of the Whigs had forgotten the great issue at stake in their admiration for his firm and liberal measures, and the courage and ability with which he carried on the struggle.

The true course for Russell to pursue was to attack the Government on the constitutional point, and beat them in a fair field—that is, to move a vote of want of confidence. Peel repeatedly challenged him to bring forward such a motion, and offered to resign if it were carried : but, by his own frank confession, Russell could not have carried it.[2] He could not count on a majority in his own party on such a point ; and he was therefore forced to adopt the plan of attacking Peel's measures in detail, and worrying him into resignation by a series of local attacks ; and even this he could not have done without the aid of the Irish Radicals. He was making a great precedent, and he had to use the weapons that were

---

[1] Russell in later life denied that any ' compact ' was made : but there must have been a fairly definite understanding.

[2] Russell, *Recollections and Suggestions*, p. 134.

ready to his hand; but the consequences of his methods were un-happy for the Whig party, for Ireland, and indeed for the whole nation.

Peel's measures being good in themselves, the Opposition could only counter them by going one better : where he offered much, they promised more. No opportunity for attack was missed, and the smaller fry among the Whigs employed tactics of delay and annoyance which their leaders discountenanced : but it was upon the Irish Tithe Bill that Russell decided to make his chief effort. The measure provided for the commutation of tithes into a rent-charge, at 75 per cent. of the old tithe, the rent-charge to be redeemable, and the purchase money to be invested in land. It therefore followed the same lines as Littleton's tithe bill, though it greatly simplified the procedure and lowered the rent-charge by 5 per cent. : but it of course contained no appropriation clause. Russell first proposed a committee of the whole House to consider the temporalities of the Irish Church, and carried it after a long debate. Next he moved a resolution that the surplus revenues of the Church should be devoted to Irish education, and carried this also. Still the Government did not resign, for the committee appointed by Lord Grey upon the Irish Church was still sitting, and until they reported it was not absolutely certain that there would be a surplus at all.

Probably Peel, if left to himself, would have resigned before this. Greville noted that this state of things could not last : ' His physical strength would not suffice for the harassing warfare that is waged against him, the whole brunt of which he bears alone.' [1] Before Russell had made his first Irish motion, the Prime Minister had in fact circulated a Cabinet memorandum,[2] urging the necessity of resigning if beaten upon this point, and the humiliation of clinging to office in such circumstances. The Tories, however, saw no objection to this policy : they clung to their places with the tenacity of barnacles, caring nothing for the consequences. They were by this time the only persons who found fault with the Prime Minister. The very Whigs who were mad to turn him out were loud in his praises, and the joke going round the town was that Peel had every virtue except resignation. The general excitement was intense, and the House rather out of hand ; but when Peel rose to speak, ' it was curious to see the

[1] *Greville*, iii. p. 252.　　[2] 25th March, 1835.　Parker, *Peel*, ii. p. 292.

lulling of the uproar, and the shuffling and scrambling into seats, till all was quiet and the coast clear.'[1] He himself seems to have enjoyed the fight, and to have been in high spirits throughout : but he sent a challenge to Joseph Hume for a piece of insolence, and extorted a reluctant apology from him. Peel as a rule seems to have regarded Hume as providing the comic relief of the House, and he certainly took great delight in teasing the surly guardian of the nation's finances ;[2] so perhaps this incident may indicate that his temper was feeling the strain. The Radicals did not fail to take advantage of it, and Roebuck attempted to move that ' it was a breach of privilege for the Chancellor of the Exchequer to call out the member for Middlesex,' but was laughed at.

At last, upon the 7th of April, Russell brought forward a new resolution that was well calculated to serve his purpose. It declared that no measure upon the subject of tithes in Ireland could lead to a satisfactory and final settlement that did not embody the principle of appropriation of surplus Church revenues. This was a positive challenge which the Government could not evade. It was carried by a majority of 37, and on the following day Peel announced his resignation in a brief speech that ended in something like a personal triumph, both parties cheering him enthusiastically for some minutes after he concluded.

It was a curious situation. Beaten repeatedly on almost every point of importance that had arisen during the session, driven from office after a tenure of only four months, he yet returned to private life with an immensely increased reputation, and with something nearer personal popularity than he had ever known. He had triumphantly demonstrated the superiority of his talents to all, opponents or colleagues ; but he had also fought a dogged and plucky fight, and that appealed to his fellow-countrymen even more.

There was a general feeling of flatness. ' I certainly never remember a great victory for which *Te Deum* was chanted with so faint and joyless a voice,' wrote Greville. ' Peel looks gayer and easier than all Brooks's put together, and Lady Holland said, " Now that we have gained our object, I'm not so glad as

---

[1] *Greville*, iii. p. 250.

[2] He once remarked to a friend that he could not imagine a House of Commons without a Joseph Hume. See also *Speeches*, iii. p. 222, and ii. p. 631, for Peel's baiting of Hume.

I thought I should be," and this I take to be the sentiment of them all.' [1]

One result of the short Ministry was very clear—Stanley's hopes of becoming the leader of a middle party were definitely at an end. His party had grown steadily smaller. His position during the session had been doubtful, and people hardly knew what to think of his intentions. He was beginning to be regarded as a flighty and unsteady politician, one who blew hot and cold and played his own game. He saw that he must abandon his hopes of leadership and, if he meant to join the Conservatives, be content to take the second place. It was probably a bitter mouthful to the brilliant and ambitious young man, but he took it gamely ; and before the end of the session he and Graham had crossed the House and ranged themselves upon the Opposition benches behind Peel.

John Russell had gained in reputation as much as Peel. Even his friends had doubted whether he was fit to lead the party in the House of Commons : but he had handled an exceedingly difficult situation with remarkable ability, and showed that he possessed equal tactical skill and political courage. Nevertheless, he found himself now in a sufficiently uncomfortable position.

Poor King William's little experiment was to prove disastrous for the nation. The Whig Ministry had been slowly sinking in 1834, and if left alone would probably have died a natural death : the King's misguided effort had given it a new lease of life. The position of the Whigs as defenders of the Constitution had a little revived their popularity, and they were now restored to office. Had this taken place under the same conditions as in 1834 little harm would have been done ; but unfortunately the general election had altered the balance of parties. The large and safe majority had been turned into a small, doubtful, and fluctuating one. It could only be maintained with the aid of the Irish members. The Government had come back pledged to carry certain reforms, and they were no longer strong enough to carry these reforms. They could, perhaps, get them through the House of Commons, but they had no longer the compact majority at their backs which would enable them to coerce the House of Lords. The Lords were fully aware of this. They knew they were safe from another creation of peers, and they exercised their

[1] *Greville*, iii. p. 259.

power with a reckless and wanton disregard of every consideration of justice and prudence, caring only to be revenged on the Whigs. This conflict between the two Houses was to be the dominant fact in English politics for the next few years. It resulted in the degradation of the character of both the great parties, the emasculation of the Whig Government, and hindrance of the most useful and necessary reforms.

CHAPTER X

THE LEADER OF OPPOSITION, 1835-1841

THE new Whig Ministry was formed on much the same lines as the old one, but with one very important difference : Brougham's colleagues could endure him no longer. He might be their best debater—he might be the real leader of the Reform movement—but he was false and flighty ; he had a savage temper and a malignant tongue ; and they decided to throw him over. They dared not as yet defy him openly : but he was told that the King had made a little difficulty, that he could not come back into office immediately ; and the Great Seal was put in commission.

Littleton also was quietly dropped and consoled with a peerage, and Charles Grant went to the upper House as Lord Glenelg. Their vacant places in the House of Commons were both snatched by Conservatives, and this was not the worst. John Russell was defeated by a Conservative in Devonshire, and had to seek refuge in the small borough of Stroud—a lamentable anti-climax. It seemed as if the majority which Peel had failed to secure in 1834 would soon arrive. The Tories in the House of Lords, however, lost no time in labouring to undo all the work that Peel had done, and they soon caused a reaction in favour of the Whigs.

Two questions required the immediate attention of the Ministry : Irish Tithes and Municipal Reform. A Tithe Bill was introduced without delay. It was very much like Peel's bill in its scheme for commutation, but it of course contained an appropriation clause—the Government was pledged to appropriation. All benefices which did not contain fifty members of the Church of England—that is to say, 860 benefices—were to be suspended,[1] and the money thus made available, which was estimated at £58,000 a year, was to be used for educational purposes.

Peel countered by proposing that the bill should be divided into two parts : he and his followers would then be able to oppose the

---

[1] Where less than fifty members existed, curates were provided so that they might not be deprived of religious ministrations.

Appropriation Clause without delaying the measure for commutation of tithes. The Government refused the compromise, Peel was beaten on the division, and the bill passed the Commons without modification.

At the same time the Government introduced a Corporation Reform Bill. The municipalities of the older English towns [1] were usually self-elected, and were therefore entirely irresponsible. In cases where they were elected, the franchise was usually confined to freemen, who often possessed special privileges or property that were the source of great abuse. The mayor and council were often corrupt and almost always incapable; so were the local courts and magistrates. The new industrial towns—Birmingham, for example—often had no municipal institutions at all, and got along as best they might without them. The new bill abolished the old corporations and all the privileges of freemen,[2] and it established new municipal councils, to be elected by all rate-payers, in 183 towns.

Peel was well aware that such a measure was the inevitable corollary of the Act of 1832, and he also realised the necessity for reform. He at once declared himself in favour of the general principle of the bill, and though he attempted, unsuccessfully, to amend one or two details, he used every effort to make its passage through the House easy and rapid—to the great annoyance of his Tory followers, who thirsted to oppose it, but dared not risk a new breach with him.

These two important measures were laid before the Lords in July, 1835, and, under the leadership of Lyndhurst, their lordships went merrily to work. They halved the Tithe Bill, as Peel had wished to do, passed the commutation measure, and threw out the Appropriation Clause. Then they turned to the Corporation Bill, and proceeded to maul it until it was unrecognisable. They introduced a high property qualification for town councillors, saved all the rights and privileges of freemen for ever, placed aldermen elected for life on every council, decided that only councillors who were members of the Church of England should administer Church property, and added a series of other amend-

---

[1] The Scottish municipalities were equally corrupt, as anyone may conclude from reading Galt's *Provost*, but they had been reformed in 1833 by the Lord Advocate, Jeffrey.

[2] It saved the rights of living freemen to corporate property.

ments of minor importance. John Campbell, a rising lawyer, took Lyndhurst aside and remonstrated with him for throwing over Peel, who had supported the bill. 'Peel? What is Peel to me? Damn Peel!' said the ex-Chancellor, elated with success, and recollecting past snubs.[1]

Peel was furious. He had known what was going to occur and had been powerless to prevent it. Lyndhurst had won over the Duke. 'They have resolved on a course quite different from that which I took,' Sir Robert wrote to his wife. 'What the consequences will be I cannot foresee. Some think the immediate adjournment of both Houses. Others, the resignation of Ministers. *I will not be made responsible for the acts of the Lords.*'[2] A few days later he bought a new flower-glass for his Julia and some bows and arrows for his little boys, and departed to Drayton, most ostentatiously in the sulks. 'It is evident he washes his hands of the entire matter,' noted Greville.[3]

Had the Tories had access to the Drayton letter-bag they might have scented danger : as it was, they were in high feather, and thought Peel had thrown up the game. In the previous year Lyndhurst had struck up a friendship with a young man of Jewish extraction, very clever and very ambitious, who had won some distinction as a writer of witty and charming fiction, and who had for some years been trying, against great disadvantages, to begin a political career. He had been a Tory democrat, a Whig, an Independent ; but in none of these characters had he caught the fancy of the electors. In the election of 1834 he had appealed to the Radical Lord Durham to get him in for Aylesbury, and this failing, Lyndhurst had tried to get him a seat through the instrumentality of Lord George Bentinck, a follower of Stanley, and a devotee of horse-racing ; but Bentinck also failed to come up to scratch, and Mr. Disraeli was still without a seat, though he was becoming known as a political journalist. This young man seems to have been Lyndhurst's chosen confidant. They had devised a scheme by which the Whigs were to be turned out on the Corporation Bill, and a Tory Ministry formed, without Peel—Lyndhurst to be Prime Minister, Brougham Lord Chancellor, Disraeli to

---

[1] Campbell, *Chancellors*, viii. p. 109.   [2] *Private Letters*, p. 154.

[3] *Greville*, iii. p. 304. Greville notes that John Russell at this time crossed the House to ask Peel if he objected to some item of procedure : Peel said, 'Oh, no, I don't object,' but called Russell back to add, 'Remember, I speak only for myself ; I can answer for no other individual in the House.'

enter the Commons, where the party was to be led, according to
Disraeli, by Graham, according to a letter of Lord Londonderry,
by Praed and Follett, ' Peel supporting of course the arrangement.' [1] The King, who had made private overtures to Lyndhurst, was said to approve the plan.[2]

It says a good deal for the state of mind of the Ultras that anyone regarded this magnificent scheme as possible : that Graham
or Follett could have maintained themselves in a House of Commons where Peel had failed ; that Graham, who shrank from a
coalition with Peel, would rush into the arms of the Ultras ; that
Peel would tamely acquiesce in his shelving and support such a
Government—these were the dreams of madness, not the plans of
statesmen.   Above all, the folly of the Ultras was shown in the
means of attack chosen : the country might have supported the
House of Lords on the defence of the Irish Church ; the whole
nation, except a few placemen, were against them on the subject
of Corporation Reform.   It is very doubtful whether all the actors
were aware of the parts allotted to them—whether Graham or
Praed knew anything of the scheme.   Brougham's case is more
doubtful : though publicly at enmity with Lyndhurst, in private
they were on most intimate and friendly terms.   Still Brougham
had not yet broken completely with the Whigs ; he still had hopes
of regaining the Great Seal from them ; and such a disgraceful
apostacy must have ruined him with the country.   The Tory
peers, however, and even Wellington himself, were ready to follow
Lyndhurst.

Upon the 31st of August John Russell came into the House of

---

[1] Londonderry to Buckingham, 17th August, 1835. *Buckingham Papers*,
3rd series, ii. p. 199.

[2] The details of the scheme rest chiefly on Disraeli's own account—Monypenny, *Disraeli*, i. p. 301.   Monypenny refers to the obituary of Lyndhurst
in the *Times*, October 13, 1863, as confirmatory evidence : but this obituary
is clearly written by Disraeli—the style and manner are unmistakable.   Campbell's *Lyndhurst* does not refer to the affair, nor does Martin's.   Parker,
Graham, says nothing of any offer made to Graham, though Disraeli says he
was ' sounded.'   Probably Mr. Kitson Clark's forthcoming book will throw
light upon the transaction.   Until more proof is advanced Disraeli's details
cannot be accepted as reliable.   He was apt to exaggerate.   In April, 1835,
he declares that Mrs. Norton and himself acted as intermediaries in a scheme
of Melbourne's for a coalition Government, Melbourne to serve under Peel.
It will be recollected that Melbourne had rejected a coalition as impossible in
1834, and it seems very improbable that he should have employed Mrs. Norton
as a go-between to Peel.   It is quite possible that the lady herself may have
invented such a plan, and that Disraeli took her political influence seriously.

Commons with the Lords' amendments in his hand and a bold and confident air. He had the authority of a mass meeting of his party, which he had just left, behind him : it is not impossible that he had also private intimations of support from another quarter. It was soon clear that he did not intend resignation at present. He offered a compromise : he rejected the proposals of the Lords to save the rights of freemen, to appoint aldermen for life, to continue the old magistrates in office, to make town clerks irremovable, and to reserve the administration of Church property to Churchmen : he consented to allow freemen the parliamentary franchise, and to impose some qualification—lower than that settled by the Lords—on town councillors. As Lord John was speaking, some of his hearers noted with surprise that Peel was in his place on the Opposition Bench—he had come back from Drayton, then ? He rose as soon as Russell finished.

He began by declaring that he had come to defend the rights of the House of Lords : and after some lip homage to that noble assembly, he proceeded, with the utmost coolness, to promise his full support to the Government on every point save the trifling ones of the permanency of town clerks and the administration of Church business. These points were conceded by Lord John, and all went merry as marriage bells.

In a few hours the word was all round the town—' Peel has thrown over the Lords.' The Whigs were in high delight ; the Tories in helpless rage. What could they do ? Some wanted to fight on : Lord Strangford declared, ' If we are to be ruined I think we had better be ruined by real Radicals than by sham Tories.' [1] But the majority realised that they were beaten : Wharncliffe again was the first to take fright, and Wellington would not go on without Wharncliffe. When Lyndhurst came to the House of Lords on August 1st, it was to find that more than half his followers had fled the field. He gave way, and the Corporation Bill, in the form settled by Russell and Peel, went through.

The matter had ended peacefully, but it had disclosed a strange state of things. A reform of the highest importance had been proposed by the Government, and only carried by the aid of the leader of the Opposition ; only his influence, too, had averted a violent conflict between the House of Lords and the House of Commons. It was clear that the Government was pitiably weak ; but it was

[1] *Greville*, iii. p. 312.

also clear that the new Conservative party was on the verge of dissolution. What was to be done when the Opposition leader was hardly on speaking terms with his own party, and hand in glove with the enemy chief ? Peel had acted throughout the session most amicably with John Russell : they had struck up a ' House of Commons intimacy,' and told each other all they meant to do on important measures beforehand.[1]

Peel was very angry with the Lords. They had flouted him and set him at defiance—even Wellington had failed him and succumbed to Lyndhurst's blandishments. Lyndhurst, in fact, had been leader in the Lords throughout the summer, Wellington a mere figurehead. Probably to this was owing the renewed coolness between Peel and the Duke, which vexed their mutual friends in 1836.

Peel was therefore faced with a difficult problem. He believed that a Conservative party was necessary to the country : he meant to be its chief, and lead it in paths of peace and moderation, not in the dangerous ways whither Tory lords would lure it. But he saw this party was on the point of breaking up : much as he disliked the Ultras and their policy, they were the material out of which his Conservative party must in some degree be formed. The maintenance of the just influence of the House of Lords he regarded as one of the most important aims of Conservatism. If he were not to lose the Tory peers, he must conciliate them. He would not abandon his principles for the sake of the party, but wherever concession was honourably possible, concession must be made. For the next two years his work consisted largely of trying to hold the party together.

Fortunately for the Conservative party, no fresh subject of controversy arose for a time. An English Tithe Bill and a Dissenters' Marriage Bill were introduced—both on the same lines as Peel's measures of 1835, but with some improvements. They passed quietly. Far otherwise was the fate of the new Irish Tithe Bill, with its new appropriation clause, and the Irish Corporation Reform Bill. These were strenuously opposed, but on both these points Peel was in general agreement with the Lords. He regarded corporation reform in Ireland as quite a different thing from corporation reform in England and Scotland.

[1] *Greville*, iii. pp. 289, 305. Greville had his information from the two Russells, Lord Tavistock and Lord John.

The Irish close corporations did not differ from those in England, except in being, if anything, more corrupt, more incapable, and more selfish, and having the added objection of being the instruments of religious intolerance—they were self-electing, and no Catholic was ever elected. Peel agreed that they ought to be swept away completely : but he did not want to set up new corporations in their places. His plan was that the nomination of magistrates and the management of the police should be transferred to the Lord Lieutenant ; that tolls (which formed the great part of corporation property) should be abolished, and the remaining corporate property administered for local purposes ; and that local needs—lighting, watching and cleaning—should continue to be, as they had been since an Act of 1829, managed by commissioners, elected by all householders and holding office for three years.

His reason for objecting to the establishment of new municipalities was, that he believed all the old abuses would reappear—only that now a Catholic majority would oppress a Protestant minority, instead of the other way round. When told that it was only fair to give municipal institutions to Ireland after giving them to Scotland and England, he replied, ' the interests of public justice are infinitely higher than nominal uniformity in the public institutions which administer it.' [1] He believed that the people of Ireland were so corrupt and so violent as to be incapable of working municipal institutions to their own advantage. It was simply throwing the administration of local affairs into the hands of ' priests and demagogues.' [2]

These views were no doubt quite sincere, and the reasoning was convincing to anyone familiar with the details of Irish government : but the fact remained that the result of Peel's plan would be to deprive the Irish people of the last vestiges of independent self-government which remained to them, and it is a question whether this loss would not outweigh all the advantages which might have been gained from a purer administration of local business. It must be remembered, too, that Peel was well aware of the tendency of such local institutions to foster national feeling and independence, and that he favoured centralisation in Ireland also because it tended to strengthen the Union with England. He had learned much since he landed in Dublin, a raw lad, twenty-four

[1] *Speeches*, iii. p. 225. [2] Parker, *Peel*, ii. p. 326.

years ago ; but he had not learned to look upon Irish questions
with any but an English eye.

In his attempts to amend the Tithe Bill and the Corporation
Bill, Peel was again defeated, but the Lords threw out both
measures, which Melbourne accordingly laid by until next session.
The commutation of tithes was therefore again postponed because
the Government was pledged not to pass a Tithe Bill without an
appropriation clause. Many of the Whigs must have cursed
John Russell's ill-advised bargain. That the appropriation clause
was in itself most just and reasonable had little to do with the
question : the point was that there was no chance of passing it.
The position of the Lords was strong here : Peel sided with them,
and the opinion of the great majority of the English people was
probably on their side. The Government, however, had to
maintain their own consistency : they had turned Peel out on this
point. They had also to satisfy O'Connell ; he had loyally supported them, he had with generous self-sacrifice waived all his
own claims to legal preferment, and he naturally insisted on his
bargain.

At the opening of 1837, therefore, Peel again found himself in
difficulties. His reactionaries wanted to fight the Corporation
Bill throughout—resist the abolition of the old municipalities, not
merely the establishment of new ones. On the other hand,
Stanley and Graham, who were now enrolled in the party, would
not agree to unconditional opposition any longer. He himself,
seeing the strong feeling in Ireland that ' the denial (of municipalities) implied inferiority and the intention to insult,' thought
the time was come to make concessions, but he was anxious to
avoid another quarrel with the Tories. He talked over the question with the Duke : he was ready to defer to Wellington's opinion
on this point : he only stipulated that whatever course they
decided upon now should be adhered to throughout. He would
not oppose the Corporation Bill now, and then when he came into
office carry such a bill himself on the plea of necessity.[1] At last
they resolved to wait until both bills were before Parliament, and
then try to drive a bargain with the Whigs : then the Duke would
give way on Corporations, in order to save the Irish Church.

The death of the King altered the situation, and postponed the

---

[1] Peel to Wellington, 28th March, 1827, Parker, *Peel*, ii. p. 344. Memorial
by Sir R. Peel, *ib.* p. 433. Sir J. Graham to Peel, 9th June, 1840, *ib.* p. 438.

crisis until 1838. Then the Tithe and Corporation Bills were again introduced, and Peel made his bargain with Russell. The Government was to abandon appropriation, and in return Peel agreed to the establishment of new municipalities in the larger towns of Ireland. Accordingly, though the Tithe Bill contained an appropriation clause, it was modified in the debate, and the measure which eventually passed was almost identical with Peel's rejected bill of 1835. It was a complete surrender of the principle on which the Whigs had entered office, and a confession that the Government was powerless to enforce its views upon the House of Lords. The Tories were triumphant, the English and Irish Radicals disgusted with the Ministry. The Corporation Bill was next introduced, and Peel carried out his side of the bargain : municipalities, elected by the £10 householders, were set up in eleven large towns, and the Lord Lieutenant empowered to grant them, with a £5 franchise, to smaller towns. Unfortunately the Lords, under Lyndhurst's leadership, introduced several amendments, including a £10 franchise for the little towns, which the Government could not accept, and the bill was lost. In 1839 the same process was gone through. Peel was indignant with Wellington, who had thus retreated from the bargain they had made.[1] In 1840 this subject, with other differences, nearly led to a complete quarrel between the two and the break-up of the party. The Duke stuck to his guns, but at last the Government consented to compromise for an £8 franchise, and the bill became law.

It is impossible to justify Peel's Irish policy while in opposition —impossible not to regret that he spent his best years defending that crying evil and injustice, the Anglican Church in Ireland. The measure of appropriation introduced by the Whigs was fair and moderate : to-day the only objection to it appears to be that it did not go far enough. There was in the 'thirties a momentary blink—due to the passing of the Reform Act—when it seemed possible to reform the Irish Church. Largely owing to the influence of Peel the chance was lost : and thirty years passed before a pupil of his took up the work again, and after a great

---

[1] Maxwell, *Wellington*, ii. p. 139. Arbuthnot wrote in June, 1840, ' He (the Duke) certainly does not appear to think he was bound to pass it (the Corporation Bill) if it should be found that in its results in would affect the general interest of the empire, and perhaps sever the connection between England and Ireland.' (Parker, *Peel*, ii. p. 440.) He must, however, have been aware of these tendencies when he made the first agreement.

struggle abolished the whole vast iniquity, at which the Whigs had cast their puny dart in vain.

It is true that Peel's resistance could have had little effect if it had not been for the strong popular feeling that backed him. A great and powerful section of the English people regarded the appropriation clause as the first step to the disestablishment of the Church and the repeal of the Union. Moreover, though Peel felt it his duty to oppose appropriation, he seems, for a time at least, to have thought he was fighting in vain : he probably thought it would inevitably come in the end, that his opposition was as useless as his opposition to the Reform Bill had been ; and he perhaps would not have been altogether broken-hearted had the Whigs succeeded in passing the measure, and got the whole disagreeable question settled before he himself came again into power. Greville tells a strange story of Russell's discussing the measure with Peel in 1835. 'Peel said to John, " If you *will* appropriate, I will show you a much better plan than your own," and he accordingly did show him a plan by which there would be a considerably greater surplus, and John acknowledged that Peel's plan would be better than his own.' Greville, who was very intimate with both the Russells, had this story from Lord John's brother, Tavistock.[1] It must be remembered, too, that Peel was already at odds with his party, and that a lapse on this point would have been unpardonable. It meant a break with Conservatism, and he would have found himself a political outcast. He would not have hesitated to face such a risk if he had thought it his duty, but unfortunately he believed his duty lay rather in defending the Church.

But when all is said, this is the darkest part of Peel's career. He used the great power that he held, from 1834 to 1841, to delay the small instalment of justice for Ireland which the Whigs offered. His action embittered and perpetuated the conflict of parties and religions in Ireland : it lessened what faint hope there was that the Irish would ever be reconciled to English rule : it increased the likelihood that if parting came between the two nations, it would be a parting without regret, without generosity, without affection.

It had been expected that the next general election would bring a Tory majority, but two things had altered the feeling of the country when King William's death caused the dissolution of

[1] *Greville*, iii. p. 305.

Parliament. The reckless and factious opposition of the Tory lords, and their attempt to throw off Peel's authority, had alarmed and disgusted many who were inclined to veer towards Conservatism ; and the popularity of the innocent young girl who had been called to the throne told on the side of the Government. It was felt that the young Queen should not have to deal with a ministerial crisis the moment she came to the throne. It was also known that the Princess Victoria had been educated in Whig principles, and surrounded by Whig companions. The election, therefore, scarcely altered the balance of parties. The Tories gained some seats in the counties, the Whigs gained some seats in the towns : still the Tories were in a minority in the House of Commons, still the Whigs could only count on a majority with Irish support.

The little Queen's first appearance in council conquered all hearts (except the cast-iron organ of Lord Lyndhurst, who remained perfectly calm while his fellows dissolved into tears and ecstasies). Victoria was not beautiful, but she was very charming, and had all the attraction of a child, who is at once entirely self-absorbed and yet devoid of self-consciousness. Her Ministers were soon deeply attached to her, and Melbourne in particular showed her a fatherly devotion, which she appreciated and returned. Unfortunately, however, the Prime Minister did not handle the political situation wisely.

The Household appointed for the young Queen consisted exclusively of Whigs, several of her ladies being the wives of Cabinet Ministers ; and she was permitted to express her preference for the party openly : she talked to Russell of ' we ' and ' our policy,' in speaking of the Government. At the general election her name was used as a rallying cry, and this was doubly unlucky, as an unusual amount of violence accompanied the polling. At Hawick, electors who had dared to vote Conservative were stripped, flung into the river, and forced to run the gauntlet naked through the town. Graham was defeated for Cumberland, was mobbed in Carlisle, and his son was seriously injured. At Tamworth, Peel challenged his Whig opponent, who had called him a liar, and the matter seems to have come nearer to bloodshed than most of Sir Robert's rather numerous affairs of honour. In the circumstances the use made of the Queen's name roused a personal feeling against her among the rank and file of the Tories, and

Croker in the *Quarterly* descanted on the advantages of the Salic Law.

The character and reputation of Parliament had for some time been sinking, and the election had not improved matters. The Tory peers, rejecting every measure of reform, irrespective of its merits, out of pure spite against the Government, had won an evil reputation for their House, and strengthened the impression made by their conduct in the Reform Bill crisis. The House of Commons was acquiring a bad name for its disorderly and lawless conduct. Abercromby had proved an incapable Speaker ; and Ministers and private members alike openly disregarded his rulings. Perhaps this insubordination accounts for the unpleasant incident in December, 1837, when young Disraeli, who had at last got a seat, was howled down in attempting to give his maiden speech. ' I say anything but failure ; he must make his way,' said Peel afterwards.[1] This need not be taken as indicating that Sir Robert, with prescient eye, discerned in the somewhat unpromising bud of 1837 the full-blown genius of 1878 ; probably a generous indignation at the cruel treatment the young man received moved him to applaud, and admiration of his pluck prompted the good-natured prophecy. After this he seems to have made a point of cheering ' Dis,'[2] contrary to his usual custom,[3] which was to look excessively bored while his friends spouted.

In this disorderly and discredited assembly, Peel's reputation was one of the few that had not suffered. It stood higher than ever, indeed, and he was merely waiting now, it seemed, for the best opportunity to turn out his adversaries. He could have done this easily enough in 1838 by a combination with the Radicals.

The trouble arose on a colonial question. For some time past Canada had been in a state of great discontent. The Upper Province, which was British, was suffering from maladministration and neglect merely ; but in the Lower Province, where the population was still mainly French, corrupt and incapable government had produced a deadlock : the House of Assembly had been driven to stop supplies, and since 1832 the revenue had been held up and no salaries paid to officials. Successive Colonial secretaries

---

[1] Monypenny, *Disraeli*, ii. p. 11.   [2] *Ib.* pp. 15, 57, 93, 111, etc.

[3] Gladstone called Peel ' the most conscientious man I ever knew in spareness of eulogium.' Morley, *Gladstone*, i. p. 280.

had done nothing to remedy the matter. Peel, when he came into office in 1834, conceived the idea of sending out an able man, with special powers, to settle the dispute. The mission was offered to Manners Sutton (now Lord Canterbury) and to Stratford Canning, and, when they refused, to Lord Amherst.[1] But the Whigs, on coming into power, sent out three commissioners instead. These had been unable to settle the trouble, and in the autumn of 1837 Lower Canada broke out into open revolt. The Whigs now adopted Peel's idea, and sent out Lord Durham with special powers.

The real difficulty of the Canada question lay in the fact that few persons in England took any interest in it, and still fewer knew anything about its rights and wrongs. On one point all parties were agreed, that the Colonial Secretary, Lord Glenelg, had shown lamentable incapacity. The Radicals, however, sympathised with the Canadian rebels and justified their action. Peel, while he condemned the conduct of Glenelg, thought it his duty to support the Government in restoring order in Canada, and maintaining its connection with Britain, even at the risk of war with the United States, which were giving the rebels unofficial encouragement.

Sir William Molesworth, a leading Radical, proposed a motion praying for the removal of Glenelg, and Joseph Hume approached the Tories to know if they would support it. Peel felt strongly that an alliance with the Radicals, who were moved by wholly different motives, would be dishonourable to himself and his party ; yet he could not vote in favour of Glenelg, whose conduct he thoroughly disapproved. At last he adopted the expedient of proposing an amendment to Molesworth's motion—an amendment which he knew the Radicals could not support. He proposed a direct vote of want of confidence in the whole Government, instead of a censure on Glenelg. There was no chance of carrying such a vote, and it was lost : but the Conservatives had avoided the fault of factious combination with opponents with whom they did not really agree.

For the same reasons Peel refused to avail himself of an ally who might have been valuable. At the opening of 1836 the Whigs had definitely broken with Brougham, and appointed a comparatively

[1] Aberdeen wanted to send Lord Howick, but Peel thought the appointment would be improper, as Howick had just made a very fierce personal attack on Aberdeen and the Duke. *Peel Papers*, British Museum, 40,312, pp. 200, 221, 223.

young and inexperienced man, Lord Cottenham, to the Chancellor-ship. Brougham's mother had always warned him that it was political suicide for him to go to the House of Lords, and now her prophecy had come true : he was helpless. Faced with ruin in the fullness of his powers, the ex-Chancellor vanished for a time from the scene. After heaven knows what hours of mental and physical sickness he had returned, animated by one desire—to be revenged on the colleagues who had used and then betrayed him. He was now the bosom friend of Lyndhurst and Croker, and his services were at the disposal of the Conservative chiefs : but Wellington and Peel would have nothing to do with a man whom they both detested and distrusted,[1] and Brougham became a free-lance, now courting the Radicals, now abetting Lyndhurst. The two scamps, ' chuckling and laughing and brimful of mischief, '[2] led the Ministers in the House of Lords a dog's life.

At last, in the April of 1839, Peel thought he had driven the Whigs to bay. A new Irish crisis had arisen, provoked partly by the Irish Under-Secretary's declaration that ' property has its duties as well as its rights,' which had driven Tory landlords to frenzy, and partly by the murder, in broad daylight, of Lord Norbury, a blameless and inoffensive old gentleman of eighty. The Lords voted an inquiry into Irish affairs. The Government countered it by a motion inviting the House of Commons to approve their Irish policy. Peel thought he had them in a corner now, and meant to push them hard ; but shortly before the debate, Charles Greville, Clerk of the Privy Council and an intimate friend of Russell's, came privately to Graham. He had information that John Russell meant to make a stand against the Radicals ; that he felt the Government must go out soon, and that he would then try to support Peel against Radical opposition. Greville entreated that Peel should hold his hand, and say nothing that could offend or alienate Russell. Peel was ' excessively annoyed and put out.' ' Why,' he said, ' I shall have to go down to the House of Commons with two speeches.' But he eventually agreed to be conciliatory, if Russell were equally so.[3] His speech was certainly mild enough to annoy his own followers. The Government got their vote of confidence with a majority of 22.

---

[1] Parker, *Peel*, ii. pp. 360, 374, 376, 414.   [2] *Greville*, iv. p. 166.

[3] *Greville*, iv. p. 190 ff. It is not clear from Greville's account whether Russell himself knew anything of this overture.

This could not last, however. The popularity of the Queen, which had served for a little to uphold the Ministry, had sunk, owing to a nasty Court scandal.[1] The only first-rate man in the Cabinet, John Russell, had lost heart and energy : his wife had died recently, and he was brooding over his vanishing popularity.[2] Melbourne now took little interest in politics : he ' seems to hold office for no other purpose than that of dining at Buckingham House,' remarked Greville.[3] Within a week or two, on a colonial question, the ministerial majority had sunk to five, and they decided to resign. The crisis was at the last sudden and unexpected : they had clung to office for so long that nobody expected them to go out on this point.[4]

Peel answered the royal summons with fear and reluctance. The young Queen had become most deeply and justly attached to her Prime Minister, and all that was best in Melbourne had risen in response to her affectionate trust. He was at once her adviser in affairs of State, and the confidant of all her girlish feelings. Melbourne was the most charming man in London—unless it were Sidney Herbert. The Tory chiefs had no attractions that could vie with his : ' I have no small-talk, and Peel has no manners,' said the Duke, with his usual directness. Peel was well aware of his own deficiencies, and if he had not been, his friends had been busy telling him for some time past. He must get over his awkwardness, they said, in dealing with the Queen ; he must abandon his caution and reserve ! No doubt these good people meant well ; but to a shy man there is nothing more paralysing than to be told that he must be frank and easy.

The Queen, on her side, was overwhelmed at the disaster which had befallen her : she could not eat, she did nothing but weep, she wrote Lord Melbourne periodical bulletins of her sensations. The first interview passed off fairly well : ' but he is such a cold, odd man, she can't make out what he means. . . . The Queen don't like his manner after—oh ! how different, how dreadfully

---

[1] The affair of Lady Flora Hastings.

[2] Walpole, *Russell*, pp. 318-9. [3] *Greville*, iv. p. 184.

[4] Parliament had passed a bill for reforming prisons in Jamaica. The Legislature of Jamaica refused to accept it. The Government then proposed to suspend the Constitution of the colony for some years. The Conservatives thought the measure too extreme and opposed it, and several Radicals crossed the House and voted with them. Of the proposal to suspend the Constitution, Peel said, ' You have got another Ireland growing up in every colony you possess.' Morley, *Gladstone*, i. p. 139.

different, to that frank, open, natural and most kind, warm manner of Lord Melbourne!'[1] Poor Victoria! Bereft of her Melbourne, whose charm and tact had been such a revelation to the home-bred girl, what could she do with this awkward, embarrassed man, with his incessant nervous fidgeting, his Lancashire accent,[2] his painful attempts to be bland?

The Queen's name had been made a party cry; she had been allowed to identify herself with the Whigs and their interests, and they had openly boasted of her partiality. The new Cabinet, therefore, decided that it was necessary to obtain a proof of her confidence. They were in a minority in the House of Commons, and now it was publicly reported that they would not possess the confidence of the Crown. In the case of a King, the Lords of the Household would have been removed: the new Ministers decided to change two or three of the Ladies of the Bedchamber, those who were the near relations of Whig statesmen. They seem to have feared that Lady Normanby, wife of the Whig Colonial Secretary, was capable of making mischief: the other two ladies selected were the Duchesses of Bedford and Sutherland. Peel went to the Palace next day with his list of appointments, and what followed is best described in the Queen's own words.

' Sir Robert said, " Now, about the Ladies," upon which I said I could not give up *any* of my Ladies, and never had imagined such a thing. He asked if I meant to retain *all*. *"All,"* I said. " The Mistress of the Robes and the Ladies of the Bedchamber?" I replied, " All." . . . Upon which he said he did not mean *all* the Bedchamber women and *all* the Maids of Honour; he meant the Mistress of the Robes and the Ladies of the Bedchamber; to which I replied they were of more importance than the others, and that I could *not* consent, and that it had never been done before. He said I was a Queen Regnant, and that made the difference. "Not here," I said, and I maintained my rights. Sir Robert then urged it upon *public grounds only*, but I said here I would not consent.' ' I never saw a man so frightened,' she added.[3]

---

[1] The Queen to Lord Melbourne, 8th May, 1839. *Letters of Queen Victoria*, i. p. 159.

[2] Peel retained his Lancashire accent, with its dropped 'h,' to the end of his life.

[3] *Letters of Queen Victoria*, i. pp. 161, 162. The new *Greville* states that Wellington told Greville that 'he had never seen Peel so gentle and conciliatory in his manner as he was to her,' and that Peel suggested that she should say who was to retire and who to stay among the ladies (vol. ii. p. 69).

Peel went off to Wellington. They came back together, and the Queen saw them, but stuck to her refusal. When they had gone, she sat down, flushed with triumph, and wrote to Lord Melbourne : ' The Queen of England will not submit to such trickery. Keep yourself in readiness, for you may soon be wanted.' [1]

Melbourne came to the Palace and saw the Queen, and the Whig leaders assembled to discuss the question. Melbourne had concluded from Victoria's account that Peel insisted on changing *all* the Ladies of the Household,[2] and only this misunderstanding can excuse their proceedings. Howick said that the negotiation with Peel must be reopened, and Spring Rice supported him ; but they stood alone. The rest of the Cabinet declared unanimously for supporting the Queen. Sir John Hobhouse swore he would sooner cut off his hand than sign such a negotiation ; Russell said ' no earthly power should induce him to hand over the Queen to Peel.' [3] Melbourne listened uneasily to the loyal effusions of his colleagues. Frivolous and cynical he might be, but he was honest : he never deceived himself and fostered his own illusions as did Lord John. He knew well enough that the course upon which they were embarking was unconstitutional, and he was well aware of the extreme impropriety of his having been in private correspondence with the Queen throughout the negotiation with Peel : but he could not bring himself to fail Victoria. He did not care a rap for leaving office, but his friendship with her had become the one joy of his lonely life, ruined by a miserable domestic tragedy. He yielded to the enthusiasm of his friends. They drew up a note, refusing all concessions, which the Queen was to send to Peel.[4] Later in the day he returned to the Palace. Victoria showed him Peel's written statement of what had passed, and for the first time Melbourne understood that there had been no question of removing all the Ladies. He was much startled, but it was too late to withdraw : Peel had declared that he and his colleagues agreed they could not go on without some demonstration of the Queen's confidence.[5] ' Hurrah for the Darling

[1] *Letters of Queen Victoria*, i. p. 162.

[2] It is not clear who was responsible for this misunderstanding. The Queen's letter (p. 162) implies *all* the Ladies ; but the account given in her diary (p. 165) states that she told Melbourne verbally that only some of the Ladies were to be removed.

[3] *Hobhouse*, v. p. 195.   [4] *Letters of Queen Victoria*, i. p. 167.

[5] It must be remembered that Peel was still actually in a minority in the House of Commons.

Little Queen! Peel is out and Melbourne is in again!' wrote O'Connell.[1]

The Queen had, in truth, made up her mind to dislike her new Minister, and snatched at the first chance that presented itself to retain her old friends in office. A keen observer, who watched her almost daily, noted that since her accession a great change had taken place in Victoria's demeanour. At first ' there was an ingenuous and serene air which seemed full of promise. At the end of a year, the change was melancholy. The expression of her face was wholly altered. It had become bold and discontented.' [2]

But if the Queen were not entirely blameless, the Whig leaders were far more guilty. They had continued to act as the Queen's advisers after handing in their resignations : Peel actually was the Queen's Minister when the Whigs were secretly counselling her to dismiss him. A spoilt and wilful girl of nineteen had upset the whole system by which the country was governed, and the Whigs had abetted her—some from personal affection and loyalty—others from desire to retain office : but none of them would have dreamed of acting as they did had the Sovereign been a stout old gentleman with grey whiskers, instead of a pretty young girl. There was no need for the *Quarterly* again to sing the praises of the Salic Law : its advantages were now sufficiently obvious. Most persons will agree with Peel, when he wrote to Croker, ' It is a real insult to the Queen, and to the Sovereign authority, to mix with constitutional arguments any appeals to the special circumstances of youth and sex.' [3]

But, indignant though he might be with his opponents, Peel had no mind to clear himself at the expense of the Queen. His explanation in the House of Commons was a masterly piece of work, though he was exceedingly nervous over it. ' Without any appearance of art or dexterity, he contrived to steer through all the difficult points and to justify himself without saying a word offensive to the Queen.' [4] His friends were not all so delicate : the sensations of the Ultras, seeing the prize thus snatched from their grasp, and their opinion of the Queen, may be better imagined than described.

The excitement which had prevailed throughout the crisis had

[1] Fitzpatrick, *O'Connell*, vol. ii. p. 178.
[2] Harriet Martineau, *Autobiography*, ii. pp. 120-1.
[3] *Croker*, ii. p. 343.   [4] *Greville*, iv. p. 219.

been extreme.   The Radicals, horrified at the result of their revolt, had, as soon as they learned that the Whigs might yet return to power, made overtures of renewed support.   A good deal of popular sentiment had been aroused against Peel's blackguardly attempt to tyrannize over the poor young Queen, and he was warned of possible attempts to assassinate him, and to attack his house at Drayton.[1]   But these emotions were very transitory : the Whigs gained no real strength from them.   ' The fact is, we have nothing to rely upon but the Queen and Paddy,' said Lady Holland dolefully.[2]

Moreover, the character of the Conservative opposition was now a little altered.   Peel, as the narrative of his life has shown, was not of a very mild and forgiving disposition : he might act very generously towards an enemy, but it was because he was incapable of anything so petty as revenge.   He had a pride in not stooping to retaliate : he did not the less resent.   He now thought the Whigs had treated him shamefully, in return for the great forbearance he had shown them ; and though he meant to conduct his opposition on the same honourable principles as before, he was ready to press them mercilessly whenever he could.   That his position with the Queen had been made impossible, he did not think should at all affect his parliamentary proceedings.   He meant to stick to his determination about the Ladies, and that, he said, ' might be a very good reason why the Queen should decline my services, but I do not think the consideration of my personal position in that respect . . . should very materially influence my parliamentary conduct.' [3]   This confidence was reasonable enough. He knew the Queen could hardly venture to provoke a second crisis on the same grounds, if he came with a majority behind him, as in the natural course of things he soon must.   A curious incident showed how Melbourne thought of the affair.   Both the party chiefs were present at a Court ball, when Melbourne went up to Peel, and whispered earnestly, ' For God's sake go and speak to the Queen ! ' But Peel, whether through obstinacy or shyness, would not go.[4]

[1] Mr. James Austin to Peel, Lord John Russell to Peel.   Parker, *Peel*, ii. p. 401.

[2] *Greville*, iv. p. 250.

[3] Parker, *Peel*, ii. p. 424.   Peel to Arbuthnot, 20th December, 1839.

[4] *Greville*, iv. p. 273.   At a later date Melbourne privately advised Peel how to deal with the Queen when he was in office, who said, ' It was very kind of Lord Melbourne, and I am obliged to him.'   *Greville*, v. p. 39.

Meanwhile internal dissensions again threatened the Tory party. The difficulties between Peel and the Duke upon the Irish Corporation Bill, which have been described, were accentuated by differences on the subject of Canada.

Durham's administration had not been very successful. His proceedings had been high-handed and illegal; when they were condemned, he came home in a huff; and he had no sooner turned his back than a fresh insurrection broke out. He had, however, drawn up the famous report, by which Britain's policy towards her colonies has been mainly directed ever since. Durham's colleagues did not defend him with any great enthusiasm; but they eventually adopted his report, and introduced a bill for the union of the two Canadian provinces under one popular Legislature, almost free from the control of the Mother Country. After some shuffling, the Whigs had put their ablest man, Russell, into the Colonial Office; and Russell was heartily of the opinion that the sooner the Colonies were got rid of the better. He adopted the Durham Report not only because its recommendations would end the trouble in Canada, but because he thought they tended towards a separation.[1] Unfortunately the Duke took the same view of the measure as Lord John: he thought it would end in separation, and so he opposed it.

Peel, as we have seen, did not contemplate the dissolution of the Empire with the same benevolent satisfaction as Lord John, but he approved of the Canada Bill, because he thought it, as it has proved to be, the best means of rendering the Canadian people contented. He thought it was his duty to support the bill—he would not even consent to delaying it. In July, 1840, he submitted to his colleagues a very strong memorandum, in which he declared that if his views were not adopted, he would undertake no responsibility for the consequences.[2] The prospect of a speedy political victory enforced the necessity for agreement; and the Duke, very much against his will, gave way. He was much hurt and displeased by Peel's conduct,[3] and the devoted Gosh was again required to bring

---

[1] In the following year Russell wrote that he had restricted the fortification of Canada as much as possible. ' If the Cabinet had disagreed with me, which they did not, I should have advised them to give up Canada at once.' Gooch, *Later Correspondence of Russell*, i. p. 43.

[2] Parker, *Peel*, ii. p. 436 ff.

[3] The Duke also seems to have been jealous because Peel consulted with Stanley and Graham instead of with him. *Graham*, i. p. 298. Arbuthnot to Graham, 12th July, 1840.

about a reconciliation. Fortunately a trifling incident aided his effort. Peel's third son, now fifteen years old, was now with his ship in the Mediterranean, and had taken part in the recent operations off the Syrian coast. His father could not resist the temptation to send ' my boy's letter ' to the Duke. Wellington was much pleased, both with the letter and with Peel's action : and this little human touch probably did more than all the efforts of friends to promote the cordial intimacy between the two Tory chiefs, which from this time forth was never disturbed. The little midshipman who unconsciously acted as peacemaker was afterwards Sir William Peel, K.C.B., V.C., whose brilliant career was prematurely cut short in the Indian Mutiny.

The Whig Ministry had now fallen very low. Until now, though their position had not been a happy one, and their efforts had often been stultified by the conduct of the Lords, still they had carried on the business of the nation, and, all things considered, they had got through a very creditable amount of reforming legislation. Now, however, they were helpless. Howick, ashamed of the position, resigned, and was succeeded by Macaulay. Even with the aid of that brilliant debater, the Government could but just maintain itself, cadging for the support of the Radicals, and at the mercy of Sir Robert Peel. They could carry no measure unless he supported it, and whether he supported or opposed, it was equally humiliating to them. A question of Privilege of Parliament arose—the famous case of Stockdale $v.$ Hansard—causing much dissension and ill-feeling. Peel supported the Government—but he supported them by taking the matter out of Russell's hands and doing much as he pleased with it, to the equal annoyance of friends and foes, displaying throughout an intemperate and domineering spirit worthy of the days of Wilkes.[1] ' It is curious,' remarks Sir James Graham, ' that Peel, who often is languid in his attack on his adversaries, puts forth superior energy and strength when he combats his followers.' [2] In much the same manner, Peel took up and settled the vexed question of election committees, which had long been a scandal, and which the Government made no attempt to deal with. Stanley, with

---

[1] Upon the general principle that official papers printed by order of Parliament should not be made the subject of actions for libel, Peel and Russell were, of course, in the right : but the methods of the House of Commons in enforcing its views were rather difficult to defend.

[2] Parker, *Graham*, i. p. 293.

Peel's support, then tried to reform the system of registration of voters in Ireland, which was subject to great abuses, but here the Whigs, driven by O'Connell, made a feeble effort to recover their position. They introduced a new registration bill of their own, which included a lowering of the franchise : it was cut to bits by the Tories. A year ago they would have resigned, but now they seemed to have lost the faculty of resigning, and dragged on their dull and disgraceful course. They had no authority anywhere, not even with the Queen. On her marriage with Prince Albert of Saxe-Coburg, she demanded an allowance for her husband of £50,000 a year. Considering the very generous Civil List that had been granted two years before, and the general depression of trade and distress in the country, there was no chance that such a grant would be made : but Ministers had not the courage to refuse the Queen, and went to the House of Commons with a proposal which in their hearts they could not approve. Peel reduced the grant to £30,000 a year.[1] In the words of an indignant Radical :

'The Right Honourable member for Tamworth governs England. The Honourable and learned member for Dublin governs Ireland. The Whigs govern nothing but Downing Street. The Right Honourable member for Tamworth is contented with power without place or patronage, and the Whigs are contented with place and patronage without power. Let any honourable man say which is the more honourable position.'[2]

No Government ever met Parliament in more desperate state than the Whigs at the opening of the session of 1841. There was no longer any semblance of unity among its members. 'A Government of departments,' one of their own men called it, ' absolutely without a chief, hating, distrusting, despising one another, having no principles and no plans, living from hand to mouth, able to do nothing, and indifferent whether they did anything or not, proposing measures without the hope or expectation of carrying them, and clinging to their places for no other reason than that they felt themselves bound to the Queen.'[3] Their difficulties had now culminated in a financial crisis.

[1] Hume tried to reduce the grant to £10,000 a year. This was defeated, and then Peel proposed and carried £30,000.

[2] *Hansard*, xlvii. p. 373.

[3] *Greville*, v. p. 49. The speaker was Charles Bulle-

For years past the national finances had been allowed to sink into worse and worse disorder. The exchequer had been directed by Spring Rice, the—let us say the unluckiest Chancellor who held office from the day when Vansittart resigned in 1823 to that when Mr. Winston Churchill took office in 1924. Baring, who succeeded Spring Rice in 1839, had not been able to retrieve the losses. He tried piling a little on the customs duties, and the yield had fallen instead of rising. In 1837 there was a deficit of £1,428,000. In 1838, it was £430,000. In 1839, it rose again to £1,457,000. In 1840, the Radicals carried Penny Postage against the Ministry and against Peel, and it took nearly thirty years for the postal revenue to recover : this year the deficit was £1,842,000. In 1841, Baring estimated the probable deficit at £2,421,000. Snatching at any remedy, the Cabinet decided to make a move towards Free Trade—or, rather, against Imperial Preference. They proposed to raise the duty on colonial timber and lower that on foreign timber ; [1] to reduce the duty on foreign (slave-grown) sugar ; and to substitute a fixed duty of 8s. a quarter on imported corn for the sliding scale of duties at present in force.

These measures were not adopted without much discussion, and especially the alteration of the Corn Laws was debated. John Russell was the advocate of the small fixed duty on corn. Melbourne had pledged himself against meddling with the Corn Laws, in the most positive language, two years before ; but Melbourne had ceased to make any attempt to control his colleagues. It was agreed to try the plan. As the council broke up, having taken their decision, the Prime Minister called after them, ' By the by, there is one thing we haven't agreed upon, which is, what we are to say. Is it to make corn dearer, or cheaper, or to make the price steady ? I don't care which ; but we had better all be in the same story.' [2]

No hint of the intention to tamper with the Corn Laws was given in the Queen's Speech : it was not announced until well into the session : and the suspicion arises that it was regarded as a

[1] Of course this arrangement would have brought no immediate gain to the revenue, though it might have ultimately caused some expansion in the timber trade.

[2] Walpole, *Russell*, i. p. 369. When Wellington asked Melbourne, in the House of Lords, whether he had changed his opinion on the Corn Laws, the Prime Minister caused a roar of laughter by replying, ' The fact is, we are always changing our minds.'

desperate expedient, and that Russell was not to be allowed to propose it unless it seemed likely that the budget would not be well received.

It was soon obvious that this was so. Accordingly, immediately before Baring brought in the budget, Russell announced that he would move for a committee on the Corn Laws a month hence. Baring, following him, produced a budget where the estimated yield of the revised customs duties only supplied half the deficiency, and declared that Russell's proposals would provide for the rest : this method of proceeding was so extraordinary that the Government was at once challenged, and Russell was obliged to communicate the details of his intended ' surprise.'

The Tories rallied against the Sugar Duties, and Peel, who had as yet said but little, led the attack. He began by condemning the admission of slave-grown sugar at a moment when the British West Indies were still ' staggering under the shock ' of the emancipation of the slaves. He would by no means pledge himself to exclude all the products of slave labour, but he thought in this particular case the moment was ill chosen : the ' great experiment of emancipation ' should be given a fair chance to succeed. He went on to make a plea for Imperial Preference, declaring that the West Indies, the East Indies, and India together could produce an ample supply of sugar for British consumption. ' I never,' he said, ' lent myself to the cry of Anti-slavery, and I will not now lend myself to the cry of cheap sugar.'

Next he passed to the general question of freedom of trade. He refused to subscribe to the principle that it was always best to buy in the cheapest market ; but if, ' by the principles of free trade, you simply mean the progressive and well-considered relaxation of restrictions upon commerce, I may venture to refer to the past. I can say with truth . . . that there was no man in this House from whom Mr. Huskisson derived a more cordial and invariable support than he did from me. . . . I did at that time cordially support the proposals made by Mr. Huskisson, and the result of those measures has confirmed me in the wisdom of that course. . . . The noble lord seems to claim an exclusive inheritance of the principles of Mr. Huskisson. Nay, he makes the awful announcement, that if he and his colleagues are driven out of office, they will pack up the principles of free trade and carry them off with them. . . . Why, what right has the noble lord to claim this exclusive dominion over the principles of Mr. Huskisson ? When did we ever hear a word of them until the pressure of the present moment ? Was there ever any public man who pronounced so positive a condemnation of the principles of free trade as the present Prime Minister . . . and did one of you dissent from that declaration ? ' As to the Corn Laws, he would say, in answer to their challenge, that he preferred a sliding scale to a fixed duty, but he would say nothing more. He would not bind himself ' to the details of the existing law.' On the timber duties, likewise, he would reserve for himself unfettered action. What did this challenge mean ? ' Now, when the aggregate of your yearly deficiencies amounts to near £8,000,000—when the burden becomes intolerable—when exposure and disgrace are inevitable—instead of penitent confessions of your own incapacity and maladministration, you represent yourselves as martyrs in the cause of free trade—and call upon me to furnish you with a budget. And I am by no means surprised at your confidence. You recollect that when I left office in 1830, I had been connected with an administration which . . . reduced the public debt by £20,000,000 of capital, and the annual charge upon that debt by more than £1,000,000 . . . (and) left a surplus of £1,600,000 of revenue over expenditure. . . . But I cannot help you now. No, great as is my commiseration, I cannot assist you. I view with unaffected sympathy the position of the right honourable gentleman, the Chancellor of the Exchequer. It has been remarked that a good man struggling with adversity is a sight worthy of the gods. And certainly the right honourable gentleman, both with respect to the goodness of the man and the extent of his adversity, presents at the moment that spectacle. Can there be a more lamentable picture than that of a Chancellor of the Exchequer seated on an empty chest—by the pool of a bottomless deficiency—fishing for a budget ? I won't bite ; the right honourable gentleman shall return home with his pannier as empty as his chest.' [1]

' And then,' says Sir John Hobhouse, with bitterness, ' he giggled, as if he had said something exceedingly funny.' [2]

The Anti-Slavery men joined the Conservatives, and the sugar duties were defeated by a majority of 36; but the Government did not resign. They had decided to dissolve—cheap bread was a good cry with which to go to the country, but for the country to

[1] *Speeches*, iii. p. 745.   [2] *Hobhouse*, vi. p. 25.

understand what was being offered, Russell must have a chance of explaining his Corn Law proposals. It was a reckless and un-scrupulous decision. Melbourne, ' almost in tears,' warned his colleagues that it would turn out badly ; but when they deter-mined to go on he yielded.[1]

On the following day, Ministers quietly announced that they would proceed with the regular business of the House. The sensation caused by the announcement was extreme ; ' Peel turned as pale as ashes.' [2] But the folly of the Whigs had only given their opponents a greater triumph. Peel countered them by proposing a direct vote of want of confidence. The struggle was fought out with extraordinary fierceness. The Whigs actually brought to the House Lord Douglas Halliburton, a member who was in a state of imbecility, and on the division wheeled him past the tellers in a bath chair, while the Tories shouted, ' Shame ! ' But in spite of all their efforts, the vote of want of confidence was carried by a majority of one.

It was impossible to delay any longer : Russell announced that they would dissolve Parliament. Peel declared that unless Russell would pledge himself to reassemble immediately, he would only grant supplies for three months ; and the Ministers were obliged to agree to this also.[3] They soon discovered that they had played into the hands of their enemy. At the general election the country returned a great Conservative majority. On the opening of the new session, Peel proposed an amendment to the Address, which was carried by a majority of 91 ; and at last the Whigs resigned.

[1] *Hobhouse*, p. 30. [2] *Ib.* vi. p. 29.

[3] *Greville* asserts that until this threat the Ministers had meant to postpone the meeting of Parliament as long as possible. V. p. 12.

CHAPTER XI

FREE TRADE AND FINANCIAL REFORM, 1841-1845

When Sir Robert Peel undertook the government in 1841, it was in a period of confusion and darkness. Abroad, prospects were threatening. The policy of Palmerston, directed to the isolation of France, had resulted in something not unlike the isolation of Britain : the French Alliance was ended, and a false and unnatural intimacy with the Northern Powers had taken its place. France, her policy checkmated and her pride humiliated, was sulking. The United States were meditating war on the question of the Canadian Frontier. The diplomats whom the jovial Palmerston had insulted and browbeaten, out of patriotic fervour or sheer *joie de vivre*, had come to curse his name, and England's for his sake. In China, a triumphant but disgraceful war, entered into in wanton abuse of strength, was not yet concluded. In India, an appalling disaster, the direct result of the reckless policy of the last few years, was already preparing. In Ireland, O'Connell was sowing the seeds of a new agitation. In Scotland, where the feeling was predominantly Liberal since the passing of the Reform Bill, any chance the Conservative Government might have of a favourable reception was diminished by the religious crisis which was convulsing the social life of the people, and threatening the disruption of the Church.

But it was the social and economic condition of the country that was most alarming. The new Minister found an empty Exchequer, a falling revenue, a growing deficit. In 1836 a crisis almost as severe as that of 1825 had shaken the financial system ; since then, trade was stagnant and industry languished. Factory, mine, and workshop closed down, or worked at half pressure. Prices fell, fell steadily : only the price of food was high. Spite of Poor Law Act and Factory Acts and Combination Law Repeal— spite of all the efforts of a reformed Parliament—the condition of the working man was more wretched than ever. Low prices brought him no relief, for wages were lower than they had been since 1815. It seemed as if the growth of population, stimulated by the old Poor Law, by ignorance and poverty, had outstripped the demand for labour and the capacity of the land to support it. The distress of 1816, of 1819, of 1826-29, had not equalled the distress that fastened on the country from 1838 to 1842. In 1841, one person in every eleven in England was a pauper. At a time when the workman was agonising, imposts, for revenue or protective purposes, were piled to the limit upon almost every article of consumption. Bread was taxed : meat, butter, tea, sugar—almost every common article of food save the potato—were taxed. The poor man lived in darkness, because there was a tax on glass : he lived in filth, not merely because sanitation and town-planning were infant sciences, but because there was a tax on soap. The introduction of the new Poor Law, at such a moment, without warning, without any attempt to soften the transition, had aggravated the suffering of the workman and roused his resentment. The indirect effect of the old system in keeping down wages had not been apparent to him : he only knew that he could go, in his distress, and get his few shillings a week, and now that wretched dole was cut off. In certain cases, administrators of the new law were callous or cruel in enforcing it. And in addition to all this, the great Reform Act had cut off the workman from any representation in Parliament.

This widespread suffering had the usual sinister accompaniments. Crime increased. Rick-burning and rioting broke out afresh. The establishment of a new Poor Law Union often required the aid of a troop of cavalry. Of course, there was political agitation, and it was no longer incoherent and disorganised. Two great movements had arisen, very different in character, one of them among the mass of the people and one among the middle class, but both alarming to statesmen who still distrusted democracy and believed that such popular organisations were inimical to the authority of the State.

The poor had long since abandoned all faith in the Whigs and their promises. They had awakened to the fact that the great reform of Parliament, which their influence helped to carry, had meant their own disfranchisement : they saw it had strengthened the influence of the middle class. They believed that, to carry the measures necessary to save themselves from exploitation, they must recover their footing in Parliament, and must swamp the upper and middle class interests with their numbers.

In 1836 the Working-Men's Association was founded in London, with the object of creating and educating public opinion for the improvement of the working classes. It obtained for a moment the countenance of the Radical leaders in Parliament, but it soon adopted notions too wild for these. In 1838 it took up a militant attitude by electing as honorary members some of the Glasgow cotton spinners who were tried for murdering a blackleg: and shortly after this it drew up and published the text of a parliamentary bill, which became known as the People's Charter.

The demands of the Chartists, as the supporters of the bill came to be called, were : Votes for all adult men (including paupers) ; Vote by Ballot ; Annual Parliaments ; equal Electoral Districts, periodically rearranged ; Payment of Members of Parliament ; and the abolition of the Property Qualification for Parliament. The country has since swallowed most of these proposals without a gulp, but in the Eighteen-forties only a few advanced Radicals were prepared to accept them.

The Charter took the imagination of the working classes to a remarkable extent, considering its purely political nature. It was popularised by travelling lecturers sent out by the London Association. The movement soon absorbed the agitation against the new Poor Law, and partly amalgamated with the Birmingham Political Union, which Attwood, still as mad as ever about paper money, had revived in 1836. A ' National Convention ' was elected, which sat for some months, first in London and then in Birmingham, and great petitions to Parliament were drawn up in 1829 and 1841, but in each case Parliament refused to receive them. This naturally turned the Chartists to less constitutional methods : the movement fell into the hands of extremists, and the moderates gradually seceded from the ' National Convention.'

John Russell in 1839 refused to interfere with the mass meetings of the Chartists, alleging that speech should be free. He was later obliged to recede from this lofty position, for the language of the leaders became steadily more incendiary. The people were openly exhorted to arm, tyrannicide was lauded, and the police denounced. Drilling began, hoards of arms were discovered in several places, and some of the ringleaders were arrested. Birmingham was again sacked by a mob, bent not on plunder, but on destruction. Shortly after a revolt was raised in South Wales : it was a miserable failure, but it appeared certain that it had been intended to give the signal for a general rising. One of the last acts of the Whig Government was to hurry through bills, setting up a municipal police force in Manchester and Birmingham, and authorising the extension of the new police throughout the country.[1]

Almost simultaneously with the Chartist movement had appeared the Anti-Corn-Law League. The popular political agitation of 1819 and 1829 had been accompanied with a demand for the repeal of the Corn Laws, but it had been entirely ineffective, and the Anti-Corn-Law Association, formed by a few Radicals in 1836, was equally futile in its proceedings. Year after year, Edward Villiers, brother of Lord Clarendon, introduced a motion for repeal, and was defeated with hardly a debate. The regular presentation and rejection of Villiers' motion bade fair to become as mechanical a proceeding as the yearly voting of the Mutiny Bill, when the leadership of the movement fell into more capable hands.

The Anti-Corn-Law Association, which soon changed its name to the Anti-Corn-Law League, was established in Manchester also. One of the original members was a young master calico printer named Richard Cobden, and under his influence the League began a systematic campaign to rouse public opinion against the Corn Laws. The Leaguers were prosperous tradesmen : they subscribed generously. At one meeting £6,000 was collected. By this means, lecturers were sent all over the country to explain to the manufacturer, the workman, and the peasant how they were being taxed to fill the landlord's pocket. In 1841 John Bright, a Quaker cotton spinner and member of the League, was sitting alone in his desolate house, with his wife lying dead upstairs. To him came Richard Cobden, and said, ' There are thousands of houses in England at this moment where wives, mothers, and children are dying of hunger. Now, when the first paroxysm of your grief is past, come with me, and we will never rest till the Corn Law is repealed.' [2]

Bright was a religious and pure-minded man, narrow perhaps

[1] Hitherto the provincial police forces had each been established by a private Act.

[2] Morley, *Cobden*, i. p. 190.

in his outlook, prejudiced sometimes, but deeply sincere : he was, moreover, an orator of incomparable power, and his sublime and poetic eloquence was all that was needed to supplement Cobden's lucid reasoning and keen, logical mind. Cobden was entirely single-minded : while he fought his battle against the Corn Laws, he was incapable of sympathising with any point of view but his own. Those who upheld the Corn Laws were to him ' murderers,' ogres feeding on the bones and blood of starving children. To propose any other remedy but his own for the sufferings of the working classes was a crime : philanthropy was all ' cant.' Ashley, Oastler, and their like were hypocrites, who merely pretended to sympathise with the poor that they might have an excuse for nagging interference with the factories of cotton spinners and calico printers.[1] These opinions were perhaps extreme, but it was all to the good of the work Cobden had undertaken. ' Open-mindedness, candour, and the careful sincerity which forbids all exaggeration, even of the truth, are admirable qualities, but they are not the virtues which obtain for a faith the adherence of mankind.' [2]

Both the Anti-Corn-Law League and the Chartist Movement meant danger, but there was a difference between them.

The Chartist Movement was less dangerous in itself than in what it hinted of. It showed that the submerged masses, since the days of Peterloo, had become more self-conscious, better organised, and more disposed towards revolution. Silly and isolated attempts like the Newport rising could easily be suppressed by a powerful State ; but the widespread discontent, of which they were a symptom, could not long be suppressed, and might in the end shake the State to its foundation.

[1] ' I cannot help attributing murder to the legislature of this country. . . . I will denounce that system of legislative murder.' Morley, *Cobden*, i. p. 187. ' I . . . observed an evident disposition on the Tory side to set up as philanthropists. Old Sir Robert Inglis sat with his hands folded ready to sigh, and if needful to weep over a case of Church destitution ; he delivered a flaming panegyric upon Lord Ashley . . . styling him *the friend of the unprotected,* after he had been canting about the sufferings of lunatics. Added to this, Peel has been professing the utmost anxiety for paupers. . . . When I told them at the close of my speech that I had been quietly observing all this, but it would not all do unless they showed their consistency by untaxing the poor man's loaf, there was a stillness and attention on the other side very much like the conduct of men looking aghast at the first consciousness of being found out.' *Ib.* p. 185. See also pp. 299, 301-2, 464 ff.

[2] Dicey, *Law and Opinion in England*, p. 438.

The Anti-Corn-Law League was doubly dangerous. A compact body of able and intelligent men, representing great interests, and commanding great resources, which it did not hesitate to spend, it was a redoubtable foe to any Government which dared to oppose it : but more than this—in the state in which society was, the propaganda of the League was exceedingly inflammatory. The leaders themselves did not advise armed resistance. Bright, it is true, anticipating the methods of Mr. Cook, proposed to enforce the wishes of the League by a general lock-out ; [1] but his comrades were too wise to accept the martial Quaker's proposal. The general tone of the League orators, however, was calculated to have the most sinister effects. To tell the working man at such a time that he was being starved to fill the pockets of a group of wealthy landowners could have but one effect. In the country districts the League lecturers were stopped on the road by labourers asking where the fighting was to be, and they reported that in Devonshire the people were ' just as ready for pikes and pistols as the most excitable people of the factory towns.' [2] There was, in truth, a vast mass of combustible material in the country : the Chartists had set it smouldering : the Anti-Corn-Law League seemed likely to blow it into flame.

The League, however, was entirely a middle-class movement. It was distrusted by the working man, and the Chartist leaders, with sublime incompetence, chose to regard it as a rival and an enemy, and incited their followers to break up League meetings with violence. Corn-Law Repeal had, of course, always been one of the desires of the working-class reformers ; it was not the object of the League, but its members, that they disliked. These men were the very masters who made them slave twelve hours a day in filthy factories, ground down their wages, refused to protect them from machine accidents, and opposed every attempt at legislation to save the workman from exploitation. [3] What did

---

[1] Trevelyan, *Bright*, pp. 77-8.   [2] Morley, *Cobden*, i. p. 156.

[3] Bright's mills were among the best managed in the country, and he paid unusually high wages ; but both he and Cobden persistently opposed all attempts at factory legislation, whether for the protection of machinery or limitation of hours, and Cobden with great inconsistency opposed trade unions with equal violence. As he felt ' bound to suggest another remedy ' on refusing these, he suggested that each working man should ' accumulate £20 ' and emigrate to the United States ! This suggests many reflections. (1) How was a working man to support a wife and family and save £20 on wages of 15s. to 25s. a week ? (2) The country would steadily lose her best workmen, as it

they mean by taking this high humanitarian tone ? They did it for themselves, said the Chartists, you might wager ! They wanted low food prices so that they might cut down wages yet further.

The war between the Chartists and the League was the security of the State. If they had joined hands, the situation would have been far more threatening.

The new Prime Minister had at least no difficulty in finding helpers to deal with these problems. In 1834 he had been unable to get the men he wanted ; now it was a case of *embarras de richesse*. The old Tories, the young Conservatives, the *ci-devant* Whigs all had their claims, and he had to make his Cabinet unusually large to find room for even a part of them. Peel could have dispensed with the services of the old Tories in the Cabinet without breaking his heart, but he had to satisfy the men who had backed him, and the Ultras were the raw material—the cannonfodder, so to speak—of his party : so Wharncliffe, Buckingham, Haddington, and Knatchbull were included. For the most part, however, Peel picked his men carefully. His two most intimate friends, Aberdeen and Hardinge, got the Foreign Seals and the War Office respectively. Graham, to whom he was becoming equally attached, was Home Secretary, and Stanley went to the Colonial Office. Goulburn was made Chancellor of the Exchequer : for Peel meant to make his own budgets, and only wanted a docile and reliable lieutenant there. The appointment of Ripon to the Board of Trade was not very happy. Lyndhurst of course was Chancellor, but his influence on affairs was negligible. Wellington sat in the Cabinet and led the House of Lords without office. The group of young men—smaller now, for Praed was dead—was not yet admitted to the Cabinet : Herbert became Secretary to the Admiralty, Lincoln Commissioner of Woods and Forests, Gladstone Vice-President of the Board of Trade. Ramsay (now Lord Dalhousie) and the young Lord Canning also received subordinate appointments.

The session of 1841 lasted but a few weeks. Everyone realised that the new Government must be given a little time to prepare its measures. Only the most necessary legislation was hurried through—a grant to cover the deficiency in Baring's budget, and

would be the most capable and enterprising who succeeded in doing this. (3) Cobden was evidently unable to understand that exile is for many men a penalty, not a reward.

a renewal of the Poor Law Act, which was on the point of expiring —and then Parliament was prorogued to February, 1842.

Rigid economy and financial reform were the Minister's first preoccupation ; and he had now colleagues who could and would give him efficient support. Graham was a politician with a reputation for shiftiness, but he was a born administrator, and a conscientious, if narrow-minded, reformer. During his service with the Whigs, he had entirely reorganised the Admiralty, producing an economy and efficiency such as were not to be found in any other office, and he had set the example of laying his accounts regularly before the House of Commons. Now, in the Conservative administration, Graham was Peel's second self, and the two were not only loyal collaborators, but devoted friends. Even Wellington recognised the need for large reforms, and as for the old Tories, they had to like it or lump it. The Duke of Buckingham did not like it, and resigned. ' No one is sorry but himself,' remarked Lady Peel.[1] The young men were speedily set to work : one of Peel's first acts was to appoint a commission of Junior Lords of the Treasury, under Gladstone, and send them to investigate personally on the spot the collection of the revenue, and decide what reductions might be made, with power to disregard all questions of patronage and so forth. ' It will be excellent practice for Junior Lords,' he wrote. ' What is the Board of Treasury for but to do these things ? '[2]

It was generally expected that Peel would introduce some grand measure of financial reform : his persistent refusal to pledge himself on the Corn Laws, and his public and express declaration that the Whigs had not a monopoly of the principles of free trade, led to an expectation that he would tamper with the system of protection. The Duke of Buckingham's resignation set all agog with curiosity ; but the secret was well kept, and was not guessed until Parliament met, and Peel himself rose to make his statement.

The Corn Law in force was that which Peel and Wellington had passed in 1828. Foreign wheat was admitted at a duty of 27s. the quarter when the price of home-grown wheat reached 59s. As the price rose the duty sank, by regular amounts, until at 69s. the duty was 16s. 8d. After this it suddenly dropped at the rate of 4s. duty for every 1s. in price, so that when the price touched 73s. the duty was only 1s. the quarter. This odd arrangement had

[1] *Private Letters*, p. 196.   [2] Parker, *Peel*, ii. p. 495.

been made under the belief that it would facilitate the import of wheat as soon as the price reached 70s., but experience showed that the rapid fall of the duty only led corn-jobbers to hold up supplies until the price rose to 73s. and then flood the market with wheat imported at a 1s. duty.

Peel also started with a duty of 1s. when the home price stood at 73s., but his scale was carefully graduated, so that there was no sudden fall to tempt the jobbers to hold back. It also rose much more slowly, so that when the home price of corn was down to 50s. the duty was still only 20s. The practical effect was to lower the duties on corn by about one half, and it was hoped that it would greatly lessen fluctuations of prices. Peel also proposed to take the average of prices from a larger number of towns, hoping that this would lessen the danger of fradulent speculation. He thought he had devised a happy mean, by which a sufficient measure of protection was given to agriculture, while at the same time the price of bread was lowered and the supply increased in time of scarcity.

Nobody was pleased. The landlords thought they were betrayed : ' He has thrown over the landed interest, as my father always said he would,' Lord Malmesbury noted in his diary.[1] John Russell invited the House of Commons to substitute for Peel's sliding scale his own fixed duty of 8s., and when it was pointed out to him that this could not be maintained in time of scarcity, proposed that it should be reduced to 1s. when the price of wheat went to 70s. He did not seem to realise that this sacrificed the whole principle for which he was contending, but his adversaries did, and Gladstone pounced on the blunder and held it up to ridicule. The Leaguers meantime refused to admit that half a loaf was better than no bread, and Cobden denounced Peel's measure as ' a bitter insult to a suffering people.' The Government, however, had a solid working majority that would have enabled them to carry a much more unpopular measure than this ; and in a few weeks the Corn Law was forgotten and its imperfections lost in a blaze of triumph.

Upon the 11th of March Peel himself introduced the budget, one of the most famous of the nineteenth century. He opened with a general survey of the financial situation of the country, in language so exquisitely lucid and simple that the most complicated

[1] Malmesbury, *Memoirs*, i. p. 139.

questions became clear, the dryest details interesting. He showed that under the existing system the revenue for 1842-3 must be estimated at £48,350,000, the expenditure at £50,819,000, making a deficit of £2,469,000 to add to the earlier deficit of nearly £8,000,000. This did not include the cost of the Chinese war or the probable necessity of a loan to Canada, while there was a deficit of £2,470,000 in the revenue of India [1] (Indian finances having of late gone the same way as those of Britain).

What remedy could be offered for this frightful state of affairs ? Were they to borrow money—issue Exchequer bills ? That might be well enough if this were a casual or temporary deficiency ; but it was not : it had steadily increased for eight years past. He himself would refuse to be a party to ' the miserable expedient of continued loans.' '

What then ? Increased taxation was the only alternative : but the taxation of articles of consumption had been pushed to its extreme limits. In 1840 Baring had raised the whole of the customs duties by 5 per cent.: the result had been that the yield had fallen instead of rising—an absolute loss. Should he impose new duties or revive old ones—taxes on leather, on beer, on salt ? But these would add to the hardships of the poor, already great enough. Should he tax railways, or gas ? That would be to place a new hindrance upon the progress of the nation.

Should he then try the plan of *reducing* taxation in hopes of an increased yield ? This, he thought, was the only solution. A long time, however, must pass before the reduction took effect and the immediate loss was recovered. How was this loss to be made up in the meantime ? He answered, by the imposition of an income tax.

All incomes over £150 should be taxed at the rate of 7d. in the £1. It was to be imposed, at present, for three years only. It would not extend to Ireland, but was to fall on the incomes of Irish landowners resident in England. (Thus did Peel fulfil an old dream, and impose something like a tax on absentees.) In return for this concession, the duty on Irish spirits was to be raised until it equalled that on Scottish spirits. The duties on exported coal were also levelled up.[2]

[1] Peel was the first British Minister to make a practice of introducing into his budget a statement of Indian finance.
[2] Coal exported in British ships went free ; exported in foreign ships it paid a moderate duty.

By the income tax and these arrangements he calculated that he would raise about £4,300,000—enough to cover the deficiency and leave a large surplus. The surplus he devoted to the reform of the tariff. There were 1,200 articles at present subject to duties : he proposed that the duties on raw materials should in no case exceed 5 per cent. ; on half manufactured articles 12 per cent. ; and on wholly manufactured articles 20 per cent. The duties on 750 articles were thus reduced, involving an immediate loss of £270,000. The duties upon coffee and timber were also largely reduced. In dealing with these Peel followed an entirely different plan from that of the Whigs in 1841. They had proposed to level up the duties on imported timber—raising the duty on colonial timber, and lowering that on foreign timber. Peel lowered the duties on both foreign and colonial timber, preserving the same proportion between them : in this way he gave the consumer the advantage of lower prices, while holding to the principle of Imperial preference. The duties on imported meat and cattle were greatly lowered, and the export duties on all British manufactures were repealed. There still remained a surplus of £520,000 to meet expenses in China and India.

Peel had at one stroke converted a deficit into a surplus, carried a sweeping measure of tariff reform, and laid the foundations of a new system of taxation.[1]

He was not guided only by financial considerations. He had looked far beyond the immediate necessity of balancing his budget, to the social and economic needs of the country.

He believed that Britain was on the verge of social revolution. To avert that danger he had shifted the burden of taxation from the poor to the wealthier classes, and he had cheapened the necessaries of life.

' Something effectual must be done to revive the languishing commerce amd manufacturing industry in this country,' he wrote to Croker, who was alarmed for the landed interest. ' Look at the congregation of manufacturing masses, the amount of our debt, the rapid increase of poor rates. . . . We must make this country a cheap country for living. . . . The danger is not from low price from the tariff, but low price from inability to consume, from the

---

[1] A recent committee on import duties had recommended several of the measures introduced by Peel, but it had not suggested them to him. Strangely enough, he had not read the report ! Parker, *Peel*, ii. pp. 508-9.

poor man giving up his pint of beer, and the man in middling station giving up his joint of meat. Rest assured of this, that landed property would not be safe during this next winter with the prices of the last four years.' [1]

When Tory friends complained that his measures had lowered prices and caused losses to the agriculturists, he answered them with passion and contempt. ' This is the first intimation I have had that the thanksgiving for a good harvest is deemed " inappropri-ate." The wheat crop of Sir Charles Burrell and that of three or four of his neighbours, who attend the parish church, failed—probably from want of draining and bad farming ; and therefore we are not to thank God for a harvest which . . . was providentially good. If Sir Charles had such cases before him as I have, of thousands and tens of thousands in want of food and employment, at Greenock, Paisley, Edinburgh, and a dozen large towns . . . he would not expect me to rend my garments in despair if " some excellent jerked beef from South America " should get into the English market, and bring down meat from . . . 8d a pound.' [2]

' For upwards of a year eight or nine thousand persons on the average have been supported each week in that one town (Paisley) . . . by voluntary charity. . . . I, who have no sort of connection with Paisley, have subscribed twice, being satisfied that if nothing were done we might take the choice either of hundreds dying of hunger, or of a frightful outbreak, and attack upon property. . . . What is to be done with these people at Paisley during next winter ? They are not fit for emigration. There have been about 150 bankruptcies among the principal manufacturers of the town. No rents are paid. No money can be raised, either by poor rate or voluntary contribution, within the district. . . . There are many other towns in a condition not very different. What is to be the end of this ? . . . My firm belief is you could not have during the coming winter the high prices of the last four years and at the same time tranquillity and security for property.' [3]

Peel had come to realise that the agricultural interest could no longer be considered first. Britain had been transformed from an agricultural to an industrial country : this might be regrettable, but there could be no going back. The fact must be accepted

[1] To Croker, 27th July, 3rd August, 30th October, 1842. Parker, *Peel*, ii. pp. 529-531.

[2] To Fremantle, 25th November, 1822. Parker, *Peel*, ii. pp. 531.

[3] To Arbuthnot, 30th October, 1842. *Ib.* p. 532.

and policy adjusted to suit altered conditions. 'If you had to constitute new societies, you might on moral and social grounds prefer cornfields to cotton factories, an agricultural to a manufacturing population,' he said. 'But our lot is cast, and we cannot recede.'[1] The 'logical consequence' of this, he admitted, was the complete repeal of the Corn Laws : but that involved a convulsion which he was not yet prepared to face : 'We take into account vested interests, engaged capital, the importance of independent supply, the social benefits of flourishing agriculture. We find the general welfare will be best promoted by a fair adjustment, by allowing the legitimate logical deductions to be controlled by the thousand considerations which enter into moral and political questions, and which . . . put a limit to the practical application of abstract reasoning.'[2]

The great budget was immediately successful. 'He took the House by storm,' says Greville. A leading Whig sat throughout the speech, ejaculating inwardly, 'Thank God, Peel is minister ! ' The effect outside Parliament was even more remarkable. 'The whole country is prepared, if not content, to take his measures, and let him have his own way without let or hindrance.'[3]

There was, however, a small, though ineffective, opposition. The Leaguers were furious. Early in the year they had sent a deputation, 500 northern manufacturers, to interview the Minister on the subject of Corn Law Repeal : when he refused to see them they paraded the streets to Palace Yard, where they were involved in a struggle with the police, who turned them back ; and, meeting Peel's carriage, they shouted at him, 'No Corn Laws ! Down with the Monopoly ! ' The new Corn Law had enraged them further, and Peel was burnt in effigy in the north. The budget was the last straw. The manufacturers wanted free trade, but they did not want to have to pay for it. Bright said an income tax should fall on 'land and buildings and canals and railroads, but not on machinery, stock-in-trade, etc.'[4]—not on cotton spinners like John Bright, in fact. 'How do our millowners and shopkeepers like to be made to pay £1,200,000 a year out of their profits to ensure the continuance of the corn and sugar monopolies ? ' asked Cobden. 'Peel is . . . putting everything in disorder without settling anything.'[5] Oblivious, therefore, of the

---

[1] Parker, *Peel*, ii. p. 529.   [2] *Ib.* p. 530.   [3] *Greville*, v. pp. 89, 90, 97.
[4] Trevelyan, *Bright*, p. 72.   [5] Morley, *Cobden*, i. pp. 240-1.

fact that the lowering of the customs duties, which he praised, could only be obtained by the aid of the income tax, Cobden continued to offer a persistent and irritating opposition to the latter measure, which could not have any ultimate effect, but caused delay and waste of time. The League, in fact, had got a bad blow. They could not help seeing that the modification of the Corn Laws and the Free Trade Budget between them must cause a great improvement in the state of the country : but every improvement, every easing of the workman's sufferings, weakened the force of the League's arguments and lessened their influence on the country.

Some of the Whigs were equally annoyed. It must not be imagined that the Whigs had any idea that their own administration had not been a complete success, or that the condition of the country, when they left office, appeared to them to be unsatisfactory. On the contrary, they were very complacent. ' The country is altogether in a prosperous and happy state,' the Duke of Bedford had written during the election. ' All interests are doing well except certain labourers in North Devon, who get, I'm told, six and seven shillings a week ! Too bad ! ' Just before the fall of the late Government, Palmerston had written, ' The country is quiet and prosperous, Ireland contented, manufacturers and trade reviving, and agriculture doing tolerably well.' They had not anticipated any very startling innovations from Peel. The Whig press had hinted that he would let himself be made the tool of the Ultra-Tories, and the Whig leaders talked in a superior tone of his weakness, his embarrassments, his incompetence. Russell and Palmerston agreed that he would never dare to propose an income tax.[1]

The budget, therefore, came as a severe shock to all these guileless hopes, and the chagrin of the critics may be imagined. Russell whispered to Hobhouse as he listened to Peel's speech, that ' his peroration lasted at least a quarter of an hour,' [2] and he and Baring at once attacked the income tax. Palmerston, on the contrary, declared it would be a disgrace to the country and the party not to support the Minister in this grand measure ; and

[1] Bedford to Russell, 9th June, 1841. Gooch, *Russell Correspondence*, p. 37. Palmerston to W. Temple, 9th February, 1841 ; Ashley, *Palmerston*, iii. p. 46. *Greville*, v. p. 89. Palmerston to Russell, 14th January, 1842 ; Gooch, *op. cit.* p. 53.
[2] *Hobhouse*, vi. p. 58.

Russell soon threw up the sponge, and went off to the country for the rest of the session. A few lesser lights continued to collaborate with Cobden in his career of obstruction.

The spring of 1842 was late and cold; but a glorious summer followed it. Day after day the sun shone, and corn grew fat in the ear. The corn-jobbers had held up supplies, in hopes of another year of scarcity. Realising that there would be a splendid harvest, they hurriedly released their stores, and the price of wheat fell like a stone. Speculators and farmers were ruined, and agricultural distress was added to commercial distress. The Chartist Movement, which had partly collapsed after the failure of the Newport rising, had begun to revive, and the leaders decided to take advantage of a strike, which, starting in a local colliery dispute, had spread through the country. In August they began to organise a general strike to enforce the Charter: [1] but falling prices made success impossible, and in September the men went back to work on the employers' terms. Rioting and violence had accompanied the strike: two policemen were killed in Manchester, and in several places the troops were compelled to fire on the mob. Drayton was threatened with attack while Sir Robert was absent in London, and Lady Peel prepared to defend the house with all the spirit of Black Agnace of Dunbar.[2]

There had been as yet no time for the reduction of duties to take effect on the course of trade, and distress and disorder caused a sudden and heavy fall—of £2,000,000—in the yield of the Customs and Excise. It was some compensation that the Income Tax yielded far more than had been expected; Peel had estimated it at £3,700,000, and it came to over £5,000,000. But it now appeared that the Minister had made a very odd mistake in his great Budget: he had forgotten that one part of the Income Tax would not fall to be collected within the current financial year. The year which had opened so fairly closed with another startling deficit.

Though his enemies might be jubilant, Peel himself was not discouraged. Far more able than most of them to understand the tendencies and significance of economic affairs, he saw that the causes of the loss were accidental and temporary, while the great

---

[1] The general strike had apparently been planned long before this. *See* Parker, *Graham*, i. p. 322.

[2] *Private Letters*, p. 204.

principles of his measures were untouched by them.   His critics
hardly noted the surprisingly large yield of the Income Tax, but
he fully comprehended all that this meant, and he refused, with
equal hardihood, the demands of the Tories for the return to
protection, and the demands of the Leaguers for the instant
repeal of the Corn Law.   He would not make the slightest concession : his reply was equally unsatisfactory to both parties : he
would only say that at present he did not intend to make any
change whatever in the Corn Law.

Unfortunately the debate produced a personal quarrel between
the Prime Minister and the leader of the League.   Just before the
meeting of Parliament, Peel's private secretary, Edward Drummond, was shot in the street by a mad Scotsman named Mac-
Naughtan : on being asked if he knew whom he had shot, the
murderer replied, ' Yes, Sir Robert Peel.' [1]   Peel was still shaken
with grief and horror at the circumstances of Drummond's death
when the Corn Law debate took place, and Cobden made a violent
personal attack upon him.   ' You passed the law,' he cried, ' you
refused to listen to the manufacturers, and I throw on you all the
responsibility of your own measure. . . . I must tell the Right
Honourable Baronet that it is the duty of every honest and independent member to hold him individually responsible for the
present position of the country. . . . I tell him the whole responsibility of the lamentable and dangerous state of the country rests
with him. . . . The Right Honourable Baronet has the power in
his hands to do as he pleases.'

Peel was at once on his feet.   ' The honourable gentleman has
stated here very emphatically,' he cried, ' what he has more than
once stated at the conferences of the Anti-Corn-Law League,
that he holds me individually responsible for the distress and
suffering of the country ; that he holds me personally responsible ;
but be the consequences of these insinuations what they may,
never will I be influenced by menaces either in this House or out
of this House, to adopt a course which I consider—— '

The speaker's voice was drowned in a general outcry.   Cobden,
in equal agitation, said, ' I did not say that I held the right honourable gentleman personally responsible—— '

' You did !   You did ! ' cried the House.

' You did ! ' repeated Peel.

[1] *Letters of Queen Victoria*, i. p. 456.

' I said that I hold the right honourable gentleman responsible by virtue of his office, as the whole context of what I have said was sufficient to explain.'

The House would not listen to Cobden. Peel passionately repeated his statement : then, Graham having handed him a note, he admitted that Cobden might not have used the word ' personally,' but added, that Cobden might hold him ' individually responsible, and induce others to do the same, but I only notice his assertion for the purpose of saying that it shall not influence me in the discharge of a public duty.'

On the following day, after Russell had made a speech conciliatory to both parties, Cobden repeated his explanation, and Peel said that he felt himself ' bound to accept it. . . . He supposes the word " individually " to mean public responsibility in the situation I hold, and I admit it at once. I thought the words he employed, " I hold you individually responsible," might have an effect, which I think many other gentlemen who heard them might anticipate.'

This very shabby apology for an unwarrantable accusation seemed to Peel himself quite sufficient. He felt that Cobden had brought against him an accusation quite as cruel as that which he had hurled at Cobden : and as the Leaguer had not withdrawn his words, but only made the ' Parliamentary ' distinction that is merely a technical apology, Peel considered that only the same technical apology was necessary on his side. Cobden, however, thought the amends quite insufficient. He, like most of the younger generation, never guessed the fire that lay beneath the Prime Minister's icy exterior : he thought Peel's passion was a sham, assumed for the purpose of discrediting him. It is rather characteristic that Peel's gust of anger blew by and left him without a trace of feeling against Cobden, while Cobden brooded over the incident, and nursed a savage resentment against Peel.[1] ' He is obliged now to assume that he was in earnest, for no man likes to confess himself a hypocrite, and to put up with the ridicule of his own party in private as a coward,' [2] he wrote. ' He is looking

[1] *Speeches*, iv. p. 149. Morley, *Cobden*, p. 257 ff. Parker, *Peel*, ii. pp. 557-8. Morley actually insinuates that Cobden was right in thinking Peel was shamming ! ' The display was undoubtedly convenient for the moment in damaging a very troublesome adversary.' He also says that this was ' the only occasion ' on which Peel lost his temper in Parliament ! *Cobden*, i. p. 260.

[2] Peel to the Queen, 27th March, 1843 : ' It may tend to remove or diminish

twenty per cent. worse since I came into the House, and if I only had Bright with me, we could worry him out of office before the close of the session.' [1]

Cobden emphatically repeated his statement that Peel was the one man responsible for the state of the country in a public letter a few weeks later.

The budget of 1843 was simple and unenterprising, and Goulburn was allowed to introduce it. Owing to the close of the wars in the East, it was possible to reduce the estimates by nearly £2,000,000. A new Corn Bill allowed the importation of Canadian corn at a nominal duty of 1s. the quarter. Peel's confidence was soon justified : another glorious summer followed, and before the end of the year a revival of trade was in full swing. The mines reopened, the factories grew busy ; the demand for labour grew steadily ; food was cheap. When the budget of 1844 was made up, it was found that expenditure had been less and income more than was anticipated : the whole deficit of 1843 was paid off, and there was still a surplus of £1,400,000. A great conversion of the National Debt, effected at the same time, made a large saving in expenditure. Taxes were remitted to the extent of £40,000, but the rest of the surplus was held in reserve, lest Parliament should refuse to renew the Income Tax when it expired next year.

In 1845 a budget almost as important as that of 1842 was brought forward, Peel again introducing it himself. There were still 813 articles on the tariff : he swept away 430 of them. He abolished the export duty on coal, which had proved injurious to the coal trade. He abolished also the duties on auctions, on cotton wool, and on glass, and he took a further 10s. off the sugar duties, which he had already reduced in 1844. To pay for these reductions, he asked for the renewal of the Income Tax for another three years.

The budget of 1845 was the complement of the budget of 1842. Together they introduced almost complete freedom of trade as far as manufacturing industry was concerned ; only a few low protective and preferential duties remained on certain articles that were specially likely to be damaged by foreign competition ; while

Your Majesty's anxiety to know that Sir Robert Peel has walked home every night from the House of Commons, and, notwithstanding frequent menaces and intimations of danger, he has not met with any obstruction.' *Letters of Queen Victoria*, i. p. 473.

[1] Morley, *Cobden*, i. pp. 263-4.   [2] *Ib.* pp. 266-8.

practically all duties on raw materials, and all export duties, were swept away.

The revival of trade was not merely one of those periodic reactions that commonly follow a time of depression. The country had taken the first step on the road that was to make her, in a few years, the wealthiest and most stable state in Europe, the foremost manufacturing country in the world, and her people the most prosperous of any. It was the coincidence of Peel's measures with the development of railway traffic that made this possible. The inventions of the industrial revolution had made almost unlimited production possible : but production had been hindered by the difficulty of distribution, by artificial restrictions on trade, and by the degradation of the working classes, which diminished their power of consumption. Now Peel removed the restraints on trade and transferred the burden of taxation from the poor to the upper and middle classes, and almost at the same moment the means of cheap and rapid distribution were provided. British trade and industry received an impulse which was hardly to be checked for forty years.

In the meantime Peel had introduced a further measure of currency reform. In 1844 the Charter of the Bank of England came up for revision, and he seized the opportunity to frame new regulations, which, he hoped, would prevent the recurrence of those periodic financial crises which had been so disastrous in the past.

The Bank Charter Act of 1844 was drawn up under the advice of Loyd Jones, afterwards Lord Overstone, himself a great banker. It divided the Bank of England into two departments, rigidly separated. One undertook the ordinary banking business ; the other dealt with the issue of notes. The Bank was allowed to issue notes against securities to the value of £14,000,000. Beyond this sum all issues must be made against coin or bullion, and the treasure of the Banking Department was not to count as part of the Issue Department's reserve.

The right of the country banks to issue was strictly limited, and no new bank of issue might be created. If any country bank surrendered its right of issue, the Bank of England might increase its own issue against securities by two-thirds of the amount surrendered.

The Scottish banking system Peel greatly admired, and he did not wish to disturb it. He merely limited the right of issue against securities to the average amount of the current year, and all notes beyond this must be issued against coin or bullion.

The Act did not touch the ordinary banking business of the country, which Peel thought should be left to private enterprise like any other business. It is usually said that the object of the Act was to secure the convertibility of bank-notes, but it is more correct to say that it was to prevent the undue expansion of the currency. This is not a distinction without a difference : the Act did secure the convertibility of notes, but it did not prevent undue inflation of credit.

Peel ' had been so strongly impressed with the evils of over-issue, the most dangerous of the abuses to which banking is liable, which had displayed themselves with extraordinary violence between 1836 and 1839, that he became almost blind to any other considerations.' [1]

In 1847, 1857 and 1866 financial crises occurred, almost as severe as those of 1825 and 1836. In each of these cases the Act of 1844 was suspended. Large demands for credit were made on the Bank; the reserve fell very low; the Bank represented to the Government that a crash must come unless they could issue notes beyond the authorised limit ; and the Government promised to introduce a bill of indemnity into Parliament if the Bank did so. The Government's letter was usually enough in itself to abate the panic, and only in 1857 was it actually necessary to issue extra notes. In each case the Bank Act aggravated the difficulty in the final crisis by limiting the issue of notes at the very moment when credit was most urgently required ; while it failed to prevent an over-expansion of credit at the beginning of the crisis.

In the series of crises between 1825 and 1866, an outburst of wild speculation had been followed by an inevitable collapse. The crisis of 1825 had been much aggravated by the issue of unsound paper by country banks, but the Act of 1826 put an end to this. In 1825, 1836, and 1847, however, the mismanagement of the Bank of England made matters much worse. They extended their advances in the beginning, when they ought to have restricted them, and restricted them at the end, when they should have been extended.[2] In 1857 the Bank restricted its issues in good time,

---

[1] Andreades, *Bank of England*, p. 285.

[2] In 1847 the Bank restricted its issues, but so slightly as to have no effect.

but the country banks and bill-brokers failed to support it, and therefore its measures were ineffective.

It will be seen that it was really impossible to prevent financial crises by any legislation. The Government could not by Act of Parliament make the bankers wise, or give the people of England common sense. Experience only could teach the bankers how to handle a crisis : education must teach the people to be prudent in speculation, and to understand that a run on the banks in difficult times would only precipitate ruin.

The Government might prevent the over-issue of bank-notes, but it could not prevent the undue expansion of credit, because bank-notes were only one form of credit. Bills of exchange, and the rapid development of the cheque-and-deposit system, deprived the bank-note of much of its importance. All that Peel's Act could do was to limit the issue of notes when other forms of credit failed, and all the demand fell on notes : and that was just the time when the note issue should have been increased.

The real test of Peel's legislation, then, is whether he anticipated that the Act of 1844 would have to be suspended in a crisis : and it seems probable that he did. In 1847 the Government consulted him before they consented to propose a bill of indemnity for the Bank, and he approved their action. In 1844, when the Act was under discussion, he wrote to the Governor of the Bank, that a crisis ' *may* occur, in spite of our precautions, and if it does, and *if it be necessary* to assume a grave responsibility for the purpose of meeting it, I daresay men will be found willing to assume such a responsibility.' [1]

' This was his way of saying that he preferred a bracing law, which might have to be suspended, to a law which by providing ways out of difficulties would encourage bankers to slide into them.' [2]

From 1866 onwards no similar crisis has occurred in Britain. The crisis of 1890, owing to the admirable management of the Governor of the Bank of England, never developed, and the public knew nothing of it till it was over. The crisis of 1907 was felt mainly in America. It would be ridiculous to attribute this to Peel's Act : the real cause was the growth of financial knowledge and experience.

The principles of the Act were sound, and this, together with

[1] Parker, *Peel*, iii. p. 140.   [2] Clapham, *Economic History*, i. p. 525.

Peel's lucid exposition in Parliament, must have helped to educate public opinion : but it set out to do what could not be done by legislation, and so far it failed. It must be remembered, however, that the Act governed British banking for seventy years, and that during those years our financial system was so solidly established that not even the shock of the Great War could destroy London's position as the money market of the world. We may perhaps conclude, then, that in spite of all that has been said against it— and much has been said—the Act, if it did not do all the good that was hoped of it, yet did not do any real harm.[1]

In the sunshine of the years 1843-1845 political agitation languished. Chartism ceased to be a danger, and the Anti-Corn-Law League lost ground steadily. With every shop and factory working at full pressure, the demand for labour exceeding the supply, wages rising and food cheap, talk of starvation and monopoly found few listeners. The League worked on, but its arguments had lost their popular force : they might convert the reasoning man, but not carry away the ignorant populace. In the autumn of 1843 they had a great victory, defeating the Government candidate in the election for the City, but it seemed, for the time being, an illusive triumph. In spite of extraordinary efforts made in 1844, ' the outlook of the cause was, perhaps, never less hopeful or encouraging.' [2]

Yet, though the League seemed to make no progress, or even to fall back, it was in reality doing work of more practical importance than anything it had done before. It had striven in vain to rouse the working classes : it had converted a large body of middle-class opinion, without having had any effect on Parliament. Now the arguments of its leaders and the logic of facts were converting Peel. There were not many men in Parliament capable of appreciating at its full worth Cobden's reasoned eloquence : but the arguments that even his own supporters might not always comprehend found their mark in the mind of his enemy, sitting apparently unmoved on the Treasury bench. When, at a League lecture, a country labourer rose and said, ' I be protected, and I be starving,'

---

[1] Even the admirers of the Act, however, admit that it had one very serious blemish, and agree that the control of the note issue could have been attained without the unnatural and inconvenient separation of the Bank into two departments.

[2] Morley, *Cobden*, i. pp. 312-3.

there was one Tory at least to whom the words, the more terrible for their simplicity, came home in their full weight.

All seemed favourable enough to superficial observers : but the leaders on both sides realised how far the continuance of prosperity depended upon accidental causes. Two good harvests had, as the Duke would have said, ' set the country on its legs.' A wet season—the failure of the corn crop—might let loose the devils of want and sedition once more. Both sides waited, watching the weather signs, the League almost with eagerness, the Minister with dark foreboding.

CHAPTER XII

THE SCOTTISH CHURCH, 1843

It cannot have escaped the notice of the intelligent reader that the Churches in England and in Ireland were among the chief sources of all the troubles that beset British Ministries, Whig or Tory. Tithes and Church rates, Catholic exclusion, Dissenters' marriages, secular and religious education—there was no end to the causes of dissension. The Church of Scotland had hitherto given but little uneasiness to statesmen : but every dog has its day, and the Scottish Church was now to show of what it was capable.

Religious problems in Scotland were in one respect simple, because the vast majority of the people practised the same form of religion, and, indeed, were members of the Established Church. The Roman Catholic and Episcopalian Dissenters were a negligible minority, and they were in no way penalised for their religion. The Catholics had been emancipated, along with their fellows, by the Act of 1829 : the Episcopalians were not subjected to any galling marriage laws : neither sect was rated to pay for Presbyterian churches ; and they had therefore none of the grievances of the English and Irish Dissenters. In Scotland the difficulties which arose were not between rival Churches, but between the Church and the State.

The Church of England was from its beginning a State Church— it was the creation of the State, and the State upheld and enforced its authority. The Church of Scotland was, on the contrary, a national Church, resulting from a popular movement, and established by the State, one might almost say, for reasons of expediency only. Certainly its recognition by the Act of Union in 1707, on which its position ever since was based, was dictated by expediency. It was necessitated by the circumstances of the time. Emerging from a long period of persecution in 1690, the Church sought the recognition of the State ; and in 1707, surrendering their independent legislature, the Scottish people still saw the need of special securities for their national religion.

It may be questioned, however, whether the State establishment was ever in accordance with the character of Scottish Presbyterianism. The religion of Scotland was a popular product —it sprang almost spontaneously from the hearts of the common people. Where the Church of England was aristocratic in constitution, the Church of Scotland was democratic. Its real strength had always lain in its hold upon the mass of the people. It is the Church of the individualist. Its tendency has always been to break away from formality and restraint.

Now that the accidental circumstances of 1707 had ceased to exist, and Presbyterianism in Scotland was free from all external danger, the relations between Church and State could be considered on their own merits. It was, however, upon a point of detail, not of principle, that difficulties first arose. The settlement of 1690 had done away with lay patronage in Scotland, and the Act of Union in 1707 acknowledged this. In 1711, however, the Imperial Parliament had restored lay patronage, in spite of the protests of the Church. Patronage in Scotland was very different from what it was in England. Under the Act of 1711 the patron had the right to present a candidate : the Church then took him ' on trials,' and if it found him qualified, it accepted him ; if it found him not qualified, and rejected him, the patron had no option but to choose another candidate.

In the words of the great judge, Lord Kames : ' Their sentence (*i.e.*, that of the Church) is ultimate, even where their proceedings are illegal (*i.e.*, illegal according to the judgment of civil law)—the person authorised by their sentence, even in opposition to the presentee (of the patron), is *de facto* minister of the parish, and as such is entitled to perform every ministerial function.' [1] But, of course, he would not receive the stipend.

This, however, was not the whole of the procedure : the ' call ' from the congregation was also necessary.

During the latter part of the eighteenth century the ' call ' had fallen into disrepute. The Church Courts and the lay patrons had both joined in forcing ministers upon violently protesting congregations. Had Scottish patronage been managed as in contemporary England, where the minister might be, and often was,

[1] Buchanan, *Ten Years' Conflict*, i. p. 140.

chosen without any regard to fitness, this would undoubtedly have produced such an explosion as that celebrated by the poet :

> Hech, sic a pairish, a pairish, a pairish,
> Hech, sic a pairish was Little Dunkeld !
> They hae hangit the Meenister, droont the Precentor,
> Dung doon the steeple, and drucken the bell.

In Scotland, however, though a person might be chosen whom the congregation disliked, he was almost sure to be of unobjectionable character and proper qualifications. Thus personal prejudice often vanished after a short trial, and the congregation would submit. The process is admirably described in Galt's *Annals of the Parish*, where the unwelcome minister, forced upon the people, becomes the darling of his congregation. Very similar conditions prevailed in Church and State at this time. The Scottish people had no voice either in political or religious affairs : the spirit of the time was unfriendly to democratic influence in every department of life.

This could not last, however. The Reform Act of 1832 for the first time made it clear that the political feeling of Scotland was predominantly Liberal—much more steadily and whole-heartedly Liberal than that of England. At the same time, democratic tendencies once more displayed themselves in the Church, and a movement began to make the ' call ' once more effective. It was not now a movement of the congregation against the Church Courts. Most of the ministers joined in pressing that the rights of the congregations should be recognised.

By 1834 practically all the younger generation of Church members, many of the older ministers, and, it was said, all the women, supported the Non-Intrusion movement, as it was called. In this year they obtained a majority in the General Assembly and passed a Veto Act, which declared that if the majority of any congregation objected to a presentee, the Presbytery should refuse to take him on trials at all, but reject him at once.

The Veto Act was soon put to the test. The Presbytery of Auchterarder rejected the patron's presentee because the congregation objected to him. The patron appealed to the Court of Session, claiming that the Presbytery was bound to admit the presentee if they found him qualified, and had no right to reject him without trial, whatever the desire of the congregation. The Court of Session found for the pursuer. The Lord President, giving judgment, used expressions that at once carried the controversy far beyond the mere question of patronage : ' That our Saviour is the head of the Kirk of Scotland,' he said, 'in any temporal, or legislative, or judicial sense, is a position which I can dignify by no other name than absurdity. The Parliament is the temporal head of the Church, from whose acts, and from whose acts alone, it exists as the national Church, and from which alone it derives all its powers.'[1] The Church took the case to the House of Lords, where the decision was even more uncompromising. It declared that the Church had no authority to reject the presentee, unless for heresy, ignorance, or immorality, and that the wishes of the congregation had nothing to do with the matter.

These two judgments ought to have opened the eyes of the Church leaders to the real significance of what was happening. Unfortunately the greatest of them, Chalmers, with all his gifts, was not a very clear or logical thinker. He had originally, while supporting the Veto Act, declared himself in favour of lay patronage. He presently joined those who wished to abolish patronage altogether, but even then he maintained that the State ought to pay all ministers, and the congregations choose them.[2]

This position was neither fair nor wise. The Church which accepts payment from the State must be prepared to allow the State a voice in the settlement of its internal affairs. It was the weakness of the Church leaders that they did not at first acknowledge this fact. There were men who saw this clearly enough. In 1829 an Auld Secession minister,[3] Dr. Andrew Marshall of Kirkintilloch, had stated in the most uncompromising terms that the Church ought to be based on voluntary contributions, and demanded its complete disestablishment : and he probably expressed the general feeling of the congregations. But the nominal leaders in the Church were as yet rather behind than in advance of the popular feeling. Their anxious desire to avoid a schism in the Church led them to cling to the hope of some settlement. By doing this they laid themselves open to the accusation brought against them by Peel, that they were trying to set the Church Courts above the law of the land. The movement was in truth one to make the Church independent of the State ; they gave it the aspect of an attempt to set the Church above the State.

If, however, their attitude was illogical, it at least offered the

---

[1] Buchanan, *Ten Years' Conflict*, p. 393.   [2] *Chalmers*, iv. pp. 270-2.
[3] The Auld Secession Kirk broke away from the Established Church in 1740.

opportunity for a settlement. They had shown that they were anxious to preserve the Church establishment : it might then be guessed that timely concession would draw them back from the path on which they had entered.

The great fault of Peel's Scottish policy was that he did not perceive this.

The Conservative Government found the question waiting for them when they came into office : but by this time it had advanced another step. The Presbytery of Strathbogie, obeying the Veto Act, refused to take a presentee on trials. The Law Courts, in accordance with the judgment of the Court of Session on Auchter-arder, ordered them to receive the presentee. The majority of the Presbytery obeyed the Law Courts, but in doing so they disobeyed the Veto Act, and the General Assembly suspended them all and put substitutes in their places.

Peel had originally been inclined to make some concession to the rights of congregations : but the affair of Strathbogie altered his mind. He called the Church leaders ' The Popish Presbyterian party,' [1] and determined that he would make no concession, and introduce no legislation whatever until the Assembly agreed to reinstate the deposed Strathbogie ministers.

Lord Aberdeen, as one of the two Scots in the Cabinet, was naturally looked to as the great authority on the subject. Peel was too conscientious not to make an effort to understand the matter, but the rest of the Cabinet, as Aberdeen remarked, didn't care sixpence about the Scottish Church.[2] It may be doubted, however, whether Aberdeen himself wholly understood what was going on. On his own Scottish estates he had settled peacefully and satisfactorily an attempt of the parishioners to reject his presentee. He attributed the success, which was really due to his personal influence, to the victory of moderate principles, and did not realise how strong popular feeling was in the country. He relied upon the information which he received from the Lord Justice Clerk, Hope, a hot-headed partisan, blind to what was going on under his very nose. ' No one will doubt,' Hope wrote, ' either (1) that they (the Church leaders) are wholly governed and moved by Whigs as their prompters ; or (2) that they are wholly devoid of all principle or consistency. . . . They may talk big, but they will do nothing.' [3]

[1] Balfour, *Aberdeen*, ii. p. 84.   [2] *Ib.* p. 90.   [3] *Ib.* p. 93.

Two courses of action had been suggested to the Conservative Ministry. The Duke of Argyll had introduced a bill legalising the Veto Act, but had not succeeded in carrying it through the House of Lords. Aberdeen had drawn up a bill making it legal for the Presbytery to reject a presentee if the objections of the congregation were, in their judgment, well founded. It was a bad bill: it conceded everything to the Presbytery and nothing to the congregation. It entirely failed to satisfy the Church. A Scottish member, Sir George Sinclair, however, suggested adding to Aberdeen's bill a clause allowing the Presbytery to reject the presentee if the objections of the congregation, though not well founded, were such as would prevent the congregation from profiting by his ministry.

Peel seems to have believed that in time the extremists in the Church would come to their senses, the moderates would gain the upper hand, and the Assembly would consent to restore the suspended ministers, in return for the addition of Sinclair's clause to Aberdeen's bill. He did not understand that that magic word, ' compromise,' which falls with such dulcet sound upon English ears, has no attraction whatever for the Scot. He had not understood, either, the character of the movement with which he had to deal: it was not a movement created or led by agitators, like the Anti-Corn-Law League, or the Repeal Movement in Ireland: it was, like almost all movements that have altered the course of Scottish history, essentially democratic, and if left alone, the official leaders were bound to fall more and more under the influence of the popular enthusiasm which was its real strength. Hence, when Peel refused to introduce any sort of legislation—refused to do anything but enter into cautious negotiations with the Non-Intrusion Committee—he was only allowing his adversaries to gather strength.

It was soon clear how things were going. The General Assembly of 1842 passed a resolution that the only solution of the difficulty was the complete abolition of patronage. But this was not all: the Assembly went on to draw up a Claim of Right, in which they affirmed the rights of congregations, and declared that ' All Acts of the Parliament of Great Britain, passed without the consent of the Church and nation, in alteration of or derogative to the government, discipline, rights and privileges of the Church . . . and also all sentences of Courts in contravention of the same government, discipline, rights and privileges, are and shall be null and void.'

This document was in the best traditions of Scottish Presbyterianism : Peden need not have thought shame to put his name to it : when Richard Cameron, drawn sword in hand, rode into Sanquhar from the high moors, and at the Mercat Cross solemnly proclaimed the deposition of Charles II., he was actuated by the same spirit as the Assembly of 1842. It seems ungracious for a Scot to find fault with a declaration so truly national in spirit, but justice compels the admission that the Claim of Right had one very serious deficiency : the only honest conclusion to such a document was that the Church should have renounced its claim to all State endowments ; and it did not do so.

The weakness of the Church leaders was once more the opportunity of the Government. In 1840 the Church would have been satisfied with the Duke of Argyll's bill : in 1842 the bill and the abolition of patronage would still have saved the establishment. The Scottish members, of all opinions, pressed eagerly the need for immediate action. Peel, however, was much displeased by the Claim of Right. All their appeals only extorted from him a statement that ' I hope . . . parties in Scotland who are moderate in their views, and sincerely anxious for a termination of the present lamentable conflicts and divisions, will pluck up courage to avow their own conscientious opinions, and to disregard the menaces of newspapers and of factious leaders. . . . You cannot be surprised, . . . after the declarations to which the General Assembly was a party, . . . if we feel the necessity of maintaining great reserve.' [1] When the Moderator requested a reply to the Claim of Right, Graham, by the advice of Peel, sent a cold refusal of all concession. ' Pretensions such as these,' he wrote, ' have hitherto been successfully resisted by the Sovereign and people of this realm ; nor could they be conceded without the surrender of civil liberty, and without the sacrifice of personal rights.' [2] Under Peel's leadership, the House of Commons voted by a large majority not to receive the Claim of Right, though a majority of the Scottish members present voted that it should be heard.

The Assembly of 1843, aware of the attitude of the Government, did not wait to hear the letter in which Graham required the withdrawal of the Veto Act, and declared that patronage would

[1] Parker, *Peel*, iii. pp. 87-8.   [2] Parker, *Peel*, iii. p. 91.

be maintained by the Government. Under the leadership of Chalmers one-half of the Assembly seceded from the Church, and, leaving the hall, set up the Free Church of Scotland.

No true-blue Presbyterian will regret the result of Peel's policy. The position of the Free Church leaders was more dignified, more sincere, and more in accordance with national feeling than it could have been had large concessions induced them to cling to the State establishment. But this cannot obscure the fact that, from his own point of view, Peel's policy was a failure, perhaps the most complete failure of his whole career. He wanted to preserve the Established Church : he could only have done so by concession, and concession he resolutely refused to make. He clung to the Act of 1711 as if it had been an integral part of the Union of 1707, instead of a contravention of it. Against the advice of many Scotsmen, he delayed action until it was too late to do anything. His policy even made it impossible to save the patronage system, which he was so anxious to preserve. The secession of 1843 made the concession of all the original demands of the Church inevitable. With the Free Church flourishing beside it, there would have been an inevitable and perpetual drain from the establishment. Accordingly, within a few years, Parliament found it necessary to agree to the abolition of lay patronage in the Church of Scotland.[1]

The dangers to civil liberty, which Peel had prophesied, did not arise. The future proved that these concessions could be made without any clash between the civil and ecclesiastical courts —it proved, in fact, that the Church of Scotland had simply wanted to be let alone.

Peel had that sort of imaginative sympathy which makes a man able to feel intensely for the sufferings of others : but he had not that wider, more intellectual imagination which makes a man able to understand and sympathise with an attitude of mind different from the traditions in which he has been brought up. That is why his Irish and Scottish policy failed. He could instinctively understand and interpret the minds of his own fellow-countrymen : he could not understand those problems which arose in Ireland and Scotland, in which distinctive national feelings came into play.

[1] It should be pointed out, too, that the measures which Peel proposed were singularly ill-calculated to attain his ends. He said that he did not want to increase the power of the Presbyteries, but Aberdeen's bill, which he approved, actually gave the Presbyteries power which they did not want and had never claimed—power which the Church wanted to give to the congregation.

CHAPTER XIII

A POLICY OF PEACE, 1841-1846

THE creeping paralysis which had attacked the Melbourne Government left one department untouched. At home, the policy of the Whigs might be feeble, wavering, and ineffectual; abroad, it was daring and imperious. Melbourne, as has been seen, made no attempt to control his colleagues; and Palmerston at the Foreign Office did what he pleased.

He had begun his career as Foreign Secretary with one of the most triumphant successes that a British diplomatist ever obtained. The skill and boldness of his conduct of affairs, the liberal principles by which he was actuated, and the tone of robust English patriotism which he assumed, had won him a popularity and reputation that set him for a time beyond the reach of criticism. The success of his Belgian policy, however, had not had an altogether beneficial effect upon Palmerston himself. His self-confidence, already great, increased; he acquired a habit of meddling and an appetite for success which he never lost. His subsequent policy had been characterised by a reckless disregard of almost every consideration save that of obtaining diplomatic triumphs—not political advantages. Even his real Liberalism was subordinated to this—he flung over the cause of the Poles for the sake of a petty piece of revenge on France. He handled each incident as it arose with consummate ability, but he seemed incapable of seeing European politics as a whole, or conceiving a national policy independent of his personal likes and dislikes. He showed also an extraordinary disregard for the susceptibilities of other Powers. He bullied the envoys of the petty States, and lectured those of the greater ones: he wantonly insulted the veteran Talleyrand, the statesman who had done so much for Franco-British friendship. His policy had gained great prestige for Britain, and had made her the best-hated country in Europe: when he left office she was at war with China and on the verge of war with the United States and with France.

The Pasha of Egypt, Mehemet Ali, had risen in revolt against the overlordship of Turkey, and defeated the Sultan by land and sea. He was in a position to dictate his own terms, when the European Powers intervened, and months of complicated negotiations followed. France proposed to give him for life the possession of Egypt, Acre, and Syria, with independence of Turkey : Palmerston insisted that Syria should be restored to the Porte. His policy was ostensibly based on the need for keeping a strong Turkey as a barrier against Russia ; but it was noticeable that Russia heartily supported him in desiring to keep Syria for the Turks. France contended that a strong Egypt would be more valuable to Europe than a rotten and decadent Turkey. The welfare of Syria (which Palmerston appears to have considered quite beneath his interest) would have been favoured by the cession : Mehemet was not an enlightened sovereign, but under his rule order had been enforced, and Syria delivered from a state of anarchy and misery indescribable.

France and Mehemet remaining obstinate, Palmerston decided to act alone. He threw over France, signed a treaty with Russia, Prussia, and Austria, and, by the bombardment of Beyrout and Acre, forced the Pasha to submit to his demands. France, isolated, was helpless. The whole matter was carried through in a manner very offensive to French feeling, and when next Parliament opened, in 1841, the Queen's Speech, which should naturally have contained an expression of goodwill to France, was ominously silent.

The flouting of France was always grateful to the English people, and the victories of the fleet in the Mediterranean would alone have been sufficient to make Palmerston's action popular at home. His policy had certainly been completely successful, as far as it went. He had preserved Syria for Turkey : in order to do so he had broken the alliance with France, and reunited Britain with the three despotic Northern Powers. Whether the game was worth the candle is a matter of opinion.

Peel thoroughly disapproved of Palmerston's ways. He disliked the continual meddling with the internal affairs of foreign States, and the encouragement indiscriminately given to revolutionary movements : he was too good a man of business to think the barter of the French alliance for some barren glory a good bargain-: he had too just a respect for the rights of others not to be disgusted by Palmerston's bullying and bravado. It was the belief of Peel and Wellington that opposition to the Government on the subject of foreign affairs should be moderate and restrained, for the sake of national interests : but at a later date, when taunted by Palmerston with his too peaceable conduct of foreign affairs, Peel gave free expression to his views :

' For six years your constant boast in this House was, that you had formed and consolidated the alliance of Western Europe. . . . The influence of despotic power in the East was to be counter-balanced by the intimate union of States in the West, governed by liberal institutions. . . . What has become of the French alliance ? . . . (The noble lord) complains of the non-ratification of treaties by France, and of her delay in admitting our just claims ; and his complaints are just ; but these things are the consequences of that alienation, of that state of irritated feeling, which, either through the fault or the misfortune of the noble lord, have been the consequences of his policy. The noble lord thinks it was necessary to incur the risk of rupture with France, in order to maintain the integrity of the Turkish Empire. " True," says the noble lord, " we have alienated France, but then we have re-established the authority of the Porte in Syria." Syria, indeed ! . . . you have delivered up Syria, not to the Porte, but to anarchy ; and my firm belief is, that it was in the power of the noble lord to maintain every interest which England has in respect to Syria without the necessary disturbance of friendly relations with France.' [1]

In 1841 he did not think it right to express his opinions quite so freely, but he took it upon himself to do what the Government had not done. He criticised the omission of any reference to France in the Queen's Speech, lamented the alienation of the late ally, said that she had just cause for indignation at the manner in which she had been treated, paid a tribute to the pacific policy of Soult and Guizot, and emphatically declared his own adherence to the French alliance. This speech, coming from a statesman whose speedy advent to power was expected, did much to neutralise the evil effects of Palmerston's policy.

The trouble with the United States was of long standing. When Great Britain acknowledged American independence, the frontier of Canada had been decided by men who had no definite

[1] August, 10th, 1842. *Speeches*, iv. pp. 133-4.

knowledge of the lie of the land,[1] and ever since that time international commissioners and foreign arbitrators had laboured in vain to settle the matter.   During the 'thirties new causes of difference embittered the controversy.   The United States refused to recognise the Right of Search claimed by Britain in suppressing the slave trade, with the result that every slaver hoisted the Stars and Stripes.   Britain had surrendered the Right of Search, but she claimed the right of visiting the ships in order to ascertain whether they were really American, and this the United States refused to concede.   Another cause of trouble was more trivial. During the Canadian revolt a band of Canadian and American filibusters established themselves on an island in the Niagara, and were supplied with munitions and food by a steamboat from the American shore.   A British force sent to root out the pirates caught the steamer in American waters and destroyed it.   In the circumstances, a conventional apology [2] would have been enough to set Great Britain right in the matter ; but Palmerston was busy, American affairs bored him, and he did not bother to send one, nor even listen to the complaints of the American Minister in London.   American statesmen were rude and hostile ; Palmerston's insolence made a trivial incident assume dangerous proportions.   In 1840, a Canadian named Macleod went to New York on business, and boasted that he had been one of the attacking party that burned the *Caroline*.   Two or three Americans had been killed in the attack on the islet, and the imprudent Macleod was arrested and thrown into prison to stand his trial for murder.

Palmerston could no longer ignore what was going on : Canada was in a ferment, the Americans were loudly calling for Macleod's execution : the affair, in fact, had become quite congenial to the British Minister.   He demanded the instant release of Macleod, declared the burning of the *Caroline* to have been fully justified by the circumstances of the case, and privately assured the President that Macleod's death would at once produce a declaration of war

---

[1] As an example of the difficulty of settling the matter, it may be said that the treaty named the river St. Croix as forming the frontier at one point.   A whole series of rivers named St. Croix irrigated the district, and it took twelve years for the commissioners to decide which one was meant.

[2] I do not mean, of course, that the burning of the *Caroline* was not fully justifiable, but surely it would have been worth while to send a technical apology for the sake of settling the matter quietly.

from Britain. This conduct, very proper in itself, came with a very bad grace from Palmerston, who a few years before had authorised the despatch of a British legion to take part in the civil wars of Spain. It was effective in so far as that the United States Government was obliged to promise that Macleod should have a fair trial—in which case, of course, his acquittal was inevitable.

These controversies were largely due to the hostile attitude of the United States, but they were embittered by the conduct and language of Palmerston. None of them had been settled when the Whig Government fell, and Palmerston was succeeded by Lord Aberdeen.

George Hamilton Gordon, fourth Earl of Aberdeen, had acquired among the Liberals the reputation of being a reactionary statesman. His opinions on home affairs were, as a matter of fact, usually more Liberal than Palmerston's : as to foreign affairs, it depends on the point of view. Trained in the old school, Aberdeen abhorred the somewhat rowdy nationalism of Palmerston and his kind, and looked on revolution rather with the eye of Castlereagh than that of Russell : on the other hand, he would have been in his element at the table of the League of Nations, and would have enjoyed a chat with Viscount Cecil.

He was a gentle, silent, melancholy man ; a scholar widely read ; a model landlord, living in almost feudal state among an adoring tenantry on his Scottish estates ; a man who impressed all who knew him with the purity and loftiness of his character. He had a great ideal, that of international peace : but he was not a strong man. Left alone, he had not the resolution to steer the country through dangerous waters : but, when guided by a strong hand and resolute will, no man could be more capable than he of carrying out a policy of moderation and justice, a policy that was truly one of peace with honour. The strong hand was not lacking now : Peel did not, like Melbourne, leave his Foreign Secretary to his own devices. He and Aberdeen worked steadily together. Aberdeen supplied the knowledge, the practical experience of foreign affairs and of dealing with foreign diplomats, which his chief lacked ; and Peel's resolution and common sense, if necessary, stiffened Aberdeen's gentle idealism.

Sir Robert Peel seems to have had a depth of sympathy that led others to turn to him when in distress. Croker, who lost his only son in childhood, found his one consolation in Peel's companion-ship.[1] Lord Lincoln, who had married at twenty, was involved in a wretched and long-drawn domestic tragedy : throughout its course, Peel was his close confidant.[2] In the same way, when Aberdeen lost, in rapid succession, his wife and four children, he turned to Peel for sympathy, and the friendship thus cemented was one of perfect confidence. ' My beloved always talked of you,' Lady Peel wrote to Aberdeen later, ' as *the friend* whom he most valued, for whom he had the sincerest affection, whom he estimated higher than any.' [3]

The first care of the two friends was to procure a good under-standing with France and America. It was clear that nothing could be done if the dispute with the United States were allowed to drag on endlessly, and they decided to send out a plenipotentiary to negotiate a settlement. Baring, now Lord Ashburton, was selected. He was especially acceptable to the United States, as he had married an American ; and by his efforts the three difficul-ties, so long the source of ill-feeling, were settled in a few months. He admitted that neutral territory had been violated in the destruction of the *Caroline*, and expressed his Government's regret that an apology had not been made at once ; and the United States accepted this as a complete settlement. The American Govern-ment then undertook to join in the suppression of the slave trade, and to send a naval squadron to the African coast for this purpose, and in return the British claim to the Right of Visitation was dropped. The frontier question was compromised : Ashburton agreed to give up some British territory in the West, in return for a cession in the East. The United States actually gained more territory, but the military communications between Quebec and St. John were secured for Canada.[4] That the treaty was really a fair settlement may be deduced from the fact that *both* Govern-ments were violently denounced by their peoples for surrendering too much. Palmerston, in a tearing rage, declared that the

[1] Croker to Peel, 1st October, 1827. Parker, *Peel*, i. p. 472.

[2] Lincoln, who was perfectly blameless, was in the end obliged to divorce his wife, after having repeatedly forgiven her.

[3] Lady Peel to Lord Aberdeen, 2nd August, 1850. Parker, *Peel*, iii. p. 555. It was, however, for Graham, not Aberdeen, that Peel asked when he was dying.

[4] The territory gained in St. John had been given to the United States by the Dutch Arbitration ten years before—and had then been refused by the United States as insufficient !

Government had betrayed the interests of the country and basely truckled to the United States. Moderate men, however, recognised the advantages of the settlement, and Ashburton received the thanks and approval of Parliament.

He had hardly returned home when a new dispute arose. The treaty had only settled the boundary east of the Rockies ; on the Pacific side it was still undecided. The ground under dispute is now partly in British Columbia, partly in the State of Washington, but it was then included in Oregon. The United States claimed the whole valley of the Columbia : Britain refused her consent to this, and proposed as frontier the 49th parallel up to the bank of the Columbia, and after that the Columbia itself to the sea. The United States had ground for their claims in so far as their subjects were actually settling in Oregon. The Canadians had until now looked but little to the Pacific coast, but the Hudson Bay Company had great interests there, and it had developed the trade of the country.

Ashburton had offered the settlement of this question also, but without effect. The conduct of the United States made it clear that difficulties were to be apprehended : the President on two occasions, in 1842 and 1843, drew the attention of Congress to the need for settlement, but in each case suppressed the fact that Great Britain had offered to negotiate. Early in 1844 Aberdeen proposed arbitration, and was refused. Soon after this the situation changed for the worse. A new presidential election took place : Polk, the successful candidate, went to the polls on the cry of ' Fifty-Four-Forty or Fight ! ' He was an ignorant and violent man, and his imprudent declarations evoked an immediate response : even the pacific Aberdeen declared that Britain would not be bullied into surrendering her rights. Peel repeated Aberdeen's declaration in the House of Commons, and the press and public opinion supported him.

Until this time a convention had been in force which sanctioned the joint occupation of the disputed territory by the subjects of both Powers. In December, 1845, Polk stated that the convention must now be denounced, and the Senate authorised him to take action. The language of the American Government was very unfriendly. ' It is a nuisance,' wrote Greville, ' to have in such a post as that of President of the United States a man who is neither a gentleman nor a statesman, and who does not know how statesmen and nations ought to and must behave to one another.' [1]

The Conservative Government resolved that they would neither be frightened into surrender nor irritated into war. Aberdeen offered a compromise : the 49th parallel should be the frontier to the sea, but the whole of Vancouver Island must be given up to Great Britain, and the navigation of the lower Columbia must be free to British subjects. It was made clear that no further compromise would be made, and at the same time the British naval and military estimates were increased.

If the conciliatory spirit displayed by Peel and Aberdeen in the earlier negotiations had encouraged the Americans to think that liberties might be taken, the resolute response to Polk's threats destroyed the illusion. Other causes predisposed the United States to accept the offer. There was danger of trouble with Mexico. It was now the spring of 1846, and it was clear that Peel's Government would not last much longer. Then there would no longer be the mild and courteous Aberdeen to deal with, but the hot and hasty Palmerston. Polk descended from his high horse, and the United States accepted the British terms without any alteration.

In the meantime the difficulties with France had been ended. Aberdeen regarded the French alliance as the first condition of European peace. By good fortune, the statesman who now directed French affairs not only shared his desire for an understanding, but was of a character peculiarly sympathetic both to the British Foreign Secretary and the Prime Minister.

Guizot had been Ambassador in London in 1840 and had seen much of Peel. He left an account of his impressions of the Conservative leader, in which a hearty admiration is occasionally tempered by that mild amusement almost inevitable in a Frenchman contemplating an Englishman. Peel, he said, had only ' vague and undetermined notions ' as to foreign affairs, ' like a man who has not made them the habitual subject of his reflections. . . . Properly speaking, Sir Robert Peel had no foreign policy that was really his own, of which he had a clear conception, which proposed to itself a special plan of European organisation. . . . Although very solicitous about the greatness of his country, and even very accessible to popular impressions in regard to national dignity and honour, he formed no design of aggrandisement for England, felt

[1] *Letters of Greville and Reeve*, p. 104.

no selfish jealousy of foreign nations, and had no mania for domination abroad. . . . He respected the rights and dignity of other States, small as well as great, weak as well as strong—and regarded the employment of menace or force solely as a last extremity, legitimate only when it was absolutely necessary. . . . He seriously desired that peace and justice should prevail in the foreign policy of his country. . . . He believed that morality and good sense are essential and practicable in the foreign relations as well as in the internal government of States.'[1]

The effect of the change of Government in Britain was noticeable. Guizot at once signed the treaty for the suppression of the slave trade, for which Palmerston had been pressing in vain for months. Palmerston's annoyance may be conceived.[2] It turned out that Guizot had moved too fast for his countrymen, for the Senate refused to ratify; but at least the new friendliness of the French Government had been manifested. In 1843 the alliance was cemented by a visit of the Queen and Prince Consort to the French King. Aberdeen accompanied the Royal party, and from this moment his close and confidential friendship with Guizot was never shaken. They took no step save in concert : they showed each other their secret despatches. It was as well, for the stability of the new alliance was soon to be put to the test.

In 1842 a French admiral had been sent to annex the Marquesas Islands : he took it upon himself, without orders, to set up a protectorate in the island of Tahiti. Guizot, when the news arrived, decided to ratify the protectorate if Britain did not object. Aberdeen replied that Britain would not at present acknowledge the protectorate, but would make no objection.

There was, however, in Tahiti an English dissenting missionary named Pritchard, who had obtained a great influence over the native queen, Pomare. Pritchard, who held the position of British Consul, had twice induced Pomare to expel the French Roman Catholic missionaries, and this treatment of the ecclesiastics had given Admiral Thouars his excuse for establishing the protectorate. Pritchard, who had been absent for a time, now returned, and was highly indignant to find Pomare turned out of her palace to make room for a French official. He called in the aid of a British cruiser which happened to be near, ejected the Frenchman, and restored the Queen. Thouars came back to the island,

[1] Guizot, *Peel*, pp. 83, 142, 143.   [2] *Greville*, v. p. 767.

was very angry, and—once again without orders—deposed Pomare and annexed Tahiti.

In the meantime Pritchard had received despatches from Aberdeen reproving him for what he had done. He at once resigned his consulship, packed the Queen off in a ship to England, promised the Tahitians that Britain would give them military aid, and raised a riot against the French. The French commandant arrested Pritchard. His superior, arriving a few days later, released the militant Christian, but put him on board the next British vessel homeward bound.

Guizot had already disavowed Thouars and his annexation; but before anything could be done, Pritchard arrived in England with a tall story of his wrongs and sufferings. Such a tale would at any time have roused a storm in England : now, however, the whole influence of the Churches (which saw in imagination Protestant missionaries superseded by Catholics) was used to inflame popular indignation. Ashley, Sir Robert Inglis, and the bishops were the leaders in Parliament. Peel was carried away with the rest, and made an injudicious speech. He said that an outrage had been committed on a British consul, and that he had no doubt France would make a proper reparation.

Guizot, in the French Chambers, had taken the wiser course of refusing, in spite of intense popular excitement, to make any statement till clearer information arrived. It would have been well if Peel had done the same. His speech was unwise at such a moment, and it was not even accurate : Pritchard was not British Consul when he was arrested, and Peel was afterwards obliged to withdraw the statement. The mischief, however, was done, and in both countries a cry for war arose.

At this moment the presence of Aberdeen at the Foreign Office was invaluable. As a Scot, he was immune from the anti-French fever which it was always so easy to arouse in England. He used all his influence to moderate the indignation of his colleagues, and he and Guizot privately resolved, that if their respective Governments insisted on going to war, they would resign on the same day as a protest.[1]

Peel had no wish for war : he had only fallen for a moment under that chronic English delusion that France wanted to fight, and he was not going to submit to be bullied ! But he soon came to his

[1] Balfour, *Aberdeen*, ii. p. 106.

senses, and set to work to undo the mischief that his hasty words had done, and to moderate the excitement of people and Parliament.

The real desire of both Governments for peace ensured the success of negotiations. Pritchard accepted a monetary indemnity ; the French Government recalled the officer who had arrested him ; and Britain admitted the right of France to remove foreigners who had disturbed public order. On the 25th of January, Guizot announced an *Entente Cordiale* to the Chambers, and in February, when Parliament opened, Peel made a similar statement, and added that Britain, in deference to French opinion, would surrender the Right of Search, so that the arrangements as to the Slave Trade might be concluded. The settlement was, of course, denounced as a pusillanimous surrender on both sides of the Channel.

' Lord Aberdeen and I can not only agree but we can differ . . . ,' said Guizot to an English friend. ' Lord Palmerston, on the contrary, concentrates all his energy on one point, and especially a point where we happen to be at variance. *Il aime la lutte*, and the place where he is least master is that where he is most anxious to become so. . . . The affair of Tahiti, ridiculous as it was, was settled with Lord Aberdeen. I doubt whether it would have been with Lord Palmerston. For if he had said, " You must quit Tahiti ! " I should have replied, " I will do no such thing." ' [1]

' We have had hard work to keep the peace,' wrote Peel to Hardinge. ' The public mind in each country was much excited, and the selfish interests of party, and the violence of newspapers on each side of the Channel, were near forcing two great countries into a war, for the most trumpery cause of quarrel (except where the point of honour was concerned) that ever led to hostilities.' [2]

It is only fair, in estimating the foreign policy of Peel and Aberdeen, to admit that they gained something from the policy of Palmerston before them. Palmerston had made Britain hated, but he had made her feared. The courtesy and consideration shown by Aberdeen shone by contrast with his predecessor's brusqueness ; the display of strength that Palmerston had made, and his great diplomatic successes, made it clear that the new policy of Great Britain was not dictated by weakness, but by a sincere

---

[1] H. Reeve to John Russell. Gooch, *Russell Correspondence*, i. p. 90.

[2] Parker, *Peel*, iii. p. 263.

love of justice and peace. There had, indeed, been no discreditable surrender of British rights, no thought of 'peace at any price.' Peel had not let Aberdeen's dreams of a political millenium prevent him from introducing Wellington's schemes for strengthening the naval and military defences of the State. He had approached international disputes in a conciliatory spirit, but he had always secured a settlement honourable to his own country. Great Britain had upheld her own rights, while showing a just respect for the rights of others.

The Conservatives came into office in time to stop the country from drifting into hostilities with France and America, but not in time to prevent war in the East.

Lord Auckland had become Governor-General of India in 1837, and in 1838 he undertook the conquest of Afghanistan and the restoration to its throne of Shah Soojah, who had been deposed by his people some years before. The excuse given for the war was that Dost Mahomed, the usurping sovereign, was intriguing with Russia against British interests in India; but it was an excuse merely. The Russian agents had been recalled from Kabul and disowned by their Government before war was declared: Dost Mahomed was an able and (compared with Shah Soojah) enlightened ruler, and was sincerely anxious to be on good terms with Britain. But Auckland and Palmerston were dazzled with notions of military glory, and resolved upon an imperialist policy. Afghanistan was invaded, Dost Mahomed was deposed and carried a prisoner to India, and Shah Soojah set up in his place. The British force should now have been withdrawn, and Shah Soojah left to his rejoicing subjects: but he was so much detested that it was clear that the evacuation of the country would be the signal for his destruction. The Dost's son, Akbar Khan, was still at large: local revolts occurred continually, and an army of occupation was perforce left to hold the country.

In later days Lord Salisbury advised his critics to study Indian politics with a large-scale map. Lord Auckland might with advantage have followed this advice. Over 800 miles of difficult country separated the army at Kabul from its base at Ferozepore. The direct way of communication lay through the wild and dangerous passes of the Sofeid-Koh, and the Punjab. The loss of the expeditionary force in camels, on the march to Kabul, had amounted to 25,000. Even if the intervening territory had been

under British control the situation would have been bad enough :
but Ranjit Singh was dead, and the Punjab was falling into a state
of anarchy. The Afghan frontier chiefs had to be bribed to per-
mit communications to pass : Auckland thought their pay too
large, and reduced it : there never was a more ill-advised piece of
economy. The British force thus isolated was mainly posted in
Kabul ; smaller bands occupied Ghazni, Jellalabad, and Kandahar.

Meanwhile the Afghan campaign had been criticised at home,
and the Government published a Blue Book to justify it. The
despatches of the British envoy at Kabul were mangled in an extraordinary manner : every sentence that told in favour of Dost
Mahomed was omitted ; the meaning of many important passages
was perverted ; and the envoy's appeal to Auckland to recognise
the Dost was transformed into a recommendation to attack him
without delay. The daring fraud was completely successful : no
one dreamed that the despatches had been tampered with, and it
was not until some years after that the truth began to leak out.[1]
While every mail brought fresh news of disorder, Palmerston had
the impudence to state in a public speech that Afghanistan was as
quiet as England.

Auckland's tenure of power expired soon after the Conservatives
took office, and Peel appointed in his place Edward Law, Lord
Ellenborough. The new Governor was a strange being. His
portrait—' his archèd brow, his hawking eye, his curls,' the
Mephistophelian nose, the smiling lip, the sparkling look of intelligence and mischief—irresistibly suggest Mr. Punch in his young
days, before he became bald ; or add a pair of tiny horns among
the luxuriant locks, and you have the perfect head of a faun. His
appearance did not belie his character : imaginative, far-sighted,
energetic and capable, he was also reckless, changeable, impatient
and conceited. He had, however, great qualifications for his
office : he had been three times President of the Board of Control,
his ability was undoubted, and he was prepared to enforce administrative reform and to attack corruption, nepotism and incompetence without mercy.

The Governor-General was virtually independent of home
control. Three months must elapse before he could receive a

---

[1] I believe it has never been established who was the person responsible for
this disgraceful transaction. Burnes, the envoy, was dead, and unable to
disown the letters. It was not until 1858 that the correct versions of the despatches were published.

reply to his letters to London, and therefore it was hardly possible to do anything but acquiesce in his decisions. He was supposed to act by the advice of a permanent Council and of the Commander-in-Chief, and Peel hoped that these would restrain Ellenborough's vagaries. Wellington, with his Indian experience, had little hope in the Council, but he thought Ellenborough's own good sense would hold his reckless impulses in check.[1]

At home, authority was divided. The East India Company was still the nominal ruler, and the Court of Directors had the right to recall the Governor-General, though they had never yet exercised it. The Government, however, appointed the Governor-General, and exercised the real power through the Board of Control.

The new Governor-General landed at Madras in the spring of 1842, to meet terrible news. The Afghans, under Akbar Khan, had risen, and besieged Shah Soojah in his palace and the army of occupation in its cantonments. There had been folly and mismanagement on one side, treachery on the other. The political envoy had been murdered under a flag of truce, and the army had accepted a safe conduct to the frontier. They surrendered the greater part of their arms, and retreated through the Khyber Pass, in mid-winter, and the whole force had been cut to pieces. The women and children were carried off captive, and one solitary man, desperately wounded, had come through alive to carry the news.

In this situation it was the bold and reckless Governor-General, and not the sedate and pacific Minister at home, who was panic-struck. Ellenborough, it is true, began by putting a bold face on it, and declared that vengeance must be taken before the Afghan policy could be reversed; but the news of a fresh defeat, and the loss of Ghazni, alarmed him, and he sent orders to Nott and Sale, who still held out at Kandahar and Jellalabad, to evacuate the country without attempting to rescue the women and children or wipe out the defeat. It was a fatal mistake, and the way in which it was received in India awakened Ellenborough to the truth. There was a general cry of indignation, and Nott and Sir George Pollock, who had taken command on the frontier, disregarded the order. Ellenborough accordingly gave permission to Nott to 'retreat' (as he called it) 'via Kabul,' but left the responsibility

---

[1] Peel to Wellington, 6th October, 1841; Wellington to Peel, 7th October, 1841. Parker, *Peel*, ii. pp. 575-6.

of the decision with the Generals. They accepted it; Nott took Ghazni, Pollock recaptured Kabul, the prisoners were rescued, and then Afghanistan was evacuated with triumphant success. Dost Mahomed was now released, and returned to his throne, and Shah Soojah disappeared from history. Ellenborough's biographers have excused him by saying that it was better for the civil authority to leave the military to decide on the best course : but the question was not one of military tactics, but of imperial policy. Such a disaster, so unparalleled and so disgraceful, might well have shaken the British dominion in India, if it had not been avenged, and the honour of the British arms vindicated. If Afghanistan had been evacuated without the recapture of Kabul, it would have appeared a base surrender, and not a wise concession.

Peel had no experience of foreign policy, no knowledge of military affairs, but it is remarkable how sure was his instinct, how true his judgment throughout. He disliked Auckland's policy, and had feared disaster from the first. ' His policy in respect to the Afghan country and the restoration of Shah Soojah will far outweigh in point of evil any good he may have effected,' he wrote ; and later, ' I am regarding all that is passing on the North-West Frontier of Hindostan with the deepest anxiety. I fear the possibility of a terrible retribution for the most absurd and insane project that was ever undertaken in the wantonness of power.' [1]

' The events at Kabul,' he wrote to Ellenborough, after the news reached him, ' are still a horrible mystery. . . . It seems to us that there was never a case wherein a desperate resolve would have been more consistent, not only with sound policy as far as the honour of the British arms is concerned, but with the personal safety of the parties taking it.' [2] While giving Ellenborough full liberty of action, he urged the necessity of retrieving the disaster and punishing the treachery of the Afghans. The order to retreat greatly disappointed him ; he agreed to it, because it was too late to do anything else, and because he thought it fair to give the man on the spot a free hand, but it was against his judgment. Ellenborough's subsequent proceedings he liked no better.

' I do not approve of Lord Ellenborough's order to General Nott. It places him . . . in an embarrassing situation, by

[1] Parker, *Peel,* ii. p. 580.

[2] *Ib.* p. 583. By ' a desperate resolve,' he means that they should have defended themselves in the Bala Hissar, a course advocated by Lady Sale at the time, and by all competent judges since.

devolving specially upon him an extent of responsibility which he ought not to bear. . . . I am convinced that nothing but very severe and overpowering necessity should induce us to abandon the prisoners. . . . Apart from any sentimental feeling—which, however, I by no means abjure—I think we should incur the risk of material loss—loss of reputation and of honour, which constitute our strength and make our name formidable—by abandoning, without one effort . . . those who are held captive by perfidious savages.' [1] He urged these views on Ellenborough, he was delighted with the resolution of Nott and Pollock, and he made it clear to Ellenborough that though the Government accepted his decisions, they did not do so with enthusiasm.

The course taken by the Governor-General had naturally given much scope to criticism on the part of the Whigs, but the final triumph destroyed the effect of this. 'The Palmerstons are still screaming themselves hoarse in their endeavours to get the credit of the success,' Greville noted. Ellenborough also was nowise backward in taking the glory to himself, and he issued a magniloquent, boastful and tactless proclamation which revived the opposition. He soon gave them further reason for talk.

The first invasion of Afghanistan had been undertaken through the province of Sind, by permission of the Amirs. Ellenborough decided that these chieftains had not been altogether loyal to their British allies. The evidence on which he acted was very incomplete : the Amirs were the corrupt and tyrannical rulers of an alien people, but they seem to have been, on the whole, true to their engagements. Ellenborough's penal measures were deliberately calculated to drive them into war : they were suppressed easily enough by Sir Charles Napier, who was in full agreement with the Governor-General ; [2] and Sind was annexed. Undoubtedly the step was a happy one for the native population, but the whole manner of proceeding was so high-handed, the treatment of the Amirs was so unnecessarily harsh and discourteous, that the news was received with almost universal disgust in Britain.

The Government were not pleased : they had no very definite information, but the transaction seemed very doubtful. They

[1] Parker, *Peel*, ii. p. 591.

[2] He wrote in his diary, 'A very advantageous, humane, useful piece of rascality it (the annexation) will be.' *Life and Opinions of General C. J. Napier*, ii. p. 218.

decided, however, that, the thing being done, it must be accepted, and Peel undertook to defend Ellenborough, so far as he conscientiously could, in Parliament. The Court of Directors, however, were not so easily reconciled.

Peel had originally appointed Fitzgerald to the India Board, and on his death had replaced him by Ripon. It was not a wise choice, but Peel probably still thought of him as the brilliant young Robinson who had been his own rival in early days, and did not realise into what abject feebleness of intellect and character he had sunk. Poor Ripon was conscious of his own deficiencies. ' I feel I am becoming more and more useless to you and to my colleagues,' he wrote rather pathetically to Peel.[1] In such hands, the Court of Directors had got out of control. Between soothing their alarms, supplementing the labours of sick or incompetent Ministers, and mitigating the effects of Ellenborough's hasty temper, Peel had had his hands full. ' The Court of Directors is becoming a very troublesome body,' he remarked, ' mainly from the want of efficient control. They presume upon the absence of it, and encroach accordingly.'[2] The ' Chairs ' were equally disgusted and alarmed by Ellenborough's conduct. They hated annexations and the extension of responsibility; they were offended by his haughty manners and hot temper; they were, above all, displeased by his attacks on official corruption and incompetence and by his favouring the army above the civil service.

A new danger was developing in India. The Punjab was sinking ever more deeply into anarchy. Gwalior was in almost as bad a state : and there seemed for a time a danger that the Sikh and the Mahratta armies might unite against the British power. Ellenborough wisely decided to nip the danger in the bud, and Gwalior, after some sharp fighting, was taken under British protection. It seemed likely that the Governor-General was meditating steps against the Sikhs also, and the Court of Directors could bear no more. For the first time they exercised their legal right, and recalled Lord Ellenborough.

There must have been mismanagement at home before things came to this pass. Peel, called away by a hundred other duties, could not compensate by his own care for the weakness of Ripon. But in truth the Court of Directors was an anomaly, and Ellenborough had realised it. He was one of the first men to under-

[1] Parker, *Peel*, iii. p. 22.　　　　[2] Law, *Ellenborough*, p. 23.

stand that the East India Company must go, and he used all his influence against it. The clash was perhaps inevitable. Peel did not approve of the conduct of the Court of Directors, but he thought they had received much provocation, and he finally told them that they would do better to recall the Governor-General than to slight him publicly and secretly weaken his position, as they had lately tried to do.[1]

He now did his best to mitigate the undeserved disgrace which had fallen on a man who, with all his faults, had rendered the greatest services to India. Ellenborough received the customary honours of retiring Governors-General, and Peel selected as his successor Sir Henry Hardinge, his brother-in-law, so that the appointment was one as flattering to the retiring Governor as any that could be made. It was also a good one in itself. Hardinge was a soldier, a Peninsular veteran, without a trace of Ellenborough's and Auckland's aggressive imperialism. Single-minded, honourable and modest, he regarded himself as a rough, uneducated fellow, because he had joined his regiment at fourteen. He had been Irish Secretary in the Wellington Government in 1830, and since that time had been one of Peel's closest personal friends.

Hardinge went out to India pledged to a policy of peace, but too clear-sighted not to be in dread of war. The aspect of the Punjab had become ever more threatening. Ranjit Singh's successor had been murdered, and the army tyrannized over the State, and plotted an attack upon British India. Hardinge's task was difficult : he must take no smallest step that might cause it to be said that he had contemplated aggression himself, or even provoked it from his adversaries ; yet he must be prepared for defence.

He carried out his plans admirably. When, in December, 1845, the Sikh army crossed the Sutlej, not the slightest provocation had been given by any word or action of the Indian Government ; yet an army of 40,000 men had been massed near the frontier, and could be rapidly concentrated to meet the attack. The campaign that followed was the hardest yet fought in India : the Sikh army was well armed and fought with desperate courage. They were defeated in three savage and bloody battles, and Hardinge marched on Lahore.

The unprovoked aggression and the internal state of the Punjab

[1] Parker, *Peel*, iii. 10, 12, 18.

might well have justified annexation : it was, in fact, generally expected, and Russia had informed Great Britain that she recognised it was inevitable : but Hardinge held resolutely to the policy of moderation on which he and Peel had determined. Only the vale of Kashmir and the territory on the left bank of the Sutlej were annexed, and an indemnity of half a million was extorted. The Sikh army was limited, and a new Government was set up under a friendly native chief. Lawrence was left as British Resident to commence his noble work of reform, and, after a few months, the British forces were withdrawn.

The concession was perhaps ill-judged. Hardly three years elapsed before the Punjab was again in arms, and, after another fierce campaign, Hardinge's successor annexed the whole State.

Undoubtedly such men as Ellenborough and Dalhousie, with their policy of territorial expansion and their clear recognition of the fact that John Company must go, showed more grasp of reality and more understanding of the inevitable tendencies of British empire in India than did Peel and Hardinge with their policy of peace and moderation. Nevertheless such a government as Hardinge's, pacific without being pusillanimous, unenterprising yet strong, was equally valuable, especially coming as it did in the midst of a series of imperialistic administrations. It is a question, too, whether the annexations of Ellenborough and Dalhousie did not help to precipitate the Mutiny. Hardinge's government showed that not mere aggressive imperialism, but considerations of justice and humanity directed British policy in India. The Governor-General had showed himself strong, but merciful. When no external danger threatened, in the hour of victory, and of his own free will, he had held his hand.

Hardinge was, of course, blamed by the Opposition for being insufficiently prepared, and for not annexing the whole of the Sikh State : but Peel, in a series of noble speeches, defended his course, and—even in the hostile House of Commons of 1846—turned opinion in his favour.

' I never can sufficiently express the warmth of my feelings for the admirable manner in which you have defended my conduct,' Hardinge wrote to him. ' I hear from several of those who heard you, that your sentiments were delivered with a depth of feeling that ought to make me proud of such a man's friendship. And so I am ; but it is quite impossible to express what I feel for the affectionate care for my character, and the generous support with which you have honoured me before our countrymen. No Governor-General was ever treated in a manner more grateful to his feelings. I owe it all to you, and the impression will never be effaced from my memory or that of my boys. . . . I observed you seized the most judicious points in justifying the delay in moving up to the frontier, and were perfectly master of all the military details.' [1]

[1] Parker, *Peel*, iii. p. 316.

CHAPTER XIV

IRELAND, 1841-1845

THE Irish policy of the Melbourne Government had been that which was most successful in itself and most honourable to them. It is true that their weakness had in part hindered them from carrying their policy into effect : they had failed to pass the Appropriation Clause ; they had equally failed in their attempt to lower the franchise ; and the Corporation Reform Act had been considerably modified. It is true, also, that their bargain with O'Connell and their dependence on the Irish vote had lowered their character and lessened their popularity. But they had at least succeeded in giving some measure of satisfaction to the Irish. They had governed Ireland for six years without passing a new Coercion Act or making use of the old one.[1] They had made an excellent impression by the judicious promotion of Roman Catholics, and they had suppressed Orange clubs. In Thomas Drummond, they had given Ireland one of the ablest, and quite the most popular, Under-Secretaries of the period. They had passed the Tithe Commutation Act, which removed a real griev-ance, by transferring the burden of tithes from the occupier to the landlord. This was a creditable record.

The success of their policy, however, was largely owing to the conduct of O'Connell. He had not only refrained from agitation, but had used all his influence to keep the country quiet. When the Whig Government was obviously drawing near its end, O'Connell changed his tactics. He saw that the Whigs were powerless ; their last measure, the Poor Law Act, he disliked ; and he could expect nothing more from them. From the Tories, he hoped nothing and feared everything. In April, 1840, he founded a new association, whose object was to be the repeal of the Act of Union of 1801. It was organised on the same lines as the Catholic Association, and was to be based, like it, on the sup-port of the mass of the people. O'Connell obtained once more the

[1] The Coercion Act of 1834 remained on the Statute Book till 1840, but was not enforced.

assistance of the village priests ; but he was anxious to enlist the moderate Protestants also on his side.

For the first two years of its life the association did very little. The Tory reaction at the election of 1841 was felt in Ireland also. O'Connell himself lost his seat in Dublin. The Repeal movement did not seem to have taken any great hold on the people, and the new Government was allowed to settle into its place quietly.

From the first, however, there were dissensions in the new Irish administration. The Viceroy, Earl de Grey, was brother-in-law to Lord Enniskillen, the Orange leader, and was himself not free from Protestant prejudice. The Permanent Under-Secretary apparently shared his views. The Parliamentary Secretary, Lord Eliot, was, on the contrary, very liberal in his opinions, but he had no influence with De Grey. The Viceroy refused to consult him, and treated him with a coolness amounting to contempt.

Peel had intended to carry out the Emancipation Act in the spirit as well as in the letter. He was anxious that the Catholics should have their full share of patronage. Even if the Protestant candidate were better qualified, he impressed upon the Viceroy, still it was better to choose the Catholic : the Protestant had an unfair advantage—for years the plums of all the professions had been reserved for him : the only way in which the balance could be restored was by promoting Catholics freely.[1] Peel carried his opinions so far that in 1845, on the resignation of Mr. Lucas, he wished to appoint a Catholic Under-Secretary, but here he was over-ruled by his colleagues.[2]

De Grey, however, would not carry out his Government's policy. To secure a single Protestant appointment, the Prime Minister and Home Secretary had to keep nagging at him unceasingly : whenever he was left alone, he appointed Protestants to every vacant place. It was impossible to exercise control of this kind effectively : and as Peel considered it a lesser evil to defend the independent action of the Irish administration than to disavow it, the Government soon acquired the reputation of being resolutely hostile to the Roman Catholics, and of failing to carry out the Emancipation Act.

No doubt Peel had hoped that Eliot's liberality would counteract the prejudices of De Grey, and had not imagined that the Secretary would allow himself to be set at nought in this manner.

[1] Parker, *Peel*, iii. pp. 54, 57, 104, 117-8, etc.   [2] *Ib.* pp. 182-6.

'I would not have held the office for an hour on such terms,' he remarked candidly to Graham,[1] while busying himself with kind encouragement to Eliot and remonstrances with the Viceroy. Graham inclined to end the difficulty by removing Eliot, but Peel would not agree to this. He succeeded in forcing a few Catholic appointments on the Viceroy, but it was not until three years passed, and De Grey was replaced by Lord Heytesbury, that the policy of fair distribution of patronage was really made effective.

De Grey was equally unsatisfactory in his administration of patronage in the Irish Church. The Government was anxious to encourage the system of national education, established by Stanley in 1831. The established Church clergy as a whole had opposed it, and now De Grey seemed anxious to fill every vacant preferment with men who had distinguished themselves for the violence and intolerance of their opposition.

The law officers were equally indiscreet. They entered upon prosecutions of Repeal agitators without consulting the Home Secretary, and magistrates who attended Repeal meetings were dismissed from the bench. Peel thought himself obliged to defend in Parliament these proceedings, which he disapproved and reprimanded in private. It may be doubted whether this was not carrying loyalty to his subordinates too far, but it was his uniform practice to make himself responsible for such blunders.

All this seems to show some laxness and inefficiency in the home control of the Irish administration. Perhaps, in such circumstances, effective control was impossible ; but in that case the Prime Minister deserves the more blame for selecting men for responsible posts in Ireland who were unable or unwilling to carry out the policy on which he himself had determined.

The effect on Ireland was very unhappy. O'Connell, who saw only the external aspect of affairs, naturally concluded that the Government was resolved upon an anti-Catholic policy ; and he threw himself with all the more eagerness into the agitation for Repeal. In the autumn of 1842 he was freed from his responsibilities as Mayor of Dublin, and he decided to withdraw from Parliament and devote himself entirely to Repeal. The movement suddenly assumed dangerous proportions. A series of monster meetings was held, at which immense crowds listened with enthusiasm, while O'Connell denounced England as the source of

[1] *Ib.* p. 60.

all the misfortunes and suffering of the Irish people. He never lent himself to schemes of rebellion, and always urged the people to confine themselves to peaceful methods, but his language was such as could not but arouse passions that were likely to seek an outlet in bloodshed. 'The time is coming when we must be doing,' he cried. ' You may have the alternative to live as slaves or die as freemen. . . . I for one defy all the Ministers of England to put down agitation. . . . If Peel forces a contest, if he invades the constitutional rights of the Irish people, then *vae victis* between the contending parties ! Where is the coward who would not die for such a land as Ireland ? . . . Let our enemies attack us if they dare. They shall never trample me under their feet ; if they do so it will be my dead body.'

At the same time, the leaders of the party known as ' Young Ireland ' were openly advocating armed rebellion. The state of Ireland began to attract attention abroad. Ledru Rollin declared that France would support the oppressed Irish if it came to war. Ledru Rollin was at that time the insignificant leader of a small minority : but in the United States, men of position, governors of states and holders of Government offices, threatened at public meetings that if the Repeal movement were suppressed by force, the loss of Canada would be the penalty. The President himself, with that disregard for international courtesies for which his countrymen are eminent, publicly declared himself ' the decided friend of Repeal.'

O'Connell himself never contemplated rebellion. He knew too well what would be the result ; he would never make himself responsible for another '98. He thought the display of force would be sufficient. He thought that now, as in 1829, he could frighten the Government into yielding ; Peel had been scared in 1829, he would be scared now. But this was a dangerous game to play.

The situation in 1843 was very different from what it had been in 1829. Peel had not thought it worth while to risk a revolt to delay the emancipation of the Catholics ; but he was ready to fight to the last to prevent the repeal of the Union. He regarded it as the first step to the break-up of the British Empire, as a movement essentially reactionary and retrogressive. There is no ground to assume that his feeling was a reasoned one ; it was rather an instinct. ' If Ireland must have federation, so must Scotland.

Why not Wales ? Why not Wessex ? and the Kingdoms of the
Heptarchy ? ' he asked, as Canning had asked before him. Arguments of this sort are easy to answer : the Heptarchy had been
dead for a thousand years : Ireland was still, in the vulgar phrase,
alive and kicking. The English people, however, did not require
reasoning to convince them that it was their duty to resist Repeal :
they were just as sure about it as Sir Robert could be. He had
thus at his back a solid body of opinion which he had not had to
anything like the same extent in 1829. Even the Whigs could not
advocate separation, and we cannot doubt that they would have
considered it their duty to put down armed rebellion with all the
resources of the Empire. As the opponent of Catholic Emancipation, Peel had been the champion of an intolerant faction ; as the
opponent of Repeal, he was the representative of the English people.

The Whigs could not in consistency attack the Government on
the grounds that Repeal should be conceded : but they attacked
it for neglecting the movement, allowing it to swell to undue
dimensions, and then putting it down with unnecessary force.

Peel did not consider it necessary to ask for special powers to
deal with the situation : Coercion Acts were for midnight murder,
not for the suppression of political agitation. In 1843, however,
the Arms Act fell to be renewed. It had been in force practically
since the Union : it was last renewed by the Whigs in 1838. It
forbade anyone to carry arms without a license, and authorised the
police, in certain counties, to search for arms in private houses.
The Act was systematically violated, and the Conservative Government decided to make it effective by adding one or two new provisions, of which the chief was, that all arms licensed by magistrates
should be registered and branded.[1] This gave the Opposition a pretext for objecting to the renewal of the Act. John Russell, while
admitting that the Act was necessary, attacked the branding of
arms as an infringement of personal liberty : when the Government pointed out that the only object of the clause was to make
the Act, hitherto a dead letter, effective, he replied that by saying
this they lost the benefit of the contention that the bill merely
renewed the Act of 1838, and that therefore ' he considered
himself at perfect liberty to oppose it.' [2] We are to conclude,

[1] These alterations had been decided on in 1842, without any reference to
the Repeal agitation.

[2] *Hansard*, lxx. 384 ff.

R.P.

apparently, that Lord John thought there ought to be an Arms Act in force in Ireland, but only so long as it was ineffective. It took the course of a long session to carry the bill through the House of Commons.

Peel took the opportunity of the debates on the Arms Bill to declare his policy regarding Repeal in bold and uncompromising terms. 'There is no influence,' he said, 'no power, no authority which the prerogatives of the Crown and the existing law give the Government, which shall not be exercised for the purpose of maintaining the Union. . . . Deprecating as I do war, but above all civil war, yet there is no alternative which I do not think preferable to the dismemberment of the Empire.' [1]

Peel rejected the idea of relying on the aid of the Protestant loyalists against the movement : and for this reason he would not make use of the yeomanry, which was almost entirely Protestant. He refused, from similar motives, to allow the Duke of Wellington to go to Ireland.[2] As the summer of 1843 passed, however, every available man was transferred to Ireland, and by autumn 35,000 regular troops were assembled there, and a naval squadron was lying off the coast. A new monster meeting had been summoned for the 8th of October at Clontarf—the scene of ' Brian's Battle,' that very barren victory which was regarded by nineteenth century Irishmen as equal to Waterloo and Bannockburn together ; and the field had been selected as the scene where Ireland's liberty was again to be won.

The monster meetings had until now been perfectly peaceable, and not the smallest act of violence had accompanied them. This was partly due to the influence of Father Mathew, who was then conducting his temperance campaign, and with whom O'Connell had been wise enough to ally himself. The meeting was not illegal in itself, but the inflammatory language employed by some of the leaders, and the use of the term ' Repeal Cavalry ' in the

[1] *Ib.* lxix. 1025 ff.

[2] ' I begin to suspect the Duke wishes to go to Ireland, and believes that the winds and waves will obey him, and that in his presence there will be a great calm. I entertain an opposite opinion. If there were a rebellion, his iron hand would crush it. I doubt very much whether his preventive measures would be of a soothing character.' Sir J. Graham to Peel, 6th September, 1843. ' I do not think it would be advantageous that under any ordinary circumstances the Duke should undertake the administration of the civil government. Such an appointment . . . would amount practically to a complete change of our policy towards Ireland.' Peel to Sir J. Graham, 18th September, 1843. Parker, *Peel,* iii. pp. 63-4.

summons to the meeting, gave a pretext for interference. The Government decided to prohibit the Clontarf assembly. The announcement was delayed until the day before, lest, if published too soon, it should precipitate a rising. ' Young Ireland ' were for holding the meeting in spite of it ; they were ready for war : but O'Connell decided that it must be stopped. Messengers were sent to turn the people back. Large bodies of persons did, in fact, appear and hover near ; but the meeting ground was occupied by a strong military force, and they dispersed without a shot being fired. In the following week O'Connell was arrested and put on trial for conspiracy. He had played a game of bluff, and the Government had called his bluff.

O'Connell's object was in itself legal. He had a perfect right to agitate for the repeal of the Union, by means of public meetings and petitions, if he desired to do so. It was contended, however, that he had intended to coerce Parliament by a display of force, and that this was illegal. He had also tried to organise a system of arbitration courts, with the avowed intention of ' taking all power out of the hands of the Government as regards the Courts of Law,' [1] and it was said that this involved a usurpation of the Royal prerogative. As a matter of fact, O'Connell *was* being tried for advocating the repeal of the Union, and as this was not a legal offence, the prosecutors were driven to manufacture more or less artificial accusations against him. As no Catholic jury would have convicted O'Connell, whatever the evidence, the law officers used their power to challenge every Catholic juryman. The whole machinery of the trial—the indictment, the jury, the judge (who is said to have been openly partisan)—was a pretence, and everyone concerned knew it. The Government was answering a show of force by the actual exertion of force.

They had taken a bold step, and they were determined that it should be successful. The packing of the jury was, of course, the work of the Irish administration, but Peel's letters, written soon after,[2] show that he was aware of the fact that a conviction in an Irish sedition trial could only be secured by such methods, and he must be held responsible. He had always thought—as did many other able men, both Irish and English—that trial by jury was not

---

[1] The arbitration courts were at first successful, until the people discovered that their decisions were not legally binding, then they collapsed.

[2] Parker, *Peel*, iii. pp. 105, 116.

suitable for the conditions of Ireland. We must conclude that when he once made up his mind to prosecute O'Connell, he determined not to stick at what was necessary to secure conviction.

O'Connell was found guilty, but sentence was not pronounced until the following term, and in the meantime he was released, and went to London to be fêted by the Radicals. At the opening of 1844, he was sentenced to a year's imprisonment and a fine of £2,000, and was bound over to keep the peace for seven years on security of £5,000. He at once appealed to the House of Lords. Peel thought the sentence ought not to be inflicted until the judgment of the Lords was known : his colleagues regarded the result as certain, and over-ruled his opinion, and O'Connell was conveyed to prison, where he was installed in the governor's house, entertained his friends to dinner every night, and had a bishop to say mass for him every morning.

The English judges called in to advise decided by seven to two that the sentence was good : but the ultimate decision lay with the Lords themselves. Such points are, of course, left to the Judicial Committee, but the lay lords have in theory, and have occasionally exercised in fact, the right to remain and vote. They were eager to do so now, and their presence would secure a victory for the Government. Peel, however, objected. ' The decision ought to be left to the Law Lords, and on no account a political vote be taken,' he wrote before the trial ; and after it, ' The permanent evil of over-riding the majority of the Law Lords by the votes of unprofessional peers would have been, I think, greater than the reversal of the sentence.' [1] Nothing is more remarkable —or more typical of English statesmanship—than this strict adherence to the spirit of the law in England and deliberate outraging of it in Ireland.

The Law Lords reversed the judgment on the grounds that sentence had been pronounced on all the counts of O'Connell's indictment, and conviction only secured on eight. The three Whig Lords, Cottenham, Denman and Campbell, composed the majority, the Tory Lyndhurst and his crony, Brougham, the minority. No doubt the Lords voted upon purely conscientious grounds, but the coincidence is curious.

The Whigs had attacked the whole course of proceedings with

[1] To Graham, 7th April, 1844 ; to Brougham, 21st September, 1844. Parker, *Peel*, iii. pp. 124-5.

great spirit : they condemned the arrest of O'Connell, and condemned the injustice of his trial. That the Whigs themselves were not above packing juries was made clear later, upon the trials of the Irish rebels in 1848 ; but their attack of the general principle on which the Government acted is even more open to criticism. On the highest moral grounds, of course, the conduct of the Conservative Government is quite unjustifiable. If we admit that no nation has a right to coerce another, then we must admit that the suppression of the Repeal movement was an act of tyranny. But the Whigs (as distinct from the Radicals) did not take this ground. They themselves never proposed to concede Repeal, either when in opposition or when in power. They attacked Peel's conduct on the ground that he had driven the Irish into discontent by misgovernment, and then had put down agitation in an unnecessarily high-handed and oppressive manner. They said the interfering with public meetings and liberty of speech was unjustifiable, and the packing of the jury a disgrace.

Critics of all schools will probably concede that the British Parliament in 1843 would no more have repealed the Act of Union than they would have given votes to women. If there was no chance of carrying Repeal by legal means, it was better for Ireland that the agitation should be effectually suppressed before it led to bloodshed. Carried on in the same manner for a few years longer, the movement must have ended in disorder, perhaps in revolt : and revolt could not have secured Irish freedom ; it could but have deepened the gulf of hatred between the two nations.

Trial by jury, the right of public meeting, freedom of speech— these are fair ideals, and the Whig statesmen rightly admired them : but the English government in Ireland was at bottom based on force, and force only, and in recognising this and acting on it, Peel showed a greater grasp of reality than did his critics. The Whigs invariably spoke of trial by jury as the best security of personal freedom ; whereas in Ireland it was as a rule simply a means of securing the acquittal of criminals in the face of the evidence. In the same way, they placed the abstract right to freedom of speech above the practical necessity of preventing bloodshed. The only logical conclusion of their arguments was that they themselves should propose to repeal the Union. Apparently, however, their idea was that the Irish should be allowed to talk as much as they liked about Repeal, but not allowed to get it.

The Conservative policy had at least the justification of success. O'Connell's release was hailed as a great triumph by the Irish, and proclaimed by the Catholic priests to be a miracle directly due to the intervention of the Virgin Mary. But O'Connell himself knew that he was beaten. He had threatened to use force : the Government had dared him to do so, and he had refused the challenge. He was now nearly seventy, and perhaps already suffering from the disease of which he eventually died : he was losing his sure political touch. He abandoned Repeal and took up a scheme of Federalism : it attracted no adherents, and he dropped it. The temporary revival of enthusiasm which followed his release did not last long. Within a year the Repeal rent had fallen to be a tithe of its former amount. O'Connell still held meetings here and there, but the heart had gone out of his agitation. He definitely declared against violence, and the declaration caused a break with 'Young Ireland.' They seceded from the association, but the mass of the people still held by the old Liberator. The split fatally weakened the Repeal movement : its influence went on, moulding the minds of the younger generation, but there was no longer any immediate danger.

The success of the Government was clinched by the fact that they had now entered into a policy of conciliation and far-reaching reform. This had been delayed by the troubles of 1843, but in the very midst of them Peel wrote to Graham : ' It is clear that mere force. . . . will do nothing as a permanent remedy for the social evils of Ireland. We must look beyond the present, must bear in mind that the day may come—and come suddenly and unexpectedly—when this country may be involved in . . . war with other Powers, and when it may be of the first importance that the foundations of a better state of things in Ireland should have been laid. Let us ponder on these things, and say nothing to others until we have talked them over.' [1]

The first measure of conciliation had been introduced in 1843: The Board which administered Charitable Bequests consisted almost entirely of Protestants, while the funds at their disposal were almost all the gift of Catholics for Catholic purposes. Peel set up a new Board instead : it was to consist of Catholics and Protestants in equal numbers, and only Catholic members were to deal with Catholic charities. The measure was the occasion of

[1] Parker, *Peel*, iii. p. 65.

another triumph over O'Connell. He opposed it, and used all
his influence to induce the Catholic Church to oppose it also.
McHale, the archbishop whose name is eminent in the annals of
bigotry and faction, worked with him. They failed. In 1844 the
Government induced the Pope to take their view of the matter, and
two Catholic archbishops and a bishop, of more moderate views,
consented to serve on the Board.

Peel, like most statesmen who have occupied themselves with
Irish affairs, had always believed that the best hope of that unhappy country lay in the progress of education. The Kildare
Street Society of Peel's young days had been superseded by
Stanley's system of national education, which, though introduced
in 1831, was founded on the recommendations of a committee of
1827. Peel's ideas on education had widened, but in one respect
he held stanchly to his old opinion : he still thought that Catholic
and Protestant children should be educated together. What hope
was there to modify religious fanaticism in Ireland if the different
Churches were to be divided even in infancy ? Childish memories
of work and play in common should work, as nothing else could,
in softening their differences.[1]

Stanley's national schools were founded on this principle.
Secular education was given in common to all sects, and the
priests of each denomination instructed the pupils in their own
faith separately. The system had not been successful, for both
the Catholic and the Anglican Churches bitterly opposed it, and
the Protestant Dissenters, more practical if less conscientious, had
by evading the rules made their schools simply Presbyterian aca-
demies. Stanley was now prepared to abandon the scheme, but
Peel would not give up the hope of co-education yet, and proposed to give it another chance, increasing the funds. He turned
his attention to the question of advanced, not of elementary,
education.

In the first place, he hoped to win over the Catholics by the
donation of funds for the education of the priesthood. The
Government already made a small annual grant to the college at
Maynooth ; Peel decided to increase it to a handsome sum.
Secondly, he intended to set up three new undenominational
colleges—one for Protestant Dissenters, two for Catholics—where
a good secular education could be obtained, while at the same

[1] To Leslie Foster, 1st September, 1829. Parker, *Peel*, ii. pp. 127-9.

time every precaution was taken to safeguard the religion of the
students and avoid all risk of religious propaganda. The University of Dublin was by this time open to Catholic students, but
its fellowships and scholarships were still reserved for Protestants.
Peel did not want to provoke an explosion of Protestant feeling by
tampering with the endowments of Dublin, but he hoped his new
Queen's Colleges would remedy the injustice.

These measures were discussed in 1843, and were finally decided
on by the opening of the session of 1844, but their introduction
was postponed in deference to the views of Mr. Gladstone, who
was now in the Cabinet. He had published a book some years
before, in which he expressed views that appeared to himself to
pledge him against such measures as these. The other Ministers
did not understand Gladstone's scruples—but then perhaps they
had not read his book. They were very tender with the conscientious young man, though they thought him an ass ; and they
allowed him time for consideration. In the meantime the public
was prepared for the Maynooth grant by a bill legalising the endowment of Roman Catholic institutions from land.

Long meditation convinced Gladstone that the educational
proposals were right and wise, but, though his mind was changed,
he still felt it his duty to resign, though he promised unofficial
support. He communicated his decision in a letter couched in
such cryptic terms that Peel remarked of it, ' I really have great
difficulty sometimes in exactly comprehending what he means.
. . . The last sentence is to me an enigma.' [1] Others have since
found themselves in the same difficulty as Sir Robert. But Gladstone, if mysterious, was resolute. His resignation was a heavy
loss, and necessitated the reconstruction of the Ministry. Dalhousie succeeded him at the Board of Trade, generously resigning
his claim to a seat in the Cabinet. Edward Cardwell became
Dalhousie's assistant. Sidney Herbert and Lincoln both entered
the Cabinet. These changes brought an influx of liberal feeling,
and it will be noted that both the new members were devoted
followers and friends of the Prime Minister. In the same year
Stanley, who was tired of playing second fiddle in the House of
Commons, at his own request went up to the Lords.

The educational bills were introduced in 1845. The Queen's
Colleges attracted comparatively little attention, though Sir

[1] Parker, *Peel*, iii. p. 164.

Robert Inglis and O'Connell, for once in agreement, denounced them as 'godless colleges.'[1] The Maynooth bill, however, aroused a storm of opposition. Many of Peel's own party—including Ashley, the Ultra-Tories, Disraeli—deserted him. The Carlton Club, full of righteously enraged Protestants, buzzed like a bees' bike. The Whigs supported the measure, but without geniality. Macaulay ended a speech in support of the bill with a denunciation of its promoter.[2] He taunted Peel with having, when in Opposition, excited the passions of religious fanaticism for his own ends, and with changing his methods whenever he came into power. 'The natural consequences follow. All those fierce spirits, whom you hallooed on to harass us, now turn round and begin to worry you. . . . But what did you expect ? Did you think, when you called the devil up, that it was as easy to lay him as to raise him ? Did you think, when you went on, session after session, thwarting and reviling those whom you knew to be in the right, and flattering all the worst passions of those whom you knew to be in the wrong, that the day of reckoning would never come ? It has come. There you sit, doing penance for the disingenuousness of years ! '

'How white poor Peel looked while I was speaking ! ' said the orator long after. 'I remember the effect of the words, " There you sit ! " ' [3]

It is hardly necessary to show that there was no inconsistency between Peel's conduct when in opposition and his proposing of the Maynooth grant. When he opposed the Whigs, he had opposed the proposal to endow education out of the funds of the Established Church : but Maynooth was not to be endowed from Church property. Nor had he ever in his speeches pandered to the spirit of religious intolerance ; his defence of Church funds was usually based on the grounds that any transfer was an unjustifiable interference with the rights of private property.

[1] Peel comments acidly on the Protestant opposition : 'Provided (Irish youths) drink and smoke and attend horse-races and lead a life of idleness and dissipation, we are utterly regardless of them and their religious instruction ; but because we try to wean them from vicious habits, to substitute knowledge for idleness and profligacy, but cannot at the same time persuade them to forswear their own religious faith and be good Protestants, then for the first time we profess to feel the tenderest care for their religious warfare.' Parker, *Peel*, iii. p. 177.

[2] Macaulay moved an amendment that Maynooth be endowed out of the funds of the Established Church, but was defeated.

[3] Trevelyan, *Macaulay*, p. 453.

Notwithstanding the heat of the Opposition, the Maynooth bill passed with large majorities ; but the healing legislation, on which many hopes had been founded, had but little ultimate effect in Ireland. The Queen's Colleges, which might have done good work, were ruined by the persistent hostility of the Roman Catholic Church.[1] Peel had taken the utmost pains to do away with all danger of religious propaganda. Every professor was obliged to take oath not to interfere with the religion of his students. Catholic bishops were offered seats on the controlling Board and on the senates of the colleges. No professorships of theology had been set up by Government, but private persons were invited to endow them for the use of their own denominations, and to establish residential halls which might be entirely under the control of their own Church. The principals of the two colleges in southern Ireland were both Catholics, and one was a priest.

All this trouble was in vain. From the beginning the majority of the Catholic priests used their influence against the colleges. A Catholic bishop refused the sacrament to parents who sent their sons there. McHale denounced the foundation as ' a penal and revolting measure,' and went to Rome to induce the Pope to pronounce against it. He was successful—the Queen's Colleges were finally condemned by the Papacy in 1851. The establishment of a system of secular education controlled by the State has almost always been resisted by the Catholic Church, just as it was resisted by the Anglican Church in England. In Ireland the control of the civil power was probably weaker than in any other European State. The higher education of the youth of Ireland was the last thing the Catholic Church desired. Poverty and ignorance had clinched the hold of that Church upon the Irish people, and it was not likely now to relax its grasp. In this struggle it was the State that went to the wall.

The Maynooth grant, if it was undertaken not as a simple measure of justice but in hopes of conciliating the Catholic Church, was equally a failure. It made for a moment a good impression on the moderate Catholics ; but the moderate party in the Church was steadily losing ground. It must be remembered, however, that the Acts of 1844-5 were to have been but the first

[1] The Dissenters' College proved very successful ; neither of the Catholic Colleges obtained any influence.

steps in a great scheme of religious endowment. When we try to estimate the importance of Peel's Irish legislation, we are estimating only the broken fragments of a whole, of whose complete form we have no very certain knowledge.

There is, however, no doubt that Peel intended to go on, and in the end to introduce a scheme for the payment of the Catholic priests by the State. In 1847 he advised John Russell to consider such a measure.[1] A letter from Lincoln to Gladstone, written in March, 1846, shows that the plan had been discussed and apparently agreed to by the Cabinet. Gladstone, as Peel remarked, is not always easy to understand, but his reply would almost lead one to conclude that they had at least considered a proposal to pay the priests out of the revenues of the Established Church, and that he (Gladstone) favoured this.[2] It may seem incredible that Peel could ever have contemplated such an appropriation of Church funds: but in 1846 Peel was going through such another crisis as that of 1829—his mind, freed from tradition and prejudice, and stimulated by a Titanic external struggle, was teeming with new and undreamed-of schemes of reform: he may have thought such a culmination possible in the end. The endowment of the priesthood he meant to undertake at once, however: in February, 1846, he offered a position in the Irish administration to one of his boy friends, afterwards Sir William Gregory. 'But remember, my good fellow,' said the Minister, 'that henceforth the days of Newmarket are over. You will have to give up racing. . . . It will be hereafter a matter of pride to you to be associated with measures of a wide and generous character which may entirely change the aspect of Ireland to England. Do not think the opposition of last year to . . . the Maynooth Grant indisposes me in the least to go much further, and to endeavour to place the Roman Catholic

---

[1] Russell, *Recollections and Suggestions*, p. 212.

[2] ' I gave no pledge to maintain the ecclesiastical property of Ireland in its present form of appropriation . . .' wrote Gladstone. ' The change of opinion, or of course, on the Irish Church will be trying to anyone,' but most to himself. ' First, because of the way in which I have declared my own preference for the system which we are abandoning ; secondly, because there will not be wanting those who will . . . ascribe it to a predilection on my own part for the Roman religion. . . . But nothing can, I think, induce me . . . to say one word implying ever so remotely an intention to persevere in maintaining permanently the present application of Church Property in Ireland. . . .' They say the condition of the Irish Church has improved. ' I should be very glad that she should have the benefit of it when the final carving comes.' Gladstone to Lincoln, 28th March, 1846. Martineau, *Newcastle*, pp. 77-9.

clergy in a position of comfort. There are other measures, too, indispensably necessary to your country' (Gregory was an Irishman) ' in which I hope you will take a part.' [1]

Whether it would have been possible to carry the endowment of the Catholic priests in Ireland through Parliament ; whether it would have been possible to induce the Catholic Church to accept the money of the British Government—all this is doubtful. We can only say, that if any man could have carried such a measure, it was Peel : and if it could ever have been done, the last opportunity was in 1846. After that time a weak Government, more deeply tinctured with religious bigotry than Peel's, was in power ; and within a few years the Ultramontanists had obtained the upper hand in Rome, and would doubtless have rejected any offer which would bring the Irish priesthood into relations with the State. The Whigs, swept away by an ignorant and fanatical popular outcry, plunged into a ridiculous but none the less violent quarrel with the Catholic Church, and the opportunity was gone for ever. When next a British Government, led by a pupil of Peel's, undertook to solve the religious problem in Ireland, it was through the disestablishment of the Protestant Church, not the endowment of the Catholics.

What were the ' other measures, indispensably necessary ' of which Peel hinted to young William Gregory ? Gladstone's letter suggests that the Prime Minister may have meditated tampering with Church endowments. Certainly he no longer regarded the rights of private property as so sacred as he had once thought them.

In 1843, Graham wrote to Peel : ' I cling to the plan of issuing a Commission for the consideration of the law and practice which regulate the tenure of land in Ireland. . . . I have seen Mr. Collis, manager of the Trinity College estates. The picture which he draws of the poverty of the tenantry, and of the exactions of landlords and their agents, is frightful and heartrending beyond measure. . . . I am quite satisfied that this inquiry, if conducted with ability and prudence, will open a distinct view of the causes of discontent in Ireland. But, alas ! I fear that the remedies are beyond the reach of legislative power.' [2]

---

[1] Gregory, *Autobiography*, pp. 128-9.
[2] Graham to Peel, 6th September, 17th October, 1843. Parker, *Peel*, iii. pp. 63-4.

In the spring of 1844, when Peel announced his first measures
for religious and educational reform in Ireland, he announced also
the appointment of a Royal Commission on the relations between
landlord and tenant in Ireland, and a bill for lowering the Irish
franchise to the level of that of England.

The franchise bill did not please the Irish members, and was for
the time being withdrawn. The Devon Commission, as it was
called from the name of its president, produced after a year's
work one of the most celebrated of Parliamentary Reports. It is
still the most reliable authority on the condition of Irish agriculture at that date, and it was the foundation on which was based
the legislation which later revolutionised the Irish land system. A
bill founded upon its recommendations was now introduced into
the House of Lords by Stanley.[1] It set up a Commissioner, who
was to inquire into all improvements projected by agricultural
tenants, and authorise them if approved. Improvements were
divided into three classes—building, fencing, and draining. The
tenant, if ejected, could claim compensation for building improvements up to thirty years, for fencing up to twenty years, and for
draining up to fourteen years. The bill never reached the House
of Commons : it was hotly opposed by a large party among the
Lords, and presently Stanley withdrew it, promising to reintroduce it at a more favourable moment.

Before the opportunity came, the Conservatives were out of
office.[2] A Whig bill, on the same lines as Peel's, was introduced
by John Russell, defeated, and withdrawn. After that the scheme
was dropped, until, after thirty years, Gladstone turned again to
the discarded Report of the Devon Commission, and produced the
great measures—going far beyond the bill of 1845—which transformed the position of the Irish and Scottish crofter and ended the
evils that had so long been the curse of Ireland.

The introduction and defeat of the Tenants' Compensation Bill
may appear a trifling incident : but it was in reality very signifi-
cant. It was the first attempt of the British Government to deal

---

[1] Lord Eversley complains that Peel courted disaster by introducing the bill
in the House of Lords. This was, of course, done in order that Stanley, who
had taken great interest in the measure, might sponsor it.

[2] A tenants' bill was introduced into the House of Commons by Lincoln in
1846, but was smothered in the excitement of that eventful session. Graham
remarks that, urgent as it is, it will have to be postponed to the Famine Relief
measures. Parker, *Graham*, ii. p. 30.

with the evil which was the chief source of Irish disorder and Irish misery—the land laws. It is true that Peel's bill seems a pitiful tinkering with details, when we consider the immensity of the evil with which it dealt ; and it has been said that it did not go nearly far enough, and that it should have introduced the principle of fixity of tenure. It is very probable, indeed, that the new bill promised in 1845 would have been an advance on the first one ; or, at least, that the measure would have been the first of a series. Peel was very cautious, but his mind was continually growing and broadening : his legislative measures show a continuous advance in liberality of outlook and boldness of conception. Once he admitted the principle that the State might interfere with the management of private property, there is no knowing where he would have stopped.[1]

In 1846, however, fixity of tenure would not have been a real remedy for the condition of Ireland, and might even have made things worse.

The misery of Ireland had in fact now grown beyond the power of legislative or human help. The population now numbered over 8,000,000, and it was calculated that there were 2,000,000 more than the resources of the country could support. The system of land tenure, the ignorance and poverty of the people, and the custom of early marriage regularly encouraged by the priests had all combined to produce this unnatural growth of population. The population per square mile was greater than in any European country save England, but in England most of the people inhabited the towns and were employed in manufacturing industry ; in Ireland they still depended on agriculture. There was, therefore, cut-throat competition for the occupation of land, and ' profiteering ' had inevitably arisen. The landlord generally let at a fair rent, but middlemen rented the land in minute plots and at exaggerated prices to the small tenants. The land had been divided and subdivided until it could be cut no more ; it had been cropped till it was exhausted. The peasant had no hope of improvement and no desire for it. He lived off the produce of his land, eking it out with a little labour at a wretched wage.

[1] He meant to accompany this bill with measures which he thought would encourage the settlement of solvent English and Scottish landlords in Ireland, who would invest capital in land instead of taking it out, and assist their tenants. This plan, which was introduced later by the succeeding Whigs Government, failed. It only resulted as a rule in transferring estates to rack-renting Irishmen.

'If I had a blanket to cover her,' said a peasant, 'I would marry the woman I liked, and if I could get potatoes enough to put into my children's mouths, I would be as happy and content as any man, and think myself as well off as my Lord Dunlo.' [1]

The most urgent need for Ireland was that this immense pauper peasantry, who were sucking the soil dry of nourishment and perishing of slow starvation, should be cleared away. Somehow or other they must be forced into another way of life. But the process had gone beyond human power to remedy. An Act against sub-letting was passed in 1826; it only led to eviction, was opposed by O'Connell, and repealed in 1832. Eviction was the landlord's only remedy, but the evicted tenant was at once dependent on charity for existence. He had no resource, once turned off his wretched plot. To introduce fixity of tenure into such a state of society would have been a grotesque mockery: it could but have encouraged over-population and sordid contentment. The obvious solution was emigration: but schemes of State-aided emigration were then in their infancy, and the priests did not encourage their flocks to a voluntary flitting. Even to-day, moreover, any Government might well quail at the thought of settling 2,000,000 of ignorant, thriftless, penniless emigrants.

Only in Ulster was there any degree of agricultural prosperity, and it was in Ulster that a customary tenant right existed. Peel's Tenants' Compensation Bill was the first step towards introducing something like tenant right into southern Ireland. It failed, and before a second attempt could be made the matter was taken out of his hands. Natural laws, long outraged, did not wait for the fumbling and uncertain efforts of men to deal with the superfluous population of Ireland: the problem was solved by a sudden and appalling calamity.

[1] *Report of the Poor Law Commission of* 1840. Quoted O'Connor, *Ireland,* ii. p. 277.

CHAPTER XV

MALICE DOMESTIC, 1841-1845

IN the spring of 1840, when it became clear that the Whigs could not maintain themselves much longer in power, Baron Stockmar had gone to work to repair the damage done the year before. The Baron had been Prince Albert's tutor, and was now his confidential friend, and the counsellor who steered him through the difficulties of his first years in England. Mr. Anson, the Prince's private secretary, came secretly to Peel, and let him know that the Queen would not refuse to change a few of the Ladies of the Bedchamber —the Duchess of Sutherland, the Duchess of Bedford, and Lady Normanby being named. Peel suggested that the ladies should voluntarily resign their offices before the Queen sent for him : in this case he would not have to make the demand, nor the Queen to concede it, and there would at least be a pretence that she had not yielded her will to his.[1] On this basis the matter was arranged, and the new Minister's induction to office took place without any further trouble : the Queen was downcast but polite, and Peel ' was more than satisfied ; he was charmed with her.' [2]

He was, however, exceedingly nervous at the prospect of dealing with the royal pair. He was frightened of the Queen, and he remembered that he had docked the Prince's allowance by almost one half. When he discovered that the Prince never showed a trace of resentment towards him he was greatly touched. Albert, in fact, demeaned himself in a difficult situation with the strictest propriety, and Peel soon found that the Prince and Stockmar were ready to act as his secret allies at Court. It was well, for the situation was for a time very dangerous.

Victoria had regarded Peel's action as to the Prince's allowance as ' a personal insult to herself,' and said that she knew Peel had meant it for that. She found his manners as trying as ever ; ' he was so shy, he made her shy too,' she told Melbourne, and Greville,

[1] Martin, *Prince Consort*, i. p. 106, seems to imply that the Prince suggested the resignation of the Ladies. Parker, *Peel*, ii. pp. 455-8, shows that the suggestion came from Peel.

[2] *Greville*, v. p. 39.

after observing the two in conversation together, remarked drily,
' He could not help putting himself into his accustomed attitude
of a dancing-master giving a lesson ; she would like him better if
he would keep his legs still.' [1]   But these were trifles : what was
really alarming was that the Queen persisted in keeping up a secret
correspondence with Lord Melbourne.

The Prince's influence was not yet strong enough to deter the
wilful little lady.   Stockmar had recourse to Melbourne himself,
appealing to his honour, his loyalty, his common sense.   No Prime
Minister would bear such treatment, and what would be the consequence to the Crown if Peel resigned on such a point ?   But it
was useless ; once more Melbourne's affections proved too strong
for his discretion.   He could not bear to give up his position as
the Queen's counsellor and friend, and, besides, he would not
forgo the political advantage of his situation.   He told Mr. Anson
that he would always advise the Queen ' To adhere to her Ministers in everything, *unless he saw the time had arrived at which it
might be resisted*.' [2]   What was worse, he even allowed Mrs. Norton
to know of what was going on, and that indiscreet lady soon set
rumours flying all over the town.

Peel had said at first that he had no objection to the Queen's
seeing as much of Melbourne as she liked : ' Nothing he could do
could prove effectual to prevent any mischief, and therefore im-
plicit confidence was the wisest course.' [3]   But the continuance of
the Queen's personal friendship with her old Minister was one
thing ; it was quite another if she asked his advice upon affairs of
State.   Stockmar called upon Peel, and was told, ' The moment I
was to learn that the Queen takes advice upon public matters in
another place, I shall throw up ; for such a thing I conceive the
country could not stand, and I would not remain an hour, whatever the consequences of my resignation may be.' [4]

Stockmar now remonstrated with Melbourne still more warmly.
The ex-Minister did not condescend to reply : but the correspondence gradually became more irregular and more innocuous.   At
the end of 1842 a paralytic stroke made it certain that Melbourne
would never be politically dangerous again ; but before that time
Peel's position at Court had become so secure as to end all his fears.

[1] *Letters of Queen Victoria*, i. pp. 306, 337, 339.   *Greville*, v. p. 45.
[2] *Letters of Queen Victoria*, i. p. 341.   The italics are Anson's.
[3] *Greville*, v. p. 39.   [4] *Letters of Queen Victoria*, i. pp. 361-2.

A year's regular association with the obnoxious Minister had conquered all Victoria's dislike. Her warm but facile affections were easily transferred, and soon 'dear Sir Robert Peel' was figuring almost as frequently as 'dear Lord Melbourne' had done in her letters to 'dear Uncle Leopold.' The Prince—though that exemplary young man does not seem to have had the capacity to care very strongly for any human being—gave Sir Robert his patronising esteem. Peel on his side became warmly attached to the young couple. At that time loyalty to the Crown was still a very active force, and Peel had his full share of it. The Prince was just of an age with his own eldest boy, and he was struck by the young man's extreme conscientiousness and real ability. He was soon the close friend of both : on meeting the Queen for the first time after an attempt had been made to assassinate her, he actually burst into tears. We may catch glimpses of him playing his part in the life of that extraordinary Court—dragged off by Albert for an hour's shooting in Windsor Park, dressed in 'thin shoes, pepper-and-salt pantaloons, and a long blue frock-coat, with borrowed gun and apparatus of all kinds' ; or playing round games in the evening, with 'watchful, cautious, characteristic sagacity, quite like his own public character all the time' ; or dancing, with other elderly gentry, at the orders of the Queen, 'much the best figure of all, so mincing with his legs and feet, and his countenance full of the funniest attempt to look unconcerned and "matter-of-course," while he was evidently both shy and cross.' [1]

But if the Minister's relations with the Court were satisfactory, those with his own party were much less so.

The name of Mr. Benjamin Disraeli did not appear upon the list of Sir Robert Peel's Ministry. Probably this occasioned no very great surprise to anyone save the owner of the name ; but 'Dis' had never pitched his conception of his own merits too low. If by any mischance the records of contemporary history are lost, and only the diary and letters of Mr. Disraeli should survive, the antiquarians of the future will certainly conclude that he was one of the central figures in Parliament in the years 1837-1841, instead of an unimportant and rather derided junior member. He had

---

[1] Peel to Croker, January, 1842. Parker, *Peel*, ii. p. 518. *Diary of Lady Littleton*, pp. 332, 357. It may be noted that the new Greville states that during Peel's ministry a new scandal, similar to that of Lady Flora Hastings, began to arise at the Court, and was immediately nipped in the bud by Peel's prompt and tactful action. (Vol. ii. pp. 211-2.)

now obtained the necessary foundations for a political career by marriage with a wealthy widow ten years older than himself, and by his tact and generous feeling had made a complete success of this rather doubtful experiment. With a fortune to back him, and considerable notoriety as a political pamphleteer and debater —and having, moreover, received some friendly encouragement from his chief—he had no doubt that he would be included in the Government. As the hours passed and no messenger came—as the conviction stole over him that he had been forgotten—he was seized with an absolute despair. He was no longer a mere youth— he was thirty-seven, and at thirty-seven Canning had been Foreign Secretary, and Pitt twelve years Prime Minister, and Peel had reformed the currency and the criminal law. He saw younger men preferred before him—Lincoln, plodding and mediocre ; Dalhousie, whose soaring spirit, bold as Disraeli's own, was still hidden under a prim and priggish exterior ; Herbert, whom he hated and nicknamed ' Peel's gentleman.' He was eaten up with ambition, he had struggled against such cruel odds, he had been so very sure that success was at last within his grasp ! He sat down and wrote to Peel :

' I will not say that I have fought since 1834 four contests for your party, that I have expended great sums, have exerted my intelligence to the utmost for the propagation of your policy, and have that position in life that can command a costly seat. But . . . I have had to struggle against a storm of political hate and malice which few men ever experienced from the moment, at the instigation of a member of your Cabinet, I enrolled myself under your banner, and I have only been sustained under these trials by the conviction that the day would come when the foremost man of this country would publicly testify that he had some respect for my ability and my character. I confess, to be unrecognised at this moment by you appears to me to be overwhelming, and I appeal to your own heart—to that justice and that magnanimity which I feel are your characteristics—to save me from an intolerable humiliation.'

It is impossible not to pity the writer of this letter. If it had been successful, Disraeli might have forgiven himself for writing it : he could never forgive Peel for having read it.

The Minister answered very gently. With delicate courtesy he spoke of the appeal as one of many similar which he had been

forced to ignore : he referred to the endless claims upon him, the
necessity of satisfying old party leaders, and those who had stood
by him in the desperate straits of 1834, and added that he hoped
those whom he could not satisfy would understand how painful
it was for him to have to refuse the offer of services, and ' how perfectly inadequate are the means at my disposal to meet the wishes
that are conveyed to me by men whose co-operation I should be
proud to have, and whose qualifications and pretensions for office
I do not contest.'   He felt it necessary, however, to free himself
from the imputation conveyed in Disraeli's letter, and he declared
that not only had he been entirely unaware of the communication
made to him by ' a member of the Cabinet,' but he should have
refused to authorise any such communication had he known of it.
He did not know who was the person referred to,[1] and ' could not
but think he acted very imprudently,' as he himself never gave
such pledges.

It seems strange that Disraeli, usually so tactful, should have
made such an appalling false step as to refer to his old plots with
Lyndhurst in such a manner as might be taken to mean that a
definite bargain had been made.   Peel, who had always abstained
from such transactions,[2] could only be offended and disgusted by
the implication.   Disraeli was obliged to write and protest that
his letter had been misunderstood, that ' no promise of official
promotion had ever been made to him,' and that such bargains
were ' utterly alien from his nature.' [3]

It is often said that Peel was blind to Disraeli's ability, and that
he committed a gross blunder when he passed over the future
leader of the Conservative party for lesser men, and so made a
dangerous enemy for himself.   Such criticisms leave out of count
the temper of Sir Robert Peel.   He may not have fully recognised

[1] It was of course Lyndhurst.

[2] Only on one occasion did Peel depart from this uniform practice.   In
October, 1842, he was informed that Lyon Playfair was meditating the accept-
ance of a Canadian professorship.   Thinking that his services ought not to be lost
to the country, Peel invited the young man (then aged only twenty-four) to
his house, and after observing him, offered him a written guarantee to give him
a situation under Government when a suitable vacancy occurred.   Playfair at
once consented to give up the Canadian post, but refused to accept the written
promise.   Peel, much pleased with his conduct, gave the document into the
keeping of a mutual friend.   It is needless to state that the mutual confidence
displayed in this affair was fully justified on both sides.   See *Memoirs of Lord
Playfair*, pp. 60, 77-80.

[3] Monypenny, *Disraeli*, ii. p. 117 f.   Parker, *Peel*, ii. pp. 486-8.

the ability of Disraeli—few persons did then—but I cannot think that if he had actually foreseen the future he would have altered his conduct.. I do not think that he would have considered the peace brought home from Berlin in 1878 to be indeed ' peace with honour,' or thought that the imperial title added a lustre to the British Crown, or that the change of policy in 1867 was justified by such circumstances as justified his own change of policy in 1829 and 1845 ; or that he would have regarded such a one as a desirable leader for the Conservative party. If he had guessed what a dangerous enemy he was making, it is still questionable whether Peel's stubborn pride and rigid integrity would have allowed him to pay this sort of blackmail to fortune.

Except for the pluck he had shown, Disraeli's political career had not been such as would appeal to Sir Robert. It is very doubtful whether Peel knew anything of his part in Lyndhurst's little intrigue of 1835 : but the *Letters of Runnymede*, with their fulsome flattery of the Conservative leader and coarse denuncia-tion of his enemies, were just the sort of production to disgust Peel ; and what was much more serious, Disraeli had on several occasions headed the factious opposition to the Whig Government, which Peel was of all things anxious to avoid.

When the agitation against the new Poor Law arose, a large section of the Tory party had eagerly taken it up, some of them, no doubt, from conscientious motives, but the greater number because it was a convenient weapon against the Government, and because it promised to get them some popularity among the work-ing class. Peel disapproved of their conduct : he had voted for the Poor Law Act in 1834, spoken in favour of it publicly, and defended it when heckled during the election of 1837. He thought it a most necessary reform, though he was ready to amend it in detail, and considered the Parliamentary opposition to it quite unjustifiable.[1] His party knew his views, but he could not restrain them ; and Disraeli, finding the subject congenial, had attacked the Poor Law as violently as any of them, and with much greater ability than most.

In 1839 Disraeli had led the Tory opposition to the police bills, measures which were in themselves urgently necessary, and which were, of course, peculiarly interesting to Peel.

[1] During his premiership he amended the Poor Law twice, abolishing the more objectionable provisions, as for example those which pressed hardly on the aged.

But Disraeli had been more than factious; he had been insubordinate. He had repeatedly taken a contrary line to that of his official chief. Early in 1840 he had been invited to an important meeting at Peel's house, and on the evening after 'he had received this signal proof of confidence, he reasserted his independence by a brilliant incursion into debate in opposition to his leader, and by voting against him in the division.' [1]

It was, of course, most creditable to Disraeli, friendless as he was, to have shown so much independence and courage in upholding his own opinions; but it could not be expected that this would commend him to his imperious and masterful chief. Peel knew well that he would have his work cut out for him to keep his party in hand: the Lords had treated him, during his period in opposition, with insolence and contempt; even his followers in the Commons had repeatedly flouted him and ignored his guidance. The Whigs were gleefully prophesying that he would be outvoted in his own Cabinet and forced to become the tool of the Ultras. He had to conciliate the Ultras, who formed the bulk of his party, by giving office to some of their leaders; but in selecting new men, he naturally preferred those whose opinions were in sympathy with his own, and who were attached to himself by ties of loyalty and friendship. Theoretically, he might admit that every man should act according to his own opinions; but practically, in forming his Government, he wanted lieutenants who would obey his orders. It has been suggested that 'Dis' in office would have been as meek as a mouse; but he had given Peel no reason to think so.

For the time being Disraeli lay low. The obvious means of retaliation—that of joining the Whigs—did not commend itself: the Whigs had never at any time showed an overmastering desire to avail themselves of the services of Mr. Disraeli. Immediate revolt would appear the outcome of pique or revenge, and would, besides, have no chance of success in a brand-new Parliament packed with Tories brimful of gratitude to the chief who had brought them a majority of ninety-one. He must wait until signs of discontent began to appear among the loyal ranks.

The budget of 1842 first disturbed the satisfaction of the Tories. They did not so much object to the reform of the tariff, though they hardly liked it; but the alteration of the Corn Law and the

[1] Monypenny, *Disraeli*, ii. p. 89. The point at issue was Stockdale *v.* Hansard.

admission of foreign meat to British markets filled them with indignation. The fine harvest of 1842, and the distress of the farmers which accidentally resulted from it, gave them the excuse to say on the one hand that the new Corn Law gave insufficient protection to the farmer, and on the other that the reduction of duty was not necessary for the sake of the consumer.

The admission of Canadian corn in 1843 and the Charitable Trusts Act, with its concessions to the Catholics, added to their annoyance, and the Old Tories became thoroughly discontented with their leader.

By this time Mr. Disraeli had begun to change his tactics. He saw the Tories were a little restive, and would not be unwilling to listen to criticism of Peel. He had also found some friends. During the course of 1842, he had drawn close to a group of young men, fresh from Oxford, and formed with them a loose sort of association, to which the name ' Young England ' was given, and which they hoped might prove the nucleus of a party. The two most important members of the group were George Smythe, heir of Lord Strangford, and Lord John Manners, younger son of the Duke of Rutland—both very young, and likely to be dazzled by Disraeli's brilliant qualities. Smythe, his first friend among them, was an ambitious, spirited, attractive young man, with a good deal of facile cleverness, and no principles at all. Manners was a sentimental young idealist, full of vague dreams of restoring England to the condition of an agricultural paradise, and less vague dislike for the sordid side of industrialism. Just as Irish poets recur continually to Conchubar and Deirdre, in default of more solid material, Manners went back to an Age of Chivalry and a Merry England that had never existed, and fed his political imagination on Scott's novels and Bolingbroke's *Patriot King*. He had published a little volume of verse, and gained a great deal of notoriety through the immortal couplet :

> Let wealth and commerce, laws and learning die,
> But leave us still our old Nobility.

This having been received with some coarse ridicule, the author was at pains to explain that he referred to abstract nobility, not the English peerage. It seems a pity, as the explanation deprives the verse of the pith and point which it undoubtedly possesses when read in the other sense.

Disraeli was quick to see the opportunity offered by the existence of this aristocratic little group. Manners was already disillusioned by the sordid opportunism of Peel, and attracted by Disraeli's sympathetic attitude to social reform. Smythe was impressed by Disraeli's cynical wit and flattered by his comradeship. The publication of *Coningsby*, where Smythe figured as Harry Coningsby and Manners as Lord Henry Sidney, and later the appearance of *Sybil*, gave to the little party a fame and importance that its original leaders could never have achieved alone.

In August, 1843, Disraeli broke into open revolt.[1] He joined the Whigs in their opposition to the Irish Arms Bill, and delivered a slashing personal attack on Peel. He declared that by his liberal policy since coming into office, Peel had forsworn his old principles, and admitted that his conduct when in opposition had been wrong. Therefore, said 'Dis,' the Minister had abdicated his position as leader, in so far as Ireland was concerned, had ' left his party in the lurch . . . thrown up the reins, and told them he had made a mistake and could give them no further advice,' so that his followers ' were plainly free from any bonds of party on the subject, for the right honourable gentleman had himself broken them.' He called the measure contemptible and futile, and abstained from voting on it.[2] Next week he attacked the foreign policy of the Government, again with sarcastic personal references to Peel.

Both Peel and Graham regarded these speeches as equivalent to a public repudiation of the Government and its policy; and when, three months later, Disraeli wrote to Graham to ask for a place for his brother, Graham was both angry and astonished, and sent him a cool refusal. He reported the transaction to Peel, who shared his feelings.

' It is a good thing when such a man puts his shabbiness on record,' said the Prime Minister. ' He asked me for office himself,

---

[1] Monypenny (*Disraeli*, ii. pp. 178-9) says that Peel forced Disraeli into opposition by giving him a public ' rebuff.' The fact is that Disraeli asked a question on foreign affairs, and was told that it could not be answered while negotiations with foreign Governments were still going on. A few weeks later he repeated the question, and Peel repeated his answer more emphatically, saying that he had no official information of the facts which Disraeli alleged. *Hansard*, lxviii. pp. 1028-9. The answer, though a little curt, is polite and quite impersonal in tone, but Disraeli chose to make a grievance of it. *Ib*. lxxi. p. 835, and see below, p. 297.

[2] *Hansard*, lxx. 430 ff.

and I was not surprised that being refused he became independent and a patriot. But to ask favours after his conduct last session is too bad.' [1]

Though Peel was quick to resent, however, no one was more quick to accept an *amende*. The first hint of a wish for reconciliation from Disraeli showed him ready to forget all his indignation. As a result of the two speeches, the party whip had not been sent to Disraeli when the session of 1844 opened, and he wrote to complain. While remarking that the severance of the party connection must be a matter of indifference to Peel, and little more than a formality to himself, he contended that his conduct had not given any excuse for such a step. He had been informed from various quarters that his speeches had given offence; but they contained merely reasonable criticism, and if they were devoid of ' hearty goodwill,' that was due to the ' want of courtesy in debate ' which Peel had shown to him.

The Minister replied with an assurance that he bore no resentment for past attacks. ' I hope I have not a good memory for expressions used in debate which cause surprise or pain at the moment, and it would be quite unsuitable to the spirit in which your letter is written, and in which it is received, were I, after the lapse of several months, to refresh my recollection of such expressions, if such were used. My reason for not sending you the usual circular was an honest doubt whether I was entitled to send it— whether towards the close of last session . . . you had not expressed opinions as to the conduct of the Government. . . . which precluded me, in justice both to you and to myself, from preferring personally an earnest request for your attendance. . . . It gives me, however, great satisfaction to infer from your letter—I trust I am justified in inferring—that my impressions were mistaken and my scruples unnecessary. . . . I am unconscious of having on any occasion treated you with the want of that respect and courtesy which I readily admit are justly your due. If I did so, the act was wholly unintentional on my part.' [2]

Immediately after these letters had been exchanged, John Russell's motion of censure upon the arrest of O'Connell was debated, and Disraeli voted with his party. He took the oppor-

[1] Parker, *Peel*, iii. pp. 424-5. This is the only remark on Disraeli's conduct made by Peel to a third party at any date.

[2] *Ib*. pp. 144-6.

tunity, however, to repeat ' every offending phrase ' which he had
used in his last speech on Ireland, as if to show ' that his criticism
had not been prompted by any feeling of pique.' [1] Peel replied
with a compliment to ' the very able speech of the member for
Shrewsbury.' But the reconciliation thus publicly sealed did not
last long : within a few weeks a large section of the Conservative
party was in open revolt, and Disraeli, though he was not the cause
or leader of the movement, did not fail to take advantage of it.

Financial reorganisation, commercial reform, the encouragement
of trade, and the cheapening of the necessaries of life, were the
main expedients on which Peel relied for improving the condition
of the working classes : but he was not satisfied with these alone.
He contemplated also large measures of social reform.

In his economic reforms Peel had found in Graham his most
able and enthusiastic assistant. On social questions, however,
Graham was a little inclined to lag behind. Peel doubted whether
the State could do much to relieve the sufferings of the poor :
Graham was sure it could do nothing.[2] Where Peel felt doubt and
hesitation, Graham cherished the black pessimism of the orthodox
political economist. Peel was very soft-hearted : Graham was
well-intentioned, conscientious, and a little callous.

Lord Ashley, the leader of the movement for factory legislation,
was a Tory, and held a high—indeed a unique—position in the
party. Between him and his leader, however, there was but little
sympathy. Peel seems to have regarded Ashley with respect and
almost affection for his high character and great ability, mingled
with impatience for what he thought his impracticability, and
distrust of his religious views. Ashley was of the stuff of which
great reformers are made : there was a strand of fanaticism in
his make-up. Single-minded, devoted, passionate, he was ready
to sacrifice every other consideration to the cause he served, and
he expected all its supporters to be equally ready. Peel was
capable of sacrifice also, but he liked to be very sure of his facts
before he threw his bonnet over the mill. He was hardly able to
understand the mental attitude that made Ashley throw away
every other political interest and every prospect of his own political distinction to press the cause of the factory child. His large
and comprehensive mind could not have borne to be confined in

---

[1] Monypenny, *Disraeli*, ii. p. 188.
[2] Parker, *Graham*, i. pp. 328-9. Parker, *Peel*, ii. p. 546.

such narrow dimensions. There was, moreover, an element of religious bigotry in Ashley that was peculiarly uncongenial to Peel. In 1839 Ashley had urged him to turn out the Whigs on ' a Protestant point '—the last thing he was likely to do.[1] On the other hand, Peel's cold caution was unpleasant to Ashley. ' What possesses that man ! ' he wrote, after sitting next to his chief at a dinner. ' It was like the neighbourhood of an iceberg with a slight thaw on the surface.' [2] It is clear that even before the Conservatives came into power Ashley was feeling dissatisfied with his leader.

In 1840 Ashley had secured the appointment of a Commission on the employment of women and children in mines. The inquiry revealed a state of affairs so appalling that little or no opposition was made in the House of Commons to the bill which Ashley introduced in 1842. The bill prohibited the employment of women, girls, and boys under twelve underground, and added various provisions for the safety and comfort of the men. It passed the House of Commons with scarcely a dissentient voice, but the Lords altered it, amd made it legal to employ boys of ten years old three days a week. It was the greatest triumph that Ashley had yet obtained ; but he was dissatisfied with his chief's conduct. Peel said he disapproved of the alterations made by the Lords, and hoped an opportunity might soon occur of restoring the clause respecting the labour of boys to its original form, but it was always his policy to uphold the right of the Lords to alter bills, and he had no intention of making the matter one of resignation. Ashley thought Peel should have ' co-operated vigorously ' instead of merely approving the bill.[3] Almost at the moment when Ashley was writing his complaints in his diary, Peel, far from being satisfied with what had been done, was planning a new inquiry.

' I wish we could appoint a Commission to ascertain the real truth as to the state of the relations between the employers and employed in collieries. I think it would be found that there are practical grievances—possibly not to be redressed by law—of which the employed have just reason to complain. What law cannot effect, exposure might. I strongly suspect the profits in many of these collieries would enable the receivers of them to deal

[1] Parker, *Peel*, ii. p. 414.   [2] Hodder, *Shaftesbury*, p. 183.
[3] *Ib*. p. 231.

much more liberally with their workmen than they do. I fear
there are galling regulations—with respect to weight of coal got,
and to deductions from wages, and to dealing with particular shops
—which justify complaint. . . . Could we get such a man as
Horner, or one of the best of your poor Law Commissioners, to
make a tour through Staffordshire and Shropshire, and get at some
part of the truth at least, without ostentatious inquiry ? ' [1]

A series of accusations have been brought against Peel by
Ashley's biographers : first formulated by Sir Edwin Hodder,[2]
they have been countenanced to some extent by Mr. and
Mrs. Hammond ; [3] and more recently Mr. Bready [4] has repeated
them in much stronger and more definite terms. Hodder con-
tents himself with saying that Peel disliked the factory movement,
and that he endeavoured to muzzle Ashley by offering him a post
in the Royal Household in 1841 and a seat in the Cabinet in 1845.[5]
Mr Bready repeats the allegation, adding that Peel offered Ashley
the Viceroyalty of Ireland in 1844 in order to ' side-track ' him,
and when he refused it, the Government recognised that he was
not to be trapped, and were at last forced to bring forward a
factory bill. Peel, says Mr. Bready, was ' the chief obstacle ' to
the protection of the factory children. Peel, finally, did not give
full support to Ashley's Mines Bill, because he had money invested
in coal.[6]

Mr. and Mrs. Hammond say that ' Peel and Graham were by
conviction as hostile to factory legislation as any two men in
Parliament.' [7]

It seems just a little unkind to Lord Ashley to assume, as
Mr Bready does, that Peel could not possibly have offered him Ireland simply because he thought Ashley would make a good Viceroy.
. . . Is it credible that, when Ireland was just emerging from a
dangerous crisis, and the situation was still doubtful, Peel would

---

[1] Peel to Graham, 30th August, 1842. Parker, *Peel*, ii. p. 543.

[2] *Life and Work of Shaftesbury*, 1887, by Sir Edwin Hodder.

[3] *Lord Shaftesbury*, by J. L. and Barbara Hammond, 1923.

[4] *Shaftesbury and Social-Industrial Progress*, 1926, by J. Wesley Bready.

[5] Hodder, *op. cit.* pp. 188-9.

[6] Of course Peel had money sunk in mines. He told Ashley that the bill
would mean a heavy loss to him, but that he thought it his duty to support it.
Bready, *op. cit.* pp. 202 note, 221, 201, 299. Mr. Bready appends a biblio-
graphy 22 pages long ; it is notable that he only considered it necessary to
consult one life of Peel—Guizot's !

[7] Hammond, *op. cit.* p. 49. See also above, pp. 73-4.

have sent Ashley there simply because he was afraid he might
introduce factory bills of which the Government did not approve ?
As a matter of fact, Peel waited, intentionally, until the Factory
Act was passed before making the offer to Ashley, lest it should
bear the aspect of a bribe.[1]   There is not a tittle of evidence that
he had any ulterior motive in making the offer, except that Ashley,
when he received it, prayed to be delivered from temptation.   I
cannot but think that Ashley's biographer has unconsciously
rationalised his mental processes, and that he regarded the offer,
not as a temptation from Peel, but as a temptation from the devil.
Mr. and Mrs. Hammond suggest that Peel chose Ashley as a suitable person to support his proposed legislation on the Report of
the Devon Commission.[2]   This is possible, but the Lord Lieutenant, after all, has but little to do with legislation.   More likely
he believed that Ashley could be relied upon to carry out a rigidly
just and scrupulous administration, while at the same time his
appointment would be very pleasing to the Protestants, whom
Peel wanted to conciliate before introducing his Maynooth Bill.

The same may be said of the offer of Cabinet rank in 1845.   A
Minister in difficulties does not offer Cabinet rank to a man whom
he fears and distrusts, but to a man whose services he values.

What is really unpardonable is the offer of the Household post
in 1841.   It was a silly mistake, but it was made not because Peel
was afraid of Ashley, but because he was afraid of the Queen.
Peel, as has been seen, was hopelessly inadequate in dealing with
such delicate situations.   What is more strange is, that he seems
to have had an idea that Ashley had some special influence with
the Queen, and could act as mediator.[3]   During the Bedchamber
crisis in 1839 he actually took Ashley to the Palace with him, in
hopes that he might influence her, a step which Greville justly
describes as ' altogether preposterous, and exhibiting the deficiency
of Peel in worldly dexterity and tact, and in knowledge of character.' [4]   His anxiety to obtain the services of Ashley as mediator is
shown by the fact that when Ashley refused to join the Queen's
Household, Peel suggested that he might take a post in Prince
Albert's !   That he did not offer Ashley political office at this time
may perhaps be explained by the fact that he knew Ashley would
refuse it : they were already at issue on the subject of the ten-hours'

[1] Hodder, *op. cit.* ii. pp. 43, 83.   [2] Hammond, *op. cit.* p. 102.
[3] Ashley had long been acquainted with the Queen.   [4] *Greville*, iv. p. 208.

day in industry. He felt he ought to offer Ashley something, and he wanted his good offices at Court, and so he committed this grotesque blunder, making an offer that was really more of an insult to Ashley than if he had simply let him alone.

Peel had been one of the chief supporters of the Act of 1819. He was the only Home Secretary who had tried to enforce that Act.[1] He had supported Hobhouse's Factory Acts of 1826 and 1831, and approved the Act of 1833. He had only voted for Poulett Thompson's motion in 1836 on the express grounds that to vote against it would be to imply that the Act of 1833 was efficiently administered, which it was not. He was one of the first British statesmen to declare publicly in favour of a restriction of hours for all workers, male and female, of every age.[2] He introduced the great Factory Act of 1844, and his Premiership saw the Mines Act and the Print Works Act passed with his approval.[3] It is, therefore, hardly just to describe him as ' the great obstacle ' to reform, and ' hostile to factory legislation,' simply for the reason that he opposed the ten-hours' day in industry.

Peel had contemplated a new Factory Act from the time he first took office. The bill was ready in 1842, but it was postponed in deference to the wishes of the Bishop of London,[4] and was not introduced until 1843. The bishop had been consulted, because the Government combined with the factory regulations a large scheme of education. Compulsory factory schools were to be established, under the management of the parish minister, two churchwardens, and four other persons elected by the justices of the peace. This scheme aroused a storm of indignation ; it gave the practical control of education to the Church of England, and the Dissenters violently objected. In deference to their protests, Graham, who had charge of the bill, eliminated the second church-warden : but the sacrifice was worse than vain. The Dissenters were not mollified, and the Church was enraged. Ashley declared that concession had gone ' to the very verge of what a man of principle could vote for.' [5] The Government withdrew the bill : the Churchmen saved their principles, the Dissenters might plume

---

[1] See above, Chapter vi.   [2] *Speeches*, iii. pp. 283-4.

[3] Edmund Peel, in 1844, complains bitterly of his brother for praising Ashley's Factory Bill ' in lavish terms.' *Private Letters*, pp. 254-5.

[4] Parker, *Graham*, i. p. 342.

[5] Ashley to Peel, 17th June, 1843. Parker, *Peel*, iii. p. 561.

themselves on the success with which they had acted dog in the manger, and the factory brats, in that most Christian country, continued to receive their education in the coal-hole or go without. Peel, who was much disgusted, consoled himself with a donation of £9000 to voluntary education.[1]

In the following year the Factory Bill was again introduced without the educational clauses, but with some important new provisions. It extended, for the first time, protection to adult women, and, also for the first time, introduced regulations for the safeguarding of machinery. The hours of children were reduced to six and a half; those of women and young persons were fixed at twelve a day. Machinery was to be inspected, and no woman, young person, or child was to clean it while in motion. The power of the factory inspectors was extended, and various minor regulations for the health and comfort of the workpeople were introduced: but in the interval Ashley had resolved to fight for the ten-hour day, and the bill no longer satisfied him.

The demand was, nominally, for a ten-hours' day for women and young persons. Practically, it involved a ten-hours' day for men also, and both the opponents and the adherents of the cause realised this. Peel was determined to make neither concession nor compromise on this point. His personal wish, indeed, was to introduce an eight-hours' day for women in industry, and to prohibit altogether their employment in agriculture except in summer:[2] but he shrank from imposing upon the just reviving trade and industry of the country what he thought was a fresh burden. In the last forty years the wages of labour in Britain had fallen: the hours of labour had also been reduced. There was no real connection between the two facts, but he thought there was. He believed that the shortening of the working day by two hours—involving, he calculated, the loss of seven weeks in the year —would mean a heavy loss to industry, and would inevitably result in a reduction of wages, probably to the extent of 15 per cent.: and wages, he said, had already been reduced to the lowest point consistent with the existence of the working-man's household. At present the textile trades produced five-sixths of the exports of Great Britain: these trades already worked shorter hours than textile factories abroad. Shorten the day still more, and there would, he believed, be a great transfer of capital from

[1] *Ib.* pp. 560-2-7.   [2] *Speeches*, iv. pp. 344, 346.

those trades to other employments.   In fine, he thought that loss, not gain, to the working man would be the result.[1]

The future proved that Peel was wrong.   The ten-hours' day, when it was introduced three years later, brought no loss to industry, for the increased health and strength of the workman made up for the time lost.   It must always be doubtful at what point the gain of increased energy ceases to counterbalance the loss incurred by shortened hours.   Peel's mistake was in drawing the line too high—probably much too high.   If, however, the Ten-Hours' Act had been passed with a contracting market and a falling export trade, it is not so certain that it might not have produced at least a temporary reduction of wages.   In 1844 the new prosperity of the country was still frail, and might be transitory : Peel feared that the ten-hours' clause might undo the work of the Budget of 1842.

The House of Commons, however, was not of the same mind as the Minister.   He pointed out to them that conditions of labour in other trades, and especially in private workshops, were far worse than in the textile trades, and that it was impossible to regulate them all.   Carried away by his own feelings, he described the sufferings of children in workshops with such effect that when he asked rhetorically, ' And will you legislate for these ? ' the whole House rose at him, crying, ' Yes ! Yes ! ' ' Oh, you will, will you ? ' said the astonished orator ; and, recovering himself, went on to ask sarcastically how they proposed to control the domestic trades, the worst of all ?   But it was of no use.   Ashley made one of his noblest speeches, and the young Conservative members, Peel's own followers, were quite carried away.   They revolted ; Disraeli and most of Young England went with them ; some Old Tories, moved by a desire to annoy the Manchester men, voted on their side, and Ashley's motion was carried.   As the result was announced there was an outburst of cheering, and one young Tory leapt up, waving his hat.   Peel looked at him over his shoulder : ' My good fellow, if you wave your hat over my head every time you beat me I shall give you a scolding, and if you wave it at all the Speaker will give you a scolding,' he said good-humouredly.[2]

It was, however, the House of Commons that was to be scolded. When the bill went into Committee, the Prime Minister came down to the House to repeat his arguments as to the danger of

---

[1] *Speeches,* iv. p. 341 ff.   [2] Gregory, *Autobiography,* p. 81.

introducing such a measure at such a time ; and he ended with an
unequivocal declaration that if the ten-hours' clause were carried
over his head he would resign. The threat was sufficient. To
Ashley's passionate disappointment, the revolted Tories returned
to their allegiance, and the ten-hours' clause was rejected.

A few days later the first reduction of the sugar duties was
brought before the House. According to the Government
scheme the duties were now to be 24s. on colonial sugar, 34s. on
foreign sugar, and 63s. on slave-grown sugar. A Conservative
member, Miles, introduced an amendment reducing the duties on
colonial and foreign sugar to 20s. and 30s. respectively. The
Whigs joined him, and once more the Government was beaten.

Peel was very angry. The alteration was trifling ; it was the
deliberate insubordination of his party that roused him, and
especially the coalition with the Whigs. When the House went
into Committee he rose and declared in the most peremptory
and resolute tone that the Government would not accept the
amendment. He would make no concession. He would not go
on unless he possessed the entire confidence and support of his
party—in fact, he said almost in so many words that if the Conservative party expected him to be their leader, they had got to
obey his orders. No Prime Minister ever made bolder pretensions : but the rebels were cowed, and came sullenly to heel.
Miles' amendment was again cut out.

Within the space of a few weeks the House of Commons, at the
command of the Prime Minister, had twice reversed the decision
they had taken upon full consideration but a short time before.
Peel had been completely successful ; but it was at the cost of a
great deal of ill-feeling. His men were indignant and humiliated.
Calmer judges regretted proceedings that must lower the character
of the House of Commons as a free deliberative assembly. Disraeli
taunted Peel with disapproving of slavery everywhere except in the
House of Commons. Tom Duncombe, a Radical member renowned for his impudence, proposed, when the sugar bill passed
the third reading, that the usual words, ' freely and voluntarily
resolved,' should be omitted from the preamble.

Peel had felt his party was getting out of hand. He knew very
well that his rule did not rest on love, and that, if he once lost his
hold on them, he had no personal popularity to fall back on. He
knew they disliked him, and complained of his coldness, his

haughtiness, his reserve. He knew that he had strained their allegiance with his Free Trade Budget, his alteration of the Corn Laws, and his Irish legislation. Of late they had been as insubordinate as they dared : the Lords had altered an important measure against his wishes ; the Commons had given him grudging and lukewarm support, and now on two occasions had defied him. He would not tolerate a state of rebellion, such as had existed in 1835. He thought the time was come to give them a lesson.

Peel was by nature imperious and overbearing, and the tendency had been increased by three years of power. He was impatient of control, and of the necessity of conciliating those whose minds were meaner than his own. He always piqued himself on never proposing legislation that he could not carry. He admitted that his conduct was thought ' very presumptuous and arrogant ' : but said, ' The fact is, people like a certain degree of obstinacy and presumption in a Minister. They abuse him for dictation and arrogance, but they like being governed.' [1]

All this may justify his conduct on the sugar duties, where the conduct of the Tories was malicious, the coalition with the Whigs very alarming, and where no principle was at stake ; but it does not excuse him for insisting on the reversal of the vote on the ten-hours' clause, where many of the rebels had undoubtedly acted from conscientious motives. Nor is it certain that he had been altogether wise. Certainly the party was now submissive, but many of its members were sullen and sore.

Ashley would not break altogether with the Government, but he dissociated himself from their counsels ; [2] and the loss of such a man, impracticable though he was, must be a blow to any party. Next year, however, the quarrel was in part made up. It was a year of many social reforms. The Government amended the Poor Law, cutting out some of the regulations that pressed most harshly on the old and feeble, [3] and they gave their assistance to Ashley in

[1] Peel to Hardinge. Parker, *Peel,* iii. p. 270.

[2] Parker, *Peel,* iii. p. 154. In February, 1845, he refused to attend a meeting on the subject of Bright's Committee on the Game Laws, feeling himself obliged to vote for it, and believing that the Government would refuse it. Peel replied (Parker, iii. p. 180) by somewhat drily saying he entirely agreed with Ashley, and that the Cabinet had decided to grant the Committee. This is typical of Ashley's misunderstanding of Peel, who as Home Secretary had been a steady advocate of Game Law Reform. *Speeches,* i. pp. 295, 345, 490.

[3] Other Reforms of the Poor Law were made in 1844. For details see Walpole, *England,* iv. p. 193.

passing three Acts—two regulating lunatic asylums, and one extending the Factory Laws to print-works. They also introduced another bill, in which Ashley was greatly interested—a Public Health Bill; but a political crisis supervened, and the Public Health Bill shared the fate of the Irish Land Bill.[1]

Much more serious than the temporary alienation of Ashley was the final and public defection of Disraeli. ' Young England ' was now tottering to its fall. Smythe, who knew which side his bread was buttered, had deserted his comrades on the ten-hours' clause, and voted with Peel. Later, the little party split again on the Maynooth grant, Disraeli opposing it, while the others supported. Soon after Smythe forsook his friends, and accepted an Under-Secretaryship at the Foreign Office. But long before this ' Dis ' had become quite independent of the support of the little group. Half the Tory party were now his unofficial backers. It was no longer dangerous to attack a leader whose own followers were estranged from him. Disraeli flung off all restraint, and commenced a series of personal attacks on Peel, equally remarkable for their brilliant wit, their spitefulness, and the skill with which the orator discovered and struck at the weaknesses of his enemy. He taunted the Minister with borrowing all his great measures from his political opponents—with having caught the Whigs bathing and stolen their clothes. He called him ' a great parliamentary middleman . . . who bamboozles one party and plunders the other.' After the Free Trade Budget of 1845, he was the first to voice the now general suspicion that Peel was no longer sound on the Corn Laws, saying that ' Protection was now in about the same state as Protestantism in 1829.'

A few years before such speeches would have been condemned. Now Tory members listened with glee, and chuckled in their seats as Disraeli flung out his gibes, and the Minister ' pulled his hat upon his brows,' in a vain attempt to hide his tell-tale change of colour.

The Whigs also hailed every telling hit with loud applause. Every weakening of Peel's influence was their gain, and they had from the first conducted a determined and unrelenting opposition. In truth, Peel's success in dealing with the difficulties which had

---

[1] The Whigs had prepared Public Health bills in 1841. These for some reason did not satisfy Peel, who appointed a new Committee on the subject. It reported in 1844, and a bill founded on the Report was introduced by Lincoln in 1845.

baffled them before had galled them cruelly. Palmerston could
not abide Aberdeen, and was furiously jealous because the Government had conducted to a happy issue the negotiations with France
and America and the operations in India, which he himself had
left in so disastrous a state. ' I never saw so much political bitterness as rankles in the hearts of himself and his wife,' remarked
Greville in 1842.[1] John Russell distrusted and disliked Peel, and
could hardly be expected to rejoice when the latter carried measures
as liberal as his own, and which he would probably have been unable
to force through Parliament.[2] The Income Tax, the Irish Arms
Bill, and Indian affairs had been made the object of successive
attacks. In the beginning of 1843 a Conservative member remarked that they were likely to have a quiet session : Macaulay,
who overheard him, said, ' Oh, will you ? We shall have five
Indian mails, and a question upon each ! '[3] Irish affairs were
handled in the same spirit. In 1844 came the discovery that the
Government had been opening Mazzini's letters ;[4] and the opportunity was taken, not merely to condemn their conduct in this
instance, which would have been perfectly legitimate, but to
attack the practice of opening letters in the Post Office as illegal,
or at least unauthorised by law. The Whig leaders had themselves
repeatedly exercised this right, which was founded on an Act of
Parliament still in force, but, though they did not countenance

[1] *Greville*, v. p. 108.

[2] See *Greville*, v. pp. 201, 239, 274, 363.

[3] Law, *Lord Ellenborough in India*, p. 61.

[4] Aberdeen was informed by Austria that a revolt was being prepared in her
Italian provinces, and from several sources he learned that owing to peculiar
circumstances the outbreak of the revolt was likely to be the signal for a
European war. Graham was therefore authorised to issue a warrant for the
opening of Mazzini's letters, and, in the words of the Select Committee which
investigated the question (*Report*, pp. 13-14), ' such information deduced from
these letters as appeared to the British Government calculated to frustrate
this attempt was communicated to a Foreign Power ' (Austria), ' but the
information so communicated was not of a nature to compromise, and did not
compromise, the safety of any individual within the reach of that Foreign
Power, nor was it made known to that Power by what means, or from what
source, that information had been obtained.' In this context a letter written
by Peel when Home Secretary is of some interest. In 1824 the Austrian
Embassy applied to the Home Office for information about one Bettera, supposed to be connected with Italian revolutionaries. Lord Sidmouth had
apparently on a previous occasion obliged Austria with such information.
The letter is docketed by Peel : ' If I had any information about Bettera's
connection with " Italian revolutionarists " I certainly would not give it to
M. de Neumann.' A polite refusal was sent. British Museum, *Peel Papers*,
40,368, p. 85.

the wilder allegations of their followers, they demanded an inquiry into the practice, and not one of them said a word in defence of Graham, who was much hurt at this treatment from his old colleagues. The Committee of Inquiry was granted, and it completely exonerated the Government from blame in every respect.

Such was the situation of the Conservative Government at the end of the session of 1845 : a party discontented and ripe for revolt, only held by a strong hand in sullen subjection ; a skilful enemy watching his chance to kindle this smouldering disaffection into flame ; a hungry and hostile Opposition, seeing with exultation that their chances of success were growing ; and the Anti-Corn-Law League waiting for the first sign of distress to renew its agitation.

CHAPTER XVI

THE REPEAL OF THE CORN LAWS—I. THE CRISIS

On the 13th of March, 1845, Cobden rose in the House of Commons to speak against the Corn Laws. The Prime Minister sat listening attentively, scribbling notes of the points which he intended to answer. As the speech went on, he grew troubled : at last he crumpled his papers up in his hand, and turning, whispered to Sidney Herbert, who was sitting beside him, ' You must answer this, for I cannot.'

For years past Peel's defence of the Corn Laws had been such as did not completely satisfy the advocates of Protection. He never upheld the principle on which they were founded : he dwelt rather on expediency—on the desirability of securing a good supply of home-grown food, on the shock that would be given to vested interests by sudden abolition of protective duties. As early as 1839 he had declared, ' Unless the existence of the Corn Law can be shown to be consistent, not only with the prosperity of agriculture and the maintenance of the landlord's interest, but also with the protection and the maintenance of the general interests of the country, and especially of the condition of the labouring class, the Corn Law is practically at an end.' [1] He had always appeared happier in attacking John Russell's scheme for a fixed duty than in defending his own sliding scale : he devoted the greater part of his speeches to picking holes in his adversaries' arguments and exposing their weaknesses, a style of criticism at which he was specially adept. Moreover, he had carefully refrained from general declarations about the future, and confined himself to the opposition of the specific measures which lay before him. Now, however, it seemed that he felt himself unable to undertake even such a limited opposition as this.

Later in the session, he was compelled to speak on Villiers' annual motion for the abolition of the Corn Law. His speech was short, and it roused the ugliest suspicions in the minds of his

[1] *Speeches*, iii. p. 591.

followers. It was justly said, that if Villiers had proposed gradual, instead of immediate, abolition, then Peel's speech would have been the strongest argument in his favour : he gave up the contention for the necessity of a home supply, frankly saying that it was no longer possible for the country to be independent of foreign supply : he declared that the principles of Free Trade, which had been so successfully applied to the manufacturing industry of the country, ought to be applied to agriculture also ; but he thought they should be applied gradually and cautiously, and therefore he would oppose Villiers' motion for immediate repeal.[1]

Peel was never the whole-hearted Protectionist that he has sometimes been represented to be. He had supported the reforms of Huskisson and Robinson ; he had reduced the duties on corn in 1828. Since that time his opinions had developed gradually and naturally along these lines ; but the development had been partly concealed from a public that had forgotten his early record by his long period in opposition, when no great commercial questions came under discussion. It is quite untrue, though it has been often repeated, that Peel turned out the Whigs in 1841 on a question of Free Trade : he turned them out on a vote of want of confidence in their general policy. The Whigs went to the hustings with a cry of Cheap Bread ! But, as a matter of fact, the commercial measures which they had proposed to introduce in 1841 were not Free Trade measures at all. The fixed duty on corn would, it was calculated, have raised the average price of corn by several shillings : the advantage of a fixed duty is that it steadies the price, not that it lowers it. The rectification of the sugar and timber duties was to level up the differential duties on foreign and colonial supplies : it did away with Imperial preference, but it did not introduce Free Trade, or anything approaching Free Trade, in sugar and timber. Peel had attacked the Whig budget only on the ground that such measures should not be introduced by a discredited Ministry as a last-minute expedient : he had expressly reserved his own right to act upon the principles of Free Trade.[2] Since that time, Peel had lowered the duties on corn, on timber, and on sugar to a far greater extent than the Whigs had proposed.

[1] *Speeches*, iv. pp. 528-532.

[2] See above, pp. 215-6. He held the same language out of Parliament, in his celebrated Tamworth speech.

Peel, however, hesitated at first to apply to agriculture the arguments in favour of Free Trade. Like Adam Smith, he thought a country to be safe should be self-supporting. Take away the Corn Laws, and would not the margin of cultivation be contracted, poor land thrown back into waste, and the labourer be driven from the land and go to swell the town population and increase the cut-throat competition for work ?

But there was another reason, far more weighty, why he hesitated to do away with agricultural protection. Let him once be sure that the repeal of the Corn Laws would bring real relief to the poor, and the Corn Laws, in his eyes, were doomed. The considerations which might justify Protection could not justify a tax, levied for the benefit of landlord and farmer, on the bread of the half-starved and brutalised population of industrial Britain. Before the supreme necessity of feeding the people, every other necessity must give way. But were the Corn Laws a tax on bread ?

Peel was still influenced by the old fallacy that wages vary with the price of bread—that they are high when bread is dear, and low when bread is cheap. The early leaders of the Anti-Corn-Law movement, including Villiers, strengthened this belief by their arguments : they contended that the Corn Laws were ruining industry by increasing the expense of production. The obvious deduction was that if the Corn Laws were repealed, wages would be equally reduced, and all the advantage would go into the pockets of the manufacturers, except that the poor might be indirectly benefited by the expansion of trade. Now to speed up the process of the industrialisation of England was the last thing Peel desired, and he did not intend to run the risk of ruining agriculture in order to increase the profits of the master manufacturers.

In this situation he characteristically determined on a compromise. He would not sweep away all Protection, but he thought the farmers could get along with much less. He reduced the duty on corn by nearly half, admitted Canadian corn free, and stood by to watch the result.

During the next three years his attitude changed, and the change was partly due to the convincing eloquence of Cobden and Bright, but more to his own observation of facts. As early as 1842 he realised that it was impossible for Britain to be self-supporting—

that was the first illusion to go.[1] Next, he saw that Protection was not always beneficial in its effects on agriculture—he saw that it fostered ignorance and waste, that there was nothing to stimulate the farmer to improvement, and that by the introduction of such methods as were already in use in Scotland, the English farmer might be able to stand against a great deal more competition. He saw that Protection was for the benefit of the landlord and the farmer, not for the country labourer : and, above all, he came to be convinced that wages did not vary with the price of food.

He had closely and carefully observed conditions in the country. He saw that in 1839-41 the price of food was high and the wages of labour very low : he saw that since the revival of trade in 1843 the price of food had fallen and wages had risen to be unusually high. ' I cannot resist the conclusion,' he said afterwards, ' that wages do not vary with the price of provisions. They do vary with the increase of capital, with the prosperity of the country, with the increased power to employ labour ; but there is no immediate relation between wages and provisions—or if there be a relation it is an inverse ratio.' [2]

In this gradual revelation Peel saw the solution of the greatest problem of the age : he saw how the sufferings of the working classes might be truly and permanently relieved.

But, though he saw the remedy, he saw also the difficulty of applying it. No man could know better than the leader of the Conservative party how strong would be the resistance offered to the repeal of the Corn Laws. His own followers would oppose it to the last : nor had he any reason to think that the Whigs would be more yielding. They had taken as their principle the establishment of a fixed duty on corn, and this he still regarded as even more objectionable than a sliding scale. The only support on which he could count was that of the Anti-Corn-Law League, which, though it had obtained increasing influence in the country, was still in a small minority in Parliament.

It was out of the question that he himself should propose to the present Parliament to repeal the Corn Laws. He was not pledged against Corn Law repeal to the extent that he had been against Catholic emancipation ; but still he was partly pledged. His party had certainly followed him under the belief that he meant

[1] See above, p. 229.　　　　　[2] *Speeches*, iv. p. 569.

to maintain agricultural protection, and, if he now abandoned
it, a large section of them would think that he had betrayed them.
He could not, however, now that his own mind was changed,
continue to oppose repeal. Some time during the spring of 1845
he came to the following decision. During the session of 1846,
when the life of the Parliament was drawing to its close, he would
confess that his opinions had changed, tell his party that he could
no longer defend the Corn Laws, and, free from all obligation,
would go to the country at the next election as a Free Trader.[1]
This might well mean the break-up of the Conservative party :
but he hoped it would not. He was always self-confident—he
knew they had no one to set in his place—what could they do
without him ? Had they not had their lesson in 1830 and 1835 ?
He hoped, too, that the logic of facts might convert his party as
it had converted him, and that he might persuade them, save for
a few extremists, to follow him in spite of all.

There was one weakness in this plan : its success depended upon
that incalculable factor, the climate of the British Isles. If the
fine weather and rich harvests of the last three years continued,
well and good : but if the corn crop failed and scarcity ensued,
then distress among the working classes would begin afresh, and
would be the signal for a new attack from the League : in such
circumstances Peel could not and would not defend the Corn Law.

Hence it was that the summer of 1845 saw the Prime Minister
poring over the weather forecasts and watching the barometer
like a child that has been invited to a picnic. Graham and Sidney
Herbert, alone of the Cabinet, shared his secret and his preoccu-
pations. ' I know not,' wrote the Home Secretary, ' that the state
of affairs is exactly sound when Ministers are driven to study the
barometer with so much anxiety. But under no law will it be
easy to feed 25 millions crowded together in a narrow space, when
heaven denies the blessing of abundance.' [2]

The early summer was fine ; but in July the weather changed,
and throughout the weeks that followed it rained, rained, rained
steadily—rain that beat down the unripened ears of wheat into
earth. It was clear that the harvest would be bad : but even this
was suddenly overshadowed by another and more frightful disaster.

---

[1] *Memoirs*, ii. p. 318.

[2] Parker, *Graham*, ii. p. 21. Graham was always inclined to attribute
disaster to the direct intervention of Providence.

In 1844 potato blight had appeared in America. This year the disease spread to Europe : in August it was reported in the Isle of Wight. It was not, however, until the end of September that the first warning of what might be expected reached the Ministers, with the authentic information that the disease was present on a large scale in Ireland. The minds of the two leaders were working so much on the same lines, that on the same day each wrote to the other, the letters crossing, to declare his conviction that the end had come.

' The accounts of the state of the potato crop in Ireland are very alarming,' said Peel. ' . . . I have no confidence in such remedies as the prohibition of exports or the stoppage of the distilleries. The removal of impediments to import is the only effectual remedy.'

' Ought (these duties) to be maintained in their present stringency,' wrote Graham, ' if the people of Ireland be reduced to the last extremity for want of food ? ' [1]

Peel's first step was to despatch two scientists, Dr. Lyon Playfair and Professor Lindley, to investigate the truth, and to find if there were any means of arresting the disease. By the 26th of October they reported that the damage was beyond all they had feared. The potato crop at utmost could amount only to three-eighths of its usual yield, and there was the greatest probability that the seed for next year would be infected. The persistent rain made efforts to cope with the disease of little use, for even sound potatoes might have rotted in the sodden soil. Moreover, the worst was not yet known, for potatoes which were put in the pits, apparently healthy, were dug up a month or two later ' masses of putrid slime.' [2]

The total population of Ireland was now over 8,000,000. Of these some 4,000,000 subsisted entirely on potatoes. So did the greater part of the inhabitants of the Western Highlands and Isles of Scotland. A small number in England and Lowland Scotland also depended exclusively on the potato, and a large number used it to supplement their diet of bread or oatmeal. Some 3,000,000 people in Ireland and an indefinite number in Britain would be entirely deprived of their usual means of subsistence : there would

[1] The letters are printed in Parker, *Peel*, iii. p. 223, and in *Memoirs*, ii. pp. 115-6.

[2] Stanmore, *Herbert*, i. pp. 44-5.

be an unusual demand for corn to supply the lack of potatoes : but the corn crop, owing to the wet season, was less than usual. How, then, were these multitudes to be fed ?

On the 31st of October, Peel met his Cabinet in his own house, armed with these reports. He had already taken various steps on his own responsibility. He had attempted to procure a supply of uninfected seed from Spain and Southern France, had instructed the Irish Government to carry out at State expense all the measures recommended by Playfair and Lindley for stemming the disease,[1] and had authorised the expenditure of £600,000 on relief works— drainage, railway construction, and fisheries. He now proposed to his colleagues to open the ports immediately by Order in Council ; to summon Parliament at once to sanction the proceeding, and to give notice of his intention to introduce a bill early in 1846 for the alteration of the Corn Laws. He said afterwards that he believed the Cabinet would have agreed if he had assured them that the suspension would only be for a limited time, and that the Corn Law would then be restored : but he told them at once that he did not think this possible, and that he would propose to admit Indian corn and all British colonial grain free, and to lower the sliding scale greatly. Graham and Herbert announced their support of the Prime Minister, and, to the surprise of most of his colleagues, Aberdeen followed them, and declared his entire concurrence with Peel's policy. The rest of the Cabinet refused to agree. Some pressed for time and more information ; others positively stated that they would not agree to repeal the Corn Law. Peel at last consented to give a short time for consideration, but said that his own resolve was taken, and that if they did not eventually support him he would resign.[2] As soon as they broke up, Peel, acting in concert with Graham and Goulburn, gave orders for the secret purchase of £160,000 of maize from the United States. This was afterwards retailed to the Irish peasantry at 1d. the pound : it was at first distrusted and nicknamed ' Peel's brimstone,' but soon proved invaluable.

A considerable difference of opinion was found among the dissident Ministers. Those of the older generation mostly objected to tampering with the Corn Laws at all. The aristocracy

---

[1] These were chiefly drying the potatoes in limekilns and applying chemical preparations, and proved ineffectual.

[2] See *Memoirs*, ii. p. 158 ff., for what happened at the Cabinet.

of England and Ireland was callous enough at that day : there were men in the Cabinet who had voted against Ashley's bill forbidding children to be employed as chimney sweepers. A few months before this a great nobleman had told the poor of England that when they had no food they could do quite nicely on a pinch of curry powder in hot water. A few months later, a Prince of the blood declared that diseased potatoes made excellent food when mixed with grass—one wonders if his Royal Highness had tried it ? Peel's aristocratic colleagues were unable to understand the disaster that was upon them, and his anguish of apprehension seemed to them ridiculous and exaggerated. ' Rotten potatoes have done it all ; they have put Peel in his damned fright,' said Wellington. Wharncliffe said Peel was panic-struck, and Graham worse.[1] That plebeian vegetable, the potato, was beneath the notice of the peers of the old school.[2]

The younger Ministers, on the other hand, were convinced of the necessity of ultimate repeal, and only differed as to time and method. Lincoln urged that Peel should wait until the dissolution of Parliament approached and then propose repeal. Dalhousie, who, though not in the Cabinet, was consulted, said that Peel ought to proclaim his change of opinion and then resign. Both agreed that the Government were pledged to maintain the Corn Laws, and could not in honour propose their repeal, but both left the Irish famine and the need for immediate action entirely out of count. Peel had no reason to believe that if he resigned the Whigs could or would propose and carry repeal. Moreover, he disagreed with his young friends as to where the obligations of honour lay : Lincoln's proposal would involve a systematic course of deception, for the Government would have to resist motions for the abolition of the Corn Laws ; Dalhousie's plan was to shirk the responsibility which fell upon the Queen's Ministers in an hour of crisis.

' I was not insensible,' said Peel, ' to the evil of acting counter to the will of those majorities (in Parliament), of severing party connections, and of subjecting public men to suspicion and reproach and the loss of public confidence ; but I felt a strong con-

---

[1] Walpole, *England*, iv. p. 263. Eversley, *Peel and O'Connell*, p. 293. *Greville*, v. p. 324.

[2] ' Wonderful times, when potatoes are converted to a political engine ! ' said the Duke of Rutland. Whibley, *Manners*, i. p. 197.

viction that such evils were light in comparison with those which must be incurred by the sacrifice of national interests to party attachments, and by deferring necessary precautions against scarcity of food for the purpose of consulting appearances and preserving the show of personal consistency. . . . The honour of public men would not have been maintained . . . if a Minister had at a critical period shrunk from the duty of giving that advice which he believed to be best, and from incurring every personal sacrifice which the giving of that advice might entail.' [1]

On the 25th of November the Cabinet met again, and Peel read to them a memorandum which he had prepared. He would not agree to issue the necessary instructions for relief measures in Ireland, he stated, unless the Corn Laws were immediately suspended and ultimately repealed. ' Suspension will compel a deliberate review of the whole question of agricultural protection. I firmly believe that it would be better for the country that that review should be undertaken by others. Under ordinary circumstances I should advise that it should be so undertaken ; but I look now to the immediate emergency and to the duties it imposes on a Minister. I am ready to take the responsibility of meeting that emergency, if the opinions of my colleagues . . . concur with mine.' [2]

Several days passed in discussion, and on the 27th of November the situation was materially altered. The succession of Cabinet meetings, held at the beginning of the month, and apparently without result, had created a great sensation, and they offered John Russell his opportunity. From Edinburgh, where he was staying, he wrote to his constituents in London, declaring that he had abandoned his contention for a fixed duty on corn, and now believed that total repeal was necessary : as the Government apparently did not mean to do anything, he thought it his duty to declare his views at once.[3]

The annoyance of Peel may be conceived : Russell had seized the opportunity which he, owing to the objections of the Protectionists, had lost. If they acted now, they would appear to be humbly obeying the Whig leader's instructions. Nevertheless,

---

[1] *Memoirs*, ii. pp. 168-9.

[2] *Ib.* p. 184.

[3] The Edinburgh letter was written on 22nd November, but it was not published in the *Times* until the 27th.

Peel determined to go on, and on December 2nd he told his colleagues the details of his plan.   It was to suspend the Corn Laws
immediately, and then when the scarcity was past to re-enact for
a short time a very low duty, only to be in force when corn was
under 58s., and diminishing annually so as to disappear in three or
four years.   Wellington's mind had been altered by Russell's letter,
and he now said that, though he still disapproved Peel's plan, he
would support it, because he felt it was above all things important
to maintain the Conservative Government in power.   The
majority of the dissidents followed Wellington : but Stanley and
Buccleuch still refused to agree.   On December 5th, on receiving
their considered decision, Peel went down to Windsor and placed
his resignation in the Queen's hands.

Meanwhile, on the previous day, the public were confounded
by an announcement in the *Times* that the Cabinet had agreed on
the total repeal of the Corn Laws.   Nothing could be done until
Lord John arrived from Edinburgh, and he did not reach London
for six days.   All this time a raging curiosity possessed the town
and fed on baseless rumours.   The *Times* stuck to its point,[1] the
resignation remained a secret.   On the 11th, Greville surmised
what was happening, at a Privy Council where the Cabinet met
in a state of wild hilarity, Peel ' full of jokes and stories,' and
Stanley remarking to a friend that ' he had probably often seen as
much patience, but never so much resignation.' [2]   The same day
Russell arrived, and the truth was known.

Lord John was excited and nervous.   He told the Queen he
must consult his friends, especially Lord Lansdowne, before he
could agree to take office, and for six days he remained undecided.
When Peel took his farewell of the Queen and the Prince, he left
with them an official statement that he would support Russell's

---

[1] It is uncertain how the *Times* came to make this odd blunder.   Aberdeen
used to carry on the necessary negotiations with Delane, as Peel, who detested
newspaper men, would have nothing to do with him.   Aberdeen told Delane
that the Cabinet was discussing the question of the Corn Laws, and Delane promised secrecy.   He then published the statement that repeal was agreed on.
In spite of this apparently flagrant breach of faith, Aberdeen continued to be
on the most friendly terms with Delane.   (See Stanmore's *Herbert*, i. pp. 62-3,
the most authentic account.)   This shows that Delane had been able to give a
satisfactory explanation.   The obvious deduction is that Delane later received
information from another source, as to which he was, of course, under no
obligation of secrecy.   It was not a reliable source, for the information was
incorrect, but Delane, owing to Aberdeen's hints, believed it.

[2] *Greville*, v. p. 322.

Government in any measure 'in general conformity' with his Edinburgh letter. In a private conversation with the Queen, he gave even stronger assurances. 'Even if Lord John goes to the full extent of his declaration in that letter (which I think goes too far) I will support him . . . and use all my influence with the House of Lords to prevent their impeding his progress. I will do more, if he likes it. I will say that the increase of the estimates which will become necessary is my work, and I alone am responsible for it.' [1]

Russell's first demand was an assurance that the Protectionists were not prepared to form a Government ; and Peel secured this for him from Stanley and Buccleuch. When, however, Russell proposed to send him his scheme for repealing the Corn Laws, he objected. Russell's Cabinet, he said, ought to retain full liberty to modify or alter the plan they decided on ; but, what was more important, 'a knowledge that a plan of adjustment had been concerted between Lord John Russell and (Peel) would increase rather than diminish the risk of failure. It would on the one hand indispose towards the support of the measure many of those friendly to the new Government. . . . on the other it would diminish the influence and authority of Sir Robert Peel in respect to the promotion of a settlement and his power to render useful service. He is convinced that previous concert, or a previous pledge on his part to support a particular measure of adjustment, would be distasteful to the House of Commons, and embarrassing to all parties. He assures your Majesty that these . . . alone are the motives which induce him to discourage such a communication as that which Lord John Russell proposes to make to him.' [2]

Meanwhile Russell had found his own party almost as much divided as the Conservative Cabinet had been. Lansdowne positively declared that he would only consent if relief were granted to the agricultural interest of at least £1,000,000 and made an integral part of the original scheme.[3] Howick (who had just succeeded his father as Lord Grey) seems to have wanted a coalition with Peel : [4] no one would agree to this, but he resolutely held to it that repeal must be immediate—there must be no transition period such as Peel's plan proposed. After long discussion, both Howick's and Lansdowne's proposals were agreed to, and Lord

[1] *Letters of Queen Victoria*, ii. p. 50.   [2] *Memoirs*, ii. p. 236.
[3] Gooch, *Russell Correspondence*, p. 94.   [4] Stanmore, *Herbert*, i. p. 55.

John considered it necessary to ask whether Peel would support immediate abolition of the duties.   Peel in reply reiterated what he had said before—he had given a general assurance of support ; he thought it better to make no preliminary agreement as to details.   ' I do not know,' he said, ' and I ought not to know, the equivalents with which it may be intended to accompany any particular plan for the adjustment of the Corn Laws ; ' he did not even know if the Whig Cabinet were all agreed as to this measure; to pledge himself in advance might be to throw away all his power of influencing his own party, who would look with the deepest suspicion upon such a bargain with the Whigs.[1]   On the 18th, Russell laid this reply before his friends, stating that he himself thought it satisfactory : they agreed, by eleven votes to five,[2] that the assurances were sufficient, and Russell, after six days' deliberation, told the Queen that he would agree to form a Government.

Internal influences, however, had been at work to destroy the new Ministry before it was made.   A week before, Howick had told a confidential friend of Russell's that he could not join the Government if Palmerston went to the Foreign Office.   The confidant did not repeat this to Russell, as Howick intended, and in consequence Russell failed to understand Howick's veiled references to the matter.   On the 19th he learned for the first time of Howick's objections, and was much taken aback.   Howick explained that he believed Palmerston would soon involve the country in war, and that his conscience would not allow him to agree to the appointment; but he offered to give up his own claims to office, and left Russell under the impression that the Ministry would be formed without him.

Russell had before this offered Palmerston the Colonial Office, and Palmerston had refused to serve in any capacity save as Foreign Secretary.   Russell felt he could not go on unless he had both Howick and Palmerston with him, and he returned to Windsor and told the Queen that he could not form a Government, thus resigning in forty-eight hours the commission which he had only accepted after a week's meditation.[3]

[1] *Memoirs*, ii. pp. 241-2.

[2] The minority was composed of Lansdowne, Bedford, Clarendon, Auckland, Monteagle ; the majority, of Howick, Morpeth, Cottenham, Macaulay, Sir G. Grey, Palmerston, Baring, Labouchere, Ellice, Hobhouse, and Russell himself

[3] See the *Historical Review*, vol. i., 1886, for the negotiation with Howick.

The cause of Lord John's failure was much debated. It was attributed by some to the obstinacy of Lord Grey, by others to Peel's refusal to give more than a general pledge of support. It was probably due to neither of these. Howick was not so indispensable but that the Government could have got on without him —they had done so from 1839 to 1841. There was no real doubt of the sincerity of Peel's support. Russell left with the Queen a written statement of his satisfaction with Peel's assurances; but it is only necessary to ask, what possible motive could Peel have for resigning if he did not mean to give Russell the support he promised? During the discussions Sidney Herbert chanced to meet Howick alone in his club, and they entered into conversation. Howick asked if Peel would support immediate abolition—'You could trip us up if you liked,' said he. Herbert laughed at him: 'Now, really, do you conceive such a thing possible? Just look at what has happened. Sir Robert Peel with a large majority in both Houses throws down a great position, breaks up his party, incurs every kind of odium for the public good. Men don't throw away brilliant positions for the purpose of playing practical jokes upon their opponents. Can you conceive that men of honour, who have made the sacrifices we have for the settlement of this question, are not prepared honestly to do their utmost to carry it through? The supposition is an absurdity.'

'No, I don't say that,' said Howick. 'I can assure you I never thought it was a trick. When I saw the letter they had written to Sir Robert, I said at once, "You must be born fools to expect him to give in to such a proposition as this." He gave the only answer he ought to give. Peel was quite right there.'[1]

The truth is that the Whigs were not strong or united enough to shoulder the responsibility which John Russell's letter had brought upon them. Some of them had approved it as a political manœuvre, but did not like it as a statement of policy. Great landlords like Lansdowne and Bedford shrank from abandoning agricultural protection. Clarendon and Bessborough declared that the potato famine was all a sham.[2] Bedford was 'ready to jump out of his skin' with delight when he heard that Russell had given up the attempt, and Lansdowne, Bessborough, Minto all wrote to the Prime Minister manqué congratulations and approval.[3]

---

[1] Stanmore, *Herbert*, i. p. 55 ff.　　　[2] *Hobhouse*, vi. pp. 157-8.
[3] Gooch, *Russell Correspondence*, pp. 96-8.

Palmerston and his circle were at heart but little inclined to Free Trade. ' If the Protectionists had but common sense and would yield what ought to be yielded,' Beauvale, Palmerston's brother-in-law and Melbourne's brother, wrote later, ' I firmly believe we should beat Johnny, Peel, and the League united.' Palmerston apparently let Russell know that he would give nothing but his vote to the service of Free Trade.[1]

Even the convinced Free Traders were doubtful whether they could succeed. ' Have we sufficient support in the country to try so extreme a measure ? ' asked Macaulay. ' . . . We are all most unwilling to take office, and so is (Russell). . . . I have no doubt that there is not a single man amongst us who would not at once refuse to enlist, if he could do so with a clear conscience. . . . My hope is that Peel will not accede to our terms, and that we shall be set at liberty.' [2]

' Can I do so wild a thing ? ' Lord John said to himself when the Queen told him the situation.[3] He was in a minority in both Houses of Parliament. His Edinburgh letter had been written as an Opposition move, and he had little guessed that he would so soon be taken at his word.[4] At that time nothing was known save that the Cabinet were discussing the Corn Laws, and it was generally believed among the Whigs that the difference among the Conservatives was caused by Peel's refusing to open the ports ! Had his party been resolute and united, Russell might have dared to meet Parliament in a minority : as it was, the task was too great for him. His worst mistake was his hesitating so long. After six days' consideration he should have realised the truth, and should have refused the Queen's commission.

Peel had been sent for to Windsor on the 20th to say his farewell to the Queen, and finally resign the seals into her hands. In the morning he received a hasty note from the Prince, warning him that difficulties had arisen, and that Russell might yet withdraw. When he arrived, Victoria met him with, ' So far from taking leave of you, Sir Robert, I must require you to withdraw your resignation and remain in my service,' and she showed Russell's statement. He looked at it and answered at once.

[1] Beauvale to Lady Palmerston, 5th January, 1846. Airlie, *Lady Palmerston*, ii. p. 105. *Greville*, i. p. 355.

[2] Trevelyan, *Macaulay*, pp. 455-7-8.   [3] Walpole, *Russell*, p. 410.

[4] Compare the Prince Consort to Peel. Parker, *Peel*, iii. p. 241 : ' Lord John knows that many of his friends disapproved of his letter,' etc.

' I want no consultation, no time for reflection. I will be your Minister, happen what may. I will do without a colleague rather than leave you in this extremity.' ' I have never seen him so excited and so determined,' said the Queen later.[1]

Peel returned to London and summoned his colleagues to a Cabinet. He told them he spoke to them as the Queen's Minister, and that, whether they would support him or not, he was resolved to carry out his policy : whether it failed or succeeded would now lie with them. ' There was a dead silence.' At last Stanley spoke, and said that he could not agree, and must resign. Buccleuch, in great agitation, said the situation had changed, and he must have time to reflect. The rest of the Cabinet with one voice declared that they would follow Peel—Wellington in great delight at his spirited conduct. ' It was exactly the same course,' the Duke told the House of Lords later, ' as I should have followed myself under similar circumstances, and I therefore determined, my Lords, to stand by him.' [2]

Peel was now in the highest spirits. ' It is a strange dream—I feel like a man restored to life after his funeral service had been preached,' he said.[3] He was much disappointed in John Russell, he told Greville, who noted that he was ' evidently elated at the advantage that had been thrown into his hands, and chuckling mightily at the pitiful figure which the Whigs had cut, and at the contrast so favourable to himself which the whole case will exhibit.' [4] Indeed, for weakness such as Lord John had shown Peel had neither understanding nor tolerance.[5] Cautious as he was in normal times, in moments of crisis his impulse was always to take any risk and face the danger boldly. ' Lord John Russell took a course quite unusual—neither accepted nor declined,' he wrote to a friend. ' There was in my opinion no alternative. I

[1] Parker, *Peel,* iii. p. 296. *Letters of Queen Victoria,* ii. p. 64.

[2] *Ib.* pp. 284-5.

[3] To Princess Lieven, *Memoirs,* ii. p. 252. He used the same expression to Hardinge (Parker, iii. p. 295) : ' The events of the last fortnight seem to be a dream.'

[4] *Greville,* v. p. 348.

[5] Sir William Gregory gives a similar instance. He was offered, and refused, the Irish Secretaryship by Peel in 1845. ' Up to the day of his death, Sir Robert Peel was not the same to me. He was as kind as ever, but he did not show the interest he always took in my doings.' The young man failed to rise to the occasion, and lost Peel's respect. See Gregory, *Autobiography,* p. 129.

might as well have hesitated in November, 1834, when King William sent for me.' [1]

It wanted now only a few weeks till Parliament should meet, and Peel, in consideration of this and of the altered situation, decided that it was better not to open the ports by Order in Council, but to submit the whole scheme to the approval of Parliament. He anticipated a struggle, but he probably did not expect that it would be so protracted as it ultimately proved, and never imagined that it would take five months to pass his bill into law.

In the meantime, the fall of the Conservative Government had flung half Europe into a panic. There was consternation in the chancelleries, and the envoys of the little states, thinking themselves delivered over to Palmerston's mercy, ' raised their tender voices like lambs to the butcher.' A great banker, rushing in a panic to Guizot, exclaimed, ' Mais, M. le Ministre, que ferez-vous de cet homme-là ? En six mois nous sommes en lutte avec l'Angleterre . . . c'est terrible ! ' [2] Peel's return to office was received with corresponding delight. At home, the Funds rose as if released from a weight, and the satisfaction in the City was extreme. Only in the ranks of the Tories terror and despair reigned. What was he going to do, this alien chief of theirs ? The resignation of Stanley pointed to the worst : but would he dare to defy and betray them—he, the son of a cotton spinner, whom they had taken and made a great man of, whom they had set above the Pelhams and the Stanleys, the Villiers and the Bentincks ?

It has often been said—both at the time and since—that Peel should have called together his party and told them what he intended to do : by doing so he might have secured their support for his measure, and by omitting to do so, he offended and disgusted them to an unnecessary degree.

It was, however, impossible for Peel to do this until he had resumed office after Lord John's failure and remodelled his Cabinet. Until that time he was in a minority in his own council : he could not communicate with the party without destroying all hope of reconciling the differences among the Ministers. After he had formed his new Government, it is doubtful whether it was not too late to do any good. The cat was already out of the bag :

[1] Parker, *Peel*, iii. p. 288.   [2] *Letters of Greville and Reeve*, pp. 134, 128.

everyone guessed that Peel was going to alter the Corn Laws, and the only doubt was, how far precisely did he mean to go ? It was too late to reconcile the malcontents by the flattery of letting them into the secret beforehand. There were two ways of proceeding. One was to call together the whole party; but that involved debating the whole scheme which was to be introduced into Parliament, and, if the decision were adverse, it would greatly weaken the position of the Government before the real struggle began. The other was to summon some twenty or thirty of the more important members and consult with them : but Peel believed that this would only give more bitter offence to those who were not invited to the council.

There is, however, no real ground for believing that the Tories would ever have assented to Corn Law repeal, even if they had been consulted beforehand. Can anyone believe that the angry landlords would have liked the prospect any the better if they had been informed of it on New Year's Day instead of on January 22nd ? Disaffection was already rife in the party : they had several times revolted; their imperious master had rated them, and they remembered it against him. They had stood much from Peel—his haughty disregard for their feelings, his Free Trade measures, his liberal reforms, his precious Maynooth grant amd ' godless colleges '—but this was the last straw. The discontent that had smouldered since 1829 only came to a head in 1846.

Disraeli afterwards boasted that he had conducted, in 1867, a great reversal of policy, without alienating his followers, while Peel, in 1829 and 1846, broke up the party. The answer to this is that the party had had its lesson : it saw it had gained nothing by revolt in 1829 and 1846—that the only result had been its own exclusion from power for many years. There is, however, a more important reason. The change of policy in 1867 involved only a sacrifice of principle—not a sacrifice of interest, as in 1846. The majority of the Tories really thought they would gain much by Disraeli's new democratic suffrage, and in the ultimate result they were right. Peel in 1846 sacrificed himself and his party in a great national crisis : his party threw him over, but the nation accepted him as its hero. Disraeli in 1867 sacrificed his principles and his party's principles for party ends : he carried his party with him, but the nation threw him over at the next election.

' It was impossible to reconcile the repeal of the Corn Laws by me with the keeping together of the Conservative party,' said Peel later, ' and I had no hesitation in sacrificing the subordinate object, and with it my own political interests. . . . I am perfectly satisfied that if at any time between the 1st of November and the day on which . . . I announced in the House of Commons the intended repeal of the Corn Laws, I had tried to gain acquiescence, either by belabouring individuals separately, or by summoning the party generally, I should have received scarcely one promise of support. I should have had on the part of the most moderate a formal protest. . . . To the most violent I should have given facilities for organised opposition ; I should have appeared to be flying in the face of a whole party, and contumaciously disregarding their opinion and advice after I had professed to consult them ; but (what is of infinitely more importance) *I should have failed in carrying the repeal of the Corn Laws*. Now I was resolved *not to fail*. I did not fail ; and if I had to fight the same battle over again, I would fight it in the same way.' [1]

There are still persons, and these include a high authority, Lord Rosebery, who, while admitting that Peel was actuated by the highest motives in repealing the Corn Laws, and that his policy was the wisest, hold that ' he was not the man to do it.' He should have resigned and left the work to others. ' Had he been sincere in his altered views he would have given his support and the leadership of the House of Commons to Richard Cobden,' says Mr. Whibley, the historian of ' Young England.' [2] ' If the Corn Laws were to be repealed,' says Disraeli's biographer, ' Russell was the man clearly designated for the task. . . . (Peel) acquiesced far too readily in Russell's failure to form a Government. . . . The excuse which he (Russell) gave for his desertion of the Queen was wholly inadequate, and would not have held against a little resolution on the part of the retiring Minister.' [3]

Such critics seem to have a curious notion of the parliamentary system in 1846. By what possible mutation of parties could Cobden have been suddenly transformed into the leader of the House of Commons ? Men are not made leaders of the House of Commons as they are made baronets. Who was to form the

---

[1] Peel to Aberdeen, 19th August, 1847. *Memoirs*, ii. pp. 323-324. The talics are Peel's.

[2] Whibley, *Manners*, i. p. 198.   [3] Monypenny, *Disraeli*, ii. p. 347.

rest of the party ? It was only with the greatest reluctance that
Russell was induced by Howick to offer Cobden the Board of
Trade in 1845 ; and Cobden refused it. The offer gave great
annoyance to the Queen and to most of the Whigs. In the same
way one may ask, how in the world was Peel to do anything but
' acquiesce ' in Russell's refusal to form a Government ? Was he
to say to the Queen, ' Oh, try again, Ma'am ! Russell only wants a
little extra persuasion. Write him another note ' ?

Mr. Monypenny goes so far as to ignore the Irish famine.
According to him, Peel ' sacrificed his pledges and his party to a
supposed necessity that had no existence.' [1] Mr. Whibley, though
he casually admits that there was a famine, insinuates that there
was no real evidence of it in 1845. Only ' scanty facts were
adduced in support of Peel's sudden conversion,' he ' yielded to
panic fear,' ' changed his mind without an adequate reason,' and
George Bentinck was ' the first honestly to investigate the alleged
famine in Ireland.' [2] The Scientific Commission, we must then
presume, investigated it dishonestly ? It was all very well for
Bentinck and Clarendon and Bedford in 1846 to deny the existence of a famine, but it is extraordinary to find these hoary arguments trotted out in 1906 and 1925. Surely a famine in which
almost 1,000,000 persons perished, in spite of vast relief measures,
was sufficient to justify anyone changing his mind as to the desirability of taxes on imported food ?

Let us be serious, however, and consider the more reasonable
accusation, that all that was necessary in 1845-6 was the temporary
suspension of the Corn Laws, and that if Peel had really been
sincere in his dread of famine he would have forbidden the export
of corn from Ireland.

The Irish corn crop was slightly below the average, but it had
not completely failed. To prohibit export would have brought
down prices with a rush, and the farmers, already hard hit, would
have lost everything, and their distress would have been added to
that of the starving cottars. The Government could have bought
the Irish corn and distributed it to the cottars, but it was much
cheaper to buy maize from America for this purpose, and let the
farmers sell their corn for a good price in England, which enabled
them to struggle on. In this way the general dislocation of trade

[1] Monypenny, *Disraeli*, ii. p. 346.
[2] Whibley, *Manners*, i. pp. 195, 193, 221, 216, etc.

resulting from a prohibition of export was avoided. There was, of course, a general scarcity of food in 1846-7, but the real problem in Ireland was not how to secure food, but how to distribute it through a marshy and mountainous country without railroads.

When it is contended that the temporary suspension of the Corn Laws was all that was required, it should be remembered that Peel wanted not merely to relieve a momentary dearth, but to prevent such a dearth from recurring again. His object was first, to prevent famine at the moment, and, secondly, to lower the price of bread permanently. The case of Ireland brought home to his mind the danger of a whole nation living upon the cheapest form of food—potatoes. He saw that if the population of Great Britain continued to increase, and food prices were not lowered, there was a possibility that a larger and larger number of people might be forced to resort to this cheaper form of food. The potato-eater lives on the very margin of subsistence; there is no cheaper substitute for him to fall back upon in times of scarcity. The repeal of the Corn Laws was, in fact, the greatest effort ever made to raise collectively the standard of life of the whole lower class.

When Peel came to realise the necessity for immediate action, should he have resigned immediately and allowed Russell to carry this great measure? He certainly could not have done this in October, 1845. At that time he had no grounds whatever for thinking that the Whigs would try to repeal the Corn Laws. They were still pledged to a fixed duty. After Russell failed to form a Government in December, there was no alternative between a Protectionist Government under Stanley and Peel's return to power. It is therefore only to the period between the publication of the Edinburgh letter on November 27 and the resignation of Peel on December 5—about a week—that this criticism can apply.

Let us for argument's sake admit that Peel should have resigned as soon as he read Russell's letter in the *Times*: the question remains, could Russell have repealed the Corn Laws? The course of events shows that he almost certainly could not. Peel would have given him his support; so would his own immediate followers, Graham, Herbert, Aberdeen, Lincoln, Gladstone: but probably that minority of the Tory party who followed Peel while he remained Minister would not have followed him when he was in opposition. The influence of Wellington carried the bill through the Lords ; but Wellington only supported the bill, which he did not approve, with the express object of *preserving a Tory Government for the country*. With Peel out of office, his one motive for supporting it would have been gone, and he would either have opposed it or let it alone. It is unnecessary to point out the danger of a conflict, however short, between the House of Lords and the House of Commons on the subject of cheap bread.

Could the bill, however, have passed the Commons ? It passed most of its divisions with a majority of over ninety ; this might have been reduced by half if Peel had been in opposition, by the desertion of some of his followers. Russell's bill, it will be remembered, was to be accompanied by very large measures of relief to the landed interest—much larger than those Peel proposed : if the League and the Radicals had opposed these, the chances of shipwreck would have increased. Russell, whose sudden abandonment of a fixed duty for total repeal was as startling a change as Peel's, would have been equally exposed to accusations of inconsistency. Peel had changed his mind when change meant the probable loss of office and ruin of his career : Russell had changed his in such circumstances as made it appear like a bid for power. Why were the accusations that were hurled at Peel never brought against Russell ?

The answer to that question is that Russell's change of opinion was comparatively unimportant. In 1846 there was but one man strong enough to repeal the Corn Laws, and that man was Peel. Russell himself knew that he had no chance of carrying repeal without Peel's whole-hearted support. Only this fact explains the bitterness of the Protectionists. They knew that only Peel could have done this thing, and so they could not forgive him.

This is the real justification of Peel's conduct. When, after Russell's failure, he took office again, he was technically freed, by his resignation, from whatever pledges he had given before. Such was the opinion of Dalhousie, who had before declared that honour demanded resignation, but now considered that they were free of all obligations. Such was the opinion of Bright, who said that Peel had been the Minister of a party, but was now the Minister of the Queen and of the people. But Peel himself did not put forward this plea. He accepted the full responsibility of his change of opinion. He had all along been prepared to propose the repeal of the Corn Laws, without offering to resign. He could, by resigning, have thrown on his successors the responsibility of repealing or maintaining the law, and could have saved himself from all these accusations of inconsistency, of treachery, of self-seeking ambition. He preferred to sacrifice his own interests at the call of what he considered his duty and the nation's need : he offered that as his only excuse, and made no attempt to shirk the consequences of what was called disloyalty to his party.

CHAPTER XVII

THE REPEAL OF THE CORN LAWS—
II. THE PEOPLE'S MINISTER

PARLIAMENT met on the 22nd of January, and Peel announced on the day of assembly that he proposed to lower the duty on corn immediately to a few shillings, and to abolish it entirely within three years. His speech was in no way conciliatory. He opened with a frank confession that he had changed his opinions, and then gave a full statement of the reasons that had influenced him, stressing particularly his belief that wages did not vary with the price of food. Then he told the House of the terrible calamity that had befallen them—the prospect of dearth in England and famine in Ireland, and stated that in such circumstances he did not believe the Corn Laws should or could be maintained. He admitted that he was not the person who should introduce such measures, and that in normal circumstances his proper course would have been to resign : but he found himself now the Queen's Minister, in a moment of peril, and he thought it his duty to consider only national interests and lay lesser considerations aside. He ended in a tone of high defiance and great excitement.

' I have thought it consistent with true Conservative policy to promote so much of happiness and contentment among the people that the voice of disaffection should be no longer heard, and that thoughts of the dissolution of our institutions should be forgotten in the midst of physical enjoyment. . . . These were my objects in accepting office—it is a burden too great for my physical, and far beyond my intellectual structure, and to be relieved from it with perfect honour would be the greatest favour that could be conferred on me. But as a feeling of honour and strong sense of duty require me to undertake these responsible functions, I declare, Sir, that I am ready to incur these risks, to bear these burdens, and to front all these honourable dangers. But, Sir, I will not take the step with mutilated power and shackled authority. I will not stand at the helm during such tempestuous nights as I have seen, if the vessel be not allowed fairly to pursue the course which I think she ought to take. I will not, Sir, undertake to direct the course of the vessel by observations which have been taken in 1842. . . . Sir, I do not wish to be the Minister of England, but while I have the high honour of holding that office, I am determined to hold it by no servile tenure. I will only hold that office upon the condition of being unshackled by any other obligations than those of consulting the public interests, and of providing for the public safety.' [1]

It was a declaration of independence; and it was received by the party in a deadly silence. Only when the Speaker mentioned Stanley there was an outburst of cheers.

When Peel ended, Russell rose to give his explanation. 'The exposition of failures is never very animating,' [2] and the House listened in a dull and half-despairing silence. It was generally expected that all discussion would be postponed: the Tories, though sullenly enraged, were unprepared with opposition, for many of them had hoped against hope to the last. Mr. Disraeli, however, had too sure a political instinct not to see that if no reply were made, the Government would have gained a great advantage. He saw no one was prepared, and rose himself. He opened in a tone of polite sarcasm, but, feeling that the House was with him, he grew more bold: with a passing gibe at the Minister's 'egoistic rhetoric,' he boldly declared that his change of policy showed a 'sublime audacity' not equalled in English history. He compared him to that Turkish admiral who steered his fleet straight into the enemy's ports, and when reproached, replied, 'I only accepted the command in order that I might betray my master.' He compared him to a nurse who in a fit of frenzy murders the darling babe in her charge—such a respectable nurse, too, never suspected of drinking until now! He ended with a passionate appeal to the Conservative party not to 'reward this political tergiversation' by supporting the Minister; and he ended in a storm of applause. [3]

It was obvious that the malcontents would not lack a leader, if they were willing to accept such a one: but Disraeli's position was still insecure. The Tories might listen with delight to his witty and exuberant denunciations; but they were not likely to acknow-

[1] *Speeches*, iv. p. 567 ff.   [2] Disraeli, *Bentinck*, p. 38.
[3] *Hansard*, lxxxiii. p. 111 ff.

ledge as their official chief an upstart and a Jew.   At this moment, however, there appeared, as if by art magic, a leader who possessed all the qualifications lacked by Disraeli, and who was admirably suited to run in double harness with him.   Henceforth he supplied the prestige and position, Disraeli the brains.

Lord George Bentinck had been for almost twenty years a member of Parliament, without ever speaking in the House.   His only title to political distinction was that he was a distant cousin of Canning's, and had once acted as his private secretary.   Lord George had, however, sought renown in other quarters ;   not Stanley's name was better known on the Turf than his, and as an owner of racehorses he had obtained a fame and influence among the rank and file of the Tory party such as many gifted and distinguished statesmen could never hope for.   Fearless, obstinate, absolutely destitute of that indefinable quality called ' good taste,' with a strangely violent temper underlying his superficial good nature, Lord George had still great, though rather undeveloped, capacity.   He had no ambition to excel in the House of Commons ;   only the urgency of the crisis called him from the innocent joys of the Turf to the toil and passions of the political arena.   In the words of one of his biographers, ' Driven by a lofty sense of duty . . . he renounced the turf without a murmur, sold his stud, and lost the chance, which surely would have been his, of winning the Derby ! . . .' [1]   Bentinck himself expressed his motives in less exalted language :   ' I don't like to be *done*,' he said simply and earnestly.

In a short time the greater number of the Tories, under the more or less official leadership of Bentinck, with Disraeli as his familiar spirit and most able supporter, organised themselves into an opposition to Sir Robert Peel.   They had not much hope of defeating the Corn Bill, but they could at least delay its passage, and they might, by some lucky chance or skilful manœuvre, by some temporary combination with Leaguers, or Irish, or Whigs, secure its rejection.   They could, at all events, revenge themselves on the leader who had betrayed them.

Peel's position was thus very insecure.   He could only count on the support of about a hundred of his own party, who soon became known as ' Peelites.'   Then there were the Whigs, a large and powerful body, generally pledged to support repeal, but not

[1] Whibley, *Manners*, i. pp. 213-5.

all of one mind about it, and most of them very unfriendly to Peel himself. The Tory Protectionists numbered over two hundred, and they were irreconcilably hostile. The sixty Irish members were always a doubtful quantity. There remained the Radicals and the Leaguers, and it might be thought that on the League at least Peel could rely with complete confidence ; but unfortunately this was not the case.

Cobden had never forgotten the old quarrel. He was addressing a meeting of his constituents at Stockport when Peel's resignation had been announced, and, excited by the cheers of the audience, he broke out into a savage personal attack upon the fallen Minister. Later, when Peel had returned to office, and it was known that he meant to repeal the Corn Laws, Villiers wrote to Cobden to propose joint support of Peel's measure, but the great agitator replied in a surly tone, ' disinclined to say what he would do, and hinting at uniting with the Protectionists to throw out Peel and his measure.' [1] He repeated his attack on Peel at a great public meeting in London ; and his followers hesitated, and held back the whole-hearted support which they inclined to give the Government, from a feeling of loyalty to their chief.

It had been open to Cobden, when he considered Peel's apology insufficient, to request a further explanation, either by a question in Parliament, by a private letter to Peel, or by the intervention of mutual acquaintances ; and so his friends had urged him to do. He had refused, under the singular delusion that he was thus pursuing a more Christian course. Three years' brooding had made the hasty retort of a sensitive man, in a moment of nervous strain and wounded feeling, appear to Cobden as ' a deliberate attempt at moral assassination, which I cannot and ought not to forget.' [2] The request for an apology, which might have been made so easily in 1843, now appeared to be impossible. Nevertheless, one of Cobden's friends determined to make the attempt, though without his knowledge. Miss Martineau was not acquainted with Sir Robert Peel, but she thought him to be a man capable of rising above petty feeling. She wrote to him, explained Cobden's feelings, and begged him now to make the reparation which had been partially withheld in 1843.

---

[1] *Greville*, v. p. 357.

[2] To George Combe, February, 1846. Morley, *Cobden*, i. p. 353. He added, ' I should forfeit my own respect . . . if I ever exchanged a word with that man (Peel) in private.'

'Most people,' she wrote, 'would say that it is now impossible for you to set the matter right, Mr. Cobden having insulted you as he has done. But I believe not only that what is just and generous always may be done, but that you are a great doer of the impossible, in the government of yourself as well as in the Government of the country.'

A few weeks before, Peel had been informed, through the agency of Fremantle and Graham, that Cobden still harboured resentment against him. He had replied then, and now wrote to Miss Martineau, that until that moment he had not had the 'slightest conception that he laboured under any such impression.' Why, he asked, did not Cobden tell him that he thought a further apology necessary ? Why did no third party inform him of Cobden's feeling ? It was impossible at this date to make an apology in Parliament—it would imply that he had deliberately withheld the apology for three years ; it would also imply (though Peel did not say this) that it was only made now in order to secure the support of the League for the Corn Bill.

Miss Martineau now wrote to Cobden, 'the most artful letter I ever penned,' not hinting that she had approached the enemy, but preparing him to expect 'some magnanimous offer of an *amende*,' for she feared that if taken by surprise he might lose his head and fail to respond. The *amende*, as it happened, was made the very next day. Disraeli—who if he had guessed the result of his words would assuredly have held his tongue—chose to taunt Peel with having once ' accused an honourable member of abetting assassination.' Peel was quick to seize the opportunity : he rose and declared he was anxious ' unequivocally to withdraw an imputation thrown out in the heat of debate, under an erroneous impression of the honourable member's meaning.' The morning's post brought Miss Martineau a copy of the *Times*, autographed by Peel and marked by him, and a hasty note from Cobden, scrawled at three o'clock in the morning, saying he could not lie down to sleep without sending her ' the blessing on the peacemaker.' Henceforth the support of the League was given without stint or reluctance to the Government, and Cobden, warmhearted and generous, had soon forgotten his old enmity in a deep admiration for the Prime Minister.[1]

[1] Martineau, *Autobiography*, pp. 259-264. Parker, *Peel*, pp. 330-3. Morley, *Cobden*, i. 351, omits Miss Martineau's part.

It was well ; for events showed that as yet the Government had little favour to expect from the electorate. The resignation of Stanley, and the death of Wharncliffe at almost the same moment, had necessitated the reconstruction of the Cabinet. Gladstone had taken Stanley's place, Dalhousie entered the Cabinet, Ellenborough became First Lord of the Admiralty, and Lincoln Secretary for Ireland. Besides these changes, Ashley and several others who followed Peel had thought it their duty to resign their seats on their change of opinion, and there was thus a whole series of by-elections in the spring of 1846. In almost every case the Peelite candidate was defeated. Gladstone lost his seat with the rest, and for the whole session he continued to act as Colonial Secretary and sit in the Cabinet while out of Parliament. The loss of his services in the Commons was one of the heaviest blows the Government had to meet.

It is difficult at the present day to realise the intensity of the feeling aroused by the Corn Law question : it not only shattered the Conservative party : it divided families and destroyed old friendships. A few instances may be given.

Lord Lincoln, the eldest of a family of motherless children, had been from childhood his father's pride and darling. He supported Peel, and the old Duke cast him off. When he stood for re-election in Nottingham, all Newcastle's influence was used against him, he was defeated, and father and son were not on speaking terms for years, and were, indeed, only reconciled at the Duke's deathbed.

Sidney Herbert was remarkable for his gentle and amiable manners. He and the Earl of Malmesbury had been from boyhood ' like brothers.' Malmesbury was one of the leaders of the Protectionist opposition in the House of Lords. Herbert encountered him in Lady Palmerston's drawing-room, and, walking up to him, said, ' that my conduct in leaving Peel was unworthy of a gentleman, that the whole Protectionist party were a set of fools, and Lord Stanley the greatest fool among us, and that Peel was delighted at having got rid of us, etc.' [1] The excited young man afterwards apologised.

Peel's friendship with Croker, though less intimate than once, had lasted until now. Finding his friend an incorrigible gossip, Peel had necessarily become less confidential about political affairs,

[1] Malmesbury, *Memoirs* i. p. 169.

but in private life they were as cordial as ever. Now Croker
attacked his old friend, not only in two hysterical articles in the
Quarterly, but in a series of private letters to mutual friends, in
which he accused Peel of abject cowardice and of inventing the
Irish famine to serve his ends. He wrote in this strain even to
Hardinge and to Wellington, whom he eagerly strove to detach
from the Government. 'My dear Croker,' replied the Duke,
'the influence of fear is certainly very strong, and it is difficult to
have evidence of it. I cannot doubt that which passed under my
own view and frequent observation day after day. I mean the
alarms of the consequences in Ireland of the potato disease. I
never witnessed in any case such agony.' 'You were not deceived,'
replied Croker, 'as to the fact, but only as to the cause. The
agony was real and intense, but it was the agony of a man who was
deluding and betraying his conscience and his colleagues.' [1]

Peel had expected a hard fight and the secession of the Ultra-
Tories : he had probably not anticipated such a powerful, well-
organised, and vindictive opposition as he had to face. The
Tories set themselves to fight every step of the Corn Bill, and the
essential part of their tactics was a savage and reckless attack upon
the Prime Minister. They accused him of the basest falsehood,
the most contemptible cowardice, of self-seeking ambition and
persistent duplicity. They declared there was no Irish famine—
that it was all a scare got up by Peel to cover his treachery. The
reckless violence of Bentinck was well supported by the coarse
invective of such men as Sibthorp and Ferrand ; but Disraeli in
particular showed an exquisite ingenuity of cruelty. 'Dis' had
got the chance of a lifetime : he could at last make a place for
himself in English politics.

He had that quality of draining every transient emotion to the
dregs, which he had so admirably portrayed in *Contarini Fleming* ; he acted his own life as Garrick acted a part, he savoured
like an epicure the taste of every dramatic moment. He saw
himself as the passionate lover of his queer wife : he saw himself,
in his momentary association with 'Young England,' as the
champion of an oppressed people : he saw himself as the devoted
Minister of a great Queen : he saw himself as the Machiavellian
statesman dictating terms to Europe at Berlin : at times, too, he
saw himself as the cynical observer, playing at life and despising it

[1] *Croker*, iii. pp. 65-6.

—Sidonia. But Disraeli was never so wholly artificial in his emotions as Contarini Fleming; he always saw the whole of the picture, he was always the artist as well as the actor; and, on the other hand, he always kept something of the affectionate, excitable boy, who had poured out his hopes and fears in artless, affected letters to his sister Sarah. So it was that under his exaggerations he had a real affection for his elderly and unattractive Mary Anne, a real enthusiasm for his dumpy little ' Fairy Queen.' And so it was that now, even while he saw himself as the gallant young statesman rallying a betrayed party against an apostate leader, he also saw the question from the other side. His sympathetic imagination had long since penetrated Peel's disguise: where others thought the Minister cold and unfeeling, ' Dis ' knew well that he was dealing with a high-strung and over-sensitive mind, and attacked the Minister's weak points with unfailing dexterity and skill. But he was at the same time too able not to see that Peel's policy was the only statesmanlike one. He himself cared not a pin for the Corn Laws: economic questions did not interest him, save where he could transmute them into romance. Now, it was partly with envy, partly with sympathy, that he surveyed his great adversary: he could not but admire and understand: [1] but he had his wounded vanity to avenge, and his ambition to satisfy, and his dramatic instincts enabled him to play his part convincingly.

A bill dealing with the revenue must be introduced by a series of resolutions in Committee. On January 27th the motion to go into committee was made: it was debated so obstinately that it could not be carried until February 16th. This was only a fore-taste of what was to come. Villiers, with singular obtuseness, insisted on proposing a resolution for immediate repeal, which gave the Protectionists an excellent opportunity for protracting the debates. It was not until March 20th that leave to bring in the bill was given. Peel accompanied the Corn Bill with a Customs Bill, removing many of the remaining protective duties on manufactures—in order that the agriculturists might not have excuse to say that they were being unfairly used—and this, of course, offered new possibilities of hindrance. When the bill went into Committee the same thing occurred—each separate clause

---

[1] I think this is very clear from the tone of *Lord George Bentinck*. One has only to contrast the hollow and unconvincing rhapsodies about Bentinck, who remains totally unreal throughout the book, with the powerful, vivid, and, in spite of many misrepresentations, sympathetic portrait of Peel.

was pulled to bits, and at each a Protectionist member would rise and move to ' report progress,' and a prolonged discussion would follow.

In the meantime the increasing scarcity in Ireland had produced an outburst of agrarian crime, and the Government thought it necessary to introduce a new Coercion Bill. It passed the House of Lords first, and reached the Commons early in March. Disraeli was quick to seize the chance. The Conservatives could not in consistency—and at present they were singing the praises of consistency night and day—refuse to support the bill : but Bentinck was put up to declare that if coercion was necessary, then the need must be immediate, and the Coercion Bill ought to take precedence of the Corn Bill, and the Government ought to show they were in earnest by pressing it before all else. This put the Government in a dilemma : they were already being accused of paltering with Irish famine by pressing another measure before the Corn Bill was passed. Peel, in spite of the risk, resolved to press on both bills simultaneously, giving precedence, however, to the Corn Bill : and the accusations of the extremists drew from him a defiant declaration that the restrictions on food, which he had once considered ' impolitic,' he now considered ' unjust,' and that if necessary he was fully prepared to dissolve Parliament in order to carry the Corn Bill.

Stimulated, as usual, by opposition—' pleased with the danger when the waves went high '—he still kept his temper and his spirits. He was not provoked into angry retort. It is noteworthy that some of the most amusing passages in his speeches occur during this stormy session, and would give a casual reader the impression that the orator was bubbling over with fun.[1] The news of the Indian victories arrived in the early spring, and gave some glory to the administration and the most whole-hearted delight to the Prime Minister. To his absent friend he poured out his hopes and fears :

' I congratulate you most heartily on the glorious battles. Your escape and that of your sons, amid all the perils that surrounded you, have filled us with delight and gratitude to God for your preservation. God bless you, my dear Hardinge. Excuse

[1] *E.g.*, the famous passage about the Recorder of Dublin's housemaid, and the reply to Mr. Miles . . . " the honourable gentleman, who takes his stand upon grease . . ."

my hurried letter. I am fighting a desperate battle here; shall probably drive my opponents over the Sutlej; but what is to come afterwards I know not.'

'I know not how a Government having only 112 supporters of its own party. . . . can stand. But you have shown that a small minority can beat a large majority, and possibly we may profit by your example. Your successes have given us moral strength. . . . The memory of Afghanistan and Kabul seemed to revive on Conservative benches, and protection of national honour seemed for a moment to outweigh protection of national wheat.'

'There never was such a session as you have had,' his indignant friend replied, 'more than enough to disgust you forever with public life. . . . What injustice attends a public man's career! I am praised, and you are scandalously abused. It really makes me ashamed.' [1]

In the House of Commons, unshaken by the storm of reprobation with which he was assailed, he steadily maintained his position, and appealed to the good sense and good feeling of his opponents.

'Do you believe,' he asked them, 'that it would be for the credit and honour of the aristocracy to say, "We throw upon the Government the responsibility of averting the evils of famine, but not one letter of the existing Corn Laws shall be altered?" Would it be fidelity to the landed interest were I to counsel this? No; I believe that, whatever might have been the outward show of consistency, such a proposal would be the real "treachery" which you impute to me, because I have thought it for your interest, and the interest of all, to relieve ourselves from the odium of stipulating for these restrictions on food in such a moment of pressure.'

The contention that the rumours of famine were exaggerated he answered fiercely with: 'Are you to hesitate in averting famine which may come, because it possibly may not come? Are you to look on and depend upon chance in such an extremity? Or, good God! are you to sit in Cabinet and consider and calculate how much diarrhoea and bloody flux and dysentery a people can bear before it becomes necessary for you to provide them with food? Is it not better to err on the side of precaution than to neglect it utterly?'

'This night,' he said to them, 'you will select the motto which

[1] Parker, *Peel*, iii. pp. 301-2, 309-10.

is to indicate the commercial policy of England. Shall it be
" advance " or " recede " ?   Which is the fitter motto for this
great Empire ?   Survey our position ;   consider the advantages
which God and nature have given us, and the destiny for which
we are intended.   We stand on the confines of Western Europe,
the link between the old world and the new. . . .   Iron and coal,
the sinews of manufacture, give us advantages over every rival.
. . . In ingenuity, in skill, in energy, we are inferior to none.
Our national character, the free institutions under which we live,
the liberty of thought and action, an unshackled press, spreading
the knowledge of every discovery and every advance in science,
combine with our natural and physical advantages to place us at
the head of those nations which profit by the free interchange of
their products.   And is this the country to shrink from competition ?   Is this the country which can only flourish in the
sickly, artificial atmosphere of prohibition ?   Is this the country
to stand shivering on the brink of exposure to the healthful breezes
of competition ?

' You may fail. . . . It seems to be incident to great prosperity
that there shall be a reverse, that the time of depression shall
follow the season of excitement and success. . . . Gloomy winters,
like those of 1841 and 1842, may again set in.   Are those winters
effaced from your memory ?   From mine they never, can be.
Commune with your own hearts, and answer me this question :
Will . . . it be no satisfaction to you to reflect, that by your own
act, you have been relieved from the grievous responsibility of
regulating the supply of food ?   Will you not then cherish with
delight the reflection that, in this present hour of comparative
prosperity, yielding to no clamour, impelled by no fear, except,
indeed, that provident fear that is the mother of safety, you had
anticipated the evil day, and long before its advent had trampled
on every impediment to the free circulation of the Creator's
bounty ? ' [1]

But of what avail were such arguments and appeals to men
inspired only by rage and fear, or moved by personal ambition ?
The opposition only grew more violent, and the strain began to
tell on the Minister.   In Committee he yielded to the tactics of
delay, confessing that he had not the physical strength to fight
any longer.   One night, after a fierce debate, he remained in his

[1] *Speeches,* iv. pp. 611, 639, 625-6.

seat sunk in thought long after all was ended and the House emptied. The Ministers left the bench one by one, with backward glances. Only one or two friends waited at a distance, watching him, but not venturing to speak. At last the attendants, entering to put out the lights, roused him from his meditation.[1]

As the struggle neared its end the rage of the Protectionists was redoubled. All their efforts had failed—the Whigs had refused every overture for coalition against the Government. On the 15th of May the bill passed its third reading, after an extraordinary scene. Peel had hitherto ignored Disraeli, but now, driven beyond endurance by a malicious attack, he at last rose to reply. With a rather pitiful attempt at indifference, he declared that the least of all the penalties he anticipated when he changed his policy was ' the continued venomous attacks of the member for Shrewsbury ' ; and went on to ask why, if Disraeli had always held such a low opinion of his character and capacity as he pretended, he should have asked him for office in 1841 ? He then passed to a fresh defence of his own conduct, and disclaimed ' any personal object of ambition.' But he had no sooner got out the words than the Tories rose at him, yelling and hooting, with gestures of execration and contempt. The Minister stopped short ; he said, ' I think it is hardly fair to interrupt me by such exclamations, but it has so far succeeded——' and his voice failed. The Speaker thought he was going to burst into tears. He stood silent, choking for a moment, and then recovered himself and went quietly on.

When he had ended, Disraeli rose, and, with little of his usual dexterity, explicitly denied that he had ever asked Peel for office. Peel quietly repeated his ' not very chivalrous taunt,' as Disraeli's biographer calls it,[2] and the incident was dropped. It left the hearers puzzled. Not until thirty years passed, and both protagonists were dead, did Peel's executors publish Disraeli's letter, and the truth was known. Peel himself never produced the letter, though he probably had it before him as he spoke—at least, he showed it to Lincoln as they walked to the House together in the morning. Disraeli took a desperate risk, but he knew the man he had to deal with, and he knew, moreover, that in 1830 (though in

---

[1] Disraeli (Bentinck, p. 143) gives a fine description ; but one would have liked to hear Carlyle on this incident.

[2] Monypenny, Disraeli, ii. p. 389.

less atrocious circumstances) Peel had refused to make use of similar evidence to confute Joseph Hume.[1] Nevertheless, his position for the rest of the session, thus completely at the mercy of his enemy, cannot have been too happy.[2]

It was now obvious that the end was near. The Corn Bill was going through the Lords without real difficulty : Stanley and Malmesbury opposed it, but without employing the tactics of Bentinck and Disraeli. The Duke of Wellington had told the House that they had no option but to pass a fiscal bill agreed to by the Commons, and their lordships were clearly disposed to obey him. It was, however, equally clear that the passage of the Corn and Customs Bills would be the signal for the fall of the Government.

The Whigs were humiliated and resentful at the pitiful figure they had cut in December. Russell was in the sulks : according to Greville, he had at first hesitated about supporting Peel. ' He saw no reason why he should do anything to assist him . . . that he (Peel) had no claim on him. I told Clarendon that the real truth was that he was jealous of Peel's popularity and the prevailing opinion that he was the best man. It is all very small, but he *is* small.' [3] Fortunately for himself, if Lord John had really had any such petty jealousy, he had overcome it, and had supported the Corn Bill throughout. Bentinck had offered him a coalition and full support, if he would adhere to the lines of his Budget of 1841,[4] but he refused them. At the end of May, a Protectionist-Whig intrigue, in which Palmerston, Bessborough, and Anglesey were said to be involved, was crushed by his vigorous action.[5] As soon, however, as the Corn Bill was safe, Lord John meant this temporary alliance to come to an end.

' If Peel should . . . propose the repeal of the Corn Laws,' Macaulay had said in December, ' my course is clear. I must support him with all the energy that I have, till the question is carried. Then I am free to oppose him.' [6] It may be assumed

---

[1] See above, p. 138.

[2] Monypenny (*Disraeli*, ii. p. 393) insinuates that Peel would have produced the letter, but could not find it, giving as evidence an anecdote of Rosebery's. The anecdote (Rosebery, *Peel*, p. 9), so far as it proves anything, proves the exact contrary. The testimony of Lincoln shows that Peel actually had the letter in his despatch-case. *Reminiscences* of Goldwin Smith, p. 177. G. S. took a note of the incident from Lincoln's lips.

[3] *Greville*, v. p. 373. [4] Disraeli, *Bentinck*, p. 167.
[5] *Greville*, v. p. 402. [6] Trevelyan, *Macaulay*, p. 455.

that Macaulay expressed the sentiments of his party, for this is the precise course which they followed.

The Protectionists were beaten, but they could at least console themselves with the sweets of revenge. A coalition with the Whigs might defeat the Government : and Disraeli selected the Coercion Bill as the occasion of it. There was a trifling difficulty in the matter : both Bentinck and Russell had supported the Coercion Bill in its earlier stages. Both, however, had safeguarded themselves in view of subsequent change. Bentinck had declared he would only support coercion if the Government proved that they considered the need really urgent—and the Government had postponed it to the Corn Bill : Russell had said he would modify the details of the bill in Committee, and it was easy to declare that on consideration he found it bad beyond all modification. Russell, however, would not move until the Corn Bill was safe, and it was therefore necessary to delay the crisis a little. Bentinck effected this by a fresh attack upon Peel.

When the debate upon the Coercion Bill was renewed, he created a diversion by accusing Peel of having ' hunted an illustrious relative of his to death,' the illustrious relative, of course, being Canning. Disraeli had contrived to rout out an inaccurate report in the *Times* of one of Peel's old speeches, and on the strength of this Bentinck declared that Peel had changed his mind on the subject of Catholic Emancipation as early as 1825, but that he had concealed it until Canning was dead, and he himself could profit by revealing his opinions. He said that Peel was ' convicted by his own verdict of base and dishonest conduct,' and that he had for a second time ' insulted the honour of Parliament and the country.' So morbid and feverish had become the political atmosphere that this grotesque travesty of the facts obtained some credit. Peel himself seems to have been almost overwhelmed at first by the sudden and vicious attack. A year ago he could have ignored it : now he was obliged to send to Drayton for his papers, and after submitting them to unprejudiced witnesses, he read all the letters bearing upon the subject to the House. It is hardly necessary to add that Bentinck himself could not have believed a word of his accusation. He had been Canning's private secretary, and must have known Canning's high opinion of Peel. He had himself served for many years under Peel's leadership, without any qualms about his ' illustrious relative.' Canning's own son was now in Peel's Government, one of his most loyal adherents. The Minister vindicated himself with complete success, and sat down amid enthusiastic cheering from a House disgusted by the injustice and malice of the attack. Only Bentinck, impervious to reason, refused to withdraw, and bawled out his accusations afresh : only Russell, while admitting that Peel had cleared himself, thought it necessary to say he had been unfair to Canning, and attacked him for inconsistency. The feeling of the House was with Roebuck, the most distinguished of the younger Radicals, when he rose in towering indignation, and expressed ' his strong feeling of gratitude to the right honourable baronet, and his supereminent carelessness and contempt for the right honourable baronet's opponents.' [1]

' Nothing could be more miserable than the figure which that choice pair, George Bentinck and Disraeli, cut . . .' noted Greville, who had come down to the House to see the fun. ' The abortive attempt to ruin (Peel's) character, which has so signally failed and recoiled on the heads of his accusers, has gathered round him feelings of sympathy which will find a loud and general echo in the country.' [2]

Peel himself was not satisfied with the result. The accusation had not been withdrawn ; and, walking home from the House, he confided to Lincoln that he was going to challenge George Bentinck, and that he must carry the cartel. Lincoln flatly refused ; but Peel was resolute—if Lincoln would not act for him, he would get someone else, but fight he would. They walked up and down, the young man anxiously remonstrating, till it was full daylight, and labourers began to pass along the streets on their way to work. At last Lincoln induced him to desist—not, as one romantic story has it, by appealing to his loyalty to Queen Victoria, but by the more prosaic expedient of threatening to inform the police.[3]

It was the only outward sign that the Minister gave of resentment. His private letters contain no complaint, and not one single reference to Disraeli. In later days, Edward Cardwell said to Lady Peel that he ' never heard him speak unkindly of his

---

[1] The debate is in *Hansard*, lxxxvii. p. 700 ff. A summary (omitting Roebuck !) is given in Disraeli, *Bentinck*, chapter xv.

[2] Greville, v. p. 408.

[3] Martineau, *Newcastle*, p. 80. *Reminiscences* of Goldwin Smith, p. 176.

persecutors.' 'Yes,' said she, ' but you cannot know that he would never allow me to do so.' [1]

The victory over Bentinck was a moral victory and no more. John Russell announced that he would vote against the third reading of the Coercion Bill ' for reasons satisfactory to himself.' On the 28th of June the Corn Bill passed the House of Lords : and on the same day the Government was beaten on the Coercion Bill by a coalition of Whigs, Radicals, and Protectionists, and by a majority of seventy-three. The Radicals had all along opposed the bill, and could do nothing else : but in justice to the Protectionists it must be stated that only some seventy followed their leader upon his devious course. Eighty absented themselves, and about a hundred, under the leadership of Lord Chandos, took the honourable course of supporting the Government which they hated rather than voting against a measure which they held to be necessary.

On the following day Sir Robert Peel announced the resignation of the Government : he announced at the same time that the question of the Canadian frontier was settled, the United States having accepted the proposals of Great Britain without the alteration of a word.

He referred with some pride to the achievements of his five years' Government : to honourable peace secured in Europe and America, to the victories in India that had repaired the disasters of the Afghan War, to reduced taxation, increasing consumption, growing trade and buoyant finances at home.

He had no complaints to make. It was natural that his friends should have withdrawn their confidence from him. When Ministers appeared to change their course, and laid themselves open to the charge of inconsistency, it was perhaps better ' for this country and for the general character of public men ' that they should be punished by expulsion from office. ' I, therefore, do not complain of that expulsion. I am sure it is far preferable to the continuance of office without a full assurance of the confidence of this House.' But he must take no credit where it was not due : he could not claim credit for the measures which he had carried, nor could the Whigs. ' The name which ought to be associated with the success of these measures is not the name of the noble lord (Lord John Russell), nor is it mine. The name which ought to be, and will

---

[1] Parker, *Peel*, vol. ii., Introduction, p. 17.

be, associated with the success of these measures is the name of one who, acting, as I believe, from pure and disinterested motives, has, with untiring energy, made appeals to our reason, and has enforced these appeals with an eloquence the more to be admired because it was unaffected and unadorned ; the name which ought to be chiefly associated with the success of these measures is the name of Richard Cobden.

' . . . In relinquishing power, I shall leave a name severely censured by many who, on public grounds, deeply regret the severance of party ties . . . severely censured also by others who, from no interested motive, adhere to the principle of Protection, considering the maintenance of it to be essential to the welfare and interests of the country : I shall leave a name execrated by every monopolist, who, from less honourable motives, clamours for Protection because it conduces to his own individual benefit ; but it may be that I shall leave a name sometimes remembered with expressions of goodwill in the abodes of those whose lot it is to labour, and to earn their bread by the sweat of their brow, when they shall recruit their exhausted strength with abundant and un-taxed food, the sweeter because it is no longer leavened by a sense of injustice.' [1]

[1] *Speeches,* iv. pp. 709-717.

CHAPTER XVIII

ABDICATION, 1846-1850

' I DO not know how other men are constituted, but I can say with truth that I find the day too short for my present occupations, which consist chiefly in lounging in my library, directing improvements, riding with the boys and my daughter, and pitying Lord John and his colleagues.' So wrote Peel to Aberdeen from Drayton, whither he had gone to idle away the rest of the session. He had resolved that Parliament should never see him as anything but a private member again, if he could help it.

' I intend to keep aloof from party combinations,' he told Hardinge, ' so far as a man can be justified in forming such a resolution, I am determined not again to resume office. I would be nothing but the head of a Government, the real bona-fide head, and to be that requires more youth, more ambition, more love of official power and official occupation than I can pretend to. I will take care, too, not again to burn my fingers by organising a party. There is too much truth in the saying, " The head of a party must be directed by the tail." As heads see, and tails are blind, I think heads are the best judges as to the course to be taken.' [1]

When it had become clear that the Government would be beaten on the Coercion Bill, two men, strangely different in character and opinion, wrote to Peel and urged upon him the same course : let him dissolve Parliament and go to the country on the strength of his own character and measures. ' The question,' wrote Wellington, ' will be, whether you are to continue the Minister, or the Queen is to look for other servants. . . . I am very much mistaken if you should not be supported by a majority of the thinking men of the country.' ' I would dissolve within the next two months,' wrote Cobden, ' . . . I would go to the country with my Free Trade laurels fresh upon my brow, and whilst the grievance under which I was suffering from the out-

[1] Parker, *Peel*, iii. pp. 457, 474.

rages of Protectionist speakers and writers was still rankling in the minds of people. . . . Whatever may be the difficulties in your Cabinet, . . . you have in your own individual will the power, backed by the country, to accomplish all that the loftiest ambition or the truest patriotism ever aspired to identify with the name and fame of one individual.' [1]

Peel replied to both his correspondents in the same sense. He had disclaimed personal ambition, and he would not now make such an appeal to the country. He would not risk the embitterment of racial feeling by going to the English constituencies on the question of a Coercion Act for Ireland. He would not combine with men who, while they agreed with him on the question of Free Trade, yet differed from him radically on other subjects of the first importance.[2]

This decision was partly due to the fact that he felt unfit to endure the strain of office again. He was, it has been said, the last Prime Minister. Since his time, the work and responsibility of the great departments have fallen on their respective chiefs: but Peel never permitted this. He controlled every branch of the nation's policy, made himself master of every problem, and entered even into details. Able as were his lieutenants, the policy of each department was Peel's policy, not Aberdeen's or Graham's or Stanley's. Ellenborough in India, owing to the difficulty of communication, had alone gone beyond his control.

The work was overwhelming. Apart from the regular official labours, there was the attendance, usually through the night, in Parliament, where all the time the Minister's faculties were strained to the utmost observing and answering his opponents, and where he must be continually on his guard against a hundred hostile glances, ready to note any weakness. ' I was not able to get anything to eat till near one o'clock last night, being obliged to sit in the House of Commons watching a debate as if I was hatching an egg,' he wrote to his wife, in an expressive simile.[3] Then there was the regular attendance on the royalties, the correspondence with the Queen and Prince, which must go off three or four times a day, all written in the Minister's own hand and

---

[1] Wellington to Peel, 21st June, 1846. Parker, *Peel,* iii. p. 365. Cobden to Peel, 23rd June. Morley, *Cobden,* i. p. 390.

[2] Peel to Wellington, 23rd June. Parker, iii. p. 366. Peel to Cobden, 24th June. Parker, iii. p. 167. Morley, *Cobden,* i. p. 397.

[3] *Private Letters,* p. 233.

best writing, and expressed in language simple enough for Victoria to understand it without difficulty; and the frequent necessity of dashing off to Windsor to dine and sleep, and squander a precious evening on inane chat and round games. George IV. and William IV. left something to be desired as sovereigns, but at least they did not subject their Ministers to such bondage as this. 'What a sad pity!' is Peel's comment to Julia, on one of these gracious invitations, 'The last day before the recommencement of the House of Commons, and when every moment of to-morrow morning is precious to me. A thousand thanks for the violets, which I had on my breakfast table this morning, a sad contrast to my blue-boxes.' [1]

For many years Peel had suffered, when over-worked, from pain and noises in the head—afflictions that seem trifling to those who have not experienced them. He was not afraid of dying in harness, but his private bogey was the fear of dying mad or imbecile, as he had seen Liverpool and Castlereagh die. The Queen pressed on him an Earldom and the Garter: he refused both, but said he would ask of her one favour—that she would not send for him again.

There was, however, another reason for his decision. He was done with the Tories at last. Deeply wounded and bitterly angry at the way he had been treated, he was resolute that nothing should make him seek or accept reconciliation. Croker, who had a little repented his first wrath, wrote to him to express a hope that, though they could not again resume their intimate correspondence, they might still meet as friends.

'Sir,' replied Sir Robert, '... I concur entirely in the opinion you express, that any personal intercourse between us would be awkward and painful. There are no doubt many cases in which personal goodwill may coexist with strong political differences, but personal goodwill cannot coexist with the spirit in which these articles' (in the *Quarterly Review*) 'were written, or with the feelings they must naturally have excited. I trust there is nothing inconsistent with perfect civility in the expression of an earnest wish that the same principle which suggests to you the propriety of closing a written correspondence of seven-and-thirty years, may be extended to every other species of intercourse. I have the honour to be, Sir, your obedient servant, Robert Peel.' [2]

---

[1] *Private Letters*, p. 184. [2] *Croker*, iii. p. 94.

' Protectionists indeed ! ' the fallen Minister wrote bitterly to a friend, ' to close their eyes to the result of every commercial experiment that has been made—to find every one of their predictions falsified—to disregard the state of public opinion—to call the Corn Laws a labourers' question, and yet listen to the appalling facts as to the condition for years past of the labourers in Dorsetshire . . . to be willing to encounter the tremendous risks of two bad harvests and the recurrence of such a state of things in Paisley and Stockport as was witnessed in the winters of 1841 and 1842— not to see that the Corn Laws would . . . be swept away with dishonour on the demand of a starving population—this is to be a *Protectionist !*

' *Thank God I am relieved for ever from the trammels of such a party !* ' [1]

With feelings such as these, it may be imagined that Peel left office without regret. ' Such a transfer of power,' wrote Greville, ' . . . the world never saw before—no rivalry, no mortification, no disappointment, no triumph, no coldness.' [2] Peel saw Lord John and astonished him by his friendly, open, whole-hearted promise of support. He was asked if he would allow his young men to join the new Government, and replied that he thought it too soon, but would make no objection. Lord John then made overtures to Herbert, Lincoln, and Dalhousie, but they all refused him.

It was, indeed, impossible that anyone but himself should accept Peel's abdication. Russell could not, and never did, believe that he was sincere. His own fondness for office made it difficult for him to take such apparent abnegation seriously. Depending, as he must, on his late rival's support, acknowledging that he behaved ' in the most fair and honourable manner ; ' [3] he still could not rid himself of the fear that Peel might emerge from his isolation, like Napoleon from Elba, and shatter the crazy structure of Whig ascendancy.

It was, to be sure, very certain that he would never again lead the Tory party. His fine tribute to Cobden, in his farewell speech, was generally regarded as a deliberate defiance of his late followers, which should make reconciliation impossible. (It had besides given great offence to his own friends, especially Gladstone, who thought

[1] *Private Letters*, p. 281.   Italics Peel's.   [2] *Greville*, v. p. 410.
[3] *Recollections and Suggestions*, p. 243. The whole tone of the book shows that Russell did not take Peel's retirement seriously.

he should have complimented them, and not the great Leaguer.)
Wellington thought that Peel 'was tired of party, and meant to
destroy it.'[1] He was, after all, only fifty-eight : he was indis-
putably the first man in the country. All classes looked to him
as a tower of strength in time of trouble. 'If the country could
be polled,' Greville noted, ' he would be elected by an immense
majority. There is a prevalent opinion that he *must* return to
power ; nobody knows when or how, but the notion is that . . . if
a crisis of difficulty and danger arrive . . . Peel is the only man
capable of extricating the country from it.'[2] Men inclined more
and more to the opinion, that he would eventually return to
power, as a more or less independent minister, supported by the
Whigs and the Radicals, and leading a ministry composed of
Peelites and Whigs.

There was, however, a section of the Tories which already
regretted their lost chief. If Peel was a general without an army
the Tory party was uncommonly like an army without generals.
Peel had taken all their best men, save Stanley, with him.
Bentinck asked a discontented Tory whether he would prefer to
see Russell in power or ' kiss and be friends ' with Peel. ' Kiss
and be friends,' said the late rebel, unhesitatingly.[3]

The leaders, however, were not of this mind. Stanley had
found himself at last. There had never been a place for him in a
party led by Peel : now he was heir-presumptive to the Premiership, and he was not likely to surrender his honours before he had
enjoyed them. His opposition had been honourable : he had
remained good friends with his late chief : but he could not serve
under him again. As for Disraeli and Bentinck, it need not be
said that they shared his feelings.

Lyndhurst, however, had lost touch with the realities of politics,
and he saw in the situation an opportunity for intrigue. One of
the first measures of the Whigs was to reduce the sugar duties all
round, and propose the gradual extinction of the preference on
free-grown sugar. Lyndhurst attempted to combine the Peelites
and Protectionists against them. He was sadly disillusioned.
Bentinck noisily denounced the plan ; Stanley declared that he
' would not touch it with the tongs ; ' and Peel, in a fury of
indignation at what he regarded as a personal insult, gave a con-
temptuous refusal and forced Lyndhurst to read it to the House

---

[1] Morley, *Gladstone*, i. p. 290.   [2] *Greville*, vi. p. 104.   [3] *Croker*, iii. p. 140.

of Lords.[1] He had meant to fight slave-grown sugar to the end : but Free Trade came before all, and he supported the Government.

But it was the Peelites, more than any, who could not bring themselves to accept their chief's altered position. Gladstone declared that Peel's resolution was ' absolutely impossible to fulfil ; that with his greatness he could not remain there overshadowing and eclipsing all governments, and yet have to do with no government ; ' [2] sooner or later, he must adhere to one party or another. Cardwell nicknamed Sir Robert ' *le mort imaginaire.*' [3] The younger men could not take up such an attitude as Peel's ; they had great careers before them. Peel left them perfectly free— would accept no vows of allegiance—but he could not induce men who were enthusiastically attached to him to forsake him while he lived. Naturally, then, they sought to draw him back to the arena. Though few in numbers, the Peelites occupied a commanding position, partly owing to their high character and ability, and partly to the state of parties. At the general election they were all returned successfully, as were the Free Trade Radicals : but the country displayed no special enthusiasm for either Whigs or Tories, and the numbers of these two parties remained almost unchanged. The Peelites, therefore, held the balance : uniting with the Whigs, they made a solid majority for Free Trade ; but by uniting with the Tories, they could have just defeated the Government.

A difference of opinion soon developed between Peel and his younger followers. They were all for a bold stroke. They wanted to force the Protectionists' hand. If the Whigs were turned out, the Queen must send for Stanley. It was not unlikely that he would not be able to form a government at all : if he did, then he must in consistency introduce a measure of agricultural Protection, there would be a trial of strength, and they believed that Free Trade principles would be victorious. It was not unlikely that there would be such a confusion of parties, such a stirring of public opinion, that Peel would be sent for : they knew that the one thing which could induce him to forswear himself and return to office would be the necessity of defending Free Trade : and probably this was at the bottom of their schemings.

---

[1] Campbell, *Chancellors*, viii. p. 164.   *Hansard*, lxxxviii. pp. 948 ff., 972 ff.
[2] Morley, *Gladstone*, i. p. 292.   [3] Parker, *Peel*, iii. p. 480.

Peel, on the contrary, believed that it was of the first importance to maintain the Whigs in power, until the results of the new policy were seen, and Free Trade was firmly rooted. He thought the Protectionist opposition was stronger than his young friends believed, and that there might yet be a fierce struggle for the restoration of the Corn Laws. Such a struggle he wished to avoid, even if victory should ultimately be with Free Trade. The country was at present plunged in deep distress : the Irish famine, the universal scarcity, the bad harvests, and the commercial crisis of 1847, had produced a new depression, and until this was past, it seemed very unwise to provoke a fresh Corn Law crisis. He, like his friends, knew that in a difficult situation he might be sent for : and, unlike them, he did not desire this consummation.

Aberdeen, who was in despair over Palmerston's foreign policy, was ready enough to join in turning out the Whigs. Graham stuck to Peel loyally, but he had a good deal of secret sympathy with the malcontents. He was ' by way of being very friendly to the Government,' noted Greville, ' but is evidently not sorry to see their mismanagement and unpopularity.' [1]

The Government, therefore, came to rely more and more upon Peel's support : only his influence restrained his followers from some demonstration against the Whigs, and even he could not always hold them back, though they never deserted him *en masse*. Men of all parties waited to see ' what Peel would say ' before they made up their minds how to vote on this or that. The Whigs acquired the habit of turning to him for aid and advice in every crisis. Already in the summer of 1846 they had consulted him, when the potato crop failed completely, even as he had anticipated, and the horrors of literal starvation began in Ireland. He had supported them on the sugar duties. His influence enabled them to repeal the Navigation Acts ; Wood, the Whig Chancellor of the Exchequer, was in secret communication with him throughout the proceedings. In the autumn of 1847, hardly a year after they had turned him out on the Coercion Bill, they were forced by the state of Ireland to introduce a Coercion Bill of their own, and Peel steadily supported it. He approved and defended their action in suspending the Bank Act. In spite of the persuasions of Aberdeen, he would not join in condemning their foreign policy. Clarendon, the new and admirable Viceroy of Ireland, came

[1] *Greville*, vi. p. 149.

privately to consult him. He helped them to carry the renewal of the Income Tax. It was small wonder that by 1848 a large section of the Whig party were contemplating a coalition under his leadership, and Bedford, Clarendon, and Auckland all declared that it must end in this.

The ranks of the Peelites were already broken. Dalhousie had accepted the Viceroyalty of India, and gone to fulfil his destiny, that four years' glorious administration, from which he returned only to die, broken-hearted, amid unmerited reproach, at forty-seven. The younger men now broke loose from Peel's guidance, and tried to put their policy in practice. The sugar duties, so fruitful of disagreement, were again under discussion. They determined to turn out the Whigs : they believed it would prove impossible for the Protectionists to form a government, and they hoped ' by a sort of gentle violence to compel (Peel) to take it.' [1] Peel was much annoyed at their recklessness and disregard of his wishes. He continued to support the Whigs ; and, rather to the surprise of all, the Government contrived to labour through the crisis safely.

Immediately after, however, the situation was changed. During the vacation, Lord George Bentinck left his house in the country to walk through the woods to the home of a friend a few miles off. He did not return ; and at length his servants, becoming anxious, went out into the night with lanterns to search for him. They found him in a woodland path, lying face downwards on the earth, dead. Some sudden seizure of the heart, consequent on his prolonged and violent exertions in the past session, had carried him off.

Bentinck was the real leader, the animating spirit, of the Protectionist party. He was the only one that was entirely sincere. Disraeli cared not a farthing for the Corn Laws now that they had served his purpose : Stanley was a Protectionist, but he was too flippant to care very much for anything : both were too able and clear-sighted to think that Protection could at this hour be restored effectively. Only Bentinck, headstrong and single-minded, had been capable of taking the task seriously.

The position of the young Peelites was now strengthened ; there was more reason to think that the policy of calling the Tory bluff would be successful. But Peel held obstinately to his course, and perhaps he was right ; for in 1850 there was, for a moment,

[1] *Greville*, vi. pp. 203-4.

a Protectionist revival.   The Protectionists moved for a committee on agricultural distress, which the Government resisted.   Most of the Peelites, including Gladstone, voted with the Opposition. The situation seemed for a little while to be dangerous, and Peel was roused to unusual energy.   Walking home from the House with Cardwell, who had supported him, he declared that he would do anything rather than allow the taxes on food to be restored. Cardwell asked as to the truth of the general belief, that he would never under *any* circumstances resume office.   Peel answered, squeezing his companion's arm with a characteristic gesture, ' I never said that.' [1]   The division was close ; the Government was victorious by a majority of 21 only ; but it was the last effort of a dying cause.   Stanley and Disraeli recognised that it was the end, and before many months had elapsed they had publicly thrown over Protection.

A few months after his support had saved the Government on the agricultural vote, Peel found himself at last forced into opposition to them.

He had not been satisfied with Russell's conduct towards him in the meantime.   In spite of the loyal support he had given them, the Prime Minister had twice attacked him, and, he thought, very ungenerously.   Upon the trial of the Irish rebels in 1848, it was found that the juries had been packed, and Russell had defended himself by declaring that Peel authorised the packing of the jury in the trial of O'Connell.   This brought up Graham, who forced Lord John to admit that the instructions issued by Peel and by himself had been identical.   Next year, Lord John thought fit to revive old controversies, and attack Peel for his opposition to the Appropriation Clause in the 'thirties.   Peel was exceedingly hurt and disgusted, but it had not shaken his resolve, and even now, when his conscience impelled him to cast his vote against the Government, his opposition was moderate and fair.

The Russell Cabinet, formed in 1846, had included both Lord Grey and Lord Palmerston.   Grey had withdrawn his opposition to Palmerston's holding the Foreign Secretaryship for several reasons.   The dispute with the United States had been settled, and there was no longer danger of an American war ; and during the interval, the versatile Palmerston had visited Paris, and,

[1] Parker, *Peel*, iii. p. 504.

exerting all his undeniable charm, had ingratiated himself with the French King and society.

Notwithstanding this, however, Grey's forebodings were soon to be justified. Within a few months of Palmerston's return to office the French Alliance was broken—broken, to be sure, by France, but only because Palmerston's conduct had given Guizot reason to believe that he did not mean to keep the engagements that Aberdeen had made. Palmerston was angry, and from that moment his influence had been employed, regardless of all other considerations, to humiliate and annoy France. The injudicious conduct of the British Ambassador in Paris certainly aided him, and such a situation arose that the Minister of France could not meet the British Ambassador in society because secrets of State had passed from the British Embassy to the leader of Opposition. In Spain also, our ambassador, by Palmerston's instructions, was intriguing with the Opposition leaders against the Government.

The Revolution of 1848 reconciled Palmerston for a moment to the French, and he hastened to recognise, even effusively, the Republican Government. In the disordered state of Europe, he flung all the influence of Britain into the Liberal scale. Unfortunately his sympathy went no further than words, and, as far as the immediate result was concerned, had better have been withheld. By the hopes of British support, Sardinia was led to protract her hopeless struggle with Austria, and to meet with worse disaster. Palmerston's interference in favour of the Hungarian rebels brought him a moderate but cutting rebuke from Austria—a rebuke which even he could not answer. In all these proceedings Palmerston had acted on his own responsibility. He made hardly a pretence of consulting the Cabinet ; he repeatedly ignored the instructions of the Prime Minister and the Queen, and even reversed decisions, to which he had agreed, without informing them.

In 1850 an Athenian mob attacked and robbed the house of one Don Pacifico, a Spanish Jew residing in Greece, who had recently naturalised as a British subject. Palmerston demanded satisfaction for the outrage, and the Greeks, acting as usual on the principle ' never do to-day what you can put off until to-morrow,' answered him with vague platitudes. In return, the British fleet in the Mediterranean was ordered to the Greek coast, and seized the shipping lying at the Piraeus. This outrage, considerably more serious than that on Don Pacifico, brought a protest from Russia. France offered her good offices, and Palmerston accepted them.

Hardly, however, had the negotiations commenced, when the fleet was ordered to employ new measures of coercion, and the Greek Government, thoroughly frightened, agreed to pay a large indemnity forthwith. France, whose friendly offices had been thus repaid with a flagrant insult, withdrew her ambassador from London.

These events caused an extraordinary sensation, not only in Britain, but throughout Europe. The House of Lords passed a vote of censure on Palmerston's conduct, and Roebuck in the Commons countered by proposing a vote of confidence.

Peel had until now supported the general principles of the Government's foreign policy, while disapproving Palmerston's methods; but he could not bring himself to support Roebuck's motion. In this he was obliged to associate himself with Disraeli, who led the Tory opposition, and he was very unhappy at the necessity.[1] He opened his speech with an explicit declaration that he was not acting in concert with the Tories: but he went on to declare that conscientious motives made it impossible for him on this occasion to support the Government, and he rested his condemnation not merely on the affair of Don Pacifico, but on the whole trend of Palmerston's recent actions.

He was no partisan of the Greeks, he said, he was ' disgusted with their evasions and their delays ; ' but he believed that redress could have been secured without recourse to violence. The Government might have asked for the good offices of France ; above all, when it had accepted them, it might have adhered to the agreement taken. They would thus have obtained the good-will of France, Russia, and Greece, and avoided the public rebukes which Russia and France had given them ; they would have avoided the necessity of making apologies and concessions to France—' I blame you not,' he said, ' for having made that concession, rather than interrupt the cordial good understanding between the two countries ; but don't ask me to vote that the course you have taken is consistent with the honour and dignity of England.' What, he asked, is diplomacy ? ' It is a costly

---

[1] *Greville*, vi. pp. 366-7, gives an odd account of Peel's efforts to avoid an appearance of concert with Disraeli on an earlier occasion.

engine for maintaining peace. . . . If . . . your application of
diplomacy be to fester every wound, to provoke instead of soothing
resentments, to place a minister in every court of Europe for the
purpose, not of preventing quarrels . . . but of continuing an angry
correspondence, and for the purpose of promoting what is supposed to be an English interest . . . then I say, that this great
engine, used by civilised society for the purpose of maintaining
peace, is perverted into a cause of hostility and war.'

He had little disposition for angry controversy, he said, and he
would make no attempt to answer the whole of the speech in
which Palmerston had replied to his critics, a speech ' which
made us proud of the man who delivered it '; he would deal only
with one topic, ' a thousand times of more importance than a
question as to the existence of a particular government ': the
principle which Roebuck and Palmerston wished to affirm by the
authority of the House of Commons, that ' We are favourable to
those efforts of man, by which he endeavours to raise himself in
the scale of nations, and . . . to govern himself and resist that
tyranny, which, under the name of legitimacy, has ever sought to
crush in him all those powers which we, as Englishmen, consider
to be the very birthright that nature has given us.' What principle would he oppose to this ? Why, ' the principle for which
every statesman of eminence in this country for the last fifty
years has contended—namely, non-interference with the domestic
affairs of other countries, without some clear and undeniable
necessity, arising from circumstances affecting the interests of
your own country.' If Britain should claim the right to interfere,
in the interests of self-determination, in the affairs of foreign
states, how could she deny a like right to other powers ? How
could she deny to France the right to introduce Republican
institutions into neighbouring states ? How could Great Britain,
the greatest of imperialist powers, logically uphold the doctrine
of self-determination in all cases ? ' We govern millions of people
in India ; are we to admit the right of other powers to inculcate
the right of self-government among them ? ' By what possible
authority, then, could Britain claim a right which she did not
concede to others ? But, more ; he was convinced that ' You
will not advance the cause of constitutional government by attempting to dictate to other nations. If you do, your intentions
will be mistaken, you will rouse feelings upon which you do not

calculate, you will invite opposition to government; and beware,'
he added, in words that seem prophetic, ' that the time does not
arrive when, frightened by your own interference, you withdraw
your countenance from those whom you have excited, and leave
upon their minds the bitter recollection that you have betrayed
them. . . . Constitutional liberty will be best worked out by
those who aspire to freedom by their own efforts. You will only
overload it by your help. You are departing from the established
policy of England, you are involving yourselves in difficulties the
extent of which you can hardly conceive, you are bestowing no
aid on the cause of constitutional freedom, but are encouraging
its advocates to look to you for aid, instead of those efforts which
can alone establish it, and upon the successful exertion of which
it can alone be useful.' [1]

It was a plea for international peace and justice. ' If he had
known what the morrow would bring forth,' said Bright afterwards, ' he would not have wished to add or to omit a word.' But
it was not a speech to suit the spirit of the assembly, inflamed by
Palmerston's gallant defiance of tyranny and high declaration that
he would make it possible for a man to claim his rights throughout
the world, with the words, ' I am a British citizen '—*civis Romanus
sum.* Roebuck's motion was carried by a majority of 36.

Sir Robert Peel walked home through the twilight of a summer
morning. He was much exhausted, and remained so long in his
dressing-room that his wife became anxious, and went to look for
him : she found him kneeling at his prayers. The next day Lady
Peel, who had been ill, remained in bed ; she sent a note down-
stairs to tell him how much pleased she was with his speech, but
did not see him until, descending in the afternoon, she saw him
starting for his ride. ' Oh, pray make haste,' she said, ' we dine
at the Jerseys, and you must not be late.' [2] He promised to return
in good time, and, as she passed on, called after her, ' Julia, you
are not going without wishing me good-bye, or saying those sweet
words, " God bless you ? " ' She went to him, and he caught
her in his arms and kissed her, ' before all the servants.'

Peel was always a bad rider, and his horses were carefully selected
for him. There seems, however, to have been some negligence.

---

[1] *Speeches,* iv. p. 591.

[2] Julia, Peel's eldest daughter, was married to Lord Villiers, eldest son of the
Earl of Jersey.

A country gentleman saw him riding in the park, and noticed that his mount was a horse which he himself had refused to buy, as it was notorious for bucking and kicking. He wondered if he should turn back and warn Sir Robert, but—perhaps recollecting stories of his cold and haughty temper—decided that it would be intrusive. At the park gates, just as Peel was lifting his hat to an acquaintance, the horse plunged and flung him over its head, and then fell forward upon him.

Assistance was at once at hand, a passing carriage was stopped, and the injured man was lifted into it. He was conscious, but seemed dazed. Before reaching home he recovered a little, and was able to walk into the house, but he could not go upstairs, and a bed was hastily improvised on the dining-room table, covered with rugs and cushions. It was found impossible to move him, and he remained there until his death four days later. His shoulder-blade and two ribs had been shattered, but all the details of the injury were never known, for the complete examination was never made. His suffering was so intense that he could bear no touch, and the doctors found it impossible to apply any remedial measures, or even to bandage the injuries. Considering that chloroform had been invented and used with entire success some years before, one cannot resist the conclusion that there was great incompetence.[1]

He remained perfectly clear-headed to the end, and was able to say good-bye to each member of his family. He asked repeatedly for Graham, and Graham and Hardinge saw him almost at the last. His wife knelt beside him, holding his hand.[2]

Meanwhile an unending stream of inquirers passed the door of the house in Whitehall Gardens ; men of all parties and of every class came anxiously to ask for news. In the street a crowd lingered, of those working men and women whom he had so grieved for, and so distrusted, and to whom he had given bread, and surged forward, as each caller left the door, to ask, How he did ? His personal unpopularity was forgotten by his political associates, in the consciousness that the greatest man in Britain was dying ; but the extent of the popular feeling displayed

[1] I am informed that such injuries would certainly not be considered fatal to-day.

[2] For the details given, see *Private Letters* ; *Diary* of Lady Shelley ; *Recollections* of Lady Georgiana Peel ; Martineau, *Newcastle* ; *Reminiscences* of Goldwin Smith.

astonished all observers. ' No man who in life was so hated and reviled was ever so lamented and honoured at his death,' wrote Greville.[1] The House of Commons met with half its members in black, and many of those who had known Peel well too much affected to speak. Russell, as Prime Minister, spoke. Graham sat throughout the proceedings with his head in his hands, crying openly. In the other House, Wellington rose, and was unable at first to get out a word. Then, in tears, and with his mind running on the cruel accusations that had been brought against his dead friend, he spoke a few abrupt sentences :

' In all the course of my acquaintance with Sir Robert Peel I never knew a man in whose truth and justice I had more lively confidence, or in whom I saw a more invariable desire to promote the public service. In the whole course of my communications with him I never knew an instance in which he did not show the strongest attachment to truth ; and I never saw in the whole course of my life the slightest reason for suspecting that he stated anything which he did not believe to be the fact.'

And by that public tribute to Peel the statesman may be set the lament of a friend for Peel the man :

' The death of Sir Robert Peel seems yet to me like a horrid dream, a thing that cannot be,' Lincoln wrote forlornly,[2] ' I cannot help, though I feel keenly the national calamity, looking at it in a selfish light. . . . The sorrows of my domestic life have been so associated with his ready and friendly counsels, and I have ever found in him so delicate a sympathy and so sagacious advice, that the termination of my married life and the simultaneous death of friend and counsellor seem to leave me in a void which yet appears bewildering.'

[1] *Greville*, vi. p. 357.   [2] Martineau, *Newcastle*, p. 99.

CHAPTER XIX

CONCLUSION

IF Peel had been ten years younger—if he had been forty-eight instead of fifty-eight when he repealed the Corn Laws—his retirement would have been impossible. Even as things stood, had he lived a few years longer, it is difficult to see how he could have maintained his attitude, and one may question whether the coalition of Whigs and Peelites, which took place under Aberdeen, would not have been replaced by a somewhat similar coalition under the leadership of Peel. It would hardly have worked well, however; it would have been much more difficult for Russell to serve under Peel than under Aberdeen; and Peel could hardly have allowed Russell and Palmerston the independence which Aberdeen permitted, and which made the arrangement possible. If Peel had persisted in refusing office it is difficult to see what could have been the future of the Peelites. Their loyalty to him was becoming a hindrance to their political career, even though he left them perfectly free. They were, by 1850, sinking into disappointment, and even despair. His death forced them to enter upon a decisive course, and give up their vague hopes of creating a third party. They could not serve with Disraeli, so, still with some reluctance, but on favourable terms, they joined the Whigs.

Peel was only sixty-two when he died : a long and honourable career might have lain before him :

> Though stripped of power,
> A watchman on a lonely tower,
> Thy thrilling trump had roused the land,
> When fraud and danger were at hand ;
> By thee, as by the beacon light,
> Our pilots had kept course aright ;
> As some proud column, though alone,
> Thy strength had propped the tottering throne.
> Now is the stately column broke !
> The beacon light is quenched in smoke,
> The trumpet's silver sound is still,
> The warder silent on the hill.[1]

[1] Scott's lines on Pitt, which were quoted by Gladstone when speaking on Peel's death in the House of Commons.

Yet, when we remember the old age of some great statesmen, it is hardly possible to regret that Peel died before time had touched him. The Palmerston of the Schleswig-Holstein War, scolding and blustering, and abandoning those to whom he had promised aid, is sadly changed from the bold and skilful statesman of the Belgian crisis. The Russell who in 1855 forsook the comrades who had loyally supported him, hardly seems to be the young enthusiast who introduced the Great Reform Bill in 1832. Bismarck at Varzin, whining, fretting, lying, suffocating in his own spite, makes one sigh for the brave days of '66. Peel died in the plenitude of his powers, his mind still elevated by a great sacrifice, his fame at its height, the last words on his lips a plea for those principles of justice and peace for which he had always contended.

The little group of men whom he had gathered about him, and trained in his own tradition of service, did not long remain unbroken. Graham, Aberdeen, and Hardinge were his elders or his contemporaries ; they had not many years of work before them ; but the younger men, his real pupils—the next fifteen years carried many of them off prematurely. Herbert, the predestined Prime Minister, had worked himself to death at fifty-one ; Dalhousie went before him, Canning and Newcastle (Peel's Lincoln) survived him but a year or two. Only Gladstone and Cardwell grew grey in the service of the State. No British statesman—hardly even Pitt—made men as Peel made them : few statesmen of any race could boast of leaving such a group of disciples behind them to carry on the traditions of their work.

They were not all great men, nor all equally able, but they were united and equal in one respect—in that loyal, steady, unselfish devotion to the interests of the nation which he had taught them. It was Herbert who abolished flogging in the army, but the Duke of Cambridge, in whose name the order was issued, got the credit for it : when his friends complained to him that this was not fair, Herbert answered impatiently, ' What on earth does it matter who gets the credit, so long as the thing is done ? '

' I was inspired,' said Gladstone, after one of his finest speeches, ' with the thought of treading, however unequally, in the ways of my great teacher and master in public affairs. . . . It was one of my keenest desires not to do dishonour to his memory, or injustice to the patriotic policy with which his name is for ever associated.'

' *He* is my leader still, though invisible,' said Lincoln, ' I never take a step in public life without reflecting how *he* would have thought of it.' [1]

More than any other individual man, Peel helped to raise the tone of political life. From his earliest days in Ireland he set his face steadily against corruption. His own administration of patronage, as Lord Rosebery feelingly remarks, is ' like a dream, like a chapter dropped from the annals of some Utopia or Atlantis.' [2] His appointments were made on considerations of merit only. The Pension Fund, which had in his young days been squandered on political bribery, had been strictly limited by the reformed Parliament, but he used it to reward long service to the nation, or to assist literary and scientific men in difficulties : Wordsworth, Hogg, Mrs. Hemans, Mrs. Somerville—such were his pensioners. In his five years as Prime Minister he created five new peers only, and these were all for supereminent service to the State. Nor was he afraid to run the risk of criticism. He always maintained that his younger brother, Jonathan Peel,[3] would have been as able as himself if he had not gone into the army ; and in 1841 he made him Surveyor-General of the Ordnance. Naturally the Opposition could not resist the temptation to ask, Why the Prime Minister had appointed his brother ? ' Because I know him to be the best person for the post,' said Sir Robert Peel briefly, and the subject dropped.

He was frequently accused of egotism by his contemporaries. ' I went to the House of Commons,' notes Hobhouse, in 1828, ' and found Peel on his legs, talking, as usual, a great deal about his own purity.' [4] Such comments are frequent in contemporary writings, and he was often publicly taunted with his ' propensity to self-praise.' There is, however, no trace of egotism in his private letters : self-confident, even arrogant, he might be, but no man was less preoccupied with himself and his feelings. He never, like so many Victorian statesmen, kept a diary, and it is very difficult to imagine him doing so. The ' egotism ' of his speeches was in truth the result of his over-sensibility. He was always most at ease, most himself, when speaking in public, and accordingly his speeches are often a more open revelation of his opinions and feelings than his private letters. He knew himself

---

[1] Parker, *Peel*, iii. pp. 559-60.   [2] Rosebery, *Peel*, p. 58.
[3] Secretary of State for War in Lord Derby's first Government.
[4] *Hobhouse*, iii. pp. 191, 260.

to be misunderstood : from his earliest days he was the member of a Government that was reviled as reactionary, corrupt, callous, and incapable. He felt this : his outburst in 1827, when he cried, ' I may be a Tory, I may be an illiberal, but at least I have reformed the law and governed the country without coercion,' shows that he felt it. Later, when he was called shifty and insincere, self-seeking and ambitious, he felt it too, and bitterly. He could not ignore or laugh at such accusations : he might make up his mind to face them, as he did in 1829 and 1846, but still he could not resign himself to be misunderstood. His passionate desire, his real ambition, was to leave an honourable name behind him ; and this explains the frequent justifications of himself and his policy, with which he bored the House of Commons ; and explains, too, the necessity he felt of writing those *Memoirs*, almost painful in their striving for exact truthfulness, and their restrained but none the less passionate demand for justice, in which he defended his conduct on Catholic Emancipation and the Corn Laws.

The caution and reserve natural to him became so extreme that it was a real fault, and a still greater disadvantage. If he had had the winning ways of Melbourne or Herbert his history might have been a little different. Russell was cold and disagreeable to his followers ; Stanley was haughty and disdainful ; but, after all, they were Russell and Stanley ; and men bore from them what they would not take from Robert Peel, whose father had been a cotton-spinner, and his grandfather a petty yeoman. No doubt Peel's apparent coldness was sometimes mere shyness, and his caution only habit. It is related that the Duke of Bedford, meeting him at a country house, wished to find out if he intended to preserve his game strictly. Peel, with perfect politeness, parried his every question as dexterously as if he had been debating in the House of Commons, and left him no wiser at the end than at the beginning.

But, when the mood took him, Peel could be a very agreeable companion. He was a brilliant talker, a raconteur, and a wit. He could keep a large company in fits of laughter with an easy succession of jokes and stories. He had an unfailing sense of humour, and a demure way of poking fun which sometimes seems to have passed unnoticed by grave companions absorbed in serious affairs. Lord Playfair relates an entertaining incident. Peel was in the habit of inviting men of science and learning to Drayton, and listening eagerly to their discussions. On one occasion George Stephenson propounded at his table the theory that the original source of power of steam-engines is the sun. This theory, now of course generally accepted, was received with scorn and ridicule by the geologists present, and Stephenson, an uneducated genius, was unable to reply to their arguments. After dinner Peel called Playfair aside and asked him if he did not think there was something in Stephenson's idea ? Playfair replied that it was not unreasonable, and explained the scientific basis of the theory. Peel then called Follett, the eminent lawyer, who was also a guest in the house, and made Playfair prime him in the scientific arguments. Next day at dinner the question was raised again, Follett took up Stephenson's cause, and with his forensic skill completely floored the geologists, while Stephenson, listening in delight, exclaimed, ' Of all the powers of nature, the greatest is the gift of the gab ! ' The quickness with which Peel detected the real value of Stephenson's suggestion, the skill and caution with which he laid his little plot, and the sense of fair play which prompted it, are thoroughly characteristic.[1]

Nothing is more striking in Peel's character than his consideration for the feelings of others. It was only on very rare occasions that he was betrayed into such a retort as he made to Cobden. In general he was unusually courteous and moderate in debate : his criticisms were confined to the political conduct of his opponents ; he never condescended to bandy personalities, he never brought such accusations against the character and motives of his adversaries as they brought against his. Frequently he surrendered advantages that he might have used against them. He relied entirely on the power of argument, and indeed the effects of his reasoning were often more deadly than any vituperation could have been :

> And Peel, decorous with his Median quiver,
> Though to wound either side humanely loth,
> Shoots each in turn, and puts an end to both.

His private life was irreproachable. In a loose-living and scandal-mongering age no word was ever breathed against his moral character. His letters to his wife show a disgust of the society in which he sometimes moved which is more like that of a woman than of a man. The perfect happiness of his own home

[1] Playfair, *Memoirs*, p. 72-3.

impressed all who saw it. ' Encore un exemple,' wrote Guizot, when he heard the news of his death, ' après tant d'autres, des plus belles existence brisées tout à coup misérablement. . . . Le bonheur le plus pur n'en est pas moins fragile.' [1]

Sir Robert Peel was a distinguished patron of the arts. He was an able classical scholar, and widely read in English literature. He extended assistance to many struggling writers and artists, and the fortune which he had inherited was employed in making a magnificent collection of pictures, a part of which afterwards passed to the British National Gallery. His private hobby was to collect the portraits of his more distinguished contemporaries, painted by Lawrence, so long as that artist lived. He liked to collect literary and scientific men about him for discussion ; and in 1848 he had the honour of being offered the presidency of the Royal Society, though he declined it.

His private charities were immense, his kindness unfailing. He had been the steady patron of the unfortunate artist, Haydon. In June 1846 that wretched man, in despair, wrote an appeal to a number of his wealthy friends. Only one answered, and that was Peel, who, though the Corn Law crisis was then at its height, sent him £50 by return of post. Haydon's last letter, written a few moments before he committed suicide, was addressed to Peel.

' Life is insupportable. Accept my gratitude for always feeling for me in adversity. I hope I have earned for my dearest wife security from want. God bless you.' [2]

The last pension given by Peel before he left office was settled upon Haydon's wife and daughters.

It has sometimes been said that Peel legislated only for the emergency of an hour, and that he did not foresee the ultimate results of his policy. ' Wanting imagination, he wanted pre-science,' said Disraeli, in an oft-quoted phrase. This was my own opinion originally ; after studying the records of Peel's life I was forced to alter it. True, his imagination was not so ' full of shapes and high-fantastical ' as that of his critic ; true, it was held close in bounds by a rarely prudent and well-balanced intellect ; but no one can say that the man whose sympathy was so boundless, who so conceived and comprehended a nation's need, who first grasped the meaning and the nature of modern industrialism, and

[1] Parker, *Peel,* iii. pp. 552-3.
[2] *Ib.* p. 449.

transformed the policy of the state to meet it, was lacking in imagination.

When he legislated for the need of a moment, it was because the need was supreme, not because he failed to foresee that circumstances might alter to-morrow.

It has been said of him, too, that he lacked originality. He could not say of most of his schemes, as the White Knight did of his mouse-trap, ' It's my own invention.' But how many statesmen can make such a boast ? When Wallace called upon serf and baron to stand together for national liberty ; when James I. said, ' I will make the key keep the castle, and the broom-bush keep the cow, throughout broad Scotland ' ; when Machiavelli devised diplomacy ; when Chatham dreamed of Empire ; when Bismarck saw Germany militant and united, ' armipotent lady, Bellona serene ; ' then, indeed, we seem to feel new ideas stirring, we hear ' the hum of mighty workings in some distant mart.' But can it be truly said, even of these great creative minds, that they created something new ? For the most part, the statesman's work is not to conceive ' great king's-thoughts,' but to adapt and apply the perpetual principles of statecraft to the needs of the time. He must translate poetry into action. It is all very well to say, Peel took the ideas of Bentham and Mackintosh, Adam Smith and Pitt and Cobden, and put them in practice—he merely had the practical ability to do it. Just so : it is Columbus and the egg over again : we could all do it if only it occurred to us.

Peel was an opportunist ; that is to say, he had that quality, common to almost all really great statesmen, of seeing things as they are, not as they ought to be, or might be ; and of applying the remedy that is practically necessary, not that which is theoretically right. If he had foreseen—though no living man then foresaw it—the vast development of communication, and the swamping of the markets with American corn, he would have said, ' That is for the statesmen of to-morrow to deal with.' As he said of his Bank Act, if it should be necessary in the future to meet a new danger with new measures, he believed ' men will be found willing to assume such a responsibility,' and he would have expected them to deal with it, as free from prejudice and tradition as he himself had been.

He was never a Free Trader of the late Victorian school, such as Gladstone and Bright became—rigidly enforcing the principles of Free Trade regardless of circumstance; looking only to the letter of the law, not the spirit. The measures which he introduced show this. The duties which he abolished were all upon articles where there was no question of foreign competition, or on the raw materials of industry, or on food. He left, it must not be forgotten, a permanent fixed duty of 1s. the quarter on imported wheat. He left a considerable duty upon foreign timber, and freed colonial timber. He left a preference on colonial coffee, pepper, and spices, and he only supported the Whigs in admitting slave-grown sugar because he could not oppose them without risking the fate of Free Trade. He left a duty on all manufactures likely to do serious harm to home industries—10 per cent. on foreign manufactures, and 5 per cent. on colonial ones, and he left a duty of 15 per cent. on manufactured silk, where the danger was most serious.[1] When he was bringing in his two great budgets, he strove to utilise the lowering of duties to obtain reciprocal commercial treaties with foreign powers.

'Have you considered,' he wrote to Ripon in 1842, 'whether it would be possible to connect with any alteration in our system of Corn Laws a preference to those countries which might be willing to admit on more favoured terms our manufactures?'

'I have frightened Bunsen out of his wits,' he remarked in the same year to Graham, 'by telling him that we would give a preference to American produce, unless Prussia and the States she can influence follow reciprocally our example of liberality towards them.'[2]

Peel's Free Trade, then, was a matter of expediency. His object was not to spread the principles of Adam Smith, not to secure universal peace, not to buy in the cheapest market and sell in the dearest: he did not confound ideas not necessarily connected, nor mistake the means for the end. His object was to encourage trade for the purpose of benefiting the people whose interests were confided to his charge, and to procure cheap food, for the time being the foremost necessity of the working class.

The great problem of the modern State is how to reconcile the new industrial system with the interests of the mass of the people. Great Britain was the first State to be confronted with this problem. Not all her statesmen understood its nature or even

---

[1] Figures from Clapham, *Economic History*, i. p. 498 ff.
[2] Parker, *Peel*, ii. pp. 504, 528.

realised its importance. With Peel himself, understanding came only gradually. He had not been trained to consider such subjects : but his mind grew into it, until it became the great preoccupation of his life. Political revolution had been the bugbear of his youth : social revolution became the ever-present dread of his later years. The thought of the famished, sullen, silent millions lay like a weight on his mind. He took up, and tried, and cautiously applied, the remedies suggested. Education, emigration, factory legislation, the mitigation of the rigours of the law, the enforcement of good order—he employed them all. But he saw, more clearly than the devisers of these remedies, both their limitations and the difficulty of carrying them out ; he saw that they were not enough. To the present day, two solutions have been devised for the problems of the industrial State : on the one hand, there is the remedy offered by the Socialist, the remedy that Germany first applied upon a large scale. Such a remedy would not have commended itself to Peel. Strongly individualistic, he believed that the aid and protection of the State, too freely offered, would sap the independence and moral health of the nation. The other remedy was that devised by Peel himself —to lower the cost of living, and above all the cost of food. He applied it, and for the time it obtained an almost complete success. It raised the standard of living in Britain far above that of any other European country. It ended, for the moment, all danger of revolution.

In 1848, when the news of the deposition of Louis Phillippe reached London, Joseph Hume crossed the floor of the House of Commons to tell Peel. Sir Robert pointed to the benches where the Protectionists sat.

' This is what would have happened here,' he said, ' if I had listened to *them.*'

' His habit of mind,' says Lord Rosebery, ' would, had he been left untrammelled, have made him a Whig,' [1] and other critics too have assumed that Peel's rightful place was among the Whigs. Probably, however, Sir Richard Lodge is right when he says, ' He was a misfit in the party system.' [2] Divergences as deep really separated him from the Whigs as from the Tories.

He never quite divested his mind of the impression made on it

[1] Rosebery, *Peel,* p. 14.
[2] Hearnshaw, *Prime Ministers of the Nineteenth Century,* p. 73.

in his early years by the unpatriotic and factious conduct of the Whigs during the war with France. It must be admitted that their later conduct did not tend to efface this impression : faction has always been the fault into which the Whig party has been most apt to fall. He disliked, also, their tendency to reckless and unconsidered experiment, and the consequent facility with which they abandoned or altered their plans. His instinct was to act with extreme caution in interfering with old-established usages, but, once he had made up his mind, to strike boldly and with all his strength. Their tentative and hesitating touch repelled him : in this respect, he would have had more sympathy with the attitude of the Radicals. He disapproved most of their principles, but their courage appealed to him more than the lukewarmness of the Whigs.

It was, however, the combination of aristocracy and pseudo-democracy in the Whigs that most displeased him. Their playing on popular passions in 1830-32, their rousing of forces, which they knew not if they could control, to further their own policy, was to him unpardonable.

Peel had no liking for modern democracy, just as he had little sympathy for the modern aggressive nationalism. Yet he was truly patriotic, and a great lover of liberty. It was only that he did not conceive of liberty and democracy as one and the same thing, as did some of his contemporaries. Of all tyrannies, he thought the tyranny of the majority the worst. He thought the liberties of his country would be better secured by a government drawn from the wealthier and more educated classes, and supported by those who had a stake in the property of the country ; but, it must be remembered, he never wished, as the Whigs did, to exclude the lower classes from representation. That part of the Reform Bill which he steadily opposed was the disfranchisement of the working man ; he defended the old constitution, because it secured to every class in the community representation in Parliament, while giving the propertied classes a preponderance.

In truth, Peel's mind was too broad, and his honesty too strict, to be confined within the limits of the party system.

His outlook was too wide, his mind too well balanced, to admit any element of fanaticism. His practical turn of mind, his respect for the rights and opinions of others, above all, his honesty, prevented him from ever running to extremes. The fault of his early training was that it had not developed the critical side of his intelligence ; and his faults and mistakes—as on the question of Catholic Emancipation—were due mainly to this. He had been taught to take his principles on trust, and he accepted them without enough consideration ; but, once his critical faculties were aroused, once he was compelled to reconsider and weigh his opinions, he was incapable of deceiving himself. This was the fundamental difference between Peel and the greatest of his pupils ; it has often been remarked, that when Peel changed his mind, he owned frankly that he had been mistaken ; Gladstone tried to persuade you—and himself—that this was what he had really thought all the time. Peel valued his political consistency as highly as other men ; but he valued his private honour above it. He would rather lay himself open to any accusation of political treachery than be false to his inward conviction of the truth.

There are few statesmen who can show such a record of great reforms as Peel. He restored the currency ; he consolidated and improved the criminal law, and much of the civil law ; he greatly increased the efficiency of the administration ; he elevated the tone of political morality ; his Irish policy leaves much to be desired, but he carried Catholic Emancipation, and passed the Maynooth grant and set up the Queen's Colleges ; he established the Irish and the English constabulary, a reform which has probably done more for the practical happiness and welfare of the country than any other individual reform ever introduced, for it may be said that every other reform is conditional upon an efficient police ; he was the first to attempt the reform of the Irish land tenure system ; he was the wise and steady promoter of factory legislation ; he reorganised the whole system of taxation ; he initiated the vast expansion of British trade by his Free Trade measures, and he permanently raised the standard of life in Britain by the introduction of cheap food.

Outside the field of actual legislation, his services were equally eminent. His loyalty and moderation steadied the reformed Parliament through its first dangerous years : he guided the Tory party from blind reaction to wise conservatism ; he showed it was possible to conduct the foreign policy of Britain with honour, dignity, and success, yet without aggression or threats, and without alienating or wounding the feelings of other Powers ; above all, he set up an ideal of an opposition leader such as has rarely been equalled, courteous and generous, able and moderate, free from faction and devoid of selfish ambition. We have only to consider what would have been the result had the passing of other measures of reform been accompanied by such a struggle as attended the passing of the Reform Bill, to see how decisive was his attitude. Peel supported the Municipal Reform Bill, he undertook the reform of the Church of England, and the Tory party was forced to acquiesce; if any one man preserved the House of Lords and the Church, it was Peel. Another conflict between the House of Lords and the House of Commons might have ended in the destruction of the former; another conflict between the Tory aristocracy and the people might have provoked a social revolution.

It is as the statesman who made Great Britain the first Free Trade country of the world that Sir Robert Peel holds his place in nineteenth-century history; but it may be questioned whether it is not another aspect of his career that has the greatest attraction for our minds to-day. It is as the party leader who took his stand above party; the politician who had no thought of self; the statesman who set the interest of the nation above every interest of class or individual, that Sir Robert Peel stands out as the noblest figure of his time.

TABLE OF DATES

1788. February 5th: Robert Peel born.
1789. Beginning of the French Revolution. Bentham's *Principles of Morals and Legislation* published.
1798. Malthus's *Essay on Population* published.
1801. Peel goes to Harrow.
1802. Peace of Amiens. Health and Morals of Apprentices Act. Jeffrey founds the *Edinburgh Review*.
1805. Peel goes to Oxford. Battle of Trafalgar. Death of Pitt.
1809. Peel enters Parliament. Formation of the Perceval Ministry.
1810. Peel becomes Colonial Under-Secretary. The Bullion Report.
1812. Formation of the Liverpool Ministry. Peel becomes Irish Secretary.
1813. Grattan's Emancipation Bill defeated.
1814. Abdication of Napoleon. Publication of *Waverley*.
1815. End of the French War. Peel challenges O'Connell. Corn Law passed.
1816-1819. Industrial depression.
1816. Canning joins the Government.
1817. Ricardo's *Principles of Political Economy* published.
1818. Peel resigns the Irish Secretaryship.
1819. First Factory Act passed. May: Peel secures the resumption of cash payments. August: 'Peterloo.'
1820. January: Death of George III. June 8th: Peel marries Miss Julia Floyd. Trial of Queen Caroline. Resignation of Canning.
1821. Death of Napoleon.
1822. January: Peel becomes Home Secretary. August: Death of Castlereagh. Canning becomes Foreign Secretary. Death of Shelley.
1823. Foundation of the Catholic Association. The Monroe Doctrine declared.
1824. Repeal of the Combination Laws. Death of Byron.
1825. Catholic Relief Bill passes the Commons, but is lost in the Lords. September: Opening of the Stockton and Darlington Railway. December: Financial crisis.
1826-1829. Industrial depression.
1827. February: Fatal illness of Lord Liverpool. April: Canning Prime Minister; Peel resigns. August: Death of Canning; Goderich Prime Minister. October: Battle of Navarino.
1828. January: Peel-Wellington Government formed. Duties on corn lowered. July: the Clare Election.
1829. Catholic Emancipation. Formation of the New Police.
1830. May: Death of Sir Robert Peel, first baronet. June: Death of George IV. July: French Revolution. November: Fall of the Government; Lord Grey Prime Minister. Publication of Tennyson's *Lyrical Poems*.
1831. First and Second Reform Bills introduced and defeated.
1832. May: Third Reform Bill defeated. Wellington's abortive Ministry. June: Reform Bill passed. Death of Sir Walter Scott.
1833. Factory Act. Abolition of Slavery.

376

1834. Poor Law Act. General Assembly passes the Veto Act. July: Resignation of Grey. First Melbourne Ministry. November: King dismisses Whigs and sends for Peel.

1835. April: Peel defeated. Second Melbourne Ministry. August: Municipal Reform Bill crisis.

1836-1842. Industrial depression.

1836. Financial crisis.

1837. June: Death of William IV. Rebellion in Canada.

1838. Irish Tithe Bill passed. Invasion of Afghanistan. People's Charter drawn up.

1839. The Anti-Corn-Law League formed. May: Government resigns; Bedchamber crisis. November: Chartist rising.

1840-1844. O'Connell's Repeal agitation in Ireland.

1840. Penny Postage adopted. February: Marriage of the Queen. Union of the Canadas. July-November: Quadrilateral Treaty and Bombardment of Acre.

1841. May: Peel carries a Vote of Want of Confidence. Dissolution of Parliament. August: Government defeated. Revolt in Afghanistan.

1842. Destruction of British Army in Afghanistan. New Corn Law. First Free Trade Budget. Income Tax introduced. Ashburton Treaty signed.

1843. Canadian Corn admitted free. May: Disruption of the Church of Scotland. October: Arrest of O'Connell. Wordsworth Poet Laureate.

1844. Party dissensions in the Ten-Hours' Clause and the Sugar Duties. O'Connell Judgment reversed. Bank Charter Act. Recall of Lord Ellenborough.

1845. Second Free Trade Budget. Maynooth Grant. September: the Irish potato crop fails. November 27th: Edinburgh Letter published. December 6th: Peel resigns. December 13th: Russell fails to form a Government; Peel recalled. December: Sikh War begins.

1846. January: Corn Bill introduced. March: Coercion Bill introduced. June: Canadian Frontier Agreement signed; Corn Laws repealed; Government resign. August: Irish famine. October: Spanish marriages; Breach with France.

1847. Irish famine. April: Don Pacifico incident. October: Financial crisis. Death of O'Connell.

1848. February: French Revolution. Revolts in Germany, Italy, etc. Collapse of the Chartist Movement.

1849. Irish revolt. Repeal of the Navigation Laws.

1850. Greek shipping seized by Britain. French Ambassador withdrawn from London. July 2nd: Death of Sir Robert Peel.

INDEX